Brief Histories

General Editor: Jeremy Black

The Romanov Empire 1613–1917

Autocracy and Opposition

Alan Wood

Hodder Arnold

A MEMBER OF THE HODDER HEADLINE GROUP

First published in Great Britain in 2007 by
Hodder Education, a member of the Hodder Headline Group,
338 Euston Road, London NW1 3BH

www.hoddereducation.com

Distributed in the United States of America by
Oxford University Press Inc.
198 Madison Avenue, New York, NY10016

British Library Cataloguing in Publication Data
A catalogue record for this book is available from the British Library

Library of Congress Cataloging-in-Publication Data
A catalog record for this book is available from the Library of Congress

ISBN 978 0 340 761 88 5

1 2 3 4 5 6 7 8 9 10

Typeset by Phoenix Photosetting, Chatham, Kent
Printed in Great Britain for Hodder Arnold, an imprint of Hodder Education,
a member of the Hodder Headline Group, 338 Euston Road, London, NW1 3BH by
CPI Bath

For Iris

Contents

List of maps

Preface

What a field modern Russian history is! And when you think that ... besides us Russians, no one can even undertake it!

(Aleksandr Pushkin, letter to Baron M. A. Korf, 14 October 1836)

Since those words were written, hundreds of non-Russian scholars, *pace* Pushkin, have essayed to undertake and understand the history of his country, particularly since the revolutions of 1917. For all its many differences from the west, Russia's past is not inscrutable, and indeed a certain amount of distance and objectivity, provided they are blended with a degree of judicious empathy, may help towards an appreciation of its unique experience. Winston Churchill may himself have been intellectually incapable of regarding Russia as no more than 'a riddle, wrapped in a mystery inside an enigma', as he said in 1939, but that is no reason why the rest of us should not try to unravel its secrets. This book is a modest attempt to penetrate the puzzle of Russia's past by providing what Steve Smith calls a 'narrative analysis' of the Romanov Empire from its inception in 1613 to its collapse in 1917. Other recent western historians have embarked on a similar enterprise, though with different approaches and angles from the present work, and within varying time spans.

Russia became officially an empire – the *Rossiiskaya Imperiya* – in 1721, when Peter the Great adopted it as the new name of the Muscovite tsardom which he had inherited at the end of the seventeenth century and massively expanded during his reign. In fact, the realm he inherited was already an empire in all but name, and arguably had been since the late sixteenth century when cossak *con-quistadores* blazed a trail through the vastness of northern Asia beyond the Ural mountains as far as the Pacific coast. It was to the throne of this hugely expanded domain that Mikhail Fëdorovich Romanov, the first of a new royal dynasty, was elected tsar in 1613. By the reign of the last Romanov, Nicholas II, the empire stretched over one-sixth of the planet's land surface, and contained a myriad of different races and peoples. When he abdicated in March 1917, his brother, Grand Duke Mikhail Aleksandrovich, refused to accept the crown, thereby bringing to an end the dynasty begun by the first tsar, Mikhail Fëdorovich, over 300 years before.

Between the first and last Romanovs, their empire went through many vicissitudes, all of which it is impossible to cover in a book of this size. Any historical account must be selective in its choice and treatment of subjects, emphases and approaches. The present study starts from two basic premises. The first, which in the current intellectual climate may be seen as outmoded, unfashionable and also deliberately provocative, is that the history of the Russian Empire is not only the history of imperial expansion and government, but also, to borrow a Marxian concept, the history of a struggle between the classes. One does not have to subscribe to Marxist doctrine to acknowledge the inescapable fact that from the time of its inception, following a period of intense domestic turmoil of civil war proportions at the beginning of the seventeenth century, right through to its collapse amid the revolutionary upheavals of 1917, the empire of the Romanov tsars was constantly riven by tensions, disturbances, revolts and a struggle between the upper ruling classes of Russian society and the lower, between the haves and the have-nots, between the government and the nobility on the one hand and the peasantry on the other, between what in Russian are known as the *verkhi* and the *nizy*. In the later decades of the Romanov period, the peasantry was joined in its confrontational relationship with the regime by the critical, increasingly militant, intelligentsia and the industrial workers. It was only in the early twentieth century that this combination of oppositional forces found sufficient strength to overcome the power of the state, the bureaucracy, the police and the military on which the tsarist autocracy leant for its support, as will be argued in the following pages. This also explains the subtitle of the book: 'Autocracy and Opposition'.

The second premise, rather less controversial, is that the history of Russia was shaped in a unique way – at least since the early eighteenth century – by the complex interplay of traditional Russian institutions, habits, religious principles, mores and values, with the thought, science, learning, philosophy, enlightenment and technology of the west. The intellectual, literary, artistic, scientific, political and ideological developments and conclusions of this process form the other major leitmotif of this book. In a very real sense, the coming together of these two themes – that of the class struggle and the mutual interaction of Russia and the west – occurred in the revolutions of 1917 with the overthrow of the traditional ruling Russian autocracy, with its origins in mediaeval Muscovy, and its ultimate replacement by a regime which had its ideological roots in the revolutionary theories of a nineteenth-century west European political economist. The present work is published in the year – 2007 – which marks the ninetieth anniversary of those revolutions, revolutions which signalled the end of the Romanov Empire and ushered in a new, but in many senses still familiar and unmistakably Russian, epoch in the country's troubled development.

Two readers of the preliminary draft of this book remarked that it seemed to take a long time to get round to the Romanovs. In fact, only Chapter 2 is concerned with the pre-Romanov period, but it seemed to me to be essential to outline the historical forces and developments which had shaped the virtual empire which they inherited at the start of the seventeenth century. The Romanovs were heirs not only to the vast geographical landmass which they were to rule for the next 300 years, but also to the political, religious and cultural traditions, as well as the social tensions and relationships, of the past, without a bare knowledge of which it is impossible properly to appreciate later developments. Similarly, it seemed important, for reasons to be explained, to place the historical evolution of the Romanov Empire within its geographical, climatic, demographic and ethnic contexts. Again, without a rudimentary understanding of these it is difficult to comprehend how the inhabitants of the country were affected by, and responded to, the environment which shaped their existence – hence Chapter 1 'Land and peoples'.

What follows does not pretend to break any new ground, or to present any startling revelations, but it will be a source of satisfaction if the arguments and conclusions provoke some thoughts, raise some eyebrows and shatter some shibboleths. The writing of Russian history, like that of any other country, is always subject to change and development, new ways of thinking and altering interpretations, and this will continue to be so as fresh archives are opened and new contours emerge on the relief map of future Russian historiography, though it is difficult to guess what shape they will take. As the writer Tatyana Tolstaya has put it: 'Russia is a country whose past is impossible to predict.'

Alan Wood
Halton-on-Lune
August 2006

Acknowledgements

Many colleagues and former tutors have over the years inspired me with an admiration for the Russian people, and the country's history, culture and character. Among those outstanding scholars, some now sadly deceased, I would like to mention in particular the following: John Fennell, Eugene Lampert, Anne Pennington, Boris Unbegaun, Richard Freeborn, Paul Foote, Harry Willetts, Dimitri Obolensky, Ron Hingley and other luminaries of the Russian academic community at the University of Oxford during the 1960s, where I was then their student. Also special thanks to my old friend, Paul Dukes.

In Russia itself I owe a particular debt of gratitude to my close friend, mentor, distinguished ethnographer and comrade, Sergei Savoskul and his family; also to the late Leonid Goryushkin, to Vladimir Shishkin, Viktor Karlov, Viktor Shilov, Vladimir Buldakov, Albina Girfanova, Nikolai Sukhachev, S. F. Koval, Nikolai Shcherbakov and many other academicians, librarians and archivists, museum curators, bureaucrats, tipplers, priests, poets and nuns in Moscow, St Petersburg, Serpukhov, Tarusa, Kishinev, Pereslavl-Zalesskii, Kaluga, Novosibirsk, Barnaul, Irkutsk, Tura, Khabarovsk, Bratsk, Vladivostok and elsewhere in that huge, fascinating country.

In the Americas, I am especially grateful for the past advice, companionship and academic discourse with Basil Dmytryshyn, Larry Black, James Gibson, Norman Pereira, John Stephan and, of course, the redoubtable and ever disreputable Victor Mote.

On a more immediate, personal level – and apart from the expert editorial and production team at Hodder Arnold – I have been aided and abetted in the writing of this book by the penetrating, nit-picking and illuminating comments of, especially, Professor Michael Mullett, Dr Steve Constantine, Dr John Swift and my sister, Sylvia Bosworth, all of whom have read and commented on the entire text; Professor Mike Kirkwood, who saw some of the early chapters, Dr Jenny Brine, who checked the footnotes and bibliography with a falcon's eye, and, finally, my wife, Iris, to whom this modest volume is dedicated. Any remaining undetected errors or infelicities are entirely their responsibility.

Notes on the text

1. All Russian forenames and patronymics are given in their transliterated version, e.g. (Aleksandr, Pëtr, Yekaterina), except in the case of the Romanov monarchs, where the more familiar, anglicised form is used (Alexander II, Peter the Great, Empress Catherine, etc.).

2. Transliteration is according to the Library of Congress system, with some emendations. Russian initial letters Е, Ю and Я are rendered as Ye, Yu and Ya. The character й is transliterated as i. The 'soft sign' has been omitted, except in italicised transliterations of Russian technical terms, titles of books, etc.

3. The stressed phoneme 'ye', pronounced 'yo', is represented throughout with a dieresis – 'ë'; thus Potëmkin, pronounced Potyomkin.

4. Dates. From January 1700 until February 1918, Russia used the Julian calendar, which, in the eighteenth century was 11 days, in the nineteenth – 12 days, and in the twentieth – 13 days behind the Gregorian calendar used in the west. Unless otherwise indicated in the text (e.g. in the case of international treaties, declarations of war, battles) all dates are given according to the Julian (Old Style, O.S.) calendar, rather than the Gregorian (New Style, N.S.).

Order of succession to the Romanov throne, 1613–1894

Eighteenth-century order of succession after the death of Peter I indicated by Roman numerals; ruling monarchs underlined.

Mikhail, 1613–45

Aleksei, 1645–76

Fëdor 1676–82

Sofya (regent) 1682–89

Ivan V 1682–96

Peter I 1682–1725 = Catherine I (i) 1725–27

Anna (iii) 1730–40

Aleksei d. 1718

Anne, Duchess of Holstein = Peter III (vi) 1761–62

Elizabeth (v) 1741–61

Catherine, Duchess of Mecklenburg

Peter II (ii) 1727–30

Paul 1796–1801 = Catherine II (vii) 1762–96

Anne, Princess of Brunswick

Alexander I, 1801–25

Nicholas I, 1825–55

Ivan VI (iv) 1740–41

Alexander II, 1855–81

Alexander III, 1881–94

Nicholas II, 1894–1917

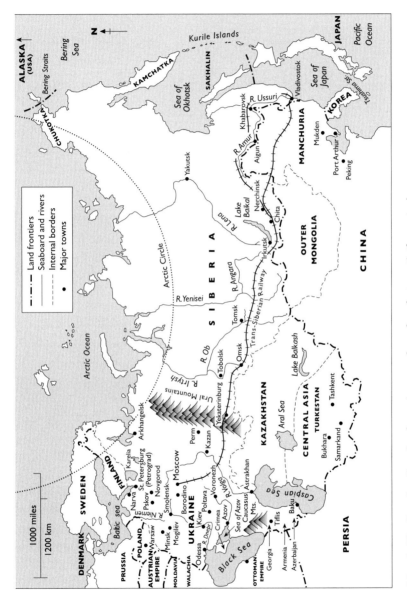

Map 1 The Russian Empire: late nineteenth and early twentieth centuries

1 Land and peoples

The historical development of any nation is to a considerable extent influenced and shaped by the physical environment and the geographical setting in which its people live, work, cultivate, trade, create, procreate, die, and also fight and kill. Such factors as spatial extent, terrain, climate, proximity to the oceans, natural resources, the fertility or aridity of the earth, relief, riverine systems, vegetation, and so on, obviously have a direct or indirect affect on patterns of behaviour, movement, settlement, diet, and of social and economic activity and organisation. This is as true of small inhabited islands – the British Isles, for example – as it is of huge continental masses, such as that occupied by the Russian Empire. In the case of Russia, among the most important geographical features to be taken into consideration when studying various facets and phases of its history and civilisation are its size, its climate, its river network, its access to seas and oceans, its natural resources (animal, vegetable and mineral), the absence of natural defensive barriers on its eastern and western edges, its Eurasian character, and its contiguity with both European, central Asian and oriental neighbours. Two of Russia's greatest historians, S. M. Solovëv and V. O. Klyuchevskii, both prefaced their monumental studies of Russia's past with a detailed explanation of the impact of the country's geography on its history.[1] It seems, therefore, quite proper to follow that tradition, though on a more modest scale, in the following pages.

Size

The focus of this section is simply on a description of the geographical immensity of the state of 'all the Russias', though it will subsequently be demonstrated how this vastness was both systematically and serendipitously accumulated by the military and political exertions of Russia's rulers. At the height of its power and territorial extent, which was also at the point of its collapse, the Russian Empire was the largest country in the world, covering roughly one-sixth of the planet's land surface (or 5 per cent of the entire globe). It sprawled across half the landmass of eastern Europe and northern Asia from the Baltic Sea in the west to the Pacific Ocean in the east, extending, in modern chronometrical terms, over eight time zones. In the far north it was bounded, as the Russian Federation is bounded today, by the Arctic Ocean and its six seas (the White, Barents, Kara, Laptev, East Siberian and Chukotskoe) which are totally ice-locked for most of the year. Its southern rim, east of the Black Sea, consists of the arid lands of central Asia and the mountain ranges of the Caucasus, Pamir, Tyan-Shan, Altai, Sayan and the Far Eastern. These uplands and highlands form a kind of orographic amphitheatre semi-circling the flatter arena of frost-bound plains, plateaux and forests further north. Roughly two-thirds of these boreal expanses are based on a vast, solid subterranean platform of permanently frozen ground, the permafrost, or, in Russian, *merzlota* (see Map 2).

It is traditional, for both geographical and historical purposes, to divide the Russian Empire into its European and Asiatic moieties, the customary physical division between the two being the medium-lying Ural mountains. These stretch from the Kazakh uplands in the south along the meridian of roughly 60° longitude to beyond the Arctic Circle in the north. European Russia, therefore, comprises the lands from the Baltic Sea and the Gulf of Finland in the west to as far as the Urals, and is basically flat. Asiatic Russia covers the vast frozen territory of northern Asia, historically known as Siberia, reaching out eastwards from the Urals to the Pacific littoral. It includes the Kamchatka peninsula, the Aleutian and Kurile archipelagos and the island of Sakhalin (the latter being shared with Japan as a condominium between 1855 and 1875, and politically divided between them from 1905 to 1945). Also, between the end of the eighteenth century and 1867, Russia's remotest northern colony consisted of her possessions across the Bering Strait in Russian America, now the largest American state of Alaska, sold by Russia to the USA in 1867 for seven and a quarter million gold dollars. As if to compensate for the

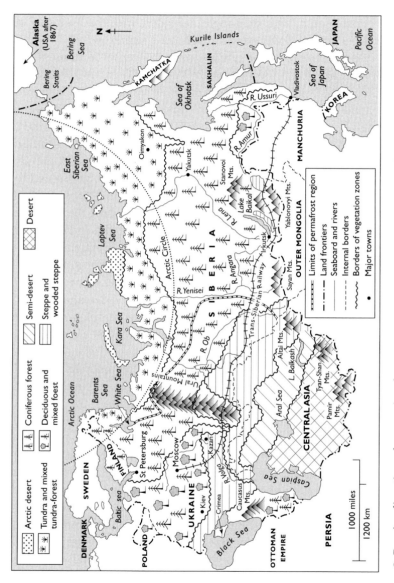

2 Russia: climatic and vegetational zones

loss of these Arctic regions, Russia had already acquired from China the Ussuri and Amur territories in the Far East under the treaties of Aigun (1858) and Peking (1860). Her new oriental possessions there were consolidated, and, seemingly, defended, with the founding of the fortress port of Vladivostok in 1860 (see Chapter 9).

At the other end of the empire, passing over for a moment the territorial wars of conquest fought by Peter the Great and Catherine the Great (see below, Chapters 3 and 4), by which Russia acquired large areas of land on the Baltic and Black Sea coasts, in the early nineteenth century it also annexed Georgia (from Persia, 1801), Finland (from Sweden, 1809) and Bessarabia (from the Ottoman Empire, 1812). Most of the ancient Christian kingdom of Armenia, sandwiched between Islamic states on east and west, was ceded to Russia by Persia under the Treaty of Turkmanchai in 1828. In central Asia the empire also extended its power by establishing the province of Turkestan (1866), creating protectorates over the independent khanates of Kokand and Bukhara (1868), and subsequently Khiva (1873). This process of imperial expansion meant that in the eighteenth, nineteenth and early twentieth centuries Russia was a major European, Baltic, Caucasian, central Asian, north Asian and oriental power. This geopolitical situation not only created problems of internal governance over such diverse territories and peoples as had been acquired by these conquests and negotiations, but also, obviously, involved the development of direct diplomatic, commercial and military interests in the affairs of the contiguous foreign states. Ethnic and religious ties, as well as political considerations, for instance, made Russia a major factor and actor in the Balkans arena during the nineteenth and twentieth centuries.

The imperial and colonial legacy of the Romanov rulers was, of course, inherited by the new revolutionary, socialist government after 1917. But even after the collapse and dismemberment of the Soviet Empire in 1991 and the loss of the former Soviet republics as newly independent states, the Russian Federation still remains the largest country in the world (the Siberian lands alone are approximately one and a third times the size of Canada). It also faces a similarly complex variety of international interests and internal problems which, ultimately, have been handed down from the imperialist activities of the Romanovs in the process of acquiring their vast domain. For example, before the modern age of instant communications, it was impossible for the rulers in Moscow or St Petersburg to *know* that their decrees were being implemented or obeyed many thousands of miles away from the capital, or that reports of local happenings were either accurate or still relevant to current policies or developments at the centre. Decrees, petitions, requests, complaints, decisions and other forms of intelligence often took months, or even years, to flow to and fro between the metropolitan core and the remote peripheries. Even in the middle of the twentieth century, chance aerial reconnaissance crews discovered isolated communities of religious schismatics living in the depths of the Siberian forests, whose existence had been unknown since the late seventeenth century. And even today, in the twenty-first century, the sheer vastness of the Russian lands presents problems of communication, human logistics and economic planning.

It is therefore clear that in Russia's historical experience, as in other vital areas of human activity, or so it is said, size matters.

Climate

To non-Russians, one of the most notorious aspects of the country's natural environment is its climate. The long duration and severity of its winters, in particular, has not only given rise to countless legends, fables, folklore and jokes, but has also had real and palpable effects on Russia's economic development, agriculture, transport and communications, building styles, migration patterns, community life, some would say even the Russian national character, and certainly its military history. In the case of the last, both the victory over Napoleon in 1812 and the defeat of Nazi invaders during the second 'Great Patriotic War' (1941–45) owed much to the role played by 'General Winter', as well as to the enemies' overstretched lines of communication in Russia's vast hinterland. These feats of arms also owed much to the resilience, stoicism and heroic courage of her fighting troops, who were more inured to the sub-zero temperatures and frozen landform than their western aggressors.

Russia's extremes of temperature are due to its predominant northern latitudes and to the vast size of its landmass, which produces a continental climate giving short, hot summers and very long, bitterly cold winters. Deep inland, particularly in Siberia, far from the moderating influence of the sea, temperatures in winter can vary from a mean of −19°C in the south (Novosibirsk) to −43°C further north (Yakutsk). At Oimyakon, the northern hemisphere's 'pole of cold', temperatures of −71° have frequently been recorded (see Map 2). Winters in central European Russia are not generally quite as severe, though even in Moscow temperatures of around −40°C are not uncommon at that time of year. However, in a country as immense as Russia, the range and change of climates and terrains obviously vary enormously, though within each sub-region there is an extensive, almost monotonous, uniformity which contrasts with the more diverse and dramatically changing environment of western Europe.

In spring, from the Baltic to mid-Siberia the landmass warms rapidly, causing the ice and snows to melt and temperatures to rise and vary from 15°C to the mid- or even high 20s. The rapid thaw and consequently increased water levels turn the typically primitive roads, paths and highways into virtual linear quagmires, which are sometimes impassable. So common is this phenomenon that this time of year is known in Russian as the *rasputitsa* ('melt-time') or season of *bezdorozh'e* (literally, 'roadlessness'). The effects of the annual, vernal snowmelt have also been described as 'an epic of mud'. The vagaries of the climate have resulted in the periodic crop failures and consequent famines that have been a recurring feature of Russia's agrarian and social history. But the brief transitional seasons of spring and autumn are also of course periods of intense agricultural activity at sowing and harvest time, which some historians have suggested has had an effect on peasant work cycles and traditions of collective labour in the Russian countryside. One of the most significant results of this was the formation and survival of the peasant commune (*obshchina* or *mir*), with its collective labour and land-holding patterns, which survived long beyond Russia's own feudal era. This subject will be returned to in a later chapter. It has also been argued that – work patterns aside – the recurring alternation between long, relatively sluggish, inactive winters and short, vigorous spurts of springtime and autumn agricultural graft has been reflected in Russia's social and political history, which has been marked by long decades of popular passivity, submission and inertia, punctuated by sudden outbursts of mass energy and dynamism, manifesting itself in such things as victorious military exertions, strenuous feats of industrial achievement, revolts and revolutions. After these climaxes, exhaustion and torpidity set in once more until the next galvanic eruption. It is not suggested that dynamic bursts of military or popular energy *coincide* with the seasonal cycle (for instance, the February 1917 Revolution occurred in the teeth of a particularly bitter winter). It is simply that there appears to be a similar pattern of extended periods of somnolence interrupted by sporadic, climacteric convulsions in both the historical and the ergonomic continuum. Readers may judge for themselves the validity of this somewhat generalised interpretation.

Geographical zones

Moving from north to south, the major climatic and vegetational parallel zones or belts are the arctic region, the sub-arctic tundra, the forest or *taiga*, the wooded steppe, the prairies and steppelands themselves, and the mountains and deserts of the Caucasus and central Asia. (In mountainous regions, more quickly changing climate and relief cause a less uniform pattern of soil and vegetation.) Virtually nothing grows in the arctic regions proper, but the tundra zone is covered with a stunted layer of dwarf vegetation consisting of small shrubs, mosses, lichens and grasses, which blossom in the short summer and provide food for indigenous wild animal life and grazing pastures for the reindeer, which are vital for the nomadic herding peoples of the far north such as the Mansi, Khanty, Eveny, Evenki and others. Further south, the tundra gradually gives way to the vast swathe of coniferous and deciduous forest, which stretches, seemingly limitlessly, though in fact from European Russia's western marches all the way across Siberia to the far eastern coast. It is the largest timber stand in the world, and the natural products of the forest, both animal and vegetable, have played a crucial role in the development of the Russian economy throughout its history. In particular, the mighty Siberian *taiga* with its teeming animal life of fur-bearing mammals – squirrel, fox, bear, marten, but most especially the valuable sable – lured thousands of trappers, hunters, merchants and fortune seekers in pursuit of Siberia's 'soft gold'. It was this 'fur rush' through the *taiga* which was one of the most important factors in opening up Siberia in the seventeenth century, thereby enabling Muscovy to spread its power ultimately throughout northern Asia (see Chapter 2). As the historical geographer, R. A. French, has properly pointed out, the forest, the timberland, the *taiga*, are the Russians' natural habitat – from wooden cradle to wooden cross. To illustrate the point lexicographically, he notes that the Russian language, augmented by a few foreign adoptions, has over 150 words that describe various subtly distinctive types of woodland, i.e. 'an area of land with trees growing on it'.[2] (By contrast, *Roget's Thesaurus of English Words and Phrases* lists only a dozen or so arboreal synonyms for 'wood' or 'forest' in modern English.)

The wooded steppe and the steppes south of the forest belt provide some of Russia's most fertile agricultural land. Much of the natural vegetation of these grassy prairies made way for cultivated crops growing in the rich black soil (*chernozem*) and providing abundant harvests, so much so that at one time Ukraine in particular was known as 'the breadbasket of Europe'. Apart from the indigenous peasants, in the eighteenth century German and other foreign immigrants were encouraged to settle and farm the southern steppes, bringing with them new agricultural techniques and breeds of livestock. Viniculture, sericulture and the rearing of fine-fleeced merino sheep from Spain, Liechtenstein and elsewhere were particularly encouraged. These newly settled and cultivated lands became known as 'New Russia' (*Novaya Rossiya* – see Chapter 6). This fertile belt also extends eastwards into southern Siberia, and a great flood of government-encouraged peasant migration at the end of the nineteenth and beginning of the twentieth centuries brought many millions of new settlers who turned the region into one of the most productive agricultural areas in the empire. Not only cereal production, but also animal husbandry was especially successful. In particular, the Siberian dairy industry (especially butter production) played an important role in the region's economy and in Russia's export trade. For instance, around 20 per cent of the butter consumed in Britain in the early twentieth century was produced in Siberia, which by 1913 contained over 4000 creameries. In fact the total export revenue from butter exports at the time was twice the value of Siberia's gold output. Even further east, the grasslands around Lake Baikal provided abundant pasture for sheep rearing carried out by the native Buryats. At a much earlier period of Russia's history, it was across these wide, open prairies that wave after wave of mounted nomadic warriors galloped in from the east, attacking the fledgling settled townships of Kievan Russia in the twelfth and thirteenth centuries (see Chapter 2). After the Pechenegs, Polovtsians and others, finally, in the early thirteenth century, came the Mongols who, following their initial destructive onslaught, reduced the Slavonic city-states to tax-paying vassals of the Mongol Empire. More than two centuries of servitude to the stern oriental despotism of Chenghiz Khan's successors – c.1240 to 1480 – was to have a profound and lasting impact on Russia's subsequent historical development. This is discussed in the next chapter.

Finally, the huge desert areas of Kazakhstan and central Asia, with their long hot summers and low precipitation, are unpropitious for extensive agricultural development except in a few irrigated valleys, and much of the land consists of large wastelands of rock and sand. However, for centuries they were the site of a thriving Muslim culture and civilisation, with flourishing administrative and commercial centres along the old silk route – cities such as Tashkent, Samarkand and Bukhara – which finally fell under Russian suzerainty in the mid-nineteenth century (see above).

River systems

Russia's network of inland waterways has been described as the 'Cinderella' of the country's communication and transport system, but while this may be true of the low budgetary provision afforded it in recent years, the description is totally incommensurate with the central importance of the system of rivers, lakes and interfluvial portages in the historical development of the Russian state from the earliest times. Despite the recent development of railways, air transport and overland oil and gas pipelines, internal shipping along Russia's huge rivers, and their use as solid ice-roads for land vehicles in winter, still remain a vital factor in the country's transport, travel and communications system. Russia contains some of the world's longest rivers and its deepest lake (Baikal in eastern Siberia, which holds one-fifth of the planet's freshwater reserves). A peculiarity of their natural disposition is that most of the major rivers in European Russia (for example, the Dnepr, Don and Volga) flow southwards, emptying mainly into the Black and the Caspian Seas, while the great rivers of Siberia (Ob, Yenisei and Lena) flow northwards into the Arctic Ocean. In the far east, the Amur, joined by its tributary the Ussuri (together demarcating the boundary between the Russian and Chinese empires from the mid-nineteenth century), flows west to east, pouring into the Tatar Strait, which separates Sakhalin Island from the mainland.

During the ninth century AD, Viking (the Russian term is *varyagi* or 'Varangian') merchant adventurers from Scandinavia, navigating the Volkhov, Dvina and Dnepr rivers, established one of Europe's major trade routes, linking the Baltic to the Black Sea. This was the famous 'road from the Varangians to the Greeks' along which the Norse invaders raided and traded their way from northern Europe to the markets of Constantinople on the Bosphorus, bringing with them merchandise – furs, honey, wax, slaves – gathered, plundered or captured from the forests of central Russia. A network of fortified riparian posts along the route, from Novgorod in the north through Kiev in the south, laid the foundations for the formation of Russia's first rudimentary state, usually referred to as 'Kiev Rus'. As long as Russia's early Nordic and Slavonic rulers commanded control of this river system, Kiev Rus survived as a relatively flourishing east European state. When, however, the combination of shifting trade routes (following the Christian crusades) and the Mongol onslaught in the early thirteenth century broke this grip, Kievan Russia collapsed, leaving the major commercial city of Novgorod in the north in a state of uneasy semi-independence during the next two centuries of the 'Mongol (or Tatar) yoke' (see Chapter 2, note 7).

It was also the skilful use of the more northerly riverways which enabled Novgorod to expand its mini-empire eastwards and across the northern Urals into north-west Siberia, then known as the 'Yugrian land' (*Yugorskaya zemlya*). The quarry, as in the later sixteenth and seventeenth centuries under Muscovite rule, was the valuable peltry acquired either through direct hunting and trading, or through the forcible imposition by the Novgorodians of the fur tribute (*yasak*) on the local native tribes, mainly the Uralic-speaking Voguls and Ostyaks (present-day Mansi and Khanty). Throughout the Mongol period of Russian history (thirteenth–fifteenth centuries, see Chapter 2), 'Lord Novgorod the Great', as it became known, managed to avoid the major depredations of the khans and their troops and tax-gatherers (though it prudently paid a regular tribute to the Tatar treasury). Moreover, through its association with the Baltic Hanseatic League, it developed into one of the most successful trading entrepôts in northern Europe.

Its ascendancy was, however, brutally curtailed by the newly powerful city of Moscow, whose Grand-Princes had, by the late fifteenth century, managed simultaneously to break the power of Novgorod and finally expel the Mongol occupiers from European Russia. The story of Moscow's rise will be returned to in the next chapter, but here it should be noted how, following the example of the Varangians and the men of Novgorod, the Muscovite rulers, their merchants, soldiers, explorers and adventurers emulated established tradition by exploiting the forests and rivers of Siberia in Russia's amazingly rapid and successful *Drang nach Osten*. Navigating the great liquid labyrinth of routes from the Urals to the Pacific, by *c.*1640 the tsars of Moscow, despite devastating domestic upheavals, had managed to establish their suzerainty over what was to become the world's largest continental empire. Many other factors, of course, facilitated this astonishing west→east anabasis, but the central role played by Russia's mighty waterways in the expansion of the Russian state across the Eurasian continent cannot be gainsaid.

Seas and oceans

As described above, the first Russian state, Kiev Rus, was established from the ninth century onwards as a result of trading links created by Norse merchants and marauders along the river system from the Baltic to the Black Sea and the Bosphorus. Whereas other European countries – France, Spain, Portugal, Britain – were developing their *overseas* empires in Asia, Africa, the Americas and the Antipodes, Russia was essentially a *land* empire, though ultimately surrounded by major seas and the world's great oceans. However, during the mediaeval period, following the expulsion of the Mongol/Tatars and the gradual rise of Moscow in the late fifteenth century, the new Muscovite tsardom remained a largely landlocked principality in the backyard of European Christendom. The occupancy of the Baltic coastal regions by other strong states, most powerfully the kingdoms of Sweden and Lithuania, cut off maritime access to the west. In the south, the Black Sea littoral and the straits were dominated by the Ottoman Turks following the fall of Constantinople in 1453 and their subsequent conquest of the Crimea. Access to the Caspian was not much use for major commercial purposes, though the fishing industry thrived. To the north, the Arctic Ocean was frozen and unnavigable for most months of the year. True, English seafarers had made landfall near the settlement of Arkhangelsk (Archangel) in 1553, and their leader, Richard Chancellor, had travelled to the court of Ivan IV ('Ivan the Terrible', r. 1533–84) and started negotiations which led to the formation of the London-based Muscovy Company. Although this gave Moscow certain trading privileges with Elizabethan England, it scarcely qualified her to be considered as a major European mercantile power.

Further eastwards, Moscow's military defeat of the Tatar khanate of Kazan in 1552 opened up the way to the Urals, Siberia and, ultimately, the Pacific coast. However, the foundation of Russian settlements on the remote Sea of Okhotsk and an egress to the Arctic Ocean can hardly be considered to have enhanced Russia's commercial capabilities. In the seventeenth century, therefore, the Muscovite empire (for an empire it had become by virtue of its vast territorial extent and its overtly colonial policies, i.e. subjugation of the indigenous peoples and exploitation of natural resources) was still denied access to north-western trade routes and was unable to reach the ancient Euxine in the south. In 1648 an illiterate Siberian cossak, Semën Dezhnëv, sailed from the mouth of the river Kolyma in the distant north-east, around the Chukotka peninsula, and through what later became known as the Bering Strait.[3] Yet his little-documented navigational feat, negotiating the treacherous narrow channel separating the most north-eastern tip of Siberia from the American continental mainland, anticipating the voyage of Vitus Bering by eight decades, did nothing to add to Moscow's maritime or mercantile reputation. Moreover, the country did not possess a navy.

All that was to change during the reign of Peter I ('Peter the Great', r. 1682–1725). Peter's exploits and achievements will be described in greater detail in a later chapter, but as far as the maritime history of Russia is concerned, his reign signalled a veritable 'sea-change' in Russia's naval, military and commercial progress, the significance of which is hard to exaggerate. Arguably, his most spectacular achievement from this point of view was his victory over Sweden in the Great Northern War (1700–21), and the gaining of a permanent foothold on the Baltic coast, symbolised by the foundation and construction of Russia's new capital, St Petersburg, at the mouth of the river Neva (see Chapter 4). After Russia's triumph at the battle of Poltava (1709), it was to remain a formidable factor in the political, military, commercial, diplomatic and cultural history of the whole of Europe. The country's regained access to the Baltic and international sea routes, the building of Russia's first military and commercial naval fleet, and her newly acquired status as a major European power were all vital factors in transforming mediaeval Muscovy into the 'modern' Russian Empire.

Later in the century, Peter's record of territorial expansion, imperial ambition and maritime achievement in the north were to be matched in the south by his illustrious successor, the Empress Catherine II ('Catherine the Great', r. 1762–96). Peter's defeat of Sweden, the opening of the Baltic to Russian shipping, and the establishment of St Petersburg as a great naval base, were to a large extent mirrored by Catherine's victories in the Russo-Turkish wars (1768–74, 1788–92), the ousting of Ottoman rule from the north coast of the Black Sea, the annexation of the Crimean peninsula in 1783, and the founding of the exciting, cosmopolitan port/city of Odessa in 1793. As Peter was the father of Russia's Baltic fleet, so Catherine was the mother of the Black Sea armada. Although her dream of driving out the Turks from Europe was never realised, Catherine's successes in the south marked another significant chapter in Russia's geopolitical realignment, based on her access to warm-water ports. Thus, by the end of the eighteenth century, the Romanov Empire's naval presence was firmly established from the Gulf of Finland to the mouth of the Bosphorus, and from Arkhangelsk to Alaska. And in 1861, the far-eastern city of Vladivostok became home to her Pacific fleet. Russia was no longer simply the world's largest land empire, but also a major naval power whose ships plied their way throughout the northern hemisphere, and even further afield into such temperate climes as California, the Hawaiian islands, Polynesia and Australia.[4]

Frontiers

Despite its enormous geographical expanse, its largely inhospitable climate and its encircling seas, Russia has nevertheless been the subject of numerous, recurring foreign invasions of its fluctuating – now shrinking, now expanding – territories. The lands occupied by the Muscovite state, the Russian Empire and the Soviet Union have over the centuries been attacked, sacked and occupied, from both east and west, by successive waves of – *inter alios* – Varangians, Teutons, Livonians, Polovtsians, Mongols, Turks, Poles, Swedes, French, Japanese, British and – more recently and most devastatingly – the armies of Hitler's Nazi Germany.

In the south, Russia is semi-circled, as described above, by a concatenation of high mountain ranges stretching from the Caucasus to Kamchatka, but – again from both east and west – the country has no natural defences. There are no impassable mountain chains like the Alps or the Pyrenees, no uncrossable sea passages and no other great geophysical barriers to impede the incursion and advance of determined foreign aggressors. The Varangians sailed blithely, if brutally, down the Baltic–Black Seas river system; the Mongol hordes swept across the steppelands of the south with impunity; the Livonian Knights simultaneously attacked from the west; Polish invaders briefly set their own ruler on the throne of Moscow; Napoleon's *grande armée* and Hitler's *Wehrmacht* reached the same city in a matter of weeks; and during the Civil War (1918–21) the armed forces of no fewer than 14 countries fought the Bolshevik Red Army on Russian soil.

A kind of 'siege mentality', a primordial fear of both the 'western threat' and the 'yellow peril', a fanatical, atavistically conditioned suspicion of foreigners' intentions has led over the last millennium to the development of a national obsession with defending 'Mother Russia', 'Holy Russia', the *rodina* (motherland) or the *Russkaya zemlya* ('the land of Russia' – *zemlya* here having the twin connotation of 'country' and 'earth'). It is therefore no surprise that what in western parlance is referred to as the Second World War (1939–45) is in Russia officially and popularly designated as the 'Great Patriotic (Fatherland) War' (as far as the Soviet Union was concerned, 1941–45). The defence of this gigantic territory therefore required a huge army that was both too expensive for the state to support and never large enough for its task, except at a terrible price for the civilian population. In the second half of the twentieth century the astronomical cost of maintaining military equivalence with the more affluent west during the Cold War was a paramount factor in the crippling process which led to the decline and fall of the Soviet Empire.

Once more it can be seen how a feature of the country's geographical peculiarities has influenced not only its military and political fortunes but also the formation of the Russian psyche and idiosyncratic national character.

The 'Eurasian' dimension

One of the most intriguing, vexatious and, in some senses almost philosophical, questions about the history of Russian civilisation is what might be called, somewhat clumsily, the country's and the people's 'geocultural orientation' (or, equally, 'occidentation'). That is to say, the question of Russia's ambivalent, dichotomous identity vis-à-vis Europe and Asia. Is she a western or an eastern nation? Does she 'belong' to Europe or Asia? Is she of neither? Is she something completely *sui generis* which does not fit easily into either category? Is the ambiguous term 'Eurasian' appropriate or sufficiently precise to identify all or any of her salient ethnic and cultural characteristics? Such questions have exercised the minds of Russian politicians, theologians, philosophers, artists, rulers, writers and revolutionaries for centuries. There is of course no model answer, and the debate continues to the present day. What one *can* do is identify a number of pertinent issues – such as geography, history, political and social development, religion, language and culture – as a starting point for informed discussion.

At the geographical level – as already noted above – it is clear that the Russian Empire, the USSR, and the present Russian Federation straddles, or sprawls across, both eastern Europe and northern Asia. Around three-quarters of its territory lies beyond the Urals, and several of Siberia's major cities lie longitudinally east of Delhi, Kathmandu and Peking. The majority of its population, however, and most of its agricultural resources and manufacturing industries are located in the European part of the country west of the Urals. Thousands and thousands of square kilometres of northern Siberia are either only sparsely populated or else totally uninhabited. While the aboriginal, native peoples of Siberia, the far north and the far east are largely of non-European stock – Mongol, Turkic, paleo-asiatic, etc. – they account today for only around 6 per cent of the territory's total population, the majority of which is composed of immigrants or the descendants of immigrants from European Russia, as well as Ukraine, Belarus and Poland. These are all part of the Slavonic group of peoples, which is unquestionably European, both ethnically and linguistically. Despite centuries of miscegenation with other, non-European peoples, the ethnic Slavs – including Russians, Ukrainians, Belorussians, Czechs, Slovaks, Bulgarians, Slovenes, Serbs, Croats, Macedonians *et al.* – are 'white' skinned, and speak the corresponding Slavic tongues which together comprise one of the major European language groups. In grammar, morphology, syntax, phonology and lexicography, Russian and the other Slavic languages are just as European as English, French, German, Latin or Greek. To that extent, there is no question but that the Russians *are* Europeans, whether they live in Vitebsk, Volgograd or Vladivostok.

However, a number of questions immediately arise. First, of course, is how one defines *Europe*. This is obviously too big an issue to discuss *in extenso* at this juncture, but it is fair to say that concepts of what actually constitutes Europe have fluctuated and altered over the centuries, and are conditioned and affected by political, military, religious and cultural considerations, as well as purely geographical factors. The former French President, Charles de Gaulle, for instance, once famously spoke of his vision of a Europe stretching from the Atlantic to the Urals – yet repeatedly said '*non*' to Britain's proposed entry into what was then the European Common Market. Very rarely do courses on modern European history at British universities include the history of, for example, Poland, Bulgaria or Finland. During the Cold War, to many westerners, Europe in fact meant just that – *western* Europe. Anything east of the Oder and Neisse rivers was in some way considered by many to be ideologically, politically and culturally alien territory. In spite of centuries of shared history and culture, Europe lay *this* side of the Iron Curtain. In the early twenty-first century, things have changed: the 'Communist bloc' has disappeared, and the European Union now (at the time of writing) consists of 25 countries, including former Communist states which share a common border with Russia. And it is well known that many citizens of the United Kingdom – a supposed pillar of western civilisation – are distinctly hostile to Britain's membership of 'Europe'.

One issue of current debate over European identity is that of a common cultural and religious legacy of Christianity. In the year 988, Kiev Rus, in the person of Grand Prince Vladimir I of Kiev (r. 978–1015), formally adopted Christianity as its official religion. The brand of that particular faith was, however, of the Eastern

Orthodox rite, with its centre at Constantinople. The schism between Byzantium and Rome therefore meant that the Russian Church (along with other Orthodox communities) followed a different path, observed a different ritual and used a different language from that of western Christendom. Thus the infant Russian state, though initially ruled by the European Norsemen, was already developing its own distinctive religious and cultural characteristics which set it apart from Europe. This was compounded by the Mongol conquest and occupation from the early thirteenth to the late fifteenth centuries. For over 200 years Russia was merely the most westerly administrative province of the vast Mongol Empire, known as the Golden Horde, with its capital at Sarai on the river Volga, and initially ruled over by the grandson of Chenghiz Khan, Baty (1208–55). It was the unique mixture of Eastern Christianity, subjection to the oriental despotism of the Mongol khans, the isolation from contemporaneous cultural developments in Europe, such as the Renaissance and, later, the Reformation, lack of familiarity with Europe's ecclesiastical and cultural lingua franca – mediaeval Latin – and ignorance of technological inventions and scientific discoveries in the west, together with her original European links, which formed the basis for Russia's idiosyncratic cultural and political development over the next few centuries. Moreover, Russia, unlike most of western Europe (including Britain south of Hadrian's Wall), had never been part of the Roman Empire, and therefore had no conception or experience of Roman law.

The distinction may also be illustrated visually by comparing the ecclesiastical architecture of Europe and Russia. The great cathedrals and small village churches of European Christendom were all (despite variations between northern Gothic and Mediterranean classical styles) built on essentially the same model – nave, transept, altar, choir, pulpit, stained-glass windows, tower, dome or steeple and attendant devotional paraphernalia. A Christian worshipper in pre-Reformation western Europe (or eastern Europe for that matter), would feel equally familiar with his surroundings in York Minster, Paris's Notre Dame or St Peter's in Rome. Russian Orthodox churches are of a totally different order, with their famous, distinctive onion-shaped cupolas, seven-pointed crosses, colourful ornamentation, painted sacred images from floor to ceiling, the iconostasis and the absence of pews. St Basil's Cathedral on Moscow's Red Square, built by Ivan the Terrible in the 1550s to celebrate his victory over Kazan, is probably the best-known example, externally at any rate, and has become almost a symbol of Russia, instantly recognisable as such. This may be an oversimplification, but the *difference*, both visually and spiritually, is there for all to see and feel.

After the collapse of the Golden Horde in the fifteenth century, Muscovy's eastwards expansion across Siberia, inheriting, as it were, the empire of Chenghiz Khan, brought her into close contact with other Asiatic peoples and civilisations – including the Chinese – which further enhanced and entrenched Russia's 'otherness' and contributed to the formation of her 'Eurasian' character.

While retaining something of their country's exclusivity in the sixteenth and seventeenth centuries, the Muscovite tsars did resume some tentative contacts with the west, dispatching ambassadors to European courts, establishing trading links and even maintaining the so-called 'foreign quarter' (*Nemetskaya sloboda*) in the suburbs of Moscow for foreign advisers, technicians and military personnel to reside. But it was really the phenomenal reforming zeal of Peter the Great and his energetic programme of far-reaching Euro-peanising change that brought a new dimension to the whole question of Russo-European relations. The impact and interplay of these reforms will be examined in detail in a later chapter, but while Peter sought to modernise the state and at any rate parts of society, Russia still retained many of the traditions and institutions of its semi-Asiatic, Muscovite past, not least the autocratic style of govern-ment, the Eastern Orthodox Church and, crucially, the mediaeval system of serfdom which had been long abandoned in western Europe. This situation remained the case even during the suppos-edly 'enlightened' regime of Catherine the Great, herself a European-educated German princess by origin.

However, it was during the second quarter of the nineteenth century, during the authoritarian rule of Emperor Nicholas I (r. 1825–55), that the question of Russia's national identity in relation to, or in contrast with, Europe came to a head and took on new propor-tions during the so-called 'Westerniser–Slavophil' controversy. In the 1840s, members of Russia's independent-minded, educated intellec-tual elite (the *intelligentsia*, see below) argued ardently and sometimes acrimoniously about the nature of Russia's civilisation, her past history, present predicament and future path. During their polemics, the Westernisers (*zapadniki*), such as Belinskii, Herzen and Bakunin, took a pro-European line, while the Slavophils (*slavyanofily*) – Khomyakov, the Kireevskii and Aksakov brothers *et al.* – stressed the unique and superior nature of Russian civilisation over that of the moribund west. The social, cultural and religious issues they discussed are explored in a later chapter, but they were to form a major leitmotif throughout the whole consequent course of Russian intellectual history, the echoes of which reverberate to this day.

Following this brief examination of some features of the country's geographical characteristics and their interaction with her special historical development – a kind of Slavic *Sonderweg*, as it were – it is appropriate at this stage to move on to describe the people, or peoples, who inhabit the Russian land.

Russian society

Since this book is principally concerned with the history of the Romanov Empire from the early seventeenth century to 1917, the social structure of the country during the Kievan, Mongol and early Muscovite periods falls outside its scope. However, some background information on the early centuries will assist understanding of later developments. Two important points need to be made. The first is that at all periods of its history until the mid-twentieth century, Russia's society was overwhelmingly peasant in composition. The general census of 1897, the only comprehensive one in Russia's history, recorded that out of the total population of the whole Russian Empire of 129 million, 81 per cent constituted the 'rural estate' (*sel'skoe soslovie* – i.e. peasants) – that is, roughly 105 million. Until 1861, the majority of the peasants were held in some kind of serf bondage to the crown, the state, the Church or to private landowners. Others, while being technically free-farming tenants inhabiting the large estates, gradually had their residual liberties eroded by various fiscal and legal mechanisms which, by the middle of the seventeenth century, had resulted in the full-fledged, near-universal enserfment of the Russian peasantry. The nature of the vassalage and the forms of feudal obligations which the peasants suffered varied from time to time and from place to place. Changing tenurial arrangements, regional variations, new legislative acts, shifting internal and external pressures means that broad, general, all-embracing definitions are impossible to make. However, following the great Code of Laws (*Ulozhenie*) of 1649, promulgated by Tsar Aleksei (r. 1645–76), the agrarian labouring classes of the Russian population were either the privately owned serfs of the landed, service nobility (*dvoryanstvo*), crown peasants living and working on the royal domains, state peasants dwelling on government-administered possessions, or 'ecclesiastical serfs', tied to either church or monastic lands. The 200-year process by which the exploited Russian serfs – whose position and relationship with their masters were not far removed from outright slavery – eventually gained their ambiguous freedom in 1861 forms a major part of the following study.

Second, a peculiar feature of Russian peasant society was the institution of the rural, or village, commune (*sel'skoe obshchestvo* – usually referred to as the *obshchina* or *mir*), briefly mentioned above. The origins of the commune are still the subject of historical debate and have long been so.[5] The communal property-owning relationship is a standard feature of many primitive and developing societies, but whereas it had long disappeared in early modern Europe, in Russia it survived well into the twentieth century and was, paradoxically, given formal, legal status under the terms of the act of emancipation issued by Alexander II (r. 1855–81) in 1861. The commune was the very core of peasant existence: it governed, determined and controlled every aspect of the peasant's life – land, work, household affairs, personal relationships, financial responsibilities, legal rights, penal liabilities and physical movement. It had its own officials, its own customs, rituals, tribunals, common laws, quasi-democratic assemblies and decision-making processes. These forms of collective organisation were not confined just to *peasant* communities; there were also similar cooperatives of craftsmen, hunters, waggoners, icon painters, lumberjacks, artisans, conscript soldiers – even criminals, convicts and exiles – in fact, in every corner of the life of the Russian common people – the *narod*. It was this collectivist tradition that led nineteenth-century 'Populist' revolutionaries, the *narodniki* (see Chapter 9), to believe that *socialism* was the natural mode of social, political and economic organisation for the Russian people. Many of the Populists maintained, too, that the Russian people were also instinctively given to rebellion, and pointed to

Russia's long, historical record of revolt against authority in the form of either spasmodic localised insurgencies or widespread peasant wars.

The upper classes of Russian society, against which these plebeian revolts were directed, consisted of: remnants of the old mediaeval landowning hereditary aristocracy, the *boyars*; the powerful service (and also landowning) nobility or *dvoryanstvo*; the higher echelons of the Orthodox Church hierarchy; and the wealthier elements of the urban-based merchant class. Of these, the most important in many respects was the *dvoryanstvo*. The term is derived from the Russian word *dvor*, meaning the royal court. (It also means a household, or a yard.) These 'courtiers' were, however, not simply servitors in the official offices and chambers of the tsar, but originally supporters of the Grand Princes of Moscow who offered their military services to them in their political struggles with other rival princes and the *boyars* at the beginning of the sixteenth century. Ivan III ('Ivan the Great', r. 1462–1505) and his son, Vasilii III (r. 1505–33), had gradually asserted the supremacy of Moscow over the other central and northern principalities, and in the process enjoyed the backing of the *dvoryanstvo*, who were rewarded for their services by landed estates (sing. *pomest'e*), often taken over from the possessions of the Grand Prince's defeated rivals. The Muscovite rulers also enjoyed the powerful support of the Orthodox Church. The distinction between the *pomest'e* of the nobility and the estates of the *boyars* was that the former were originally held in life-tenure, reverting to the state for redistribution after the owner's death, whereas the *boyars'* lands (sing. *votchina*) were traditionally hereditary and passed on down the family line. However, during the course of the sixteenth and seventeenth centuries, the distinction began to be blurred and virtually disappeared. This was partly because the powers of the old *boyar* class had been eroded as the autocracy gained in strength, and partly because the *dvoryanstvo*'s original tradition of service to the state had fallen into desuetude. Such was the reliance of the Muscovite tsars on the nobility's continuing allegiance and support that the latter's privileges – including greater powers over the enserfed peasants – were enhanced and entrenched without the distraction of perpetual military or civilian service obligations. Peter the Great was soon to jolt them out of their relative complacency. Throughout the empire's existence, both before and after the end of serfdom, it was the *dvoryanstvo* from which the state continued to recruit its military leaders, its governors, its senior bureaucrats and its diplomatic personnel. Though compulsory life-long service obligations re-imposed by Peter the Great were to be lifted by Catherine II, the *dvoryanstvo* (including the surviving descendants of the old *boyar* class) continued to be essentially Russia's ruling elite until the revolutions of 1917, and the status of nobleman (*dvoryanin*) still remained the reward for distinguished service to the state in the military or the civil bureaucracy. The 1897 census records the 'noble estate' (both personal and hereditary) as numbering 1.2 per cent of the population.

So, on the eve of those revolutions, Russian society still consisted essentially of the five official estates (*soslovie*) – nobility, clergy, merchantry, burghers and peasantry (*dvoryanstvo, dukhovenstvo, kupechestvo, meshchanstvo, krest'yanstvo*) – which had formed the basis of the mediaeval Muscovite social order. However, from the mid-nineteenth century onwards, three new significant forces appeared in Russian society, which, while none of them constituted an official *soslovie*, were nevertheless absolutely central to the social and political history of late imperial Russia, and ultimately to have a crucial impact on the fate of the Romanov Empire. These were the intelligentsia, the industrial working class, and what Marxists term the 'bourgeoisie'.

Although the exact date of the word's first literary usage cannot be pinned down, the term *intelligentsia* is a Russian coinage dating probably from the late 1850s. Obviously derived from the Latin part-icipial adjective *intellegens* ('that which understands'), in the Russian context it did not mean simply intellectuals, still less the educated, nor even members of the 'free professions'. It was origin-ally and in essence what Isaiah Berlin once described as the *intelligentsia militans* – i.e. a kind of secular order of dedicated, rad-ically minded 'left-wing' intellectuals, passionate in their belief in freedom, justice and humanity, fiercely opposed to the tsarist social and political order, devoted to what they saw as the cause of the Russian peasant masses (*narod*), and determined to bring about the total transformation of Russian society, if necessary by the means of violent revolution. Although this critically thinking and often implacable fraternity was often out of tune with the conservatism and popular monarchism of the common people on whose behalf they claimed to be acting, there is no doubt as to their sincerity, zeal and sense of revolutionary purpose in the mid- to late nineteenth century. Over the years many gave up their own lives or liberty in the struggle to ensure that the Russian people could lead their lives in liberty. And, around the end of the century, the intellectual gulf that had separated the militant intelligentsia and the originally suspicious *narod* began to narrow, ultimately resulting in an unstoppable alliance of revolutionary proportions.

The traditional object of the radical intelligentsia's concern had been the plight of the Russian peasantry. However, the belated, rapid industrialisation of the economy at the turn of the nineteenth and twentieth centuries created the largely urban labour force which manned Russia's booming new industrial enterprises, mines, mills and swiftly expanding railway system (see Chapter 10). Compared with the enormous class of agrarian workers – the peasantry – the industrial proletariat comprised only a very small percentage of the population. Figures vary according to different sources, and are complicated by the actual definition of 'working class', since many of its members still technically belonged to the peasantry, and often returned to their villages to assist with the spring sowing or autumn harvest. According to one source, the number of workers employed in manufacturing, mining and metallurgy rose from 1.4 million in 1890 to 3.1 million in 1913.[6] This, of course, was tiny in comparison with the enormous rural population. However, its strategic location in a handful of large urban centres such as Moscow, St Petersburg, Baku and Warsaw, its concentration in overcrowded, unsanitary living quarters, the great size of the workforce in individual factories, dangerous and unhealthy working conditions and gross economic exploitation all led to the speedy development of a corporate identity or class consciousness based on common grievances and common suffering. Russian workers did not need the ministrations of Marxist revolutionary agitators to teach them the evils and inequalities of capitalism or the tsarist police state. Consequently the discontented and increasingly organised proletariat was to play a leading role in the nationwide unrest and social upheavals which peaked in the early twentieth century. It is significant that the revolutionary explosions of 1905 and of both February and October 1917 were all initially detonated, not by revolting peasants or the restive middle class, but by the radicalised *industrial workers* of the imperial capital, St Petersburg (Petrograd).

Until the Industrial Revolution in the late nineteenth century, Russia did not possess anything like an economically powerful professional or business class, owners of industrial capital or entrepreneurs which were in any way analogous to the European middle classes or bourgeoisie. Richard Pipes, in his book on Russia under the old regime, talks of 'the missing bourgeoisie' and analyses possible reasons for this hole in the social fabric of Russia: the largely agrarian economy, the small amount of money in circulation, the retarded development of towns and cities, and so on.[7] What urban population there was in Russia's very few large pre-industrial towns consisted mainly of administrative and military personnel, artisans, shopkeepers, merchants and clergy.

It was only with the development of capitalist relationships following the end of serfdom that something approaching a European-style bourgeoisie began to develop. Unlike the case of their western counterparts, however, the newly accumulated economic prosperity of the Russian middle classes was not matched by any great political ambition on their part. Ideas of democracy, parliamentarianism, constitutional government, although being long admired and advocated by more moderate members of the intelligentsia, had no real solid social or economic base. There was, consequently, no strong tradition of 'liberalism', of the politics of the centre, in autocratic Russia. (It is perhaps significant that there is no native Russian word for 'compromise'.) Against the background of her own belated industrial revolution, however, liberal aspirations began to twitch and stir. And after the introduction of institutional reforms in the wake of the revolutionary upheavals of 1905, moderate, constitutionally-minded parties such as the Constitutional Democrats ('Kadets') and the so-called Octobrists (see Chapter 11) were to play a prominent, if ultimately ineffectual, role in the political play-acting during the dying years of the regime. In comparison with the parties of the left, such as the Socialist Revolutionaries and the Social Democrats, the feeble plant of Russian liberalism stood little chance of success or survival in the face of the vigorously blooming revolutionary movement of peasants and workers.

It is clear, then, that Russia had a highly polarised social structure. It was a country and a society of extreme contrasts and contradictions. Peter the Great had in fact effectively created two societies. On the one hand was the semi-Europeanised, cultured elite, and on the other were the peasant masses, exploited, fleeced, conscripted and mired in ignorance, superstition, fear of the knout and periodic famine. This great divide was recognised in the Russian language, which uses two different words to describe, on the one hand, 'society' (*obshchestvo*) – what in English might be called 'high society' – i.e. the upper, privileged classes, and, on the other, 'the people' (*narod*), i.e. the lower classes of peasant and proletariat. In that sense of the terminology, 'society' did not include 'the people', and 'the people' were not part of 'society'. As stated in the Preface to this book, one does not need to subscribe to Marx's theory of class struggle to see that the whole course of Russia's modern history is shot through with the constant conflict between her upper and lower classes – in Russian, the *verkhi* and the *nizy*. As the present author has written elsewhere:

> The Russian Empire at the beginning of the twentieth century contained a highly volatile mixture of ostentatious wealth and grinding poverty; power and debility; backwardness and modernity; despotism and urgent demand for change. Examples everywhere were to be found of juxtaposed barbarism and sophistication; European and Asiatic traditions; advanced technology and primitive techniques; enlightenment and ignorance … [which] led the great Russian writer, Leo Tolstoy, to remark ironically that Russia was 'the only country in the world where Ghenghis Khan enjoys the use of the telephone'.[8]

Non-Russian peoples

In his *The Course of Russian History*, Klyuchevskii famously observed that: 'The history of Russia is the history of a country which is being colonised … Migrations, the colonisation of the country, constituted the fundamental fact of our history.'[9] While one may reasonably point to other fundamental facts that have shaped Russia's history in similar measure, nevertheless the movement of peoples, the colonial expansion of the Russian state into distant territories, the settlement of remote, alien lands, and intercourse with myriad non-Russian peoples of many differing ethnic origins is clearly central to the exponential development of the original petty princedoms of Kiev Rus into the massive Russian Empire.

The early settlement of the European steppe and forest zones by the eastern Slavs and Nordic incomers was retarded by the Mongol occupation, but after the lifting of the 'Tatar yoke', expansion and colonisation resumed northwards towards the White and Kara Seas, and eastwards beyond the Urals through the fur-rich forests of Siberia. As Muscovy expanded, her new territories were protected by a peppering of small stockaded wooden fortresses – *ostrogi* (sing. *ostrog*) – which formed the nuclei of future towns. These were originally military, administrative and trading centres, and also rudimentary bastions from which the advancing Slavs established their control over the indigenous peoples who inhabited their newly conquered possessions. Resistance to the Russians' onward march was minimal, and the native tribes of Siberia and the far north were quickly, easily and brutally reduced to submission. Their primitive weapons were no match for Muscovite powder and shot, and in many cases it was simply a matter of switching payment of tribute from their erstwhile Mongol masters to the new Russian tsars. Also, as long as the aboriginal peoples remained docile, as they largely did, and continued to deliver the *yasak*, the Russian authorities interfered little with their traditional lifestyles. However, there is a long-standing controversy over what benefits, or blights, the victorious newcomers visited on the non-Russian peoples (*inorodtsy*) with whom they came into contact during their inexorable eastward advance. Was Russia the bearer of a superior civilisation bringing economic progress, modern technology, agriculture and Christianity to a primitive patchwork of backward and mutually belligerent tribesmen? Or was she simply a rapacious plunderer, ransacking the forests of their fur, screwing the natives, and bringing only brutality, bad liquor and pathogenic bacilli which in some cases resulted in creeping genocide? The answer may be that while there was no deliberate policy of extermination, there is no doubt that the conquering Russians inflicted untold suffering on the subjugated aboriginals through such practices as hostage taking – which denuded villages of their ablest hunters, chieftains and shamans – abducting native women and children, depleting natural food stocks through over-hunting, and introducing virulent alien diseases such as smallpox, leprosy and syphilis. On the other hand, there were genuine attempts to integrate native leaders into the local administration, the introduction of superior tools and appliances, innovatory agricultural practices, and legislation which afforded some protection from the more extortionate forms of exploitation. Also, both forcible and voluntary sexual intercourse between the Russians and the *inorodtsy* led to interbreeding, metisisation, and, over time, a limited mutual absorption, or at least respectful recognition, of each other's values, practices and customs. This process, of course, lent an extra dimension to the question of Russia's Eurasian identity discussed earlier.

Statistical tables in a government publication of 1914 put the number of non-Russian peoples inhabiting the territory of Asiatic Russia at over 50, divided into two larger sub-groups of Ural-Altaians (including Finnic, Tungus, Mongol and Turkic), and the Paleoasiatic (among them the Eskimo, Chukchi, Koryak, Yukagir, Aleut, Ainu, Gilyak, and other peoples of the Arctic north and far eastern coastline). According to the 1897 census the total population of Siberia and the Far East (but excluding Turkestan), was around 5.8 million, of which 4.9 million were composed of Russian and other European incomers, while the *inorodtsy* numbered just short of 900,000 (i.e. about 15.5 per cent). By 1911, the corresponding figures were: total – 9.4 million; Russian – 8.4 million; 'native' – 973,000.[10] The proportion of the latter had therefore dwindled to 10.3 per cent of the total. The reason for this percentage decrease was the massive movement of government-sponsored peasant migration from central European Russia and Ukraine into Siberia during the first decade or so of the twentieth century, which was, of course, facilitated by the completion of the Trans-Siberian Railway.

Aside from Russia's vast northern empire, during the eighteenth century her rulers shifted their attention to the west and south. Peter I's conquests on the Baltic littoral have already been touched on, but apart from the maritime aspect, Russia's new possessions in this region brought within her boundaries the non-Slav, Catholic and Lutheran populations of present-day Lithuania, Latvia and Estonia, with their own old civilisations, cultures and western traditions. Although they were infinitesimal in size compared with the limitless expanses of Siberia, the acquisition of the Baltic provinces, together with the new capital of St Petersburg, went a long way towards consummating Peter's desires and ambitions to turn his country to the west. It also added another element to the ethnic composition of his subjects.

Equally ambitious in her territorial designs, Catherine the Great extended the Russian Empire even further westwards by her military and diplomatic role in the three partitions of the ancient Catholic kingdom of Poland in 1773, 1793 and 1795. While the subjection of Poland to Russian rule certainly added to the empire's territories and its tax-paying population, it was also to stir up an angry storm of bitter anti-Russian emotion and hostility over the next century and beyond. It also added considerably to the Jewish population of the Russian Empire. In the south, although Catherine never achieved her ambition, fuelled by her lover, Prince Grigorii Potëmkin, of ousting the Turks from Constantinople, she had considerable success in the Russo-Turkish wars, and, as mentioned above, established Russian dominion over the north coast of the Black Sea (see Chapter 6). In ethnic terms this now brought a further contingent of Turkic-speaking Muslim Tatars under Russian imperial rule.

In the nineteenth century Russia continued its imperial expansion and colonial policies, acquiring successively Georgia, Finland, Bessarabia, Armenia and Azerbaijan, and the large central Asian territories which nowadays comprise Turkmenistan, Kazakhstan, Uzbekistan, Tadjikistan and Kirgizstan. Russian America (Alaska) with its sparse North American Indian population was acquired in the late eighteenth century, though abandoned in the 1860s. Large tracts of far eastern territory were ceded by China to Russia on the eve of the emancipation of the serfs, and the Amur and Ussuri districts thus became the scene for further Russian settlement and colonisation (see Chapter 9). The transaction also served to augment the oriental population of the Romanov Empire with tens of thousands of mainly Chinese and Korean subjects.

On the eve of its collapse this huge continental empire was therefore made up of a motley, multi-ethnic, polyglot collection of many peoples, traditions, religions and cultures in various stages of economic and social development, from the Palaeolithic to the modern industrial, but only two-fifths of which were ethnically Russian. The distinction between the 'truly' Russian, and the other nationalities which made up the empire, is exemplified by the two adjectives in Russian for 'Russian'. One – *russkii* – derives from the old name of 'Rus' and denotes what is quintessentially and ethnically pure Russian (*chistyi russkii*) – whatever that might be. The other – *Rossiiskii* – comes from the Latinate term 'Rossiya', which is of later provenance and refers not so much to the nation as to the state. Thus, a native Russian would speak of the *russkaya zemlya* ('the Russian land') and the *russkii yazyk* ('Russian language') but of the *Rossiiskaya Imperiya* (the Russian Empire), which was made up of many nationalities, but all under Russian rule.[11] (The distinction is not entirely dissimilar from that between the terms 'English' and 'British'. It is also interesting to note in this respect that the Soviet national anthem, or 'State Hymn', composed under Stalin, had as its first line: 'An indestructible union of free republics has been created by Great *Rus*' [not "Rossiya"]'. On the other hand, both in Soviet times and at the present day the Russian state is officially called the *Rossiiskaya Federatsiya*.) And, like all other imperial powers throughout history, the builders of the Russian Empire never questioned the morality of, or justification for, their territorial aggrandisement at the expense of other nations. Avarice, military glory, curiosity, power-lust, 'manifest destiny' and the 'urge to the sea' – all played their part in the imperial imperative. Like the Roman Caesars, the Spanish *conquistadores* and the British colonialists, successive Russian governments and the Russian people seemed to assume they had a 'natural', emphyteutic right to occupy, settle and profit from the usufruct of other peoples' homelands, regardless of the interests of the original inhabitants.

But whatever the differing levels of development of the multifarious peoples of the *Rossiiskaya Imperiya*, they all shared one thing in common. They were all of them – whether Russian or Tatar, Estonian or Eskimo, gentile or Jew – subjects of the same autocratic Russian tsars, emperors and empresses of the royal house of Romanov. How these absolute monarchs originally established and consolidated their imperial sway in the sixteenth and seventeenth centuries is the subject of the next two chapters.

2 Kievan, Mongol and early Muscovite Russia

The *periodizatsiya* ('periodisation', to use a rather awkward word) of Russia's past is generally agreed on by historians who otherwise adopt different methodological approaches, and start from varying ideological or intellectual premises. If one ignores the very earliest times when nothing that could properly be described as a Russian nation, state or even people existed, then five major generally accepted periods of the country's historical development can safely be identified: (i) Kievan (ninth to early thirteenth centuries); (ii) Mongol or Tatar (early thirteenth to late fifteenth centuries); (iii) Muscovite (sixteenth and seventeenth centuries); (iv) Petrine, St Petersburg or Imperial (eighteenth to early twentieth centuries); and (v.) Soviet (twentieth century). As yet it is too early to come up with a word that satisfactorily designates the 'post-Soviet' period, but that term itself will suffice pro tem. While the main focus of the present chapter is on the early Muscovite period, it is useful to preface this with a brief analysis of Kievan and Mongol Russia, in so far as both epochs left their own distinct imprint on developments in later centuries.

Kiev Rus

The history of Russia proper is traditionally dated from the ninth century AD, and any reconstruction of the history of the eastern Slavs before that date 'can only be conjectural'.[1] The major Russian source for the early history of Kiev Rus is 'The Primary Chronicle' (*Povest' vremennykh let*) – part historical record, part legend, part saga – written over a number of decades by many hands. The entry for the year 862 records that the unruly Slavs of the Novgorod region summoned three brothers from among the Scandinavian Varangians (Vikings) to come and rule over them, 'For our whole land is great and rich, but there is no order in it.'[2] Accordingly, the eldest of the brothers, the semi-mythical Ryurik, with his headquarters at Novgorod, became the founder of Russia's first ruling dynasty, the *Ryurikevichi* (sons, or descendants, of Ryurik), from which all Russia's later rulers until the late sixteenth century traced their descent. The first of the Varangian princes to make Kiev, if not exactly the capital then at any rate the most important of the fortress towns in the lands of Rus, was Oleg (r. 882–912), known in folklore as 'Oleg the Far-seeing' (*Oleg Veshchii*), and renowned for his wisdom, military prowess and diplomatic skills, not least in his dealings with Byzantium. He may properly be regarded as the first 'real' ruler of Kiev Rus.

Never in its entire history could Kiev Rus be regarded as a unified, still less a unitary, nation-state under a single, all-powerful monarch. The petty princedoms of Kievan Russia formed a loose congeries (even 'federation' is too strong a term) of semi-independent tiny city-states dotted along the waterways from the Baltic to the Black Sea, from Novgorod in the north to the mouth of the Dnepr in the south. Though a successful trading power with its own flourishing culture, close religious ties with Constantinople, and dynastic alliances through marriage into other European royal houses, Kiev Rus was racked throughout its history by internecine, fratricidal warfare among the Ryurikevich rulers, and constantly harried by the incursions of warrior neighbours from the steppes, such as the Pechenegs and Polovtsians. True, there were some outstanding figures among the princes who brought military victory and brief periods of peace and some prosperity, but overall the pattern of politics in this era is one of dynastic rivalries, conspiracy, family feuds, alien invasions and murder.

Perhaps the two most successful rulers were Vladimir I (r. 980–1015) – later canonised by the Orthodox Church as St Vladimir – and his son Yaroslav I ('Yaroslav the Wise' – *Yaroslav Mudryi* – r. 1036–54). Vladimir was originally a fierce pagan warrior, reputedly with a taste for hard liquor and human sacrifice, and serviced by a multitude of concubines strategically sequestered in a number of handily located seraglios. 'He was,' says the chronicler, 'insatiable in vice (*I bye nesyt' bluda*)', habitually violating female relatives, virgin girls and nuns.[3] A confirmed and practising satyr, Vladimir was hardly the most obvious candidate for sainthood, but he eventually attained this celestial status by formally (and often forcibly) converting his subjects to Christianity, officially in 988. Commercial, military and diplomatic calculations, rather than religious zeal, natural piety or divine, Damascene revelation were the main motivating factors behind Vladimir's decision, but the alliance with Byzantium, now sanctified by a shared nominal faith, was to have incalculable repercussions throughout the whole course of Russia's future development. Not only in matters ecclesiastical, but her entire civilisation – governance, culture, literature, art, ideology, morality, even the quotidian routines of Russian community life – were to be profoundly affected and shaped by tenth-century Kiev's conversion to Eastern Orthodox Christianity by the violent libertine, later saint, Vladimir.

The reign of Yaroslav the Wise was possibly the high point of Kiev Rus's power and prestige. 'The Primary Chronicle' shows him in a very rosy light, but his path to the throne, like that of many of his predecessors and successors, was littered with the bodies of his rivals and opponents. For a while, Rus was divided between him and his challenger and brother, Mstislav of Tmutorokan, who ruled lands to the east of the Dnepr, while Yaroslav himself held sway over the territories to the west, including Kiev. When Mstislav died in 1036, the country was reunified, and during the rest of Yaroslav's reign remained more united than it possibly ever had been during its history. This, though, was at a cost: ten of his eleven brothers were dead, and the surviving one remained imprisoned until Yaroslav's death. However, his sobriquet was probably well deserved, at least judged by the barbaric standards of the time. He forged shrewd alliances with other rulers, including the Byzantine Emperor, sealing them with the marriages of his various offspring with the sons and daughters of other royal families. In this way, politico-nuptial relations were forged between Kiev and, for example, Poland, Hungary, France and Norway. He also managed to secure the appointment of the priest, Ilarion, as the first native Russian metropolitan of the Orthodox Church in Kiev, thus demonstrating his independence from Byzantium. Ilarion himself is credited with being one of the most outstanding authors of homiletic literature in the Kievan age, in particular his *Sermon on the Law and Grace*, which includes a grandiloquent encomium to the 'great "kagan" [*sic*] Volodimer', the Christianiser of the Rus.[4] Yaroslav was also a great patron of the arts, and under his 'wise' rule Kiev developed into an important centre of mediaeval learning. Outwardly, too, his city began to rival the architectural splendours of Constantinople, with which contemporaries admiringly compared it, including the Great Golden Gates of Kiev, constructed in 1037, and the magnificent St Sophia cathedral, to which Yaroslav added Russia's first library, also in 1037. Finally, as legislator, Yaroslav the Wise earned his reputation for sagacity by his compilation of the earliest Russian code of laws, the *Pravda Russkaya*, which, for certain offences, introduced some humane provisions for the substitution of monetary fines for blood vengeance.

Blood, however, was to be a recurring feature of the next period of Kievan history following Yaroslav's death. Despite the claims of some historians, such as Klyuchevskii, that he attempted in his testament to ensure some kind of continuing unity under his heirs and successors, the next half century or so was marked by the same pattern of family in-fighting, sibling slaughter and rivalry among the Ryurikevich princelings as in the earlier period. Only the reign of Vladimir II (Vladimir Monomakh, r. 1113–25) restored some kind of short-lived unity to the fractious state of Kievan Rus. After the death of his son Mstislav in 1132 the country degenerated into a century of renewed political confusion and internal mayhem during which – to use Florinsky's image – 'ambitious princes … came and went amidst disorder and torrents of blood'.[5] So enfeebled were the Russian principalities by the eternal feuding, the internal haemorrhaging, and the routine ravages of the steppe horsemen from the east, that they were in no fit state to parry the final *coup de sabre* administered by the Mongol warlords in 1237.

Before examining the effects of the Mongol invasion and occupation of Russia, three questions concerning the Kievan period need to be briefly addressed. The first is the issue of the so-called 'Normanist controversy'. This revolves around the problem of whether the first organisers and rulers of the primitive Kievan state were the Scandinavian, Varangian, invaders, referred to by the chronicler as the '*Rus*', or the indigenous Slavs. Ever since the argument first flared up in the eighteenth century, it has been bedevilled by fierce patriotic, nationalistic and ethnicist emotions, the evidence adduced by both sides often resting on fairly flimsy historical, annalistic, archaeological or philological data. True, many of the names of the early rulers of Kiev are recognisably Nordic – Oleg, Olga, Igor, etc. – but it is also clear that some form of rudimentary civil structure and political administration must have been in place before the coming of the Varangians. It seems sensible to conclude that some kind of conflation of the incoming northern merchant adventurers and the leaders of the settled Slavic tribes took place, which led to the emergence of a ruling, if internally dysfunctional, dynasty and a mixed governing class of princes, chieftains, magnates and their entourages.

This leads on to the following question – that of the Kievan economy. Was its basis trade or agriculture? There is little doubt, as already mentioned in this and the preceding chapter, that the riverborne incursions of the Varangians were motivated by the quest to establish commercial relations with the markets of the eastern Roman Empire, most prominently Constantinople, where the blonde, fair-skinned Slavs were highly prized on the Byzantine slave markets. (The words 'Slav' and 'slave' are in fact etymologically related.) However, it is obvious that this lucrative commercial business was transacted, not by the mass of the people or petty peddlers, but by wealthy merchants, ship owners, government agencies and professional traders – in other words, the rich and powerful upper classes of Kievan society, backed by military support. The hoi polloi of ancient Rus would be engaged in the basic, traditional modes of agricultural production and their associated crafts and skills, including hunting and gathering. Again, it seems safe to reach the conclusion that Kievan Rus's economy was a mixed one which combined both mercantile and agrarian activities, the latter including the development of a prosperous landowning class and a toiling peasantry.

Finally, there is the subject of political institutions and rulership. As indicated in the preceding pages, the Kievan polity was not an absolute monarchy. Apart from two or three brief periods, the early Russian state, such as it was, was non-centralised, disunited, fissiparous and crudely governed by a disparate bunch of squabbling, ambitious, treacherous, homicidal chieftains. The major centres of this primitive political patchwork, apart from Kiev itself, were Ryazan, Vladimir, Suzdal, Chernigov, Pereyaslavl, Tver, Tmutorokan and Novgorod. The emergence of a single, absolute sovereign was obstructed not only by the princely pastime of serial assassination and brotherly backstabbing, but also by the existence of popular town assemblies, called the *veche*. These civic congregations exercised a form of rudimentary, quasi-democratic influence, if not control, over the activities and indeed the personages of their princes. The *veche* of Novgorod in particular was renowned for the regular role it played in the city's public affairs, periodically *electing* its own governor (*posadnik*) and even its own bishops. That is not to say that the people of Kiev Rus were unfamiliar with the concept, or even the institution, of supreme monarchical power. Most obvious was the example of the emperors of Byzantium, successors to the Roman Caesars. The Russian word for Constantinople was in fact 'Tsargrad' – 'City of the Caesars' – and the extent and nature of the omnipotence enjoyed by the rulers of the Byzantine *imperium* was well known to their Russian contemporaries. During Moscow's rise to power in later centuries it was in fact back to the ancient Roman and more recently the Byzantine emperors that the Muscovite tsars looked as their exemplars. Before that process took place, however, Russia was to undergo its own, more direct experience of subjugation to the tyranny of despotic rule in the shape of the Mongol khans. The 'destruction of the Russian land', as described, for instance, in *The Tale of Baty's Destruction of Ryazan*,[6] may not, however, have been as devastating as surviving mediaeval accounts suggest.

The 'Tatar yoke'[7]

The first mention of the Tatars appears in the chronicles under the year 1223. It reads:

> In the year 6731 ... peoples (*yazytsi*) appeared, and no-one knows clearly who they are, whence they came, what language they speak, of what race they are, or of what faith; they call them Tatars (*tatary*) ... [but] God alone knows who they are or from where they came.[8]

The reference is to the first military encounter of Russian forces with an advance guard of Chenghiz Khan's troops on the banks of the river

Kalka, nine days' eastward march from the Dnepr, close to the sea of Azov. In the ensuing battle, the Russians were slaughtered, and the Tatars vanished as swiftly and as suddenly as they had appeared. The engagement on the Kalka was a frightening foretaste of what was to come, though in fact the defeat had little immediate effect on the course of events in southern Rus. Despite the casualties, it was just another unfortunate, unsuccessful skirmish with steppelands horsemen – identity unknown. However, in 1237, the armies of Baty Khan, grandson of Chenghiz, returned and began to 'lay waste' the Russian lands in deadly earnest. There are many chronicle accounts and martial tales about the widespread butchery and pillage inflicted by the heathen Asiatic hordes on the Christian people of Rus. Much of this was deliberate propaganda, emphasising the barbaric cruelty, perfidy and terrifying bestiality for which the Mongol invaders became legendary. Horrific accounts of mass slaughter, rape, plunder, torching towns, gruesome forms of torture, mutilation and execution all added to the bloodcurdling Mongol myth which was seared for generations into Russia's collective historical memory.

However, while it is no doubt true that the capture of several townships and the massacre of their populations were the occasion of much brutality and bloodshed, such occurrences were after all part of the standard pattern of mediaeval (indeed, modern) warfare. There is no reason, still less evidence, to suppose that the Tatars were any more or less cruel or unusual than their contemporaries in their conduct of war, the treatment of their vanquished victims or their rapacious indulgence in the spoils of battle. In fact, the written historical record of the two and a half centuries of Mongol rule is fairly short on solid information. Much of it is stylised, formulaic, couched in the trite commonplaces of medieval chronicle writing in general – hyperbolic, pietistic, factually fuzzy, impressionistic, and largely unreliable as an accurate picture of events, still less as an analysis of their causes and consequences. What we do know, apart from the necrology of dead Russian princes, dates of battles and sieges, and the odd gory anecdotal or apocryphal titbit, is that between 1237 and 1240 the whole of central and southern Russia had been subdued, and its major princedoms – Ryazan, Vladimir, Suzdal, Chernigov, Pereyaslavl and Kiev – reduced to vassal status. Baty abandoned any plans he may have entertained for further expansion into western Europe, withdrew to the Volga and there established his capital at

Sarai, to where a procession of Russian princes journeyed over the next 140 years to pay both homage and taxes, and to kow-tow before the Great Khan of the Golden Horde. For a century beyond that, until *c.*1480, although the obsequious embassies to Sarai declined in frequency, and despite the occasional reckless challenge to Mongol suzerainty (always followed up by automatic and merciless reprisals), the Russian princes still continued to deliver tribute and depend on the patronage of their Tatar overlords for their own precarious and figuratively parochial power.

The Mongols' swift and successful subjugation of Kievan Russia can be partly explained by a number of factors. The superior numbers of their forces (though the chronicles are not particularly helpful in their supply of precise figures), their skilful horsemanship, sophisticated strategy, the deployment of cunningly devised mechanical engines of war – battering rams, missile launchers, combustible projectiles ('Greek fire'), clever intelligence gathering, the element of surprise and the toughness of the troops who were able to survive on minimal, easily transportable rations (pemmican, cheese, fresh horse blood) – all these played their part. However, the basic, underlying cause was the sheer incompetence, disunity, absence of central leadership and command, ignorance of enemy tactics, lack of internal liaison, and mutual bickering among the Russian princelings. The price of their petulance and unpreparedness was military defeat, decimation of the population, over two centuries of foreign domination and what Soviet Marxist historians referred to as the 'feudal disintegration' (*feodal'naya razdroblennost'*) of the Russian lands.

As the Tatars struck from the east, Russia's western enemies seized the opportunity to attack in the north-west. The successive incursions of Swedes, Lithuanians, the German Knights of the Catholic Order of Livonian Swordbearers, and the Teutonic Knights in the areas around Novgorod, Pskov and the Finnish Gulf meant not only that the highly vulnerable and volatile Russian state was fighting simultaneous wars on two fronts – Catholic Teutons on the west, pagan Tatars from the east – but also created a lasting national legend around the name of one of Russia's great mediaeval heroes: Prince Aleksandr Nevskii (1220/21–63). Grand Prince of Vladimir, and later of Novgorod (1252–63), Aleksandr is celebrated for his victory over the Swedes in the battle by the river Neva in 1240 – hence his honorific sobriquet, 'Nevskii' – and over the Teutonic knights on the frozen surface of Lake Peipus (Lake Chud; Chud being the ancient name for Estonia) in 1242. These two victories over the treacherous western foe have been blown out of all proportion and transformed into mighty epics of Russian arms by both his anonymous mediaeval hagiographer (Nevskii was later canonised), and by the great twentieth-century Russian film director, Sergei Eisenstein (*Alexander Nevskii*, 1938). In both of these portrayals, Aleksandr is depicted as a fearless defender of Holy, Orthodox Russia against her heretical western enemies, who, as Christians of a sort, but unlike the heathen Tatars, did not even enjoy the privilege of being infidels. Like many of Eisenstein's cinematographic images, his frame-shots of the sinister, iron-helmeted German cavalry grimly galloping with their Catholic crosses over the frozen waters of Lake Peipus, but halted and triumphantly defeated by the stalwart, Orthodox defenders of the *Russkaya zemlya*, have acquired iconic status in the Russian popular imagination. (They also presented a remarkably prescient allegorical portrayal of the Soviet Union's imminent struggle against Nazi German aggressors in the Great Patriotic War (1941–45).) The truth, however, is almost certainly of less titanic dimensions. The battles of 1240 and 1242 were in no way mediaeval dress rehearsals for the defence of Stalingrad in 1943, but rather minor clashes involving a minimal number of combatants on both sides, the results of which had no significant impact on the course of Russia's later history. More important than Aleksandr's military victories on the western front was his successful policy of ensuring the relative independence of Novgorod by playing the obedient toady of Sarai in the east. In the final analysis, as the late John Fennell has demonstrated with his typically level-headed acumen, Aleksandr of the Neva was not so much a great military hero or scourge of the papacy, but the successful resister of a couple of minor border raids, a crafty, self-serving negotiator, and a deft wheeler-dealer in the politics of appeasement. 'It would indeed be generous,' concludes Fennell, 'to call his policy altruistic.'[9]

The oppressive burden of the 'Tatar yoke' has become something of a historiographical cliché. In actual fact, after the traumatic shock of the initial invasion, and despite the regular punitive expeditions which followed various instances of rebellion on the part of a few uppity princes, Russia experienced an era of comparative internal tranquillity under a kind of *pax mongolica*. That is not to say that there was no spirit of resistance or a supine acceptance of foreign domination. As hinted above, there were indeed a number of rebellions and insurgencies against Tatar rule. But on the whole, provided that the Russian princes paid their regular tribute, supplied conscript troops for the Mongol armies, and generally kept their letters patent clean, the khans of the Golden Horde interfered very little in the local government, administration of justice, social relationships or, importantly, religious observances of their Russian subjects. And it is doubtful that the day-to-day existence of the wretched Russian peasants would have been altered in any fundamental or dramatic way as a result of the Mongol occupation. Despite their relative freedom of action within their own fiefdoms, however, the loyal Russian satraps of the Mongol khans were left in no doubt as to who was in overall charge. That is, until the year 1380.

That was the year in which Prince Dmitrii of Moscow (r. 1359–89), at that time a relatively minor fortress town, scored a significant military victory over a Mongol army at the battle of Kulikovo on a tributary of the river Don. This by no means signalled the beginning of the end of Mongol rule in Russia, nor did it announce the immediate ascendancy of Moscow. Indeed, the Mongols' defeat was soon avenged by the sacking and burning of Moscow by a punitive expedition in 1382. However, the battle of Kulikovo field has gone down in the annals of Russian military history as one of the country's most glorious achievements, on a par with Poltava (1709 – see Chapter 4), Napoleon's retreat from Moscow (1812 – see Chapter 7), and Stalingrad (1943). It demonstrated that, notwithstanding future punitive attacks on Russian towns, the Mongols were not invincible. For his exploit, Dmitrii was later dubbed 'Donskoi' – i.e. Dmitrii of the Don, echoing the accolade previously bestowed on Aleksandr Nevskii – and the unprecedented victory celebrated in the Russian military epic, the *Zadonshchina* ('The Deeds beyond the Don'), the earliest manuscript of which dates from *c*.1470.[10]

It was to be, however, another 100 years before the Tatar yoke was finally lifted, and that was not so much a result of determined Russian opposition or military prowess as the internal weaknesses and process of debilitation within the Mongol Empire, the Golden Horde and the court at Sarai itself. It was as if the occupying power had become infected with the same malaise of internal disunity, inter-princely rivalries and enervating struggles for dominance as had earlier afflicted the rulers of Kievan Rus. It should be noted that similar rivalries also continued to be a feature of relations among the central and northern Russian principalities such as Tver, Rostov, Suzdal, Vladimir, Novgorod and, most portentously, Moscow. The story of Moscow's steady rise to hegemony towards the end of the fifteenth century, and the progress of what some historians have called 'the gathering together of the Russian lands' under the tsardom of Muscovy, is too complex and intricate a tale to go into in any great detail at this juncture, but will be returned to briefly in the following section. It remains to note here, however, that by the year 1480, Ivan III, Grand Prince of Moscow (r. 1462–1505), had presided over the final withdrawal of the Mongol occupying powers, and – by a mixture of military conquest, shrewd diplomacy, a prestigious marriage and the backing of the Orthodox Church – had managed to establish Moscow as the 'capital' of post-Mongol Russia, underpinning his city's hegemony by espousing the fanciful theory of 'Moscow the Third Rome' (see below).

But what of the legacy left to him by the departing Tatars? Historians' interpretations naturally differ as to both the profundity and the longevity of the Mongol impact on Russia. Some have seen it as having no real long-term significance, while others regard it as having left an indelible mark on the Russian state and the Russian people: 'Scratch a Russian, and find a Tatar', as the popular aphorism has it. In terms of religious toleration, a reluctance to impose their own social conventions and a controlled licence for the vassal princes to order their own affairs, the Mongols did not impinge too heavy-handedly on the conduct of everyday life. So long as there was a steady influx of taxes and troops, then – punishment raids apart – Russia under Mongol domination did not, on the surface, suffer any major changes. However, there are two significant aspects of the Mongol legacy which did leave a lasting impression, and infused Russia with a different spirit from that of the pre-Mongol period.

First was the institution of absolute fealty to a single, autocratic, sovereign ruler. In Kievan Russia, the power of the princes was to a certain extent moderated, first, by their own self-inflicted rivalries, which precluded the domination of one individual monarch; second, by a powerful aristocracy of boyars, magnates and members of the prince's retinue (*druzhina*); and, third, by the semi-democratic citizens' assemblies (*veche*). But, by the end of the fifteenth century, the concept of the concentration of political power in the person of one supreme ruler had become part of the national *Weltanschauung*, or – in Russian – *mirovozzrenie* (there is no exact English equivalent, but it approximates to something like 'world-view'). The amalgam of oriental despotism from the Mongol khans, the Byzantine tradition of αὐτοκρατεια ('autocracy', Russian *samoderzhavie*), and the idea of service to the state – or its personification in the ruler of the state – all entered into the peculiar Russian version of tsarist absolutism, and was clearly part of the legacy of the Mongol period. In their political behaviour and ideological assumptions, the Muscovite tsars and the Russian emperors did not act in a very different spirit from that of their Tatar precursors. Excruciating forms of physical torture, corporal and capital punishment were also part of the Mongols' legacy. Indeed, the nineteenth-century Russian criminologist, I. Ya. Foinitskii, states:

> Our country became the classical land of corporal
> punishment, though this was under the influence
> of the Tatar yoke, before which we did not resort
> to this measure.[11]

Mention has already been made of the relatively tolerant attitude taken by the Mongols to the religious beliefs and practices of the peoples whom they conquered. In the case of the Russian Orthodox Church, the period of Mongol domination brought many benefits and helped to consolidate the Church's commanding position within the later power structure of Muscovite and imperial Russia. Pious churchmen exploited the Mongol invasion as a sign of God's wrath for the sinful ways of His people, and urged their superstitious listeners to repent and turn to the way of the Lord, if possible bestowing sizeable chunks of their moveable and immoveable property on the churches and monasteries for good measure as they did so. Appropriate prayers would be intoned in order to ensure that such munificence would be rewarded with a place among the angels. The Church also bolstered its position by acting as impartial intermediary in negotiations between the Christian, warring princes of the appanage states and the Mongol authorities, thereby considerably augmenting their political power and influence. Also, the monastic movement made enormous strides during the Mongol period, when revered clerics and monks would periodically abandon their original monasteries and wander off into the northern forests, and establish their own hermitages. There they would gain a reputation for piety, wisdom, healing powers or other thaumaturgical feats, and attract their own following of supplicants and suitably grateful worshippers. Eventually a new monastery would gradually develop, after which another seeker after solitude, meditation and holy contemplation, shunning the clamour of the cloisters, would wend his eremitic way even deeper into the *taiga* and start the whole process over again. In this way the Russian Orthodox Church expanded in its worldly wealth, political influence and geographical coverage during two and a half centuries' service to its pagan, later Muslim, overlords. With the Mongols' retreat, it was therefore in a position to play a powerful role in establishing the political hegemony of the Muscovite tsars over contending appanage princes, boyars and other sundry rivals.

The rise of Moscow

In comparison with some of the other historical so-called 'Greats' – Alexander of Macedon, Peter I of Russia, Frederick II of Prussia, for example – Ivan III, Grand Prince of Moscow from 1462 to 1505, although a redoubtable ruler, was not a spectacularly outstanding figure. His most enduring achievement was to end the 'feudal disintegration' of the Russian vassal dependencies of the Golden Horde, gathering them together under his own increasingly autocratic rule, destroying the power of the thriving, semi-independent trading city of Novgorod, and overseeing the gradual withdrawal of the Mongols from central Russia. The liberation of Russia from the rule of the Tatars was not, however, the result of any great military victory, so much as the consequences of the latter's own gradual debilitation and disintegration caused by internal factions and rivalries, as described above. The Golden Horde itself broke up and was replaced to the east of Muscovy by the small independent Tatar khanates of Kazan, Astrakhan and western Siberia. To Moscow's west and south, she was hemmed in by the kingdoms of Poland, Lithuania and the Ottoman Empire, and was also harried by the Crimean Tatars. Ivan did, however, gradually outwit, conquer or outdo his more immediate Russian neighbours, subdue the ambitious boyars, and with the full backing of the Orthodox hierarchy and the rising class of military state-servitors – the *dvoryanstvo* – succeed in having himself recognised in diplomatic correspondence as not merely Grand Prince (*Velikii knyaz*') of Moscow but as 'Lord of All Russia' (*Gosudar' vseya Rusi*), occasionally referring to himself as 'tsar'. The embryonic imperial status of his domain was also marked by symbolic appurtenances such as the adoption of the Byzantine double-headed eagle as the Muscovite ruler's heraldic device, the forging of a direct link with the last emperor at Constantinople, Constantine XI, through his second marriage with Constantine's niece, Sofiya Palaeologa, and the appearance of a corpus of preposterous panegyrical literature tracing the descent of the Moscow princes from the earliest Roman emperors (see below). A number of points need to be made about these conceits.

First, Moscow was not alone in using the double-headed eagle as a symbol of earthly power. It was not uncommon in the heraldry of other principalities and not too much significance need be read into it. In fact, as Gustave Alef has persuasively argued, it is more likely that the model for the two-headed aquiline emblem was taken not from the Byzantines, but from the Hapsburgs. Whatever its provenance, the imperial symbolism of the crest is unambiguous.[12]

Second, the marriage with Sofiya was not without its political difficulties. A Byzantine princess, she was born just five years before the fall of Constantinople and the death of her uncle, Constantine, who was killed defending the walls of his city. Her father, Thomas Palaeologus, fled from the advancing Turks in 1460 and sought refuge in Italy, where he soon died. His three children, including Zoë (as she was originally named), were made the wards of Pope Paul II, and their education entrusted to the Greek scholar and Roman Catholic convert, Cardinal Johannes Bessarion (1403–72). The initiative for the proposed marriage of his protégée with the widower Grand Prince of the increasingly powerful Moscow came from the pontiff himself, seeking an alliance with Muscovy against the Ottomans, then threatening western Christendom in Europe. While this diplomatic stratagem was unsuccessful, the marriage at any rate went ahead, Zoë journeyed to Moscow and was betrothed and married according to the Orthodox rite under her adopted name of Sofiya. Her Catholic upbringing, her approval of the Union of

Florence in 1439, which sought to reunite the western and eastern branches of Christianity under the Roman papacy, and the popish practices of her entourage bought her few friends in bitterly anti-Catholic Russia. She was, however, a very sophisticated, educated lady of imperial blood who was sufficiently versed in the ways of courtly intrigue to secure her position without too much harassment. And it is doubtful that the foreign policies of her husband were significantly influenced by such blandishments as she may have brought to bear.

In one area, though, her presence at the Moscow court did have a visible and enduring effect. That was in persuading Ivan to engage the services of Italian architects and engineers to design the refurbishment, fortification and embellishment of the Moscow Kremlin. The wood- and stone-built Kremlin (in Russian, *kreml'*, meaning a fortress or citadel) – administrative centre of the state and home of the Grand Prince – did not really offer its incumbents the protection or afford the pomp that was commensurate with the city's metropolitan status. Accordingly, for over a quarter of a century, roughly from 1475 to 1505, the Kremlin underwent an intensive reconstruction programme under the guidance of Italian masters such as Fioravanti, Novi, Solari and Ruffo, employing a unique blend of traditional Russian and western Renaissance styles. The resultant cathedrals, topped with their glittering gold cupolas – the Dormition (*Uspenskii*), the Annunciation (*Blagoveshchenskii*), scene of the coronation of all the Muscovite tsars and Russian emperors, and the Archangel Michael (*Arkhangelskii*), where all the Muscovite tsars are buried – the Faceted Palace (*Granovitaya palata*), as well as the soaring belltower of Ivan the Great and the familiar huge red-brick walls, towers and turrets overlooking Red Square, are still today one of the most spectacular architectural ensembles in the world.

If Moscow was now architecturally equipped to take its place as a recognised capital city, at the same time the ideological underpinning for its claims to international status began to take shape. Towards the end of the fifteenth century and in the first half of the sixteenth, a body of publicistic, 'panegyrical' literature began to accumulate which sought to establish Moscow's legitimacy, not just as an independent, sovereign state, a political entity in its own right, but also one whose paramount position was based on both historical and ecclesiastical authority. In such fanciful works as the late fifteenth-century 'Tale of the Princes of Vladimir' (*Skazanie o knyaz'yakh Vladimirskikh*) and later concoctions, ingenious, imaginative genealogies were devised which sought to trace the lineage of the Muscovite rulers, through Kievan princes to the Byzantine emperors and even further to the Ancient Roman Caesars. One legend, for instance, has it that Ryurik, the fabled Varangian founder of ancient Rus (see above), was the direct descendant of one Prus, purportedly ruler of the land of Prussia (Lithuania), and the brother of Augustus Caesar. From such fabrications arose the repeated claims of Ivan's grandson, Ivan the Terrible, to derive his legitimate pedigree from the early Roman emperors. Needless to say, these purely fictional family trees had no roots in any kind of historical reality, and were in any case similar to other dynastic dream-tales current elsewhere in Europe. In an age of near-universal illiteracy, ignorance, superstition, and a healthy respect for the wrath of kings, these legends, many of them compiled by distinguished, devout ecclesiastics, served their avowed political purpose of both bolstering and beatifying the absolute power of the Moscow Grand Princes.

A central part was played in this process by the doctrine of 'Moscow the Third Rome', briefly mentioned above. Unlike the genealogical fictions just referred to, this piece of politico-religious propaganda did have at least a scintilla of plausibility. It was at any rate based upon a couple of historical facts. Fact one: the old Roman Empire had sunk into a state of decline and finally fallen to the barbarians at the onset of the Dark Ages. Fact two: the site of the second Rome, Constantinople, centre of the Eastern Roman Empire, had in turn succumbed to the heathen Turks in 1453. Added to this is the third fact that, following the spread of Ottoman rule throughout the Balkans, and the Tatar withdrawal from Russia, Moscow was now the only surviving, independent, true Orthodox Christian principality in the world. The main ideologue of the theory of Moscow's religious hegemony – an otherwise obscure monk of Pskov, named Filofei (Theophilus) – added conjecture to fact by suggesting that the reasons for the collapse of the first two Romes were: the first's falling into the Apollinarian heresy which denied the human side of Christ's dual nature; and the second's apostasy at the Union of Florence in 1439.[13] In his classic formulation: 'Two Romes have fallen; the third still stands; a fourth there shall not be' (*dva Rima padosha, tretei stoit, a chetvertomu ne byti*), he went on to describe Moscow as 'Thy Christian Tsardom' (*tvoe khrist'yanstvoe tsarstvo*).[14]

Towards the end of his reign, Ivan III was faced with a problem of succession. This was due to the existence of two claimants to the throne. The 'natural' heir, 'Ivan the Young', Ivan's son by his first wife, Maria of Tver, had died in 1490, leaving him a grandson, Dmitrii. His oldest son, Vasilii, by his second wife, Sofiya Palaeologa, also had a powerful claim, backed by his ambitious mother. The result was a decade or so of plots, counter-plots, royal intrigues, courtly conspiracy and religious interference, which was finally resolved by the disgrace and later imprisonment of Dmitrii and his mother. Vasilii Ivanovich – great-nephew, through his mother, of the last Byzantine Emperor – was duly proclaimed heir to the Grand Principality of Moscow, to which he succeeded on his father's death, apparently through natural causes, in 1505. Despite the unquestionably bogus nature of the panegyrical pedigrees referred to above, here at least there is genuine genealogical evidence that the blood of the Byzantine emperors ran in the veins of the monarchs of Muscovy.

Vasilii inherited a nominally unified domain, three times the size of that to which his father had succeeded, but one which was still riven with internal tensions and religious conflict, and surrounded by hostile neighbours. Although his reign (1505–33) was not especially remarkable in comparison with those of his father, Ivan the Great, and his son, Ivan the Terrible, he generally consolidated the former's achievements by continuing the process of unification, further curbing the residual opposition of the remaining appanage princes, and conducting a reasonably successful foreign policy in his relations with Lithuania, the Holy Roman Empire, the Ottoman Turks and the Vatican. He also dealt effectively with sporadic border spats with the Tatars, though the khanates were not brought under proper control until the more decisive actions of his successor, Ivan IV.

In all his activities, Vasilii, like his father, generally enjoyed the support of the Orthodox Church hierarchy. There was, however, a complication in the fact that the Church was not totally united either spiritually or in its attitude towards what, if not involving its own internal affairs, would otherwise have been a purely secular, literally terrestrial, matter. Put simply, the problem (which originated during the reign of his father, Ivan III), revolved – both doctrinally and materially – around the question of the ownership of church and monastic lands. This is usually referred to in the literature as the conflict between the 'Possessors' and the 'Non-possessors' (*styazhateli* and *nestyazhateli*). The leader and acknowledged spokesman of the former (also known as the Josephans) was Iosif (Joseph, 1439/40–1515), abbot of the monastery of Volokolamsk, and of the latter, a revered holy man known to his followers as Nil Sorskii (*c.*1433–1508), leader of the so-called Trans-Volga Elders.

To take the Possessors first: despite some earlier ambiguity about his position vis-à-vis support for Ivan, Iosif eventually emerged as the leading ecclesiastical spokesman for the divine provenance of autocratic power, and unequivocally lent the formidable backing of the Church to both Ivan the Great and his successor, Vasilii. However, he was also a vociferous advocate of the monasteries' right to own vast tracts of land and to accumulate material riches. Although he made it clear in his writings that individual monks must abjure worldly possessions and observe the rule of absolute poverty, nevertheless it was the prerogative, even the duty, of the Church to maintain large, profitable estates in order that the monasteries could be in a position to offer Christian charity, succour and refuge to the needy and the suffering. This notion of the monasteries as local clinics, borshch kitchens and social welfare centres was of course a convenient, eleemosynary justification for the Church to defend itself against the possible encroachment on its territories by the state. Thus, the astute abbot successfully combined the concept of the divine right of tsars with the notion that the Church's possessions are God's possessions, thereby guaranteeing the sacrosanctity of monastic estates in return for lending political and religious support to the semi-theocratic sovereign.

Nil Sorskii was of an altogether different persuasion, arguing that preoccupation with land, property and the management of large, organised communities was no part of the monastic calling. On the contrary, as a disciple of the fourteenth-century Greek mystical hesychast school of individual contemplation and prayer, with which he had become acquainted during a pilgrimage to Mount Athos, Nil insisted that only by a life of spiritual concentration, mental and physical discipline, constant devotion and rejection of all carnal and material temptations could one enter into a direct knowledge of God. Subsequently, eschewing the cœnobitic life of the prosperous monasteries, he established a number of tiny hermitages on the river Sora, beyond the Volga (hence 'Sorskii'), and pursued a middle path between the busy life of the large religious communities and that of the complete anchorite. Although Sorskii did not make a direct, written attack on the evils of monastic landholding, his implicit condemnation of the institution provided a useful theological foundation for Ivan's territorial ambitions. Apart from the monarchy, other sections of Muscovite society, from the lowly peasants to wealthy landowners and boyars, also viewed with resentment the spiritual estate's continuing interest in real estate. At a Church council in 1503, Nil Sorskii, possibly at Ivan's instigation, raised the matter of monastic property rights, while also criticising the Josephans' attitude to such things as corporate worship, prayer, iconolatry and the current, ongoing 'heresy' of the so-called 'Judaisers' (*zhidovstvuyushchie*).[15] If the Grand Prince hoped that the Non-possessors would carry the argument, he was disappointed. The Josephan faction's support of the autocratic principle, along with the self-interested property-owning instincts of the powerful hierarchy, allied to Sorskii's personal disinclination to engage in the business of political in-fighting, ensured that both the political and ecclesiastical policies of Iosif of Volokolamsk won the day. It was a victory which was to be used to great advantage by Vasilii's son, heir and successor, Ivan the Terrible, who inherited the throne of Moscow on his father's death in 1533.

Ivan the Terrible (i)

How 'terrible' was Ivan the Terrible? The first problem to sort out is one of semantics and translation. The Russian adjective '*groznyi*', which became Ivan IV's sobriquet, is usually translated as 'terrible', and yet the term may also be rendered, according to the context, as 'awe-inspiring', 'menacing', 'redoubtable', 'ferocious' and 'stern'. One could argue that all applied in equal measure to Russia's first crowned tsar. The American, Russian émigré scholar, Michael Florinsky, follows the British historian Sir Bernard Pares in adopting the term 'Ivan the Dread'; this, he says, 'seems to render more accurately the meaning of the Russian epithet *Groznyi*'.[16] Dreadful as the sum total of Ivan's activities may have been, it seems unnecessary to tinker with the well-established and more familiar 'Terrible', in so far as one can quite justifiably regard his years in power as a 'reign of terror'.

Ivan was only three years of age when his father, Vasilii, died. Throughout his minority the court of the Kremlin became the scene of renewed squabbling, inter-boyar family bickering, copious bloodshed and general mayhem – much of which the young and therefore impressionable Ivan personally witnessed. Whether this early exposure to the murderous activities of the brutal and ambitious boyars and princes such as the Belskii, the Shuiskii and the Glinskii clans, wrapped in a blood-soaked web of intrigue, arrest, torture and executions, had a lasting psychological or psychopathological effect on the boy-prince's mind is difficult to judge in the absence of any professional clinical evidence. However, stories appear in the admittedly rather patchy literature about the cruel and sadistic streak already observable in the adolescent Ivan's nature. A perverse pleasure in the infliction of pain was at any rate a prominent feature of both his youthful and adult behaviour, which expressed itself in bizarre aberrations from what would nowadays be considered 'normal'. From boyish pranks like dropping live animals to their death from the top of his grandfather's bell tower in the Kremlin, the more mature Ivan was to graduate to more thoughtfully planned campaigns of systematic rape, floggings, burning and butchery. At the same time, he was also – and this was also part of the convoluted, contradictory character which he carried over into adult life – something of a phenomenon of pious and precocious erudition. His eventide sorties, full of violent sexual excesses, alternated with long periods of almost eremitic study and prayer that later bore exotic fruit in his own literary outpourings, which were themselves a remarkable mixture of often erroneous biblical, patristic and historical allusion with startling displays of verbal pyrotechnics.[17]

In 1547, at the age of 17, Ivan IV, Grand Prince of Moscow, was duly crowned in the Kremlin's Uspenskii cathedral as 'Tsar of All Russia'. Although both his immediate forebears had on occasion coyly alluded to themselves as 'tsar', this was the first time that a Russian ruler was formally and ceremoniously anointed, crowned and enthroned as such amidst the full pomp and pageantry of Orthodox ritual. Ivan's coronation had the full backing of the solidly Josephan hierarchy, led by the metropolitan Makarii, who officiated at the proceedings. It is unlikely, however, that other European monarchs, or the Turkish sultan, were impressed by such imperial pretensions. In the same year he married the daughter of a minor boyar family, Anastasiya Romanovna Zakharina, by all accounts a demure and modest girl, to whom Ivan remained apparently devoted until her death, possibly through poisoning, in 1560. Her patronymic, *Romanovna* – daughter of Roman Zakharin – was to have long historical reverberations throughout the coming centuries, for it was, of course, from the Romanov line that a new ruling dynasty was to be formed at the beginning of the seventeenth century (see Chapter 3).

The first decade or so of the new tsar's reign, 1547–*c*.1560, is generally regarded by historians in a relatively positive light, and not marked by the same seemingly gratuitous, unpredictable and cruel eccentricities as his later years. There are many gaps and lacunae in the evidence, but a general pattern emerges of a ruler, who by the standards of his age, appears to have pursued a steady policy in domestic, foreign and ecclesiastical affairs. He established new laws to regularise the conduct of public officials, curbed the continuing caprices of the boyars, and attacked corruption at local level by limiting the system of *kormlenie* (literally, 'feeding'), by which provincial administrators (*namestniki*) battened off the local populations within their jurisdiction by the arbitrary imposition of taxes, tribute, and other dues and services. This practice, which was obviously wide open to abuse and a virtual licence for extortion, was brought under closer central scrutiny, though not totally eradicated. Adjustments were also made to the complex system known as *mestnichestvo*, an untranslatable term betokening an arrangement whereby top military and civil appointments and promotions were made according to a protocol of genealogical precedence, which ensured that a particular appointee should not hold a rank lower than that of any of his ancestors.

Although now officially recognised as absolute autocrat, Ivan was also apparently assisted in his decision- and law-making policies by an unofficial, so-called 'Select Council' (*Izbrannaya rada*), of which the most prominent members were the two civil servants, Aleksei Adashev (?–1561) and Ivan Viskovatyi (?–1570), the archpriest Silvestr (?–*c*.1566) – the tsar's spiritual mentor, and the Metropolitan of Moscow, Makarii (1482–1563). Apart from this inner circle, the tsar was also responsible for convening a wider consultative assembly called the Assembly of the Land (*zemskii sobor*), which represented most of the more powerful interest groups in Muscovite society. Not that its deliberations had any noticeable effect on the conduct of state affairs; nor could it possibly be regarded as voicing the will of the people.

A similar piece of congressional window-dressing was provided by the Church council of 1551 (the Council of a Hundred Chapters, or *Stoglav*). This ecclesiastical assembly confirmed the concordat between church and state, passed the routine agenda items condemning licentiousness, corruption and superstition, made certain decisions regarding the order of holy service, ecclesiography, marriage, remarriage and the punishment of children, slotted in a couple of chapters on such weighty issues as beards and buggery, unsportingly prohibited the cohabitation of monks and nuns, and banned the eating of black pudding ('sausages' (*kolbasy*), made from 'animal blood' (*zhivotna krov'*)). Most importantly for the monasteries, the Council came down firmly on the side of the abbots' right to continue exercising their divinely ordained prerogatives as owners of large, lucrative *latifundia*. In his introduction to a recent reprint of *Stoglav*, Will Ryan concludes: 'From a consideration of what the *Stoglav* thinks desirable or undesirable, we obtain a picture of a Muscovite state that is violent, autocratic, isolationist and obscurantist.'[18]

If that is indeed an accurate picture of the Muscovite state in 1551, then it is difficult to find words adequate to describe the condition of the country in the truly terrible years of Ivan's later reign.

Before turning to this grim chapter of Russia's internal history, a few words need to be said about Ivan's foreign policy. In the west, he continued to be preoccupied with the Livonian Knights, Lithuania, Sweden and Poland, and in the south and east with the continuing nuisance of the Tatar khanates. Muscovy was in a state of almost permanent warfare with her western neighbours, and gained only scant reward for her military efforts with the acquisition of a very tenuous foothold on the Finnish Gulf, laying down a few strategic duckboards over the Karelian swamps along which Peter the Great was later to stride. Trading relations, as mentioned in Chapter 1, were established with Elizabethan England with the founding of the Muscovy Company following Richard Chancellor's pioneering voyage in 1553. Ivan also made overtures to the Virgin Queen about the possibility of cementing even closer ties through a proposed marriage with one of Elizabeth's relatives, Lady Mary Hastings. Neither she nor her sovereign showed any inclination to entertain the proposal, and the tsar's attempt to consummate his alleged anglophilia by bedding an English bride came to nothing. Nor were his approaches to other European royal households any more fruitful in this respect. All in all, Ivan's foreign relations with the west cannot be regarded as having been particularly distinguished.

More successful was his thrust to the east, which put down the foundations for Muscovy's transformation into the future empire. The process began in earnest with the capture of Kazan in 1552, followed by Astrakhan in 1556. The victory over Kazan was to be of enormous significance, going well beyond simply mopping up the remnants of Russia's erstwhile Mongol masters. The way now lay open for Muscovite expansion across the Urals and on into the fur-laden forests of Siberia. After the fall of Kazan, for the time being the tiny khanate of Sibir, otherwise known as Isker, on the river Irtysh, remained unmolested. This was partly because its rulers prudently continued to pay an annual tribute to the Russian tsar, and partly because at that time Ivan probably had no definite ambition for further expansion into what was still a remote and inhospitable *terra incognita*. However, after a series of dynastic rivalries within the ruling clan the new khan, Kuchum (?–1598), finally cancelled delivery of tribute to Moscow, and was possibly responsible for instigating a number of raids into Muscovite territory during the 1570s. In retaliation, the powerful Russian merchant family of the Stroganovs, which owned enormous territorial and commercial interests along large stretches of the Urals, were granted a series of royal charters authorising them to fortify their eastern boundaries and mount military expeditions against the rebellious Siberian Tatars.

It is at this point that the celebrated cossak *ataman* and free-booter, Yermak Timofeevich (?–1585) – sometimes extravagantly described as the Russian Cortez or Pizarro – makes his portentous appearance in the annals of Russian history. Despite some chronological controversy over the date and the precise provenance of his orders, it seems clear, at least according to the distinguished Russian historian R. G. Skrynnikov, that Yermak and his band of cossaks, probably acting as agents for the Stroganovs, launched their initial campaign against the Siberian khanate in 1582.[19] Although Kuchum was forced to withdraw from his capital, Isker, the cossaks soon lost control and Yermak himself was later drowned during a skirmish on the Irtysh in 1585 – dragged down, according to legend, by the weight of his armour, which had been a personal gift from the tsar. Khan Kuchum carried on a courageous guerrilla campaign against the Russian occupying forces that followed in Yermak's wake until his final defeat and death in 1598. The struggle was carried on by his successors, but they were no match for the Russians' superior fire-power and their establishment of a network of wooden fortresses protecting their newly conquered territories. What had originally begun during the reign of Ivan the Terrible as the private enterprise of merchant adventurers and cossak *conquistadores* now had the full backing of the Muscovite state. By the middle of the next century, not just the tiny khanate of Sibir, but the whole continent of northern Asia lay at Moscow's feet.

Ivan the Terrible (ii)

The quarter century from the death of Ivan's first wife, Anastasiya, in 1560, and his own in 1584, is marked by a series of quite extraordinary, baffling episodes which still defy logical explanation from both the historiographical and psychological points of view. Among these are: his decision to retire from the throne in 1564 and his immediate recall to office by popular acclaim; the disastrous division of his kingdom into a private and a public domain (the *oprichnina* and the *zemshchina*) with its attendant atrocities; the slow, public torture and execution of a number of his former close advisers; the purge of Novgorod; Ivan's second 'retirement' and his appointment of a Tatar prince to the throne of Moscow; and his killing of his eldest son, the tsarevich Ivan, in 1581. Before examining each of these events in turn, an important point needs to be made concerning the nature of Ivan's political support.

It has already been seen that the nominally omnipotent tsar enjoyed full support from the dominant, Josephan, faction of the Russian Orthodox Church (provided, at any rate, that he kept his royal hands off the monasteries' estates). Equally, the increasingly powerful civil bureaucracy provided vital backing – for which it was duly rewarded – as well as being responsible for actually implementing the tsar's policies. During Ivan's reign a number of new administrative bureaux or chanceries (*prikazy*) were established, staffed by more or less influential civil servants and secretaries (*d'yaki*) who, by virtue of their managerial position, played an important role in the country's governance. It is an indication of the power of the bureaucracy that it managed to survive the depredations of the *oprichnina*, and the upheavals of the 'Time of Troubles' (see below, and Chapter 3), and carried on to play a crucial role in the revival of the autocracy under the new, Romanov dynasty in the next century.

Apart from the support of the civil administration and the religious hierarchy, all governments, ancient, mediaeval and modern, have needed the support of the military. The role of both the influential officer class and the common soldiery at crucial moments of Russia's later history will be constantly referred to throughout this book. The Russian military was essential not only for fighting foreign wars, but also for maintaining internal discipline and control over the tsars' own subjects. It was also a prime factor in the making and unmaking of monarchs, as will be seen. Apart from some minor reforms in the *mestnichestvo* system referred to above, Ivan also established a permanent militia of armed musketeers called the *strel'tsy* (literally, 'shooters') which was the first time Russia had anything like a standing army. These innovations aside, Ivan's greatest reliance by far was on the services and loyalty of the *dvoryanstvo*, the origins of which have already been explained in Chapter 1. This caste, or class, of military state-servitors (variously referred to in contemporaneous accounts as *sluzhilye lyudi* [serving men], *deti boyarskie* [minor boyars] or *dvoryane* [nobles]) was really the backbone of the autocracy. And although the relationship between the two institutions – monarchy and nobility – was to fluctuate considerably in later years, particularly in the eighteenth century, the troughs and peaks of that strained, though symbiotic, interdependence remained a permanent feature of Russia's social and political landscape until the revolutionary earthquake of 1917.

Although the *dvoryanstvo* later developed into a powerful, semi-independent class of land- and serf-owners, its military function in the service of the Grand Prince was its original *raison d'être*. In their battle with the boyars, Ivan III, Vasilii III and Ivan IV were all dependent on the active, committed support of the military nobility in their implementation of firm central government. This theme of strong government, of the danger to the state posed by quarrelsome self-serving grandees, and of the need for a loyal body of fighting men prepared to take merciless measures to preserve the authority of the sovereign ruler is stressed in a number of literary compositions in the mid-sixteenth century, which are traditionally attributed to the pen of one Ivan Peresvetov, a much overlooked figure in the historiography of the period. Despite some attempts to suggest that Peresvetov did not in fact exist, and was merely a collective pseudonym for a group of political agitators, responsible scholars such as Rzhiga and Zimin are confident about the authenticity of both the literary works and their author.[20] The details of his career need not detain us. But what emerges from such writings as his 'Tale of Sultan Mohamet' (*Skazanie o Magmete Saltane*), written around 1547, is a political programme for an authoritarian, centralised, military quasi-police state based on the use of terror. It is interesting that Peresvetov picks on the Muslim Sultan Mohamet, the conqueror of Constantinople, as his ideal ruler, and blames the Christian emperor Constantine XI for being too soft and irresolute in the face of his quarrelsome, selfish aristocrats (*velmozhi*), thereby losing his kingdom through lack of internal discipline. The greed, venality and treachery of the Byzantine aristocracy are an obvious analogy for the scheming and intrigues of the Moscow boyars during Ivan's youth. In Peresvetov's view of things, Constantine's downfall was not the result of religious degeneration, but of political pussyfooting and lack of resolution. In a later composition, the 'Tale of Tsar Constantine' (*Skazanie o tsare Konstantine*), Peresvetov is even more scathing of the Byzantine ruler's pusillanimity – even though Ivan was indirectly descended from Constantine – and holds up for admiration the resolute dictatorship of the Turkish sultan, ruling through the agency of a trained, ruthless military bureaucracy from whom he demands absolute obedience. Essential for the smooth operation of government, the unity of the state and the correct dispensation of justice (*pravda*) is the unflinching use of terror. This emphasis on physical coercion is repeated like a murderer's mantra throughout Peresvetov's works: terror, he says, is indispensable for the administration of justice, for 'Like a horse without a bridle beneath a tsar, so is a tsardom without terror' (*Kak kon' pod tsarem bez uzdy, tak tsarstvo bez grozy*).[21] There are too many obvious similarities between the contents and references in Peresvetov's work and the policies of Ivan the Terrible not to interpret it as a blueprint for absolute autocracy, based on terror, and implemented by an obedient, faithful military service nobility. In the words of the Soviet scholar, Budovnits: 'In their struggle with the boyars for power and influence, the nobles (*dvoryane*) henceforth relied not only on their economic and military position, but had also received into their hands an ideological weapon.'[22]

The use of terror (*groza* – hence *Groznyi*), so highly recommended by Peresvetov, is nowhere more grimly demonstrated than in Ivan's creation of the *oprichnina*. This sinister, death-dealing institution was set up by Ivan after his return to Moscow following the strange business of his apparent abdication and recall in the winter of 1564/5. In a deliberately calculated move, the tsar expressed his displeasure at boyar opposition to some of his policies, mainly, though not entirely, in the conduct of foreign affairs. He had also been badly shaken by the defection of Prince Andrei Kurbskii (*c.*1528–83). Kurbskii – previously a member of Ivan's intimate circle, a distinguished military commander and a highly educated scholar of languages and history – chose to defect from Muscovy to Lithuania, whence he entered the service of King Zygmunt II of Poland in 1564. Ivan's bitter resentment and venomous anger caused by this act of betrayal at a time of war is vividly illustrated in the famous correspondence between the two men, in which the tsar's increasingly apoplectic paranoia is vitriolically expressed (see note 17).

Ivan left Moscow in December 1564 accompanied by a large, loyal entourage, and set up headquarters at Aleksandrovskaya Sloboda, some 60 miles north of the capital. From there, he sent two missives addressed to the people of Moscow, one denouncing the boyars and the corrupt clergy, the other absolving the common people from any blame for causing the tsar's wrath. He did not set out an ultimatum dictating terms for his return, but such was the general consternation caused by his unusual behaviour that a delegation was despatched to Aleksandrovskaya, begging him to re-assume his throne, which is probably what Ivan had counted on in the first place. Having deigned to return to the Kremlin, Ivan then set about reorganising his domain in a most bizarre fashion. He divided his kingdom into two unequal halves, one called the *oprichnina*, the other the *zemshchina*. The former, derived from an old

Russian term for a portion of land set apart as the property of a prince's widow, was to be in effect the private domain of the tsar, run according to his personal whims and wishes, and staffed by his own hand-picked henchmen, guards and officials – a kind of private security force or militia. The *zemshchina*, 'the public land' as it were, continued to be administered by the ordinary officers and institutions of the Muscovite state, and inhabited by those not of Ivan's personal elect. The members of the *oprichnina* were termed the *oprichniki*, and their sinister purpose was symbolised by their black uniforms, their black horses, and the dog's head and broom which each man carried on his saddle, an indication of their mission to savage the tsar's enemies and sweep them from the land. Thus accoutred, the *oprichniki* launched a systematic campaign of pillage, rape, arson and murder throughout the lands of the *zemshchina*.

It has been suggested that these horrific activities were an exercise in social engineering deliberately designed to liquidate the boyars as a class, in much the same way that Stalin was later to unleash the Soviet Communist Party *oprichniki* on the kulaks during the collectivisation drive of the 1930s. The comparison is far from exact, and the 'class struggle' analysis is simply untenable. There were many members of the petty service gentry among Ivan's victims, as well as highly placed members of old aristocratic families in the ranks of the *oprichnina*. Where the analogy *is* closer to the mark is in the fact that both despots utilised their respective campaigns as a means of ridding the country of those whom they perceived as enemies and opponents of their will, whether real or imagined. To this extent both Ivan the Terrible and Iosif Stalin were driven by an irrational paranoia which led them to commit, through their subordinates, what nowadays would be described as crimes against humanity. What made the *oprichniki*'s purges even more grotesque was their habit of relaxing after a good day's slaughter by evenings spent in a mixture of pious devotion, reciting orisons for the souls of those whom they had just dispatched to a better world, and indulging in drunken sexual extravaganzas which were only interrupted by recreational trips to the torture chamber. The terror came to a dreadful climax in 1570 when scores of Ivan's already tormented victims were dragged in chains to the scaffolds on Red Square and there publicly boiled, butchered and beheaded. Among the condemned was Ivan Viskovatyi, the tsar's former confidant, whose manner of execution was as ingenious as it was revolting.[23] In the same year, the citizens of Novgorod were subjected to an equally sadistic orgy of mass murder and 'urban cleansing'. Seemingly sated, Ivan finally called an end to the activities of the *oprichnina* in 1570, and even banned the use of the word. The result of this sorry sequence of events was a national tragedy, the dismemberment of society (as well as that of many of its unfortunate individual citizens), economic crisis, depopulation of whole areas as people fled to the borderlands for refuge, and deep psychological trauma.

Ivan's call for a halt was not, however, the end of the domestic violence. In 1575, he once more embarked on a series of savage executions, and it seemed that the country was about to be subjected to the horrors of yet another *oprichnina*. However, in a kind of re-run of the events of 1564, he once more abdicated and enthroned one Simeon Bekbulatovich, a Tartar prince in Russian service and a descendant of Chenghiz Khan, as tsar of Russia. One year later, Ivan changed his mind, relieved Bekbulatovich of his position, appointed him as Grand Prince of Tver, and resumed the throne yet again. One can only speculate as to what abnormal twists of his abnormal mind led Ivan to stage this weird pantomime. It is typical of the tsar's aggressive and irascible nature that he should be personally responsible for a further act of violence which was to have serious consequences for the future of the Ryurikevich dynasty.

Ivan had in all seven wives, though the precise legal status of at least two of them is in question. His oldest surviving son by his first wife, Ivan Ivanovich, did not have an easy relationship with his father, and although still heir to the throne, is known to have been opposed to some of the old man's policies, particularly over the ongoing war with Poland. In 1581, whatever the immediate trigger for their final confrontation – almost certainly Ivan *père*'s physical assault on his pregnant daughter-in-law – the two of them became engaged in an emotional scuffle during which Ivan struck a fatal blow to his son's head with his iron-tipped staff. He died a few days later. Somewhat surprisingly, perhaps, Ivan is said to have been racked with grief and remorse over the incident, but his evil, mercurial temper had finally sealed the fate of his own dynasty. On his deathbed in 1584, the fast-failing tsar consulted a number of astrologers as to what the precise date of his death would be. When they predicted 18 March, Ivan considerately warned them that if the forecast proved untrue he would have them all burned alive. No doubt the astrologers thanked their lucky stars when on the appointed day, Ivan duly passed away, and was straightaway posthumously tonsured as a monk. This was as Ivan had himself decreed, though one can only surmise as to whether he intended it as a parting act of belated atonement for his terrible sins, or as a final gesture of that monstrous blend of affected piety and genuine perversity which had been the hallmark of his life.

Ivan was succeeded as tsar by his physically feeble and mentally retarded son, Fëdor (r. 1584–98), under the unofficial regency of his brother-in-law, Boris Godunov (r. 1598–1605). Fëdor's death in 1598 marked the end of the Ryurikevich dynasty and plunged the country into more than a decade of internal strife, traditionally known in Russian as the *smutnoe vremya*, and in English as the 'Time of Troubles'.

Before examining the events of those years in the next chapter, a final, brief appraisal of the reign of Ivan the Terrible seems appropriate. In a recent book, Maureen Perrie described him as 'probably the most controversial figure in Russian history'.[24] While the use of the superlative is certainly open to challenge – in view of other obvious contenders for the title – there is no doubt that the reign and character of the first Russian tsar has raised a good deal of historical controversy. Some scholars have tried to adduce mitigating circumstances, justifications, sophistic explanations and specious excuses for his bizarre and barbaric conduct. During the equally barbaric dictatorship of Iosif Stalin in particular, Ivan the Terrible was held up as the model of a wise, strong and beneficent reforming Russian ruler.[25] However, while it is true that one needs to judge historical figures by the standards of their time, rather than by the ethical codes and supposedly more humanitarian principles of a later age, it is equally true that on occasion there appears in the blood-soaked arena of history a monster in human form whose deeds defy any kind of sympathetic consideration. One might, at the limit, concede that Ivan's mental capacities were strained in later life by the chronic physical pain he suffered through the combined effects of advanced osteosclerosis and, possibly, syphilis, posthumous medical evidence of which was discovered during scientific examination of Ivan's exhumed skeletal remains by the Soviet anthropologist M. M. Gerasimov during the 1960s.[26] But the sheer scale of the human suffering, excruciating physical torment and social dislocation inflicted on his contemporaries, and the dreadful legacy of national agony left to posterity by this demonic despot is difficult to comprehend, let alone condone.

3 The early Romanovs, 1613–1682

In 1588, the English scholar and diplomat, Giles Fletcher, arrived in Moscow as Queen Elizabeth's ambassador to the court of Tsar Fëdor I of Russia (r. 1584–98). On his return from his embassy, Fletcher, an astute and erudite observer, composed an account of the government and manners of country he had just departed, which he addressed and dedicated to his sovereign. His *Of the Russe Commonwealth* was first published in 1591, and contains a wealth of information about the then current state of Muscovy, and some remarkably percipient remarks about its future. In particular, his chapter on the nobility, which includes comments on the activities of the former *oprichniki* (see Chapter 2) contains the following passage:

> … this wicked and tyrannous practice (though now it be ceased) hath so troubled that country and filled it so full of grudge and mortal hatred ever since, that it will not be quenched (as it seemeth now) till it burn again into a civil flame.[1]

Less than a decade after Fletcher composed these words, Russia was indeed enveloped in a sequence of acute political crises, social unrest, dynastic turmoil, economic ruin, cossak rebellion, peasant wars, famine and foreign invasion that it is difficult to find a more adequate description for them than the traditional term 'The Time of Troubles'. (The Russian term – *smutnoe vremya* – conveys an even more confused and murky picture of total chaos and disorder.) But even that expression scarcely encapsulates the complex, shifting and seismic proportions of the upheavals which contained all the ingredients of a nationwide civil war that more or less eviscerated the Russian state and society at the time, but which in fact changed surprisingly little when the turmoil had temporarily subsided. The most thorough and detailed scholarly post-Marxist analysis of the period, by the American historian Chester Dunning, is entitled *Russia's First Civil War*,[2] and its subtitle, *The Time of Troubles and the Founding of the Romanov Dynasty*, is the subject of the present chapter.

The Time of Troubles

Scholars variously date the beginning of the Time of Troubles from either the death of Ivan the Terrible in 1584, or that of his successor, Fëdor, in 1598. In either case, Giles Fletcher's prediction, made in 1591, about the 'civil flame' which would soon reduce Russia to virtual ashes was based on his first-hand knowledge of the deep crisis from which the country was already suffering during his brief embassy. As indicated in the foregoing chapter, the devastation wrought by the *oprichnina* and the unpredictable calamities of the last period of Ivan IV's reign had sown the deadly seeds of the harvest of sorrow which was soon to be reaped from the Russian land. The corny metaphor is in this case indeed appropriate in view of the indisputable link between the dreaded tsar's misbegotten policies and the chain of disasters and miseries which overwhelmed the country in the years after his death.

In contrast to his ferocious father, Fëdor was a physically weak and dim-witted character with an unsteady gait, suffering from dropsy, and given to vacuous smiles and fits of inane giggling. If descriptions of such unfortunate traits are true (and the impeccable Giles Fletcher is one of the reporters), then this, combined with his reputedly deep piety and fondness for religious pilgrimages, would qualify Fëdor to be regarded as something of a *yurodivyi* – a 'holy fool' or saintly simpleton, a familiar and popularly revered character in mediaeval Russian society. Recognising his heir's bodily and mental infirmity, if not his immanent spirituality, Ivan had appointed a regency council to oversee the business of government after his death, out of which the most powerful figure to emerge was the recently elevated boyar, and former *oprichnik*, Boris Godunov (r. 1598–1605), whose sister, Irina Godunova, had married Fëdor in

1580. Fëdor reigned in name only, and failed to set the stamp of his own authority on any recognisable policy. Under Godunov's guiding hand Moscow maintained good relations with England, less so with Poland and Sweden, and continued the eastward march across Siberia. Domestically, the country was still racked with civil strife, famine and the serious problem of depopulation and labour shortage as peasants continued to flee to the peripheries of Ukraine and western Siberia, often joining the peculiar freebooting, self-governing communities of the 'cossaks' (*kazaki*), which comprised a motley collection of runaway serfs, brigands, mercenaries, horsemen, farmers and pirates. The unruly, warlike cossaks were to remain a thorn in the flesh of the tsarist authorities throughout the seventeenth and eighteenth centuries. Many of the great popular rebellions during those years were led by charismatic cossak *ataman*s, or chieftains, such as Ivan Bolotnikov (1606), 'Stenka' Razin (1669–71), Kondratii Bulavin (1707) and, most notoriously, Emelyan Pugachëv (1773–4). The exploits of these champions of the exploited, whose names are still preserved in folklore, legend and song, will be returned to below.

Impotent as he may have been in other respects, Fëdor did manage to produce an offspring: a daughter, Feodosiya, born in 1592. However, he left no male heir and failed to designate a chosen successor by the time of his death in 1598. His half-brother, Dmitrii, Ivan IV's son by his last wife, had died in mysterious circumstances in the town of Uglich in 1591. The official version, put out by the boyar Vasilii Shuiskii, who was sent by Godunov to investigate the affair, was that Dmitrii's death was the result of a self-inflicted, though accidental, stabbing during an epileptic fit. Whether this was true, or whether he was in fact murdered by an assassin acting on behalf of Godunov in order to remove the last possible obstacle to his own regal ambitions, has never been firmly established. What is known is that the citizens of Uglich reacted to what they believed to be Dmitrii's murder by themselves killing the suspected perpetrators. Godunov himself retaliated by arresting and executing many of the town's inhabitants and exiling many more to Siberia.[3]

Ivan the Terrible had killed his eldest son, Ivan Ivanovich, in 1581 (see Chapter 2). The tsarevich Dmitrii was (allegedly) murdered in 1591. The halfwit Tsar Fëdor died heirless in 1598. The Ryurikevich dynasty had therefore finally fizzled out, and the throne of Russia was now Godunov's for the taking. He took it. After feigning some initial reluctance in his retreat at the fortified *Novodevichii* (New Virgins') Convent on the capital's south-western limits, he eventually succumbed to the solicitations of the people of Moscow, and, at the third time of asking, agreed to be crowned as tsar. The ceremony took place in the Moscow Kremlin's *Blagoveshchenskii* (Annunciation) Cathedral on 1 September – the Russian Orthodox calendar's New Year's Day – 1598. Despite continuing domestic disturbances, while regent, the future Tsar Boris had built up a limited amount of good-will and guided the country through a period of *relative* stability, at least in comparison with the murderous upheavals and uncertain-ties of Ivan the Terrible's reign. He had continued to placate the *dvoryanstvo* by tightening up the system of serf ownership, though no doubt the serfs themselves viewed the legislation which restricted their freedom of movement with rather less enthusiasm. The Russian Orthodox Church, too, had reason to lend the autocracy its continu-ing support, having gained autocephalous status with the establishment of the independent patriarchate of Moscow in the person of Godunov's crony, Iov (Job), in 1589. During the first few years of his own incumbency, the new tsar pursued an ambiguous policy which has been the subject of widely differing interpretations by subsequent historians, who have variously cast him as either 'tragic hero' or 'evil tyrant'.[4]

What *is* unarguable is that Boris was elevated to the throne at an extremely fraught period of Muscovy's history. The country was still suffering from the effects of Ivan the Terrible's depredations, in the throes of a ruinous famine, ravaged internally by endemic brig-andage, politically in a state of constant disequilibrium caused by continuing rivalries among leading boyar clans – in particular the Shuiskii, the Romanov, the Mstislavskii and the Nagoi – and faced with an ever-present threat of attack by the Crimean Tatars on its southern borderlands. In these inauspicious circumstances, Boris was forced to undertake a number of draconian measures in a vain attempt to maintain some kind of albeit fractious unity in his realm. These included greatly increased taxation, severe restrictions on peasant mobility, more burdensome fiscal and service obligations on the townspeople, and the physical elimination, either by assassi-nation or exile, of opponents and potential rivals. Despite Chester Dunning's critique of Marxist, class-based, analyses of the Time of

Troubles mentioned above, even by his own admission the policies of Boris Godunov resulted in a much more highly polarised, almost caste-ridden, society in which the struggle between the *verkhi* and the *nizy* (see Chapter 1) became more acute.

Apart from flight and rebellion, another increasingly common consequence of the people's growing impoverishment was the practice of selling oneself into slavery – thereby avoiding payment of taxes – or joining the volatile cossak communities in the south. The tightening bonds of serfdom also meant that both bandit gangs and cossak bands contained an increasing number of runaway peasants who joined in the frequent manifestations of popular opposition to the central government and its highly, if precariously, placed beneficiaries. Dunning's repeated dismissals of Soviet, and also some western historians', claims to detect in these manifestations of mass disaffection and protest the seeds of an incipient peasant war against the ruling classes are not particularly convincing. His attempts to make subtle distinctions among the participants in these insurgencies as slaves, dispossessed gentry, brigands, cossaks, mutinous soldiers (as opposed to 'real' serfs and peasants) do not really alter the picture of a society that was deeply and traumatically divided, one in which the upper classes, consisting of boyars, wealthy merchants, the Church, state dignitaries and the military elite were the recurring object of the resentment, rebellion and retribution of the lower social categories, or classes.

Between 1601 and 1603, it was the turn of the forces of nature to conspire to hurl the country into even deeper turmoil and human misery. In what has been described as 'a little ice-age', Russia, like other parts of Europe at the time, was struck by a series of meteorological catastrophes – severe rains and flooding, preternaturally early summertime frosts, an unusually cruel winter, even by Russian standards – which rapidly led to harvest failure, food shortages, famine and starvation on a massive scale. Hundreds of thousands perished, the countryside was littered with emaciated corpses, looting was rampant, fathers sold their wives and children into slavery for food, refugees flooded the towns in a vain search for succour – thereby compounding the problem of urban starvation – and acts of cannibalism were not uncommon. Tsar Boris and his officials did what they could by distributing limited amounts of alms and loaves to the starving, but ultimately it was the civil and ecclesiastical authorities which were blamed for this national disaster in which some sources claim that between one-third and two-thirds of the country's population died of hunger and disease.[5] There is no doubt that Boris's claims for popular legitimacy were undermined by the devastating effects of the famine, though whether a national movement demanding his removal from office would have occurred but for unexpected outside intervention is problematical.

That outside intervention took the shape of a rival claimant to the throne in the person of a pretender (*samozvanets*), usually referred to as the False- or the pseudo-Dmitrii (*Lzhedimitrii*). The precise origins and identity of the pretender are still the subject of historical debate and conjecture, but the general consensus is that he was a runaway monk, named Grigorii Otrepev, who had previously served in the Kremlin's *Chudov* (Miracles) monastery, and in the household of the boyar Romanov family. After a period of wandering, he fetched up in the kingdom of Poland-Lithuania and announced to his patron, a minor Polish nobleman, that he was in fact the tsarevich Dmitrii, son of Ivan the Terrible, who had miraculously survived the plot to assassinate him at Uglich in 1591. He, therefore, was the legitimate ruler of Russia, rather than the usurper, Godunov. While his claim was patently absurd, in a credulous age and in the heat of international rivalry and political intrigue, the False Dmitrii secured the backing of the Catholic Poles, and in 1604 invaded Muscovy at the head of an army of Poles, cossaks and Russian opponents of Godunov. Among his Russian supporters were members of the disgraced Romanov clan, some of whom had been exiled by Godunov, who suspected them of plotting against him, and one of whose senior figures, Fëdor Nikitich Romanov (*c*.1553–1633) had been forced to become a monk, under the name of Filaret, and incarcerated in a monastery. (Godunov's bitter enemy, he was later to become one of the most powerful men in Russia as Patriarch of Moscow, and father of the first Romanov tsar, Mikhail Fëdorovich – see below.)

Given the spurious nature of the False-Dmitrii's claim, it may seem remarkable how much support he could command, but the appearance of popularly backed pretenders was a common phenomenon in seventeenth- and eighteenth-century Russia. Their acceptance is partly explained by the deep well of popular resentment and opposition to an unpopular incumbent tsar on which the impostor could draw; by the widespread myth of the 'good tsar' returning to save his people from a tyrannical ruler; and by very real grievances which made the pretender a rallying point, or catalyst, for action by widespread disaffected elements of the population. Whether this was the result of false consciousness, simple naivety or a manifestation of genuine popular monarchism is open for debate.[6] At all events, after some initial successes, the pretender's forces were eventually trounced by troops loyal to Godunov under the command of Prince Vasilii Shuiskii. The False-Dmitrii escaped the field of battle and managed to evade capture by Shuiskii, who failed to press home his advantage.

Godunov, it appeared, had survived the most serious threat to his rule, which was in any case brought to an end by his death from a fatal haemorrhage in April 1605. He was immediately succeeded by his son, Fëdor II (r. April–June 1605). However, the 16-year-old tsar was rapidly betrayed by his boyars, who transferred their allegiance to the False-Dmitrii, arrested and murdered Fëdor and his mother, ejected Patriarch Iov from office and opened the gates of Moscow to the pretender's advancing forces. With the backing of the boyars, and of Filaret Romanov, recently restored to favour as Metropolitan of Rostov, the False-Dmitrii now became recognised as Tsar Dmitrii (r. 1605–6). (The whole Godunov/Dmitrii imbroglio has received both literary and musical immortality in Aleksandr Pushkin's play, *Boris Godunov* (1825) and in Modest Musorgskii's operatic master-piece of the same title, composed in 1869 and first performed in St Petersburg in 1874.)

The trappings of divinely ordained, autocratic power notwith-standing, permanence of tenure in that exalted office was far from guaranteed in those troubled times. This was particularly so in Dmitrii's case, who was rumoured to have converted to Catholicism, had a Polish wife, was clean-shaven, and – perhaps most difficult for most good Russians to accept – was alleged to be teetotal. It was not long before the fickle Muscovite magnates, led by the venerable Vasilii Shuiskii, once more shifted their loyalty, deposed Dmitrii, duplicitously acknowledged the falsity of his claim, had him mur-dered and his cremated ashes, mixed with gunpowder, fired from a cannon in the direction of Poland, whence he had come. In his place Vasilii Shuiskii himself, a distant descendant of Aleksandr Nevskii (see Chapter 2), was proclaimed tsar (r. 1606–10).

During his short reign, Shuiskii faced two major threats to his position. The first, starting in 1606, was in the form of a large cossak and peasant rebellion under the unlikely combined leadership of the aristocratic Prince Gregorii Shakovskoi, a personal enemy of Shuiskii, and Ivan Bolotnikov, a runaway former slave and cossak chieftain. In his inflammatory propaganda, Bolotnikov preached bloody social revolution and the overthrow of the people's oppressors, but, unsurprisingly, had no properly articulated programme of reform or legislation. After briefly threatening Moscow, and weakened by internal divisions and defections, Bolotnikov's motley hordes were finally crushed in 1607 and their leaders executed. That was not the end of Shuiskii's troubles, and over the next year or so a grotesque parade of further pretenders to the throne continued to fan the flames of popular revolt. These unlikely impostors were, in Florinsky's words, 'merely a pretext for a continuation of the struggle against a hated regime'.[7]

The second threat came from a second False-Dmitrii, of even more obscure origins than the first, who, again with opportunistic Polish support, achieved some success by setting up a rival tsardom in 1608 with its headquarters at the village of Tushino, not far from Moscow, and exercised his rule over large areas of southern Russia. The confrontation between Shuiskii, sometimes referred to as 'the boyars' tsar', and the so-called 'brigand of Tushino', was not resolved until 1610, when invading Polish forces aided the Romanovs in deposing Shuiskii, who was then promptly tonsured as a monk. He died as a prisoner of the Poles in Warsaw in 1612. The problem of political power, however, failed to be resolved, and over the next two or three years, the throne of Moscow became the object of bloody contesting rivalries among Polish royalty, boyar cliques, cossak armies, yet *another* False-Dmitrii, ephemeral provisional governments and various factions in the Orthodox Church hierarchy, during which the whole country was in a state of perpetual anarchy and civil war.

Among the most anarchical and volatile elements in this conflict were the cossak insurgents, whose preferred choice as tsar was the second pseudo-Dmitrii. The boyars and the old aristocrats, however, had different ideas. They were stuck between the Scylla and Charybdis of, on the one side, an unpredictable 'cossaks' tsar', backed by what they regarded as an unruly rabble of fugitive serfs, brigands and free-booting champions of plebeian liberties; and, on the other, a foreign, *Catholic*, ruler in the Kremlin, who might nevertheless protect or restore their aristocratic privileges. Faced with this dilemma, the more influential members of the Muscovite elite threw in their lot behind the candidacy of the Polish king, Zygmunt III (1587–1632), or more precisely his 14-year-old son, Władysław (r. 1632–48). A hastily convened assembly of Moscow's rich and powerful accordingly offered the crown of Russia to a pubescent Pole, and the forces of the second False-Dmitrii were forced to withdraw from the outskirts of Moscow to the town of Kaluga, where he was finally murdered. The threat posed by the 'brigand of Tushino' was at an end, and for the next two years the throne of Russia was occupied by an adolescent Polish prince. The new regime immediately inaugurated a programme of authoritarian, oppressive government which rapidly alienated its Orthodox subjects, reinforcing traditional, Russian xenophobic hatred of their ancient Catholic foe, and leading to further civil unrest.

The crisis came to a head in the autumn of 1611, when a patriotic appeal by the patriarch of Moscow, Hermogen, then imprisoned by the occupying Poles, led to the formation of a national militia (*opolchenie*), headed by two very different men, a wealthy butcher from Nizhnii-Novgorod, named Kuzma Minin, and a distinguished military commander, Prince Dmitrii Pozharskii. At that stage in the continuing civil war, the choice before the country seemed still to be between foreign rule by a Polish tsar, or social revolution led by the insurgent cossaks. The boyars, the propertied and the privileged classes appeared to favour the former, and not even Hermogen condemned his Polish captors in his message. But Minin and Pozharskii offered a third way. Appealing to Russian patriotic and religious emotions, they called on the country to unite in driving out the Catholic Poles and reject a foreign king, but also to quell the rebel cossaks and bring peace and order to the land under a new, popularly elected Orthodox Russian tsar. On receiving news that a Polish relief army was on its way to assist their countrymen besieged inside the Moscow Kremlin, Minin and Pozharskii's new citizens' militia moved from their strongholds on the Volga and attacked the capital. An uneasy and bumpy patriotic alliance of sorts was forged between the leaders of the *opolchenie* and the cossak command. At the end of October 1612, their combined forces finally captured the Kremlin, and the exhausted Poles were defeated and driven out of Holy Russia. A major lesson was drawn from the conflict – that it was the Russian people under popular leadership, rather than the self-seeking, landowning Russian *dvoryanstvo*, who had delivered the country from foreign conquest and further domestic chaos. However, the country still required firm direction and an end to the crisis of government. To this end Minin, Pozharskii and the cossak commander, Trubetskoi, issued a summons for the convocation of a *zemskii sobor*, an Assembly of the Land, delegates to which gathered in Moscow in January 1613 to elect a new tsar. The choice fell on Mikhail Fëdorovich Romanov, first of the new dynasty which was to rule the Russian Empire for the next 300 years. Regarded as popular national heroes, 'Citizen Minin and Prince Pozharskii' were later commemorated for their services to the fatherland by the erection of a neo-classical statue, sculpted by the Rome-educated Ivan Martos in 1818, which still adorns Moscow's Red Square close by St Basil's Cathedral. (It may be considered ironic that the sculptor of the monument celebrating the expulsion of the Catholic Poles was educated in Rome.)

The Time of Troubles, it appeared, was over. But the immediate solution to the political problem of who was to rule Russia did little to assuage the continuing economic and social difficulties. In fact, Russia in the middle of the seventeenth century was scarred by so many instances of riot, mutiny, rebellion and religious schism that it became known, even by its contemporaries – after the Time of Troubles – as the 'Time of Revolts' (*buntashnee vremya*).[8] How the new tsar handled his daunting legacy is the subject of the following section – but first, a final appraisal of the effects of the Time of Troubles.

Given the extent of the civil upheavals, cossak rebellions, foreign invasions, devastating famine, class warfare, dynastic mayhem and murderous military conflict, it is truly remarkable how unscathed and unchanged, though not unaffected, Muscovy emerged from its 'first civil war'. First, despite the deadly game of 'musical chairs' which was played with the Russian throne during this period, the *institution* of autocracy survived intact, and the opportunity for establishing a mode of more participatory government, whether patrician or plebeian, was lost. How Mikhail Romanov successfully managed to restore and reconsolidate the tradition of tsarist absolutism is discussed below. Second, for all the vigour and the violence of the popular protests and rebellions, the potential for real social revolution was similarly dissipated. After 1613, the class structure of Muscovite society remained unaltered, the cossaks by and large scuttled back to the southern badlands, the peasant serfs were returned to their masters' estates, and both the battered boyars and the double-dealing *dvoryanstvo* easily retained their privileged positions in society. The latter, in particular, had shown themselves to be not so much a state-serving nobility of merit, as a self-serving freemasonry of the meretricious. Finally, the Orthodox Church, which had already survived, indeed prospered, under the pagan Tatars, which had successfully warded off the secularisation of their estates and outlasted the *oprichnina*, had now come through the devastation of the Time of Troubles with its prestige, its status and its considerable property intact. And – led by a powerful patriarch – it retained the faithful following of an overwhelmingly devout population.

The destructive, though potentially creative, forces unleashed during the Time of Troubles, it seemed, were now spent. More troubles, however, lay ahead.

The first Romanov tsar

One of the main reasons for the successful candidacy of Mikhail Romanov as tsar was, according to Florinsky, his 'utter insignificance'.[9] That is to say, the somewhat sickly youth entertained no grandiose personal ambitions, and could be relied on – in so far as anyone could be relied on – to pursue policies which were in the interests of the most influential and powerful sections of Muscovite society. While not being exactly a stooge of the merchants, the nobility and other assorted nabobs, he was at any rate, and at best, a puppet ruler, a marionette monarch whose strings were pulled by manipulative forces behind the throne. Of these, the most powerful puppet-master was the new tsar's own father, Filaret (the quondam Fëdor Nikitich Romanov), who enjoyed some popular kudos for the role he had played as acting patriarch in the camp of the second False-Dmitrii, and his imprisonment by the Poles, in whose custody he still languished at the time of the *zemskii sobor* which had elected his son to the throne. An ambitious, scheming and still influential figure on the Russian political scene, Filaret was released from captivity in 1619 and returned to Moscow, where he was elevated to the patriarchate. From his lofty position, he became the *éminence grise* of his offspring's regime, and virtual ruler, or co-ruler, of Russia in this dynastic diarchy.

Until his death in 1633, it was Filaret, rather than Mikhail, who guided the domestic and foreign policies of the country with all the firmness and authority of a genuinely absolute autocrat. After the chaos and uncertainty of the Time of Troubles, the centralised power of the Muscovite autocracy, as it had developed in the sixteenth century, was revived and reconsolidated with fresh vigour. What little power remained with the boyar council (*boyarskaya duma*) was further whittled down, and the *zemskii sobor* convened less frequently, as Filaret (who had assumed the same honorific title of 'Great Sovereign' – *Velikii gosudar'* – as his son, the tsar) relied more on the advice and assistance of a tiny clique of close senior confidants.

However, such a vast realm as Russia had now become, chiefly as a result of its steady eastwards expansion through Siberia, could not be properly governed by a small handful of Kremlin courtiers, and the first few years of Romanov rule witnessed the fairly rapid proliferation of an administrative bureaucracy composed of rudimentary ministries, chanceries or *prikazy*, each with its own area of responsibility, though with sometimes overlapping and imprecise functions. For instance, the *Razboinyi prikaz* (Criminal Bureau) was responsible for the restoration and maintenance of law and order – a kind of embryonic 'ministry of internal affairs'. The *Posolskii prikaz* (Ambassadors' Bureau), in charge of diplomatic relations with foreign powers, was the corresponding 'ministry of foreign affairs'. The office responsible for maintaining coach drivers' settlements (*yam*), post-houses and communications was known as the *Yamskoi prikaz*, or Bureau of Post and Communications. The whole, huge territory of Siberia was nominally administered by the *Sibirskii prikaz*, established in 1637, though in actual practice the vast area and its constituent provinces became the personal, albeit temporary, fiefdoms of rapacious local military governors (*voevody*). From the mid-seventeenth century to the central government reforms of Peter the Great (see Chapter 4), around 50 government *prikazy* were established, the operations of which were, however, often distinguished more by bureaucratic ineptitude than administrative efficiency.

Among the major preoccupations of any government is the business of revenue raising, and one of the first tasks of the new

Romanov regime was to attend to the parlous state of the nation's economy after the ravages of the Time of Troubles. This it sought to improve by the usual mixture of raising loans (for example, from the immensely wealthy Stroganov family), increasing direct taxation and granting generous financial privileges to the powerful merchant class. Not a small part in this process was the imposition of further restrictions on peasant movement, tying them more closely to the estates on which they worked, increasing their indebtedness to their landowners and, in short, raising the level of their exploitation while simultaneously lowering the portcullis of enserfment. In general terms, the reign of the first Romanov saw an improvement in the country's central finances (though, as is commonly the case, at the cost of popular suffering), an increase in foreign trade and the establishment of new manufacturing industries. All this was achieved despite the never-ending drain on the exchequer caused by Russia's continuing foreign wars.

Military conflicts with Sweden, Poland-Lithuania, rebel cossaks, Crimean Tatars and the Ottoman Turks placed a permanent strain on the country's financial and human resources, and, despite the conclusion of a number of temporary truces and short-lived treaties, throughout the seventeenth century Russia's rulers had perforce to reconcile themselves to the foreign occupation of what they regarded as their ancient territories in the west and south, and to the denial of a permanent maritime exit to the Baltic. It was not until the wars of Peter the Great in the early eighteenth century that Russia was to gain the degree of internationally recognised status and respect which was commensurate with the country's enormous territorial dimensions, natural resources and military potential.

Domestically, although the subterranean rumblings that were a legacy of the Time of Troubles continued to reverberate throughout Mikhail's reign, it was during that of his successor, Tsar Aleksei (r. 1645–76), that the social, economic and religious problems of the country erupted during the 'Time of Revolts'.

Tsar Aleksei and the Time of Revolts

Like his father, Aleksei was only 16 years of age when he succeeded him and ascended the throne on 13 July 1645, the oldest boy of ten siblings born to Mikhail's second wife, Yevdokiya Streshneva. In comparison with some of his more violent and bellicose predecessors, Aleksei's generally pacific temperament, his piety and assiduous attention to learning earned him the sobriquet 'most quiet tsar' (*tishaishii tsar'*). However, the placidity of his personality belied the tumultuous nature of the times through which he lived and the pandemonium over which he presided.

The first major rebellion of the Time of Revolts occurred in 1648, just three years into his reign. Increased taxation, lack of military pay for the *strel'tsy*, a three-fold hike in the price of salt, further encroachments on residual peasant freedoms, and popular discontent at the arrogant and high-handed caprices of the tsar's favourites led to a mass urban rebellion. In June the Moscow mobs were besieging the gates of the Kremlin, bellowing for redress of their grievances and the surrender into their vengeful hands of the hated magnates, senior monks and merchants. Singled out for particular venom was Boris Morozov (1590–1661), the tsar's brother-in-law, erstwhile tutor and author of the detested economic reforms which had sparked the disturbance. A characteristically tearful public appeal from the terrified tsar failed to calm the anger of the mob, until two of his advisers, Leonid Pleshcheev and Pëtr Trakhaniotov, were finally delivered up for execution and Morozov banished to a remote monastery. Further urban insurgencies followed over the next few years, including one protesting against the debasement of the metal coinage – the so-called 'copper revolt' (*mednyi bunt*) of 1656. The government responded to these manifestations of popular insubordination, including another mass uprising in Moscow in 1662, with a sustained campaign of torture, floggings, executions and exile. The obvious failure of this 'most quiet tsar' to satisfy the demands of the populace, and his ruthless determination to implement the most draconian reprisals against his opponents is again evidence of the chronic inability of the autocratic government to bring any degree of social harmony, domestic tranquillity or justice to the Russian land.

An ambitious attempt was, however, made to bring a degree of order and regularity to the state of the Russian law. That was the promulgation of the great Code of Laws (the *Ulozhenie*) of 1649. While it is difficult to establish any direct link between the popular revolt in Moscow in the previous year and Tsar Aleksei's efforts to establish a firm legislative foundation for the future political administration, dispensation of justice, social relationships, moral values and religious practices within his kingdom, it is a fact that the new code was published only a few weeks after the public manifestations of dissatisfaction with the status quo which must have been rawly fresh in the minds of its drafters. Whether the new laws were meant genuinely to address popular grievances or simply to give a legal framework to measures designed to prevent or punish any further breaches of public order is, again, difficult to establish with any certainty. It is, however, clear that the contents of the *Ulozhenie* did embellish the regime with a relatively clear set of approved procedures, principles and provisions which would act as the basis of all future legislative activity, whether of a jurisprudential or decretive nature. The appearance of the new codex did not, however, suddenly transform the Russian autocracy into a 'nomocracy' – that is, a system of government based on a legal code. So long as the autocrat possessed the sovereign legal power to alter, rescind or abolish the law at his absolute discretion or personal caprice, then the *de jure* nature of the government's authority was totally undermined by the *de facto* reality of unfettered tyrannical rule, and exposed as spurious, pseudological and a sham.

Despite its deficiencies, it is, however, worthwhile examining briefly the actual contents of the *Ulozhenie*. Its overriding aim was to enhance the central powers of the autocratic state at the expense of the individual rights and freedoms of its citizens through a mixture of social designations, fiscal imposts, service obligations, severe penal sanctions and the final consolidation of peasant bondage – serfdom – as the bedrock of the entire tsarist social, political and economic order. Russian society was now formally divided into a hierarchical stratification of classes, or estates (*sosloviya*; sing. *soslovie* – see Chapter 1), each with its own legal obligations, duties and hereditary status. In case of failure to fulfil the required obligations, most articles of the code helpfully provided an indication of the appropriate punishment which the perpetrator of a particular offence might confidently anticipate. These ranged from fines, restrictions on movement or confinement, to the most gruesome forms of corporal and/or capital punishment.

Interestingly, it is in Aleksei's *Ulozhenie* that the first legally formulated reference to exile (*ssylka*) to the peripheries of Russia, including the remotest parts of Siberia, was formally mentioned as the penalty for a variety of felonies or crimes from hooliganism to homicide. Often the period of banishment would commence only after a preliminary scourging with the knout – Russia's favoured instrument of flagellation – and some form of minor physical mutilation, disfigurement or amputation. The lopping off of ears, slitting of nostrils, excising the tongue and slicing off a finger or two were fairly routine practices. Flogging with the knout was prescribed in 141 articles of the *Ulozhenie,* either for a designated number of strokes or 'without mercy' (*neshchadno*). The apprentice public executioners of Muscovy had obviously learned the savage lessons of their Mongol predecessors, as pointed out by Professor Foinitskii (see Chapter 2, note 11). By comparison, the gruesome nature of some Muscovite punitive practices makes the severest application of the Islamic *Sharia* penal code look positively therapeutic.

Under the terms of the *Ulozhenie,* all classes of Russian society were in effect the corporate servants of the state and were compelled to adhere to its dictates, primarily in order to maintain the steady flow of revenue into its coffers and recruits pressed into its armed forces. And, under a later edict of 1658, the registered townsfolk (inhabitants of a township, or *posad*) were required to dwell permanently in their place of residence and forbidden to migrate and settle in another town on pain of death. In this way, to put it simply, the tax collectors knew who the urban tax-payers were, where they were, and how they were to be found. Moreover, in order to sustain the tax-paying ability of the town dwellers, restrictions were placed on the entrepreneurial activities of other sections of the population living on the fringes of the *posad,* such as petty nobles, foreigners, commercially minded clerics, suburban squatters and even slaves.

Members of the *dvoryanstvo,* so crucial for the survival of the autocracy, were also limited in the exercise of their personal freedom, but were compensated, as it were, by the award of certain rights and privileges. They lost the right, for instance, to pledge themselves into slavery, a curious ploy which was commonly used to avoid tax and service obligations while simultaneously gaining the protection of a new owner. The nobility was also transformed into a *hereditary* service caste, by a provision in the *Ulozhenie* that no newcomers from other social groups were to be admitted to that estate. Moreover, the right to own lands cultivated by the servile labour of bonded serfs was made the exclusive preserve of the *dvoryanstvo,* thus completing its gradual metamorphosis into an exclusive class of land- and serf-owning nobility. The downside, however, was that compulsory military service to the state, in which the *dvoryanstvo* had its origins, but which had fallen somewhat into abeyance during the Time of Troubles, was now rigorously reinforced. The corollary to the landowning military nobility's privileged position was the final consolidation of serfdom. As mentioned above, over the last half-century or so, the flimsy remaining freedoms of the peasantry – to migrate, to change masters, to hire themselves out or to take up new tenancies – had been progressively (or regressively?) curtailed. Under the terms of the code of 1649, these last, threadbare liberties were finally abolished, and peasant labourers, together with their families, were henceforward firmly tied to the estates on which they dwelt and also thereby to the person of the noble owner of that land. In effect, from 1649 on, the enserfed peasants had become the private property, the chattels, of their noble masters – their legal position, their personal circumstances and their social status being akin to simple, unadulterated, primitive slavery. And that, with some minor amendments – some for the better, but most for the worse – was to remain the situation for the next two centuries.

Such, in brief, were the long-term consequences of the Russian government's attempt to introduce the country's first comprehensive legislative code, an enterprise which succeeded in creating a tyrannical, semi-theocratic, feudal police state, based on serfdom and resting on the tripod support of the military, the bureaucracy and the Church.

Foreign policy, eastern expansion and western influences

While wrestling with divisive domestic difficulties, Aleksei also had his fair share of foreign policy and military problems. In 1654 Russia went to war with Poland, the major objective being to oust the Poles from Russia's southern and western borderlands and retake Kiev and Smolensk under Moscow's rule. At the same time, Aleksei joined battle with Sweden in an attempt to regain for Russia the Baltic littoral and an exit to the western seas. Both wars were long, bloody and unspectacular in their conclusions. In the south, under the terms of the Treaty of Andrusovo (1667), Russia regained large areas of what later became designated as Ukraine, east of the river Dnepr, including Kiev. Turkey, too, had its own ambitions in this region, but after a long series of hostilities, Russia's earlier gains were reconfirmed by the Treaty of Bakhchisarai in 1681. To the west of Moscow, Smolensk had already fallen to Aleksei's forces in 1654 after a siege in which he personally led his troops. Though not realising all of his objectives, Aleksei had nevertheless laid the foundations for the more decisive military and territorial gains of his as yet unborn son, Peter, in the Great Northern War (1700–21, see Chapter 4). In this respect Aleksei displayed a rather more robust side of his personality, which offsets his traditional reputation as 'the most quiet tsar'. However, the expansion of Russian possessions in the south brought her into closer proximity with the Crimean Tatars, the Ottoman Empire and the ever-contumacious cossaks, whose fickle allegiances and mercenary military services switched mercurially between Russia, Poland and Turkey. The swashbuckling Ukrainian cossak commander, Bogdan Khmelnitskii (*c*.1595–1657), was a typical example of the shifting nature of cossak loyalties, and his posthumous stature as a great national hero – now Ukrainian, now Russian, now cossak, or all three – is based on equally shifting grounds. As will be seen, Moscow's (and, later, St Petersburg's) quadrangular relationship with Warsaw, the cossaks and the Sublime Porte in Constantinople were to be a constant preoccupation of Russia's foreign policy makers and military commanders over the next two centuries.

In the east, the relentless drive through Siberia, the subjection of her native peoples, the rapacious imposition of fur tribute, and the exploitation of the territory's animal, vegetable and mineral resources continued at breakneck pace. By the 1680s, Russian hunters, trappers, merchants, militiamen and Muscovite officials had established a network of fortified townships, fortresses, trading posts and local commercial centres stretching all the way from Omsk to Okhotsk, from the Urals to the Ussuri, and the intrepid seafarer, Semën Dezhnëv, had already navigated the Bering Strait (see Chapter 1). The epic story of this process of discovery, exploration and colonisation is not widely known in the west, or even by many Russians, outside a relatively small number of specialist scholars. While most reasonably well-educated westerners will have at least heard of Magellan, Marco Polo, Drake, Columbus, Pizarro and Cortez, how many are familiar with the contemporaneous expeditions of Yermak, Khabarov, Perfilev, Pashkov and Dezhnëv? Yet their achievements were no less spectacular and opened up a vast alternative 'New World' in a very short period of time. A variety of factors contributed to this amazingly swift 'conquest of a continent'.[10] The spirit of adventure, scientific curiosity, territorial imperatives, the discovery of other natural riches, imperial prestige, flight from oppression, insatiable greed, 'manifest destiny' and sheer serendipity may have all contributed to the process, but the major motivating factor was unquestionably the economic determinant of fur, as indicated in Chapter 1. In his pioneering work on the trade in precious pelts, Raymond Fisher estimated that, in the seventeenth century, the fur business accounted for as much as 10 per cent of Moscow's total state revenue, a significant proportion of the whole.[11]

On the other hand, fur alone cannot account exclusively for the huge influx of Russian migrants and settlers into Russia's new frontierlands. There has been a long historical debate in an attempt to explain the population dynamics of Siberian settlement from European Russia. The basic question seems to boil down to this: was Russia's penetration and settlement of Siberia the result of state-sponsored, government-directed initiatives, or did it owe more to the spontaneous movement of the Russian people migrating freely and voluntarily to fill up the huge vacuum across the Urals in search of wealth and land, or freedom from an increasingly coercive central government? What is clear is that there is no mono-causal explanation. While many Siberian regionalist historians and some Soviet scholars, notably V. I. Shunkov, have argued in favour of the mass peasant migration theory, N. I. Nikitin has persuasively demonstrated that in the early period of colonisation, by far the largest category of the Russian population of Siberia was represented by military personnel (*voennosluzhilye lyudi*). Not confining themselves to purely military matters, these trailblazers brought with them a variety of crafts and manufacturing skills which contributed much to the civic development and economic diversity of the territory.[12] In the final analysis, the argument over 'which came first, the *muzhik* or the militia?' becomes a circular one. It is, therefore, difficult to contest the conclusion of N. V. Ustyugov that 'government-directed and free colonisation [of Siberia] are two parallel, mutually dependent and closely connected processes which are impossible to understand one without the other'.[13] What is certainly indisputable is that, contrary to popular misconceptions, the exile of common criminals and political offenders against the state played only a minimal role in the colonisation of Siberia. The major factors were always a combination of state service, voluntary migration, eager miscegenation with the native peoples, and the consequent process of natural procreation.[14] At all events, it was the conquest, or 'assimilation' (*osvoenie*), of Siberia in the late sixteenth and seventeenth century which transformed mediaeval Muscovy into the largest continuous land empire in the history of the world.[15]

While Muscovy was busy extending its interests in the east, she was at the same time cautiously becoming more receptive to the gradual encroachment of European influences, ideas and inventions from the west. As in the case of the later, more dramatic, reforms of Peter the Great, many of the piecemeal western innovations in the middle of the seventeenth century were introduced as a result of military imperatives. The need for more sophisticated weaponry, foreign technicians, experienced army officers, and general European 'know-how' led to the gradual influx of western experts, scientists, doctors, designers, linguists, engineers and artisans skilled in modern techniques of smelting, forging, gunsmithery, textile manufacture and masonry. Traditional Russian suspicion of foreigners, however, meant that these alien specialists, working in the service of Moscow, were segregated in a special suburb of the city called the German, or Foreign, Quarter (*nemetskaya sloboda*), in order that the Orthodox Christian population of the capital should not be contaminated with diabolical alien customs, unhealthy habits and tastes or heretical ideas. (In Russian, the term *nemets*, adjective *nemetskii*, meaning 'German', is cognate with the word *nemoi*, literally meaning 'dumb'. In the seventeenth century it was applied more or less indiscriminately to all non-Russian-speaking resident foreigners.) Despite the cultural quarantine, it proved impossible to utilise European techniques and expertise without being infected by the bacilli of intellectual inquiry, scientific thought and secular education of which they were the products. As a result, familiarity with the temporal learning of the west, along with its social and cultural accompaniments, against the ambiguous background of government prompting and official disapprobation, led to a whole range of bizarre anomalies. These included, for instance, the encouragement of modern mathematics and ballistic technology, while prohibiting the taking of snuff or trading in tobacco (*tobach-nichestvo*), on pain of having the septum ripped from one's nostrils. (This may safely be regarded as the first official government warning that the use of tobacco may seriously damage one's health.) The peculiar blend of barbaric practice with a simulacrum of civilised behaviour, typical of seventeenth-century Muscovy, provides a fair foretaste of the menu of mediaevalism and modernity which was the distinguishing feature of Peter the Great's style of government in the coming century.

Aleksei, the second Romanov, died in 1676, to be succeeded by his eldest son, Fëdor (r. 1676–82), but not before having to grapple with two further major challenges to his regime. A double whirlwind of widespread civil tumult and deep religious schism was to cause havoc in the remaining years of the reign of 'the most quiet tsar'.

Rebellion and religious schism

Mention has already been made of the Bolotnikov rebellion of 1606 during the Time of Troubles. Of greater significance and even greater notoriety was the massive revolt of 1669–71 led by the celebrated Don cossak *ataman*, Stepan Timofeevich ('Stenka') Razin (*c*.1640–71). Like so many popular uprisings in the seventeenth, eighteenth and even nineteenth centuries, Razin's revolt was not directed so much against the autocracy as such, as against the members of the governing classes of Russian society who were viewed by the masses, no doubt justifiably, as a breed of privileged, exploitative parasites. The insurgency began in 1667 as a localised campaign of piratical plundering along the waters of the Caspian Sea and the lower reaches of the river Volga, standard behaviour for the lawless cossak gangs in that area and at that time. By 1670, however, Razin's followers had swelled into a significant military force which threatened to march on Moscow in an effort to lift the oppressive yoke of the nobles and boyars. The ragamuffin army of runaway serfs, cossaks, native tribesmen and other social dissidents was, however, no match for the more disciplined regiments of the newly modernised Muscovite military. In 1671, with only the fortress of Astrakhan still loyal to him, Razin was finally betrayed by members of his own entourage, arrested, and taken to Moscow for torture, execution and the familiar gory pageant of public dismemberment. The

hitherto constituent parts of his mutilated corpse were finally transformed, quite literally, into a dogs' breakfast. In the insurgent
regions, thousands of his followers were savagely slaughtered,
hanged, hooked or impaled in an effort to restore tranquillity, calm
and civic order.

The rebel hordes were duly suppressed, but what the authorities
were incapable of suppressing was the lasting legend of Stenka
Razin, whose drunken, bloodthirsty adventures in support of
popular freedom are still celebrated in Russian folklore and song to
the present day. In particular, his boisterous display of fraternal
machismo by drowning his new Persian bride beneath the waves of
the Volga river in the interests of maintaining the camaraderie of his
cossak boatcrew is the subject of one of Russia's most popular folk
songs. This apart, his buccaneering exploits along the coasts of
'Mother Volga', his championship of the people's cause and his bold,
if misbegotten, challenge to authority remained an epic symbol of
popular resistance to tyranny, emulated by future rebel rousers,
which was never far from the mind of Russia's later rulers. Nor was
the choice between Razin or Romanov ever far from the minds of
Russia's later revolutionaries.

An altogether different, though related, example of popular
challenge to authority, both civil and ecclesiastical, was provided by
the great Schism (*raskol*) within the Russian Orthodox Church,
which had its origins in the 1640s and still exists in so-called 'Old
Believer' Christian communities, both in Russia and in emigration,
even today. Although lip service to the occurrence of the *raskol* is regularly paid in general histories of Russia, the long-term social and
symbolic significance of the phenomenon is too often given less
attention than it unquestionably deserves.[16] The reader's notice has
already been drawn to the deep social, economic and political crises
from which Russia continued to suffer in the mid-seventeenth
century. Added to these was now a religious controversy of such
apparent abstruseness but obvious magnitude as to require some
explanation at this point. More was involved in the schism than
questions of purely religious dissent, though this was not necessarily
appreciated by the dissenters at the time. The shambolic state of
public life, instances of malfeasance in high office, widespread corruption and popular tensions were nowhere more acutely felt than
within the Russian Church. During the 1640s a group of civil and

clerical leaders and activists gathered in Moscow to discuss the general need for moral and spiritual reform in the country. These were known as the 'zealots for piety' (*revniteli blagochestiya*), and counted among their number the tsar himself, his personal confessor Stefan Vonifatev (dates unknown), the future patriarch Nikon (1605–81), and a number of provincial clerics, including one Archpriest Avvakum (*c.*1620–82), who was to become the most vociferous, articulate and obstreperous leader of the schismatic movement, and also mediaeval Russia's unchallengeably most brilliant and blistering writer. Among the objects of the brotherhood's attention was the need to eradicate lax habits which had crept into the performance of church services, to extirpate immorality, superstition, witchcraft, pernicious western influences, corruption, alcoholism (never an easy task to eliminate in traditionally unabstemious Russia), and to reintroduce stern moral discipline into public and private life (equally problematic).

It was also felt that the time had come to inaugurate a thorough overhaul of religious practices and liturgical texts into which a number of discrepancies had developed over the centuries, and which placed the Russian Church somewhat apart from the observances of other Orthodox communities. However, a dispute soon arose over which direction the necessary revisions should take, or rather, from which source they should flow. On the one hand were those who believed that the reforms should be modelled on the contemporary practices of the Greek Orthodox Church, whose centre, though now under Muslim rule, was still Constantinople. It was thought by some of the 'Graecisers' that Moscow's claim to be the 'Third Rome' and leader of Orthodox Christendom would be better founded if her practices were more in line with those of her sister churches. Moreover, on a more doctrinal level, it was also argued that the preservation of the idiosyncratic nature of ancient Russian customs, which for historical reasons had developed along a separate path from that of other ministrations, was in some way a betrayal of the œcumenical traditions of original Christianity. The Russian traditionalists, on the other hand, and despite the original provenance of their own faith, nurtured a long suspicion of Byzantium, and believed that, at least from the Council of Florence in 1439, the Greeks had fallen into apostasy, for which God had duly punished them by abandoning them to the infidel Turks in 1453.

Also, since 1589 the Russian Orthodox Church had enjoyed its own autonomous patriarchy. There was thus no justifiable reason – historical, doctrinal or administrative – for Russia to fall in step with the despised Greeks.

The fact that the reforms, when eventually implemented, moved in the direction of the Hellenophils, rather than the Russian traditionalists, was the result not so much of religious as of political considerations, particularly in the realm of foreign policy. The more Moscow could be seen to be at one with other Orthodox churches under Catholic or Muslim political rule in the south, the greater was her claim to the leadership of the entire Orthodox Christian world, in conformity with the doctrine of 'Moscow, the Third Rome'. In terms of *Realpolitik* there were obvious advantages for Moscow along this route. The fact that Tsar Aleksei and the newly appointed patriarch Nikon (from 1652) both favoured the Greek tendency, meant that the 'Old Believers' (*starovery*), or 'Old Ritualists' (*staroobryadtsy*), could do little to resist the combined powers of crown and altar in their introduction and enforcement of the hated reforms. Between 1653 and 1656 Nikon, supported by his secular sovereign, forced through his programme with a ruthless campaign of persecution against the recusants which was of such ferocity as to turn the initially purely religious dissent into a movement of mass opposition to the official church and the autocratic state.

What, though, was involved in the reforms which was to provoke such fanatical resistance on the part of the schismatics (*raskolniki*)? It must be stressed that no changes in the fundamental beliefs or dogmata of the church were involved. The revisions were purely formalistic in character and concerned such *apparent* trivialities as the number of fingers used in making the sign of the cross, whether two – as in the old Russian style – or three, according to then current Greek practice. This was only the most notorious of the alterations, and became a kind of symbol for the whole gamut of reforms. Others were to do with the number and manner of genuflections to be made at a particular moment in the church service; whether the word of glorification, 'alleluia', should be chanted two or three times during the doxology; whether the holy name of Jesus – '*Isus*' or '*Iisus*' – should be spelt with one letter 'I' or two; whether the ceremonial procession of priests should move round the church clockwise, or anti-clockwise; and so on. Over the next century Old Believers were to be slaughtered in their thousands for their refusal to alter the position of their fingers and perform the tridigital cross and all that it represented. But what *did* it represent? Why did it matter if no changes in basic beliefs and theological principle were involved? To understand the answer to this question one must appreciate the central importance of ritual in the life and worship of Orthodox Christianity. The lack of any tradition of scholasticism or exegetic analysis of text in the history of the Russian Church had succeeded in surrounding the outward ceremonial with an aura of sacrosanct, almost magical, mystery. The observance of regular ritual, of rehearsed performance, of traditional totemism and respect for ancestral symbols was a core essential of the true faith. The central issue was not, therefore, what one western commentator ignorantly described as a piece of 'nominalistic nonsense', but the whole heritage of Russian Orthodoxy and, in a sense, the Russian way of life. In a largely illiterate society, ritual *was* doctrine, and to tamper with a single gesture, to move the merest jot or tittle, was for many a diabolical heresy which struck at the heart of their whole religious belief. To compel a seventeenth-century Russian peasant or village priest to cross himself with three fingers rather than two would be like forcing an Irish Jesuit to deny the divinity of Christ or the virginity of His mother. In the long, often brutal history of Christianity, many have been burned on the bonfire for less.

More complex social and national issues, however, have to be taken into consideration in order to understand the true nature and wider implications of the *raskol.* The underlying causes of the deep distemper of Russian society mentioned above were not addressed by any programme of reform, articulated by any political leadership or formulated in any kind of intellectual critique. What the recently enserfed peasantry, the recalcitrant cossaks, the poor parish clergy and the urban lower classes did recognise, however, was the steady concentration of economic power and political privilege in the hands of the secular and ecclesiastical authorities, and their own increasing degradation and exploitation. These hierarchies were now seeking to impose a whole range of religious reforms which the commonality was not intellectually or constitutionally conditioned to absorb. The language of their revolt was therefore naturally the language of their religion, which they *could* understand. In this way, the *raskol* was marked from the beginning by class antagonisms between the lower clergy and their peasant congregations on the one hand, and the powerful and wealthy church aristocracy, backed by the power of the state, on the other. Whether they were conscious of it or not, the revolt of the *raskolniki* in the name of their old faith represented a popular rebellion against the civil and religious establishment of Muscovy. There is, however, no paradox in the phenomenon of mass rebellion against what were apparently the forces of progress and cultural change. While those who defied the tsar and patriarch seemed to be suffering and sacrificing themselves for an essentially obscurantist ideal, in reality the two-fingered cross became a symbol of revolution and a rejection of political authority. In the words of one eminent scholar: 'The heavy artillery of obscurantism and rigid ritualism which the Old Believer directed against the mind concealed a plebeian revolt against a gentry-ridden state, and a state-ridden church.'[17]

Although the leaders and followers of this revolt were anathematised, exiled or executed over the following years, and a Church Council of 1666, attended by the patriarchs of Antioch and Jerusalem, approved the Nikonian reforms, their chief author, Nikon himself, was stripped of his office and banished to a remote monastery. The reason for this was that his overweening political ambition had brought him into open conflict with the tsar and consequent disgrace, once more demonstrating the superiority of the secular over the ecclesiastical authorities. Peter the Great was later to complete the job by abolishing the office of patriarch altogether.

As will be seen, Peter's reign was also the period of the most vicious and unrelenting persecution of the schismatics, many of whom, imbued with an eschatological sense of doom at the approaching end of the world, believed that they were living literally in the age of the Antichrist, of which the Romanov tsars were the corporeal manifestation on earth. Throughout the eighteenth and nineteenth centuries, although they were not subjected to the same degree of torture and persecution as in the early years, the Old Believers continued to be regarded not only as a disturbing manifestation of religious dissent, even heresy, but also as a serious threat to the constituted authority of the secular state, and, as such, remained the object of many forms of legal and fiscal discrimination. In those areas to which they fled in order to escape their persecutors, the *raskolniki* were considered to be a hotbed of opposition to the

Romanov regime. Even in the 1880s, the notoriously reactionary Procurator of the Holy Synod, Konstantin Pobedonostsev (1827–1907), effectively Russia's minister of religion, described the Old Believers as a more dangerous menace to the government than the activists and terrorists of the revolutionary movement. It has also been suggested that as many as one-third of the Christian peasant population of the Russian Empire may have been members of one schismatic sect or another, and it is well known that many wealthy Old Believer merchants and industrialists – most notably the textile manufacturer, Savva Morozov (1862–1905) – contributed thousands of rubles to revolutionary organisations, including the Bolsheviks.

What began, therefore, as the protest of a conservative opposition to a number of ecclesiastical reforms became transmuted into a serious and widespread movement of religiously disguised civil rebellion against the autocratic state. Nowhere is that spirit of rebellion more starkly and vividly exemplified than in the life and works of the turbulent archpriest Avvakum, referred to above. It is impossible to give a satisfactory account of the nature of Avvakum's inimitable contribution to the religious, cultural, social, linguistic and literary history of Russia in the present context. Suffice it to say that through his astonishingly outspoken, courageous and persistent opposition to authority, his terrible personal sufferings and excruciations in tsarist prisons and Siberian exile, Avvakum personified the centuries-long struggle of the Russian people against their oppressors. From his frozen subterranean cell beyond the Arctic Circle, the indomitable rebel priest launched a barrage of sermons, letters and tracts in which he continued to berate and condemn those whom he persisted in regarding as the agents of the devil. He also wrote, in a number of redactions, his own autobiography – *The Life of the Archpriest Avvakum: Written by Himself.* Though little known in the west, it is without rival as the most dynamic, vivid and sinewy piece of Russian prose literature written before the nineteenth century. It is at the same time a historical chronicle, a profession of deep religious faith, a heroic, epic account of the times and places in which the author lived, a stylistic pioneer of the modern realistic novel, a detailed travelogue, diary, testament, tract and a magnum opus of extraordinary literary power, imagination and linguistic force which is impossible to capture in translation. Avvakum's *Life* (*Zhitie*) is not only a literary masterpiece, but also a triumph of the human will to resist, protest and survive.[18]

Sadly, however, Avvakum did not survive to his natural end. Finally driven to exasperation by his unstoppable, cantankerous outpourings, the Muscovite authorities condemned him to death, and on 14 April 1682, Avvakum and three of his fellow prisoners were led from their frozen dungeons to an elaborate pyre of straw and pinewood billets, and there burned alive. According to a not necessarily reliable eye-witness account, as the flames leapt around Avvakum's body, he lifted his right hand in the traditional signing of the cross and, with a last defiant gesture, raised two fingers against his state-appointed executioners.[19] Less than two weeks later, following the death of Tsar Aleksei's successor, Fëdor III, the Muscovite throne passed into the joint hands of the two Romanov half-brothers, Ivan V and Peter I. The chronological coincidence of the execution of Archpriest Avvakum, a fanatical champion of the religious beliefs and social practices of a passing era, and the accession of Pëtr Alekseevich Romanov, the tsar who did more than any other to drag his reluctant realm into the arena of European history, is a poignant symbol of the transition of Russia from belated mediaevalism to limited modernity.

4 The age of Peter the Great, 1682–1725

One of the west's leading experts on eighteenth-century Russia, Paul Dukes, borrowing Thomas Hobbes' famous description of the life of man as 'nasty, brutish and short', classifies Tsar Peter I of Russia as 'nasty, brutish and extremely tall'.[1] The physical dimensions of his lofty stature are not in dispute. According to contemporaneous observations and physiological evidence, Peter stood around 7 feet (2.1 metres) tall. In comparison with his height, he had a small head and tiny feet, the space between being occupied by an elongated torso and lanky legs. Military records of conscript soldiers in Europe at the time indicate that the height of an average adult male was just over 5 feet. Peter, therefore, towered literally head and shoulders above his subjects. While the term 'extremely tall' is therefore not in question, the 'nasty' and 'brutish' nature of his actual methods of implementing policy, when compared to his spectacular achievements in the fields of foreign, domestic and cultural affairs, are still the object of historiographical debate.

Partly as a result of his natural inclinations and temperament, but also as a consequence of his youthful experiences both in the Kremlin and the *nemetskaya sloboda* (see Chapter 3), Peter grew to adulthood with a determination to transform the country over which, from 1696, he held absolute personal sway, from being a semi-mediaeval, demi-Asiatic, economically retarded backwater of seventeenth-century Europe into a modern, westernised, recognisably European state. In order to accomplish this ambition, a whole range of military, institutional, financial, educational and administrative reforms needed to be introduced in order to try to force Russian society into an alien, heretical and unfamiliar mould. If drastic methods of compulsion were required to achieve this aim, then Peter was neither squeamish nor over-fastidious in the means he chose to threaten, flog or otherwise coerce his subjects into conformity with his autocratic will. Both the policies and the punitive methods of implementing them are examined below. However, the circumstances in which Peter came to the throne require some preliminary attention.

Dynastic turmoil, 1682–1696

Tsar Aleksei died in 1676, and was immediately succeeded by his son, Fëdor (r. 1676–82), the offspring of his first marriage to Mariya Miloslavskaya, who bore him 12 other children. Aleksei's frequent absences from Moscow and his preoccupations with affairs of state had obviously not impaired his ability to perform his patrimonial or matrimonial duties. After Mariya's death in 1669, the tsar remarried, this time to Nataliya Naryshkina, daughter of a minor noble family, and destined to be the mother of the boy who became, arguably, Russia's most controversial ruler, Pëtr Alekseevich Romanov, born in 1672. The reign of his older half-brother, Fëdor, was not remarkable for any major feats of foreign policy or domestic reform. Like the members of so many royal families and imperial dynasties, he was not personally endowed with any great intellectual capacities, and he consequently left no noticeable trace on the conduct of government, much of which was dominated by the members of his mother's powerful Miloslavskii clan. Nor, when he died in 1682, did he leave an heir to the throne of the Romanovs. This created a dynastic dilemma, not the first or last in Russia's history, which was solved by the creation of the joint tsardom of Ivan V (r. 1682–96), the son of Aleksei and Mariya Miloslavskaya, and his half-brother (*not* step-brother as is often erroneously stated), Peter I, eldest child of Aleksei's second marriage to Nataliya Naryshkina. Since both of Russia's new co-rulers were in their minority (and one of them, Ivan, blind, lame and mentally incapacitated), a regent was appointed to deal with the everyday business of government. That regent, unprecedentedly in Russian history, was a woman, Ivan's sister and Peter's half-sister, Sofiya Alekseevna (née Miloslavskaya). Neither the accession of Ivan and Peter, nor the inauguration of Sofiya's regency went without the accompaniment of factional and right royal family violence in the Kremlin. The volatile and uncontrollable Muscovite militia of *strel'tsy* largely supported the Miloslavskii faction in this regal tug-of-war, but the rioting which attended the revolts of 1682 spared neither side, and the ten-year-old tsar-designate, Peter, was a terrified witness to the slaughter of his relatives while the Miloslavskii supporters, the Naryshkins and the militia battled for the throne. Eventually, a compromise was agreed which led to the establishment of the dual monarchy, under Sofiya's regency, as described above.

Despite the social and domestic disadvantages of being a female in late seventeenth-century Russia, Sofiya acquitted herself with a measure of competence, intelligence, firmness of purpose and success, which easily matched that of some of her male predecessors.[2] She was responsible for the introduction of a number of enlightened domestic reforms, including the abolition of some of the more barbaric forms of capital punishment and the continuation of a well-intentioned programme of land registration (obviously for reasons of fiscal and financial advantage to the state). In foreign affairs, two significant events should be noted. First was the unrealistically entitled Treaty of Eternal Peace with Poland in 1686. Under its terms, Russia agreed to provide support for Poland's war against the Ottoman Empire, as well as an indemnity payment of 146,000 rubles, in return for Warsaw's recognition of Moscow's possession of Kiev, east-bank Ukraine and Smolensk. Poland's offensive against Turkey, as well as Russian efforts to provide military assistance, came to nothing, and relations among the three powers continued to be fraught over the next century, culminating in the Russo-Turkish wars and the partitions of Poland during the reign of Catherine the Great in the late eighteenth century (see Chapter 6). Second was the signing of the Treaty of Nerchinsk with China in 1689, which facilitated free trade between the two countries and established mutually recognised borders in that remote and practically undefinable far-eastern territory.

As Peter matured into early manhood (a process which included his marriage – at age 16 – to Yevdokiya Polukhina in 1689), and given his co-ruler's incurable infirmities, Peter's own ambitions grew to such an extent that they clearly threatened the position of his half-sister and regent, Sofiya. It should be said, however, as Lindsey Hughes has pointed out, that, despite an abundance of opportunities, Sofiya apparently never did anything to menace the life or the current role of Peter as the legitimately recognised joint tsar. In fact, as Hughes goes on to demonstrate, the boisterous, inquisitive and hyper-active teenaged Peter was spared many of the duties of his regal office, except for the odd ceremonial appearance at court, and spent much of his time at the settlement of Preobrazhenskoe on the outskirts of Moscow, or consorting and cavorting with an assorted company of foreign experts, technicians, military officers, wine merchants and wenches in the Foreign Quarter.[3] Both of these adolescent experiences were to have an important formative influence on his future ambitions, passions, preferences and policies.

In Preobrazhenskoe, Peter was able to develop and put into practice his youthful zeal for military affairs. For instance he recruited, drilled and trained regiments of boy soldiers (*poteshnye*) which formed the nucleus of his later crack imperial guards regiments, the Preobrazhenskii and the Semënovskii. Typical of Peter's preference, most of the hired officers responsible for instructing their young charges were foreigners, and Peter himself was content to play the part of a student soldier in the ranks, rather than taking on a commanding role. The later, complete overhaul of Russia's military machine, leading to her victory over Sweden in the Great Northern War, owed much to Peter's early enthusiasm and expertise acquired during these adolescent manoeuvres. But it was not just the arts of warfare in which the young tsar was interested. In the *nemetskaya sloboda* he immersed himself in the strange and fascinating world of the foreigners in Moscow's service. Their arts, crafts, skills, technological and scientific knowledge, as well as their instruments and artefacts, not to mention their freewheeling, promiscuous social activities – all whetted Peter's appetite to enlighten, educate and Europeanise his domain.

By the summer of 1689, the jealousies, rivalries and personal tensions between Peter and Sofiya had reached crisis point. Ivan, Peter's sickly and afflicted half-brother, was really out of the frame. Although only 17 years of age, Peter held all the important cards. Apart from his own powerful physique and personal charisma (and, it must be said, the advantage of being male), Peter was now married, his wife pregnant and likely to produce a healthy heir. There was thus no longer any need for a regent. Moreover, he had his own loyal troops, well drilled and expertly commanded at their headquarters just north of Moscow, and he had the backing of the patriarch. Sofiya's own standing, in so far as she had enjoyed any, was tarnished by the humiliation of military failures in the anti-Turkish campaigns in the south, which had been led unsuccessfully by her military commander, adviser – and, possibly, lover – Vasilii Golitsyn (1643–1714). Nor could the *strel'tsy* be relied on to back her in any serious confrontation. Indeed, who *would*, given the precariousness of her position? The *strel'tsy* were in any case a notoriously fickle, vacillating and volatile crew, rather than a properly organised, unified military force. In the event, the regent was forced to bow to the inevitable, her supporters faded away, Golitsyn was banished, and Sofiya confined in the *Novodevichii* convent where she finally took the veil, dying there in 1704. Though not able to be declared sole tsar in his own right until the death of Ivan in 1696, Peter was now in effective command.

The 'Great Embassy' and the revolt of the *strel'tsy*

With Sofiya securely locked in her nunnery and Ivan dead and buried, Peter was now able to take things firmly into his own powerful hands without – as he thought – serious challenge to his rule. Uniquely, his first departure as sole tsar was to depart from his tsardom altogether, embarking on his 'Great Embassy' to western Europe in March 1697. Before leaving, however, Peter managed to succeed where Sofiya had failed by capturing the Turkish fortress of Azov on the Sea of Azov in 1696. Though not technically in operational command of the campaign, Peter's single-minded determination to wipe out the humiliation of an earlier, disastrous expedition in 1695 secured the first military victory of his reign, and was also the first demonstration of the importance of using naval power to contribute to that victory. During the winter of 1695 the tsar, whose 'un-Russian' passion for seafaring had already been aroused during visits to the port of Arkhangelsk in 1693 and 1694, ordered the rapid construction of a naval flotilla at Voronezh on the river Don (see Map 1). By ruthless methods of conscription, lavish expenditure, less divided command, and the deployment of the hastily built galley fleet, Peter seized the garrison and gave Russia a southern maritime outlet. However, Turkey's continuing hold on the fortress of Kerch at the eastern tip of the Crimean peninsula still blocked Russian access to the Black Sea, and in any case Russia was forced to abandon Azov to the Turks once more in 1711 (see below).

The ostensible purpose of Peter's Great Embassy of 1697–8 was to secure the cooperation of his fellow monarchs in Europe in an anti-Turkish coalition, in which he was ultimately unsuccessful. However, underlying this diplomatic mission was a more pragmatic and perhaps ambitious objective. Peter's voracious enthusiasm and insatiable curiosity for all things western had been stimulated, as mentioned above, by his youthful escapades and personal experiences in the Foreign Quarter of Moscow. This was, however, only second-hand knowledge. With his military victory at Azov behind him, Peter now felt confident enough to venture abroad – the first Russian ruler to do so since the tenth century – and discover the science, practise the skills and study the technology of western civilisation for himself, though Klyuchevskii considers he was interested more in the technology (*tekhnika*) than the civilisation.[4]

This was typical of Peter's 'hands on' approach to the conduct of whatever enterprise he was engaged in, whether leading his troops in battle, building ships, pulling teeth, cobbling boots or executing opponents. If his immediate object were learning from Europe, then Peter would *go* to Europe and *be* in Europe; and not just in the courts, academies and chanceries, but in the wharves and shipyards, the observatories, the smithies, the Mint, the arsenal and the manufactories. Moreover he would live not just in palaces, but in the houses of ordinary citizens, converse with commoners, get drunk in foreign taverns and fornicate with western women. To facilitate this purpose, Peter entrusted the formal leadership of the Embassy to his three 'Great Ambassadors' (*velikie posoly*), the Swiss adventurer Franz Lefort, the seasoned diplomat Fëdor Golovin, and senior civil servant Prokopii Voznitsyn. Peter himself made a vain attempt to travel incognito, disguised as a common workman under the name of Pëtr Mikhailov. Not surprisingly, this bizarre stratagem was unsuccessful. The tsar's personal feverish involvement in every activity of the expedition, his negotiations with foreign monarchs, his boundless physical energy, and his eccentric personal traits made it impossible to maintain any kind of alias, and in any case, at seven feet tall in his clogs, he could hardly fail to stand out among, and above, his companions.

The Embassy left Moscow in March and travelled to the Dutch Republic by way of Riga – Peter's first view of the Baltic – Mittau,

Königsberg and Berlin, where Lefort signed mutual trade and friendship treaties with Prussia, though these did not have any military implications. Peter stayed for over four months in Holland, where he spent most of his time inspecting and labouring in the shipbuilding yards of Zaandam and Amsterdam, and also observing the workings of other minor, but technically based industries. From Amsterdam, he was invited by King William to visit Britain, where the gangling Muscovite giant and his retinue caused much consternation by the uncouth, raucous and uncivilised nature of their behaviour. Notoriously, they managed to vandalise the town house of the English diarist, John Evelyn, where they were temporarily lodged. Just as notoriously, Evelyn's manservant was to describe their Russian guests as 'right nasty', a comment, no doubt, on both their behaviour and their personal hygiene.[5] Obviously, public etiquette and the genteel manners of polite European society were not among the lessons learned by the crude visitors from Moscow.

Yet, Peter packed an impressive programme of activities into his English visit. He furthered his practical interest in shipbuilding on the wharves at Deptford, attended the Houses of Parliament, visited the Greenwich Observatory, the Royal Arsenal at Woolwich, the Royal Mint, the Tower of London and Lambeth Palace, and travelled to Oxford and to Portsmouth where he watched a mock naval battle in the Solent. He went on tours of factories and workshops, shipyards, and even the theatre, conducting a brief liaison with an English actress named Laetitia Cross.[6]

Restless as ever, Peter quit Britain in May 1698, intending to visit Vienna and Venice. While in Vienna he received news of serious disturbances in Moscow in the shape of yet another uprising of the vexatious *strel'tsy*. He immediately set off for home, but on receiving further intelligence that the insurgency had been suppressed, dawdled for a while at Rawa in Galicia where he found congenial company and established a personal rapport with Augustus, Elector of Saxony (r. 1694–1733) and newly crowned King of Poland (r. 1696–1704 and 1709–33). Discovering a shared interest in wine, women and war, the two monarchs reached an informal agreement that it would be to the advantage of both their countries to turn their attention to Sweden's continuing occupancy of the Baltic territories, though at this stage no formal military alliance was formed. This reciprocal understanding with Augustus was just about the only diplomatic success of the Great Embassy, which was otherwise unproductive in terms of international relations. Most of the other great European powers had their own preoccupations without being over-concerned with the importunities of a country which was still regarded, with some justification, as rather peripheral to their own immediate interests. Besides, Peter's eccentric behaviour and outlandish antics bewildered many of his foreign hosts to such an extent that it may have been difficult to take his proposals seriously. However, his forthcoming military triumphs were soon to alter dramatically those purblind perceptions.

In other respects, however, Peter's mission successfully bore fruit in the acquisition of western expertise and the recruitment into Russian service of scores of foreign specialists, technicians, engineers and craftsmen. He also brought back a rich booty of modern weaponry, scientific instruments and mechanical appliances, as well as chestfuls of other more trivial, though no less intriguing, novel and educative commodities which had more than a curiosity value. Despite Peter's inquisitiveness, he was not interested in exotica simply as exotica, but for their usefulness and potential practical application, though what precise pragmatic purpose he had in mind for a stuffed crocodile must remain a matter of speculation. More seriously, Peter's own personal experiences in Europe, building on his early experiences in Moscow's Foreign Quarter, and reinforced with the knowledge and skills of his western recruits, mercenaries and experts, were to have a powerful effect on his later programme of modernisation.

When he finally arrived back in Moscow in August 1698, Peter immediately set about the deadly process of mopping up the mess left over in the aftermath of the revolt of the *strel'tsy*. Whereas the conduct and the results of the Great Embassy had been symptomatic of the tsar's desire to acquire at least the accoutrements of apparently more progressive cultures, his treatment of the Moscow *strel'tsy* revealed, in awful, bloodcurdling unambiguity, the darker, savage, even sadistic, side of his nature, which his awesome predecessor, Ivan the Terrible, would no doubt have quietly applauded. The reasons for the mutiny were a mixture of grievances over pay arrears, suspicion at increasing foreign influences, offended religious sentiments, residual loyalty to the Miloslavskii, vengeance for the sufferings they had endured during the Azov campaign, and an opportunistic bid to vent their hostility towards the impetuous, unorthodox young tsar during his absence in heathen lands. Although the rebellion was forcefully suppressed by loyal troops under the command of Peter's faithful Scottish officer, General Patrick Gordon (1635–99), and suitable reprisals applied, the tsar was not satisfied with the thoroughness of the original investigation into the causes. He therefore inaugurated a relentless campaign of systematic, mass torture of such unspeakable fiendishness as had rarely been seen even in the most horrific days of the *oprichnina* (see Chapter 2). Hundreds were flogged, roasted and carved into pieces in the public squares of Moscow and Preobrazhenskoe, hundreds more were decapitated, hanged or broken on the wheel, their severed heads impaled on row upon row of wooden stakes. The corpses of the mutilated victims dangled from their gibbets for days and weeks, including those of three ringleaders whose bodies swung outside the window of the ex-regent Sofiya's cell in the *Novodevichii* Convent. According to the diary of Johann Korb, an Austrian envoy who witnessed the butchery, Peter himself personally led in the interrogations and executions, and showed himself to be as proficient at wielding the axe as were his most accomplished headsmen.[7] Reportedly, a little levity was also added to the hideous proceedings by the active participation of the court jester. Following these scenes of unbridled barbarity, Peter next set about enforcing the compulsory cutting and shaving of the beards of his boyars and nobles, a visual sign that his ruling classes were now to take their place alongside their civilised, smooth-chinned European peers. Within a few weeks of his return from his European Embassy in search of western culture, Peter had revealed himself to be barbarian, barber and butcher.

Peter's wars

It has been calculated that of the 25 years from the defeat of Russia at the battle of Narva in 1700 to Peter's death in 1725, for less than 18 months was Russia not at war. In a very real sense, all the rest of Peter's reforming activities – administrative, fiscal, social, educational, cultural, etc. – were predicated on and driven by his military ambitions. While it is not the purpose of this section to give a blow-by-blow account of his battles, campaigns, defeats and triumphs, it is essential to understand the overwhelmingly martial environment and military imperatives which formed the fundamental leitmotif of his entire reign.

Having dealt with the domestic problem of the *strel'tsy* in his inimitable manner, Peter rapidly turned his attention to foreign affairs. Put simply, following the unwritten accord formed between Peter and Augustus II at Rawa, Russia's old adversary, Poland, was for the time being no longer a problem. To the west, Sweden still dominated the Baltic littoral, barring Russia's exit to the sea. In the south, Peter still faced a hostile Turkey and the Crimean Tatar khanate, preventing access to the Black Sea. On the face of it, a successful war with Sweden, under the leadership of its teenage king, Charles XII (r. 1697–1718), seemed to present the easier option and offer the greater immediate rewards. Peter not only wished to establish a maritime outlet for Russian trade with Holland, England, France, Denmark, even Spain, but also sought justification for his ambitions in the desire to reclaim lands around the Finnish Gulf which were historically Russian territory. Logistically, too, war on the Baltic would theoretically be easier to sustain than in the more distant southern borderlands. Russia also had the support of an anti-Swedish coalition consisting of herself, Saxony-Poland and Denmark, each with its own agenda, each with its own axe to grind.

The first confrontation between Russia and Sweden in what came to be called the Great Northern War took place on 20 November 1700 at the Baltic coastal town of Narva, and ended up in a costly and humiliating defeat for Peter's numerically superior forces. (Unaccountably, Peter himself had left his troops on the night before the battle.) Had Charles of Sweden decided to press home his advantage and pursue the retreating Russians into their heartland, even moving on Moscow, it is entirely possible that the whole course of European history might have been very different. However, probably in the belief that his swift and crushing victory at Narva was enough to settle Peter's hash, and sensibly wishing to avoid a long winter campaign in Russia's vast hinterland, Charles chose to turn south and carry the war to Augustus of Saxony-Poland. The decision ultimately cost the Swedish king dear. He had not calculated on the determination, ambition, resilience and ruthlessness of Peter in using the post-Narva breathing space to recuperate, reorganise, recruit and re-equip his forces with a wide-ranging programme of military reforms, intensive conscription methods, new systems of command, communication and control. These military measures, fuelled by massive new revenue-raising devices, both of which will be examined in more detail below, totally transformed his fighting forces into the triumphant engine of war which was to turn the tables on Sweden at the battle of Poltava in 1709.

The astonishingly rapid recovery after the near-annihilation of Narva, as well as Sweden's failure to secure a decisive victory against Saxony-Poland, allowed Peter – with Charles bogged down further south – to make a small but very significant number of gains around the mouth of the river Neva and further down the Baltic coast. Most significant of all was the capture of the Swedish fortress of Nöteborg (1702), giving access to the lower reaches of the Neva where Peter established a fortified bastion on an island close to the exit to the Finnish Gulf. This was to be named the Fortress of SS Peter and Paul, which represented the first stage of Peter's foundation of his future new capital city, St Petersburg (*Sankt Peterburg* – see below). Meanwhile, other Swedish strongholds on the Baltic – now not so strong, and weakly held by insufficient forces – fell to Russia's remodelled army (see below).

Charles was able to do little about this process as Russia became increasingly entrenched along a line stretching from Livonia in the south to Karelia in the north. Peter also began to lay the keels of Russia's future Baltic fleet. However, in 1706, having signed the Treaty of Altranstadt with Saxony, under the terms of which Augustus relinquished the Polish throne, Charles decided the time had come to deal with Peter, and turned east to invade Russian territory. Despite his reputation as a brilliant strategist, Charles faced a number of setbacks on the campaign, which ultimately proved fatal. Swedish support forces on their way from Riga to join up with Charles were thrashed by Russian battalions at the village of Lesnaya in September 1708, thereby depriving him of expected reinforcements. Another blow was the failure of the cossak *hetman* (chieftan, cf. *ataman*), Ivan Mazepa (1644–1709), to live up to Charles' expectations of his support. Mazepa, acting in what he thought to be the interests of Ukrainian independence, betrayed his earlier uneasy allegiance to the tsar and threw in his lot with the Swedish king. He was, however, poorly supported by his own cossaks and soundly defeated by Peter's favourite, Aleksandr Menshikov (1673–1729), and his headquarters razed to the ground. Peter's scorched-earth policies also deprived Charles of much needed supplies for his exhausted troops. In the event, Charles misguidedly ordered the investment of the fortress town of Poltava in Ukraine, where vastly superior Russian forces counter-attacked and decimated the Swedish army. Narva had been avenged, Charles fled to Turkey, where he remained until 1714, and the military power of Sweden was finally broken.

Further south, Peter was less successful in confronting the Ottoman Turks. The Sublime Porte viewed with alarm Russia's growing strength after Poltava, and declared war in November 1710. At this point, Peter, no doubt flushed with his recent victory over the Swedes, invaded Turkish territory, but, rather like Charles before him, bereft of promised military support and suffering from over-stretched lines of communication, was hammered by the Turks at the battle on the river Pruth in July 1711. In a sense, Peter was totally at the sultan's mercy with nowhere to run. However, he came out of the crisis surprisingly unscathed. He was allowed to withdraw, and merely forced to abandon both the fortress and the fleet at Azov and a number of frontier posts on the lower river Dnestr. He was, astonishingly, free to return home and continue the ongoing war with Sweden.

Although the battle of Poltava had been won, Russia's Great Northern War dragged on for more than another decade, but was eventually brought to an end with the signing of the treaty of Nystadt in 1721. Poltava was, however, the turning point, as Stalingrad was to be the turning point in the Great Patriotic War in 1943. Its significance is hard to exaggerate. It is possible to study the history of Europe before 1709 with only passing reference to events in far off Muscovy. The history of the eastern Slavs during the Kievan, Mongol and Muscovite periods impinged only peripherally on the affairs of the major European powers. Similarly, although passing reference has been made to occasional links between Russia and Europe during the same centuries, it is possible to study the history of pre-Petrine Russia without taking too much cognisance of major developments in the west. After Poltava, that is an impossibility. From that time on Russia has been inextricably involved in the political, economic, diplomatic, military and cultural development of Europe as a whole. From Poltava to Potsdam, the boundaries of European states have been defined and redefined only with the direct or indirect involvement of or interaction with Russian interests. No major war has been fought in Europe in which Russia's national affairs have not been a part. And in the field of the arts and sciences, Russia's apprenticeship to the west, beginning in Peter's reign, laid the foundations for the tremendous contribution made by her literary, musical, artistic and scientific geniuses to the later development of pan-European culture. This in itself may be regarded as an astonishing achievement, given Peter's own personally unsophisticated, vulgar and even barbaric nature. Whatever view one might take about the virtues of military conquest as a mark of 'greatness', it is difficult to deny that it was by dint of his victory over Sweden that Peter once and for all placed his country fairly and squarely on the map of Europe, and made it an inextricable factor in the history of modern European civilisation.

A final foray in the south, this time directed against Persia, whose weakening grip on the trans-Caucasian kingdoms of Georgia and Armenia presented an attractive opportunity for further Russian acquisitions, was frustrated by the intervention of the Turks during the costly campaigns of 1722–3. The region was finally partitioned, with Russia gaining only a narrow strip of the western Caspian strand, which in any case was abandoned in 1732. Meanwhile, negotiations with China to enlarge on the trading agreements in the Far East under the terms of the Treaty of Nerchinsk met with little success, though Peter's continuing interest in his Asiatic possessions was clearly signalled by his authorisation shortly before his death of the 'Great Northern Expedition' to explore Siberia (see below), and his annexation of the Kamchatka peninsula and Kurile Islands. Given the relative failures or inconclusive results of his southern and eastern military and diplomatic démarches, Peter's claim to greatness in the arena of foreign policy must ultimately rest solely on his triumph over Sweden in the Great Northern War.

Peter's reforms

Military

It is generally accepted that all of Peter's other reforms were in one way or another based on or rendered necessary by his transformation of his military machine. In Lindsey Hughes's words, 'in Peter's case, the links between war, domestic policy and the man himself were quite explicit'.[8] Despite the traditional image of Russia's seventeenth-century soldiery as a rather ramshackle body or an 'uncouth rabble',[9] the forces of the sixteenth- and seventeenth-century Muscovite tsars were not without some form of rudimentary organisation and military success. Ivan the Terrible's conquest of Kazan, Minin and Pozharskii's campaign against the Poles, Tsar Aleksei's recapture of east-bank Ukraine, and Peter's taking of Azov in 1695 are cases in point. However, it is nevertheless true that, compared with European armies of the period, Russia's military resources were relatively unsophisticated and inexperienced in the techniques of modern warfare. Peter therefore embarked with a zeal unprecedented among his predecessors on the task of radically rebuilding his armies into a formidable, battle-worthy and ultimately victorious instrument of war.

After the shock of Narva, complex, though comprehensive and comparatively efficient, new conscription methods were introduced, fresh regiments were raised, experienced foreign generals and senior officers were recruited, 'state-of-the-art' weaponry was acquired or manufactured, and fearsome forms of discipline applied to punish or deter evasion, cowardice and desertion. Among other simple innovations, the introduction of the fixed-ring bayonet made it possible to set aside the traditional division of the troops into pikemen and musket bearers, thereby doubling the combat power of the infantry at a stroke. A new central arsenal and the establishment of metallurgical industries produced the heavy cannon and other ordnance which greatly enhanced the effectiveness of the Russian artillery. Some indication of the scale of Peter's military expansion and recruitment programme is provided by the calculations of the German Resident of Brunswick (Braunschweig) in St Petersburg, Friedrich Weber. He reckoned that, on average, Peter recruited around 20,000 fresh troops every year, and that towards the end of his reign, the full complement of the regular army, both infantry and cavalry, stood at nearly 200,000 men, in addition to irregulars, cossaks and naval personnel. Massive annual levies were necessary not only to replace troops fallen in battle, but to make up for the even greater numbers who had been lost through hunger and hypothermia, disease and desertion.[10]

The organisation, command structure, discipline and general routine of the armed services were spelled out in detail in Peter's

'Military Regulation' (*Voinskii ustav*), based on an amalgam of European military manuals and promulgated in 1716. Matters such as general expectations of obedience, of pay, supply of uniforms, duties, relations between officers and men, religious observance, grounds for leave of absence, mutiny, espionage and guidance on maintaining physical fitness were all addressed in detail, as were the prescribed punishments for such offences as buggery, rape and bestiality. As in all matters, though not always successfully, Peter was concerned to regulate all his military enterprises and initiatives with a properly and unambiguously formulated code of practice, with appropriate penalties in case of default.

As has already been mentioned, Peter always evinced an especial fascination with things nautical, and his foundation of the Russian navy is one of his most spectacular and lasting achievements. Beginning with the creation of his modest flotilla on the river Don in 1695, which played such a decisive role in the siege and capture of Azov, Peter was to leave at his death a military and commercial fleet on the Baltic which established Russia as a naval power to be seriously reckoned with in northern Europe. Starting from absolute zero, but building on his first-hand experience in the shipyards of Holland and England, and assisted by foreign naval architects, Peter was to create a sizeable armada which by the end of the Great Northern War numbered over 50 warships, 70 in-shore oar-propelled galleys and almost 300 other vessels. A number of naval manuals, of even greater complexity and detail than the 'Military Regulation', were published, foreign skippers and other senior officers were hired, young Russian nobles were sent unwillingly abroad for naval training, and a flood of nautical neologisms and foreign borrowings entered the Russian language in order to identify the myriad items and contrivances in the unfamiliar naval technology. Although the Russian people did not display a great affinity with the sea, and although the Baltic fleet fell into disrepair after Peter's death, nevertheless his pioneering work laid the foundations for the development of Russia as a formidable naval power, though never really achieving the same international maritime status as, say, Britain, Holland or Spain. If the pun may be forgiven, command of the high seas was never Russia's main forte.

Central and local government

In the previous chapter mention has been made of the burgeoning bureaucracy and proliferation of *prikazy* during the seventeenth century. By the time of Peter's accession, the whole system of central government administration had become unwieldy, cumbersome and chaotic. Therefore, in the same spirit in which the military machine was modernised, Peter attempted to streamline the civilian organs of government in order to make them more efficient and workable.

Because of the tsar's frequent and protracted absences on his various military campaigns, and undoubted reluctance to appoint a powerful single viceroy to act for him, in 1711 Peter established what was to survive – with some vicissitudes – as the principal political and legal governmental body in the empire until 1917. This was the Ruling Senate (*Upravitel'nyi senat*), composed of nine of Peter's advisers, with two secretaries, which was charged with a number of fairly comprehensive legislative, revenue-raising, administrative and commercial duties. Peter's, and, vicariously, the Senate's, financial and military priorities were made quite explicit in Article 3 of the decree establishing the new body, which ordered succinctly and unambiguously: 'Collect as much money as possible, because money is the artery of war.'[11] Orders and *ukazy* of the Senate were to be obeyed in the same way as those of the tsar, on pain of death. However, in actual practice Peter had abrogated none of his absolute powers, and the distinguished senators were not only prone to internal bickering and corrupt practices, but also subject to covert surveillance by a body of regulators, called 'fiscals' (*fiskaly*), whose job it was to spy on, investigate and report instances of embezzlement, illegal activities and malfeasance in office. When in St Petersburg, Peter also frequently attended, intervened and interfered in the business of the Senate, impatiently chiding and reprimanding its members for inefficiency and time-wasting. On one occasion he even had two of the senators flogged and their tongues branded. Finally disillusioned by the incompetence of his designated legislators, Peter appointed – in addition to the *fiskaly* – a high official, the Procurator General, to keep a close watch on the deliberations and activities of the Ruling Senate. Not for nothing was the Procurator known as the 'tsar's eye' (*nashe oko* – literally, 'Our eye'). Like so much of Peter's legislation and new institutions, the well-meaning intentions did not necessarily square up with the actual results. However, despite the rather mediocre nature of the original Senate's performance, it did remain as one of the most senior institutions of Russian government until the revolutions of 1917.

While the Senate was theoretically responsible for initiating and implementing policy, the actual administration of the various affairs of state was removed from the hands of the multifarious *prikazy*, some of which were simply abolished, and placed under the jurisdiction of a small number of what were in effect ministries, called 'colleges' (sing. *kollegiya*, pl. *kollegii*). Not all of the *prikazy* disappeared, and indeed several continued to function in one capacity or another throughout Peter's reign. Their authority was, however, overshadowed by the new collegiate bodies, nine of which were created in 1719. Not surprisingly, the structure of the *kollegii* was based on foreign models, most closely on the Swedish system of collegiate administration, investigated on Peter's behalf by Heinrich Fik (von Füch), a civil servant from Holstein in Russia's employ.[12] Nine colleges in all were initially established. It will come as no surprise that seven of them were concerned with financial and military affairs. They were: Foreign Affairs (*Kollegiya chuzhestrannykh del*); State Revenue (*Kamor* or *Kammer kollegiya*); Justice (*Yustits-kollegiya*); Financial Control (*Revizion*); Army (*Voinskaya*, dealing with land forces); Admiralty (naval affairs – *Admiralteiskaya*); Commerce (*Kommerts-kollegiya*); Mines and Manufactories (*Berg i manufaktor kollegiya*); and State Expenditure (*Shtats-kontor*). (Notice the overwhelmingly non-Slavonic, western nomenclature.) Each college was assigned its own staff of clerks, notaries, scribes, book-keepers and sundry other officials, and orders issued for the proper recording of agenda, protocols and minutes of meetings, which were to be held on a regular basis. The personnel of the colleges comprised 11 members, including the chairman and two foreign officials, and, in contradistinction to the *prikazy*, their remit covered the entire country, rather than being limited to specific territorial-administrative regions. On the face of it, this was a genuine attempt to introduce a measure of simplification and rationalisation to the governance of the country. Again, however, as with the Senate, the power of the autocrat, and the delegation of individual missions and items of state business to his closest cronies often overrode, ignored or obstructed the formal proceedings and responsibilities of the new government institutions. In any case, very few Russians were able to understand how these new-fangled institutions were intended to operate.

Another complication was in the overlapping functions of central and provincial government agencies. In the seventeenth century the collection of taxes, recruitment of soldiers and dispensation of justice at local level were in the hands of regional military commanders, or *voevody*. These appointments, as under the old *kormlenie* system mentioned in Chapter 2, were tantamount to an official licence to batten on the local population, and to indulge in all kinds of extortion, malpractice and self-enrichment. In an attempt to bring some kind of well-regulated management to the regions and some devolution of central power, in 1708 Peter divided his realm into eight, later 12, 'governorships' (sing. *guberniya*, pl. *guberbnii*), each headed by a *gubernator* (governor) with near plenipotentiary powers in his own region, but still directly responsible to the tsar. The day-to-day running of these often vast territories (Siberia, for example) was an impossible task for one official, who in any case often had other important responsibilities, and in 1719 the *gubernii* were further subdivided into 50 'provinces' (*provintsii*), whose leaders theoretically had more direct local control over their smaller geographical units. In practice, 'local control' by the heads of provinces meant a return to, or continuation of, the old system of regional *voevody* which it was meant to replace. Lack of funding, inadequacy of personnel, continuing corruption, absence of policing and the fact that, like the central government reforms, the local changes were based on foreign models which had developed naturally over a long period of time and were the result of traditional, indigenous practices, all resulted in confusion, misunderstanding and general disorder. These problems were compounded by the introduction of 'military districts' whose officers were responsible for recruitment and collection of the poll tax (see below), but whose territorial jurisdiction overlapped with that of the local civilian governors and provincial officials.

In Russia's few urban centres, municipal government was in the hands of local 'magistrates', under the general supervision of the

'Chief Magistracy' (*Glavnyi magistrat*) in St Petersburg. On paper, their official duties comprised a wide range of activities including collection of tolls, promotion of trade and small-scale manufacturing, gathering of statistics, fire-fighting and prevention, road and bridge maintenance, 'social cleansing' – that is, controlling the activities of tramps, beggars, drunkards and whores, and promoting public health and hygiene. Accounts from the time suggest, however, that the conditions of life among the urban lower classes remained perilous, insalubrious and overwhelmingly grim.

It is indisputable that Peter did make a genuine effort to modernise and make more efficient the governmental and administrative apparatus of his empire. At the end of his reign at least the outline of a more up-to-date (that is, in comparison with European systems) machinery of policy making and policy implementation was in place, elements of which were, with suitable adaptations, to survive for many decades. However, it is equally indisputable that the mentality and the practices of mediaeval Muscovy, the crudeness of the methods employed to effectuate the new, alien institutions – which were often incompatible with traditional custom and usage, more often than not simply relying on physical coercion – led to a situation in which the relationship between the intention and the operation, the outward shape and the inner substance was frequently blurred.

Fiscal policies and public finance

Keeping the blood circulating through the 'artery of war' was, for Peter, an obsession. Throughout his reign he and his inland revenue officials devised and introduced an assortment of new, sometimes bizarre, methods of levying exponentially increasing amounts of taxes from an already overburdened population in order to finance his various grandiose projects, both military and civilian. Apart from direct taxes raised from each peasant household (*dvor*), Peter's newly established corps of revenue raisers or 'profit makers' (*pribyl'shchiki*), established in 1699, dreamt up a whole gamut of items, commodities and practices on which duty was payable. Extensive, if not exactly interminable, the list included at various times, and in alphabetical order, barrels, bathhouses, beards, bee-hives, cabbages, coffins, cucumbers, fisheries, horse-trading, legal fees, liquor, note-paper, playing cards, salt and tobacco (English and Russian; Turkish was exempt). Hardly surprisingly, this curious inventory of taxable goods or appurtenances scarcely scratched the problem of Peter's need for more cash receipts. Nor did the imposition of state monopolies on trade in such commodities as potash, tar and Siberian furs, which of course greatly riled the merchant class, and were soon abolished.

Eventually, the introduction of the most hated and iniquitous of Peter's taxes succeeded in multiplying state revenue three-, four- and in some years even five-fold. This was the notorious so-called 'soul tax' – *podushnaya podat'* – usually translated into English as the poll tax, first implemented in the year 1719. The mathematics of the new tax were simple. In 1718 a Senate decree ordered a census of the entire male peasant population. The resulting total was then divided into the estimated military expenditure for the coming year, and the sum arrived at became the tax liability for each male peasant 'soul', regardless of age, and regardless of ability to pay. Moreover, the revenue thus raised was earmarked, or 'ring-fenced', specifically to defray the costs of the military budget. What appeared to be an egalitarian fiscal measure was in fact totally inequitable and placed yet a further financial burden on the servile population. However, from the state's point of view the new levy was entirely successful and resulted in a more than doubling of government revenue from 1.8 million rubles in 1701 to 4.6 million in 1724.[13] Taxation is never a popular item of public policy, but the poll tax was regarded with particular loathing by the Russian people, not only because of its onerous nature in financial terms but because of its blatantly discriminatory quality. It was not abolished until 1887, exactly 101 years before a similarly divisive poll tax – the speciously named 'Community Charge' – was introduced by the Conservative Government in Britain.

Other areas of economic policy, equally geared to the country's war needs, were the encouragement of industrial development, particularly the mining and metallurgical industries, and, influenced by contemporaneous western theory (and practice), the promotion of mercantilism. Of all the classes of Russian society it was the merchantry which, even in comparison with the nobility, probably enjoyed the greatest privileges under Peter's administration, though the extent of free economic enterprise was always limited and controlled by the state. This has given rise to a good deal of historical controversy as to whether Peter's economic policies helped or hindered the emergence of a truly mercantile, proto-capitalist, entrepreneurial free-market economy. Certainly, with access to the Baltic ports secured, commerce with the major European powers increased in significant proportions, boosting both the export and the import trade, though a number of protectionist measures were introduced to limit the import of certain commodities, thereby safeguarding the interests of indigenous producers and suppliers. Most Russian exports were in the shape of raw materials – including flax, hemp, tallow, leather, grain, timber and furs, and such imports as there were consisted of various metals and luxury items, including French wines and English beer.

In the final analysis, controversies over the precise nature of the Petrine economy – whether it was 'merchant capitalist' – as early Soviet Marxist economic historians such as M. N. Pokrovskii (1868–1932) maintained – proto-capitalist, state controlled or simply still feudal – are at best inconclusive, and at worst ultimately sterile. It therefore seems sensible to conclude that no single all-embracing formula is satisfactory, and that economic formations during this period represented a complex amalgam of different stages of development, but all of which were harnessed to the overriding interests of the state. What *is* incontrovertible is that at the heart of the Russian socio-economic order lay the relationship between the service nobility and the peasant serfs.

Nobles and serfs

It will be remembered (see Chapters 1 and 2) that the origins of the *dvoryanstvo* lay in the late fifteenth and early sixteenth centuries as a result of the Moscow Grand Princes' practice of bestowing parcels of land (*pomest'e*) on those who performed military service in support of the rising power of the Muscovite autocracy. For reasons explained above, the expectation, if not the habit, of continuous state service had somewhat atrophied during the seventeenth century as the nobility's control over the serfs on their estates was gradually increased, and as the distinction between the lands held in service tenure, and the traditionally heritable estates (*votchina*) became blurred. In his furious drive to create a fully mobilised society, Peter introduced a number of measures designed to reinstitute the practice of compulsory, life-long service to the state in either a military or civilian capacity in order to achieve noble status.

Among these measures were the compulsory registration of all noble youths between the ages of 10 and 15 years, and their assignment to an institute of secular education. On satisfactory completion of their courses, mainly in the mathematical sciences (hence 'cipher schools', *tsyfirnye shkoly*), the reluctant young graduates were further assigned to one or another branch of government service. Service was for life, and all forms of evasion, malingering, and shirking of duties and responsibilities were severely punished. The penalty for failure to complete one's education successfully was to be banned from marrying, and in extreme cases evasion of government service could lead to 'public disgrace' (*shelmovanie*), which meant that the unfortunate lead-swinger was placed beyond the protection of the law, thereby becoming literally an 'outlaw' who could be robbed, attacked or even murdered without retribution. In order further to encourage enrolment in state service, in 1714 Peter introduced the Entail Law (*Ukaz o edinonasledii*), under which, on a landowner's death, the estate must be inherited *in its entirety*, and not divided up between the various offspring or relatives of the deceased. The heir need not necessarily be the eldest child. It was not therefore, as it is often mistakenly described, a law on primogeniture, but designed (a) to maintain the integrity of large, more productive estates *in toto*, and thereby prevent the impoverishment of the land, and (b) to force those not eligible to inherit to seek a livelihood in government service. The law was very much resented, often flouted, and in any case repealed soon after Peter's death.

The final buckle and strap in the *dvoryanstvo*'s harness to the state was provided by the introduction, in January 1722, of the so-called Table of Ranks (*Tabel' o rangakh*). This was a scale of ranks in the military service and civil bureaucracy up which everyone must clamber who aspired to the status of hereditary noble (*dvoryanin*). Each would-be nobleman was expected to commence his perpetual service on the lowest rung, thereafter being promoted according to ability and merit to a higher rank, with appropriately corresponding honorific forms of address. There were 14 grades, the highest being number one, and attainment of eighth grade and above entitled one to the status of hereditary noble. The equivalent miltary and civilian ranks are shown in Table 4.1.

Table 4.1   Table of ranks, 24 January 1722

Grade	Military	Civilian
I	Field Marshal	Chancellor
II	General	Active Privy Counsellor
III	Lieutenant General	Privy Counsellor
IV	Major General	Active State Counsellor
V	Brigadier	State Counsellor
VI	Colonel	Collegial Counsellor
VII	Lieutenant Colonel	Court Counsellor
VIII	Major	Collegial Assessor
IX	Captain	Titular Counsellor
X	Staff Captain	College Secretary
XI	————————	Senate Secretary
XII	Lieutenant	*Guberniya* Secretary
XIII	Sub-lieutenant	Provincial Secretary
XIV	Ensign	Assistant Assessor/College Registrar

There were also equivalent, corresponding ranks in the navy and in the Guards regiments.

The fact that entry to, and progress through, the Table of Ranks was open to all classes, including commoners and foreigners, regardless of lineage, was very much resented by the 'traditional' nobility, but this new device, together with the abolition of the ancient system of appointment according to hereditary precedent (*mestnichestvo*), meant that ennoblement by birth and ancestry was now replaced by ennoblement through state service and merit. Wealth, powerful patronage, 'crony-ism', backstairs influence (a practice known in Russian as *blat*), could of course smooth the way for more rapid promotion, or the blocking of a rival upstart. But the principle, if not of total meritocracy then of something approaching it, was now established. The chivalric concept of *noblesse oblige* was now strictly applied to a Russian nobility which was literally obliged to serve. For the next half-century after Peter's death it was the ambition to disentangle itself from these compulsory service obligations that was the main driving force behind the nobility's corporate relationship with the Russian state (see Chapter 5). But it is to its relationship with the Russian peasantry that we must now turn.

Put very simply, Peter's reforming activities in effect created two societies, or at least one that was deeply divided. Not only in Russia, but also in Europe and elsewhere, the glaring differences between high society and the 'common herd', the contrasts between the *haut monde* and hoi polloi were a stark fact of life. In Russia, however, as a direct result of Peter's innovations, an extra dimension was created by the simultaneous existence of two very different worlds and distinct ways of life. These were almost hermetically sealed off from each other in terms of habitat, lifestyle, mentality and even language. The only common denominators between them were subjection to an absolutist state, and a shared faith in the Russian Orthodox Church. (Even in the latter case, large swathes of the Russian peasantry remained in opposition to the official Church as a result of their adherence to the 'Old Belief', or their membership of one schismatic sect or another.) On the one hand was the semi-westernised, rudimentarily educated, European-oriented privileged nobility, compelled to perform state service, it is true, but nevertheless, provided they fulfilled their duties and broke no laws, enjoying all the legal, cultural and personal advantages of superior social status, and the financial security of serf ownership. In their sartorial appearance, in the foreign tongues with which many now became familiar, in their slowly developing more cosmopolitan view of the world, in their literacy, their secularism, social habits and albeit shallow sophistication, the Russian nobility was, figuratively and hyperbolically speaking, living on a different planet from the world of the Russian *narod.*

The peasant *soslovie* included privately owned serfs (i.e. those belonging to an individual landlord or *pomeshchik*), state peasants, crown peasants, ecclesiastical or monastic serfs, and serfs who were ascribed (*pripisannye*) to work in industrial enterprises such as mines and factories. Together they accounted for around 90 per cent of the population. Whatever their technical or legal status, the circumstances of their life and work, their physical environment, their collective liability to swingeing forms of taxation – most infamously the poll tax – and to military conscription were shared in common by all Russian peasant communities. Their mutual responsibilities and feudal obligations, their religious beliefs and practices, their subjection to personal indignities, lack of individual freedom, and vulnerability to a savage system of physical punishments, were also similar, and set them entirely apart from their lords and masters. They were parochial in their horizons, almost universally illiterate, super-stitious, and subject to diseases of epidemic proportions and to periodic famine. Their wretched position has often been likened, with some justification, to that of slaves. Russian serfs, like slaves, could be bought and sold, auctioned off, given as gifts and gambled away, in the same way as goods, chattels and livestock. But their situation was also in a sense like that of colonial natives, aboriginal 'savages', exploited for their labour and resources by some alien imperial power: except in this case, the imperialists, the colonialists and the exploiters were not foreign *conquistadores*, settlers and planters, but were themselves native Russians, their own countrymen and fellow-Christians. It is therefore hardly surprising that the enserfed peasantry should have protested against their miserable lot by peri-odic, spontaneous, violent rebellions, or else by flight to the relative freedom of the Russian borderlands. The various other forms of oppo-sition to Peter's oppressive impositions will be discussed below.

Ecclesiastical, educational and cultural change

Unlike mediaeval Europe, Russia had no history of serious caesaro-papist confrontation. That is to say, there were no gravely damaging major conflicts of interest or power struggles between the secular and the ecclesiastical authorities. The collision between Tsar Aleksei and Patriarch Nikon in the middle of the seventeenth century (see Chapter 3) had resulted in the disgrace of the latter and the firm sub-ordination of the interests of the Church to those of the state. Peter, as one might expect, went one step further. In order to ensure that the Church – still a powerful, rich and influential organisation – would never again be in a position to challenge or rival the ultimate power of the tsar, Peter abolished the office of patriarch altogether, and, after the death of the last patriarch, Adrian, in 1700, placed the management of the Russian Orthodox Church in the hands of, first, the 'Monasteries Office' (*Monastirskii prikaz*) and finally those of a new institution named the 'Most Holy Governing Synod' (*Svyateishii Pravitel'stvuyushchii Sinod*), created in 1721. As in the case of the military and various navy regulations, the Church now, too, had its own set code of rules and procedures, spelled out in the 'Spiritual Regulation' (*Dukhovnyi Reglament*), published in January 1721. The inclusion of the adjective 'governing' in the title of the new body implied that it had a similar status to the 'Ruling Senate', though both in composition and jurisdiction it was much more akin to the secular *kollegii*. Throughout its existence, the membership of the Synod was almost invariably made up of an equal number of lay and clerical officials, though the chairman – the 'Over-Procurator' (*Ober-prokuror*) was always a layman. The Spiritual Regulation set out a comprehensive code of rules for the internal governance of the Church, its recruitment policies, educational, financial, tenurial and devotional responsibilities in such a way as to ensure that its activities and its ministrations always served the interests of the state. Limitations were set on the number of entrants into the monastic calling (Peter always regarded the monasteries as at best a respectable avenue of escape from 'real' state service and, at worst, dens of idleness and moral incontinence). Church bells were sequestered for their metal; taxes on church property were increased; priests were required to report potentially seditious comments heard during confessions; monasteries were required to provide humanitarian assistance to the needy at their own expense; and Peter personally intervened in the appointment of bishops and other senior prelates. Henceforth, the Church was in effect reduced to the position of a rather elaborate and ostentatiously embellished organ of the secular government. Moreover, one of Peter's most influential and highly educated spiritual mentors, and author of the Spiritual Regulation, Feofan Prokopovich (1681–1736), provided an eloquent quasi-theological justification for the exercise of Peter's absolute monarchical power in what Florinsky has described as the 'dogma of the divinely guided police state'.[14]

A less authoritarian, though altogether more grotesque, manifestation of Peter's involvement with meta-religious matters was the institution of the 'Most-crazy, All-joking, All-drunken Assembly' (*sumasbrodneishii, vseshuteishii, vsep'yaneishii sobor*). This was a gluttonous, ribald, shameless charade of religious rituals in which jesters, dwarves, naked mock-bishops, Peter's comrades, court officials and fellow revellers, lewd impersonators of civil and clerical dignitaries, some bearing nicknames with none-too-subtle priapic connotations, accompanied by dogs, pigs and goats, cavorted and caroused together in regular, sacrilegious public saturnalia. What the exact purpose of these impiously obscene pantomimes was is still a matter of speculation, although similar types of irreligious horseplay, with a mixture of pagan rites, satirical send-ups of officialdom, cross-dressing and social role-swapping have a long pedigree not only in Russian but also in other folk customs and traditions. At all events, such displays were a not uncommon feature of Peter's leisuretime activities, and another indication of the deliberately shocking, iconoclastic nature of his character.

What primitive sources of literacy and rudimentary institutions of education there were in mediaeval Russia were almost exclusively the preserve of the Church. However, Peter's growing demand for technical and mathematical skills, familiarity with foreign languages, and more than basic standards of literacy and numeracy among his ruling elite led to the obvious necessity of providing the pedagogical infrastructure and educational opportunities for the process of enlightenment and instruction to take place. As in so many other areas of reform and development, the westernising tsar was dependent on the expertise of foreign scholars, scientists and professional practitioners to provide the tuition and staff for his embryonic academies. Consequently, a system of secular schools was introduced, the so-called 'cipher schools', where the basic principles of arithmetic, geometry, astronomy and navigational techniques were instilled in their pupils. Shortage of trained teaching staff, insufficient funding, lack of basic equipment, as well as a general unwillingness to learn and fear of a possible naval career among the student body, meant that the enterprise was rather limited in its success. However, one must allow for small beginnings, and there is no doubt that Peter's innovations in this area, as in so many others, laid the proper foundations for the future development of Russia's educational system, albeit one that was long limited to the upper classes of Russian society. In addition to the provision of tuition at home institutions, both secular and ecclesiastical, many noble youths were sent abroad for technical training, though by some accounts their colourful experience of foreign parts was not always particularly edifying, and amounted to little more than a series of harum-scarum escapades. Lindsey Hughes cites the reminiscences of one Ivan Neplyuev, sent to study abroad in 1717–18, among whose Russian companions 'one ran off to Mount Athos to became a monk, another was stabbed in a brawl in a tavern, and another went mad in Spain'.[15]

In addition to the cipher schools, Peter also set up naval, artillery, engineering and medical academies, and, although he never founded a university, the establishment of the Academy of Sciences, opened shortly after his death by his illiterate widow, Empress Catherine I (r. 1725–7), provided the foundation stone for the edifice of what is still Russia's most prestigious and world-famous institution of scientific research. Shortly before he died, Peter also commissioned an ambitious scientific and naval expedition, under the command of the Danish seafarer, Vitus Bering, to explore the northern ocean around Kamchatka, and establish whether a landbridge existed between north-east Siberia and the American continent. The so-called First Kamchatka Expedition, which lasted from 1725 to 1730, set the pattern for further great journeys of exploration through Siberia later in the eighteenth century.

By no stretch of the imagination could one argue that Peter's educational reforms transformed his country into an enlightened, sophisticated centre of cultural, artistic and scientific excellence. Most of the population, including a fair proportion of the nobility, was still illiterate. There was no university. Merchant families unaccountably eschewed schools which taught their children how to count. Knowledge of geography and the outside world was minuscule. Compasses, quadrants and even crayons were in short supply. Russia's first 'scientific' museum, the *Kuntskamera*, consisted largely of an eclectic assortment of pickled monsters, teratological freaks and polycephalous abortions preserved in bottles (visitors were helpfully plied with free vodka). *Belles-lettres* were almost non-existent. And literally hundreds of foreign lexical borrowings, clumsy transliterations of European terms, calques and neologisms suffused the Russian language with outlandish words which to most people were utterly incomprehensible. The situation must have been similar to the non-intelligibility of present-day 'cyberspeak' to twenty-first-century computer neophytes and technophobes.

On the other hand certain innovations were successfully introduced in order to facilitate the dissemination of knowledge and information more widely. Among these was the reform of the Cyrillic alphabet with a more Latinised 'font', which simplified the printing of secular textbooks and translations. (The Old Church Slavonic script was retained for publications of an ecclesiastical nature.) The adoption of Arabic numerals, replacing the Cyrillic alphabetic system, encouraged the numeracy drive. Russia's first newspaper –

basically a government information bulletin entitled simply 'News' (*Vedomosti*) – was designed to keep the population informed of military victories and new government decrees, but provided the prototype for the later development of Russian journalism. Finally, the mediaeval Russian calendar, which dated the years from the mythical creation of the world as described in the Old Testament book of Genesis, was abandoned and replaced with the western, Julian, calendar, which was formally introduced, to the accompaniment of compulsory fireworks, decorative fir trees and fusillades on 1 January 1700, the first day of the new century.

There were other, apparently superficial, but powerfully symbolic indications of the new, Europeanised, identity that Peter was seeking to impose on Russian society. The shaving of beards, the introduction of western sartorial styles and uniforms, the encouragement of tobacco smoking, the compulsory holding of western-type social gatherings, balls and *soirées – assemblées* (the French word was used) – as well as the attendance of females, forced from the mediaeval purdah of the *terem* (women's quarters) and dressed in deeply *décolleté* gowns, were all visible signs of the cleavage between old Muscovy and Peter's brave new Russia.

Most visible, of course, was the foundation and construction of the country's new capital city, St Petersburg. There is insufficient space here to do justice to this grandiose project, which, perhaps more than anything else, gave literally concrete substance to the concept of Peter's 'window on Europe'. The term is taken from Aleksandr Pushkin's famous poem, 'The Bronze Horseman' (*Mednyi vsadnik*), written in 1833, and the relevant stanza is worth quoting in full. Peter is standing on the bleak banks of the river Neva:

> And thus he thought:
> 'From here we shall threaten the Swede.
> Here shall a city be founded
> To the harm of our arrogant neighbour.
> Here we are destined by Nature
> To hack out a window on Europe,
> And gain a firm foothold by the sea.
> Hither, on unaccustomed waves,
> Shall sail the ships of every flag,
> And we shall feast without restraint.'[16]

Pushkin's choice of the verb 'to hack' (*prorubit'*) nicely captures the brute force, the energy and the sheer human effort which went into the construction of his northern 'paradise'. Foreign architects were hired to design new buildings on western models; swamps and marshes were drained; canals were dug with convict labour; nobles were drafted in from elsewhere in the country and compelled to build new domiciles; wagoners entering the city were made to pay a kind of toll in stone paving slabs; the beginnings of fortifications and embankments were laid in granite in this Herculean task of creating a modern metropolis on the hitherto deserted, pestilential swamp-lands of the Finnish Gulf. Hundreds of thousands perished in the enterprise, but it still stands as a proud civic memorial to Peter's European vision. Étienne Falconet's famous equestrian statue of Peter the Great, commissioned by Catherine II and celebrated in Pushkin's poem; the emperor's elaborate tomb in the SS Peter and Paul Cathedral, adorned with his bust and daily decorated with fresh flowers; the decision of the citizens of Leningrad to revert to the original name of St Petersburg in 1991 – all bear testimony to the pride with which present-day Russians still regard the city together with the memory of its illustrious founder. Here, though, there is something of a paradox. Despite the widespread adulation which Peter's legacy has enjoyed in the centuries following his death, during his own lifetime he was regarded with almost universal fear and loathing as a tyrant, an alien changeling, a murderer, a slave-master, and even as the Antichrist.

Opposition and obituary

The hatred of Peter and the opposition to his policies referred to above took on multifarious forms. The rebellion of the *strel'tsy* in 1698 provided a vivid preview of the confrontations which Peter could expect during the rest of his reign. His relentless and ruthless punishment of the participants provided an equally horrific fore-taste of the manner in which Peter would deal with any further manifestations of opposition to his rule. But opposition there was. On the part of the *dvoryanstvo*, despite the ineluctable punishments which followed detection, instances of tax and service evasion were legion, as large numbers of the noble estate resorted to various stratagems in order to avoid the detested restrictions on their privileges and private pursuits. Peter seemed constitutionally unable to comprehend why each and every one of his subjects did not share his own fanatical enthusiasm to dedicate their entire life to the service of the Russian state. Equally, many were prepared to risk life, limb and liberty to evade those impositions. At the bottom of the social heap, as has already been indicated, the enserfed peasantry constantly expressed their dissatisfaction, their resentment and their fury with their brutal exploitation by a mixture of flight and fight. Continuing religious dissent, cossak mutinies – most spectacularly the revolt led by Kondratii Bulavin in 1707 – isolated insurgencies from Kiev to Kamchatka, and suspected political conspiracies continued to be thorns in Peter's flesh throughout his reign.

One purported plot involving his own son and heir, the tsarevich Aleksei, was to have a particularly tragic denouement. Whether Aleksei was personally involved in an alleged conspiracy to overthrow his father, or whether indeed such a conspiracy ever existed, is not known. What *is* known is that there was little reciprocal filial/paternal affection between Peter and his son, and in 1718 the latter, having returned to Moscow from temporary refuge in Austria, was arrested, imprisoned and questioned under torture. After several days of simultaneous interrogation and knouting, Aleksei finally expired in the dungeons of the SS Peter and Paul fortress. Whatever the precise circumstances of the Aleksei affair, the death of Peter's eldest son created a situation which prompted Peter to issue a decree (in 1722) which declared that, in view of Aleksei's 'wickedness' and his manifest unfitness to rule, every monarch would henceforth personally name and formally appoint his own successor. The fact that Peter himself omitted to do so before he died was to create yet another of Russia's recurring crises of succession (see Chapter 5). The immediate pathological cause of Peter's death in January 1725 has not been precisely established, though it is known that he had for some time been suffering from a severe infection of the urinary tract, for which he had recently undergone vesicular surgery to relieve pressure on his bladder. This was possibly aggravated by a venereal disease and the onset of gangrene. Nor was his already debilitated physical condition helped by his wading into the icy waters of the Finnish Gulf in an attempt to assist in the rescue of some seamen whose boat had capsized.

Peter's deathbed failure to fulfil the requirements of his own decree and nominate his successor was in a sense curiously typical of the dichotomy which can so often be observed between the first Russian emperor's intentions and his accomplishments. In an earlier chapter the question was posed: 'How terrible was Ivan the Terrible?' One might similarly ask: 'How great was Peter the Great?'

Tentative answers to this question have already been hinted at in the pages above. Both Russian and western historians have generally dealt favourably with Peter's achievements, though by no means uniformly so. The mid-nineteenth-century Slavophils were particularly critical; Klyuchevskii left an unflattering portrayal of the man, though paying lip-service to the 'necessity' of Peter's reforms; while Pokrovskii and his Marxist school were scathingly dismissive. However, the history of his reign was mainly written by members of Russia's educated elite and her official establishment who had had most to gain from the 'progressive' reforms he had inaugurated in the face of what to a lesser mortal would have been overwhelming odds. And, on the 'profit' side of the historical ledger, Peter did unquestionably leave his country a very different place from the one he had inherited. He had transformed it into a major European state with a powerful army and navy, and considerable diplomatic clout. He had created the framework of a moderately more efficient modern government administration, and laid down the infrastructure of an industrial and commercial economy. The upper classes of Russian society had received at least an elementary education in the science, technology and learning of contemporary Europe. The Russian Empire stretched from the Baltic to the Pacific, and from the Arctic Ocean to the borders of Central Asia and China. Although there was little visible sign of change outside St Petersburg and Moscow, no longer could contemptuous foreigners regard Russia as a remote, semi-oriental terra incognita, or as a 'rude and barbarous kingdom'.

On the 'debit' side, Peter's undoubted military and territorial gains, his genuine efforts to don the mantle of western civilisation, and his cultural innovations were realised only at the cost of the incalculable suffering, torment and physical ruin of his own subjects. At the personal, physical and psychological levels, Peter was a man of gargantuan appetites and uncontrollable emotions. He was subject to sudden fits of temper, violent behaviour, epileptic seizures, facial twitches, nervous convulsions and swings of mood, which ranged from bouts of outrageous exuberance to periods of deep, dark melancholia. And to some extent these personal traits are reflected in the uncertain, imperfect and unpredictable nature of his public policies and the savage nature of their implementation. One fundamental paradox concerning Peter's achievements or failures, which is often overlooked, is that while attempting to *modernise* his country according to the pattern of his contemporary European exemplars, he still preserved intact, and indeed even reinforced, as the basis of Russia's socio-economic system, the essentially *mediaeval* system of serfdom.

Finally, it is a well-worn cliché that Peter was attempting to drive out barbarism from his country by the use of barbaric methods. But for all its over-usage, the axiom still contains more than a granule of truth. All the available panoply and paraphernalia of a primitive police state, the instruments and agents of a reign of terror, the systematic scarification of the entire population, ghastly forms of punishment and execution, and the gratuitous torment of his myriad victims make the reign of Peter the Great not only a defining epoch in the evolution of modern Russia, but also a monument to human monstrosity. If the formation of the Russian Empire, the fancy architecture of St Petersburg and the founding of the Academy of Sciences are part of Peter's legacy, then so are the fetters, the scaffold and the knout.

5 The period of palace revolutions, 1725–1762

Peter the Great ruled as sole tsar for 29 years. Catherine the Great was to reign for 34. Between the death of the one and the accession of the other – a period of 37 years – Russia had no fewer than six successive monarchs, though one, the Empress Elizabeth (r. 1741–61), managed to survive for 20 of them. This interval between the two 'Great' sovereigns, was, by comparison, a time of no spectacular or especially remarkable achievements, and is usually referred to in the literature as the 'period of palace revolutions', or the 'time of favourites', rather than an epoch memorably associated with the name of any outstanding individual. While not being an era of total insignificance or stagnation, the accomplishments of the rather mediocre Romanov rulers of mid-eighteenth-century Russia cannot really be compared with the dramatic reforms of Peter I or the important developments in both domestic and foreign policy that took place during the reign of Catherine II (see Chapter 6). In the case of a couple of them, they barely qualify as even 'figurehead' monarchs, such was the brevity of their incumbency and the nugatory nature of their impact. And in the case of the two longest lasting, the empresses Anna (r. 1730–40) and Elizabeth, they were both ladies who, in the words of Isabel de Madariaga, 'preferred to reign, and leave ruling to others'.[1]

Peter's intestate death left the country without an obvious, designated successor. However, the choice ultimately fell on his widow, Catherine, whom Peter himself had personally crowned with the title of Empress in 1724. Despite the rather trifling nature of their ephemeral possession of imperial power, the reigns of Catherine I and her immediate successor, Peter II, do require some attention. After all, they were both, nominally at any rate, rulers of the Romanov Empire.

Catherine I and Peter II

Peter's marriage to his first wife, Yevdokiya Lopukhina, daughter of a minor noble family, was an arranged match, and one which never prevented him from conducting a number of extra-marital affairs, most notoriously with Anna Mons, daughter of a German vintner in the *nemetskaya sloboda*. Yevdokiya nevertheless bore him three sons: Aleksei (1690) whom Peter later had tortured to death (see Chapter 4), Aleksandr (1691) and Pavel (1693), both of whom died in infancy. Finally discarded, Yevdokiya was eventually confined to a convent and made to take the veil, though whether a proper legal divorce took place is uncertain (which raises a question surrounding the legitimacy of Peter's second marriage, to Catherine). Peter also had a brief liaison with one Mary Hamilton, a lady-in-waiting of Scottish descent, whom he was later to have decapitated and her head affectionately preserved in a jar of pickling fluid.

His most lasting, apparently genuinely loving and fecund relationship was with the future Catherine I, who, rather in the spirit of Peter's Table of Ranks, worked her way up from the obscure status of a Lithuanian, or Livonian, peasant girl, through the roles of housemaid, military camp follower, concubine, mistress, wife, mother of at least ten of Peter's children, and eventually empress. Hers was thus a shining example of how energetic and meritorious labours in Peter's service could literally be crowned with success. However, Catherine, *née* Marfa Skavronskaya, was not only of dubious paternity, illiterate, of vulgar tastes (though no more vulgar than Peter's) and unschooled in affairs of state, but also temperamentally unsuited to the demands of high office, preferring to spend her time at the banqueting table or in various beds. The explanation for her choice as empress must presumably be sought elsewhere. Or must it? Catherine's well-known sociability, her generous nature and the unparsimonious distribution of her favours had earned her many friends in high places, not least among whom was her former lover, Peter's closest companion and colonel of the Preobrazhenskii Guards, Aleksandr Menshikov, reputedly the son of a Moscow pieman, though his father was more likely an ostler in the royal stables. At all events, Menshikov was from as lowly a background as Catherine, but had risen to be one of the most powerful members of Peter's immediate entourage, though under something of a cloud during the last few weeks of Peter's life. A similarly dark cloud also loured over Catherine's head, as a result of Peter's discovery of his wife's adulterous affair with William Mons, brother of his former mistress. Mons was promptly beheaded, though any action the emperor may have been contemplating against Catherine – and Menshikov – was prevented by his own sudden death. Menshikov had, however, prepared his ground, and immediately called in the favours of the imperial guards to support the nomination of his ex-paramour as empress. Catherine was swiftly so acclaimed in the first of Russia's eighteenth-century palace coups. Thus began the brief, inglorious reign of the quondam peasant girl under the virtual regency of the former ostler's lad.

Realising that his power needed a more secure foundation than simply his personal intimacy with Catherine, Menshikov established a body known as the Supreme Privy Council (*Verkhovnyi tainyi sovet*), consisting of six highly placed military and civil dignitaries, including, of course, himself. This eclipsed the Ruling Senate as the supreme organ of state, acting on the empress's behalf while she continued to debauch herself with the pleasures of the boudoir and the bottle. These eventually took their toll on Catherine's ravaged and over-ravished body, which finally expired on 6 May 1727. Of the government's actual policies carried out in her name, little need be said other than to note that nothing of great moment on either the domestic or foreign policy fronts occurred beyond a slight reduction in the poll tax, and the marriage of Peter's and Catherine's daughter, Anna, to the Duke of Holstein-Gottorp. The offspring of this union was later to become the emperor Peter III, husband of the future Catherine the Great (see the dynastic chart on page xvi).

The obvious successor to Catherine was Pëtr Alekseevich, the child of Peter the Great's eldest son, Aleksei, killed under torture in 1718. The young heir was only 11 years of age on Catherine's death, which meant that effective power still lay with the Supreme Privy Council, which confirmed its own authority, and Peter's accession, once more to the noisy acclamation of the palace guards. Again, the resourceful Menshikov sought to consolidate his personal position, this time by securing the betrothal of the boy-emperor to his own daughter, Mariya. Yet, though seemingly now at the peak of his power as the future father-in-law of the Romanov tsar, Menshikov was in fact teetering on the brink of a rapid fall. He had not achieved his present position without making enemies on his way to the top, and there were many in influential places who resented him as an upstart and a hubristic Jack-in-office. Nor did Menshikov's murky role in the interrogation and death of Peter II's father, Aleksei, exactly win him the affection of the youthful emperor. Scarcely three months after Peter's accession, a cabal of aristocratic conspirators, in which a leading role was played by the ancient Dolgorukii family, persuaded the guards regiments to support a plot to arrest Menshikov and strip him of his offices. The ostensible reason for his disgrace was his alleged involvement in treacherous negotiations with the defeated enemy, Sweden. (This was not the first nor the last time that a Russian government was to eliminate a perceived threat or rival by using the pretext of treason.) Menshikov was thereafter exiled, first to his estate and later to the remote, freezing fastness of Berëzov on the lower reaches of the river Ob in north-west Siberia, where he was accompanied by his son and two daughters, including Mariya, the boy-tsar's once bride-to-be. (His own wife died on the journey.)[2]

It was now the turn of the Dolgorukii to resort to the stratagem of the royal marriage to further their own ambitions. Consequently, in 1729, Prince Aleksei Dolgorukii arranged the engagement of his daughter, Yekaterina, to the young emperor, and the wedding was scheduled to take place in the Moscow Kremlin – whither the royal court had already moved from St Petersburg – on 19 January 1730. However, the grim reaper, who had been cutting a swathe through the population of Moscow with the lethal implement of smallpox, added another victim to his toll with the death of the now 14-year-old Emperor Peter II on the very day of his planned nuptials. Peter's sudden demise threw the Supreme Privy Council, the nobles, magnates, dignitaries and prelates gathered in Moscow for the marriage ceremony and celebrations into another crisis of succession, the third in five years. With his death, the legitimate male line of the Romanovs, as it were, petered out.

Anna Ivanovna

Though no doubt sexually active – despite his youth – Peter left no issue, and the governing elite of Moscow was forced to scramble among the branches of the Romanov family tree in pursuit of a suitable successor. After rejecting a handful of candidates on the grounds that they were unreliable, ineligible, illegitimate or dead, the Privy Council's choice fell on Anna, daughter of Ivan V, Peter the Great's dim-witted elder half-brother, and widow of the deceased Duke Friedrich-Wilhelm of Courland, a petty Baltic principality over which Russia and Poland vied for political power. Claiming some form of legitimacy in a probably bogus testament left by Catherine I, the councillors, headed by Prince D. M. Golitsyn (1665–1737) and senior members of the Dolgorukii clan, finally offered the crown to Anna, but only on condition that she accept a number of restrictions on her exercise of royal power.

The 'Conditions' (*Konditsii*) to which Anna was asked to consent prevented her, without the approval of the Supreme Privy Council, from marrying or appointing a successor, declaring war (or peace), raising new taxes, making senior appointments to state or military office, confiscating a noble's property or disposing of state revenues. It was further required that Anna's lover, Ernst Biron (von Bühren, 1690–1771) should be left at Mitau in Courland, and forbidden to accompany her to Moscow. The government of Russia was, in effect, to be transformed from an autocracy into an oligarchy of aristocrats. Initially, Anna agreed to the 'Conditions', including the abandonment of her favourite, but on arriving in Moscow she was approached by apprehensive representatives of the service nobility, originally gathered in the city for Peter II's wedding, who, fearing the supremacy of the oligarchs, begged her to ignore the restrictions on her absolute authority and to assume the throne as sovereign autocrat in her own right.

Their pleas received the support of the guards officers and of the senior clergy, including Feofan Prokopovich, the influential churchman who had so clearly enunciated the divine provenance of autocratic power under Peter the Great (see Chapter 4). On ascertaining that the 'Conditions' to which she had earlier agreed had *not* had the 'support of the entire nation' (which she had been mendaciously led to believe), she promptly tore into pieces the document she had previously signed, announced her absolute right to succeed to the throne of her ancestors, and declared that 'whosoever opposed her sovereignty should be punished as guilty of high treason'.[3] According to Christoff von Manstein (1711–57), a German official in Russian service and later memoirist, although the announcement of her accession was joyfully received by the people of Moscow, the manifestation that same night of a blood-coloured aurora borealis struck terror into the population, which later regarded it as a presage of the bloody circumstances of Anna's reign under the oppressive ascendancy of her reunited lover, Biron, a foreign adventurer who did not even condescend to learn the Russian language.

Rather like her female predecessor, Catherine, Anna – despite her defiant display of sovereign power – showed no great predilection for the cares or duties of her royal office, which were largely discharged throughout her reign by a clique of Germanic barons and princelings, led by Biron, who has lent his name to Anna's regime as the *Bironovshchina*. It is traditional to depict the years of Biron's influence as something of a reign of terror, with increased taxation, brutal administrative practices, total neglect of the welfare of the population, gratuitous persecution of the disgraced oligarchs, and a cavalier disregard for anything other than the immediate interests of the German-dominated imperial court. To be fair, however, while these charges do have some substance, it is difficult to make any fine distinction between the activities of Anna's sycophants and those of many of her predecessors or successors. Even the power of Biron himself may have been somewhat exaggerated by his later detractors, and his position as the empress's 'favourite' was undoubtedly and intimately shared by other courtiers of German extraction such as Count A. I. Ostermann (1686–1747), Karl Löwenwolde (16??–1735), and her military commander-in-chief, Field Marshal Burkhard Münnich (1683–1767). During the reign of Elizabeth (see below), all these once-powerful high officers of state (except, of course, the deceased Löwenwolde), along with Biron, were to follow the same dreary road into Siberian exile already trodden by Menshikov and the Dolgorukii.[4]

While Anna shared Peter the Great's predilection for freaks, frolics and cruel practical jokes (she once forced one of her courtiers into marriage with an extremely ugly Kalmyk woman and had them spend their wedding night in a palace sculpted out of ice on the frozen river Neva), at least she looked favourably on the interests of the Russian nobility who had supported her assertion of unlimited power at the time of her accession. Among the concessions she granted was a repeal of Peter the Great's resented Entail Law in 1731, which now allowed the nobility to divide their estates among their heirs. In the following year she established the Imperial Corps of Cadets (*Kadetskii korpus*), which provided a full education for noble youths and immediate entry on passing out into a commissioned officer's rank. In 1736 she decreed that one son from every noble household could be exempted from state service in order to manage the family estates, and, finally, the nobles' period of compulsory state service was reduced from life to 25 years. These were important stepping stones along the road that was to lead to Catherine the Great's legislation, which brought about the final 'emancipation of the nobility' from state service altogether in 1785 (see Chapter 6). Needless to say, there was nothing in Anna's legislative programme which did anything to ameliorate the miserable lot of the enserfed peasants. If anything, their condition was worsened by the increased rate of taxation.

In foreign policy, Anna's achievements were minimal. Russia retained her influence in Polish affairs by securing the succession of August III of Saxony as king, but, in return for Persian assistance in renewed war against Turkey, was made to abandon the territorial gains on the Caspian Sea made by Peter the Great (see Chapter 4).

Herself childless, Anna nevertheless wished to retain the throne of Russia in the hands of the descendants of the Miloslavskii side of the Romanov family, and in her dying days nominated the baby son of her niece, Anna Leopoldovna, wife of Duke Anton Ulrich of Brunswick-Wolfenbüttel, as her successor. Named Ivan VI, the infant emperor was to have as regent none other than the egregious Ernst Biron. Biron's ascendancy was, however, short-lived, and only three weeks after his former imperial mistress's death he was arrested, exiled and replaced as regent by Ivan's mother, Anna Leopoldovna, a woman of giddy disposition who spent much of her time in the secluded company of her lady-in-waiting, Julia Mengden, with whom she was in all probability locked in a lesbian relationship. Her tiny son was little over one year old when Elizabeth (Yelizaveta Petrovna), surviving daughter of Peter the Great, acquiesced in being protagonist in yet another palace coup, involving the imperial guards and anti-German foreign diplomatic interests, which led, in 1741, to the arrest of the regent Anna, the imprisonment of the baby Ivan VI, and the banishment of Counts Ostermann and Münnich to exile in Siberia. According to Manstein, the only true crimes of the latter were 'their having incurred the displeasure of the new Empress and having too well served the Empress Anna'.[5] That Anna had been well and truly served by them is not in doubt, but German power behind the Russian throne was seemingly now at an end.

Empress Elizabeth

At the time of her accession on 25 November 1741, Elizabeth was 31 years of age. She had spent her adolescence and early adulthood in frivolous pastimes and the energetic pursuit of carnal gratification and dogged dissipation. Her assiduous application and physical exertions in this area were to reap their own reward in the devoted support of the powerful guardsmen with whom she had disported herself and who now gave her their unstinting support as their imperial dominatrix. Her dalliances with a succession of lovers, which continued throughout her reign, created a situation in which individual favourites, rather than the empress herself, exercised a preponderant influence over the conduct of both internal and foreign policies, although she did take more interest in the responsibilities of her office than either Catherine I or Anna.

Her reign is generally remembered as one in which the life of at least the upper classes of Russian society became more refined and sophisticated, and some of the coarser elements of public activity less obviously brutal. This did not, however, prevent the empress from having two ladies from the grandest circles of St Petersburg's high society, suspected of being engaged in an intrigue to replace Ivan VI on the throne, publicly flogged and their tongues branded. Systematic application of the pincers and the knout still continued to be used as the favoured form of punishment for a wide variety of crimes, though Elizabeth did, in practice, abolish the death penalty, to which she expressed an aversion, for criminal – not political – offences. In the place of capital punishment, those who would previously have been so condemned were instead publicly scourged with the knout, branded, often suffering some other form of physical mutilation, placed in fetters and exiled to life-long hard labour (*katorga*) in Siberia or elsewhere. In 1760, she also issued a decree which granted owners the right to hand over their recalcitrant, disobedient or otherwise unwanted serfs to the civil authorities for exile to Siberia. In return, they were issued with a military recruit quittance (*kvitantsiya*) – that is, a receipt-note verifying their exemption from providing an equivalent number of peasant conscripts for the army. The fact that the wording of the decree stipulated that only able-bodied serfs under the age of 45, accompanied by their wives and, sometimes, children, should be so exiled, suggests that this measure was undertaken as much as a colonising as a penal policy. This was reinforced by a further law of 15 March 1761, which stated that peasants who were publicly flogged before departing on their exile journey should not be so savagely beaten as to 'render them unfit for work' (*tol'ko by godny ostavilis' k rabotam*).[6] These humanitarian provisions were re-enacted in similar legislation passed by Catherine the Great, who obviously shared Elizabeth's delicate feelings.

Despite her relatively long incumbency of the Russian throne, Elizabeth's period of office is not distinguished by any particularly remarkable achievements, save in the lavish disbursements of barely affordable public funds on the architectural embellishment of the capital and its environs, her constant pandering to the corporate interests of the *dvoryanstvo*, and the energetic pursuit of her personal pleasures in the form of hunting, dancing, extravagant entertainments, a succession of passionate sexual liaisons, and a fetishistic predilection for transvestism. To take her building programme first: the two most famous architectural monuments to her reign are the Winter Palace in St Petersburg, official residence of all succeeding Romanov rulers, and site of the world-famous *Ermitazh* (Hermitage) museum; and the sumptuous Summer Palace, also known as the Catherine Palace, a short journey from the capital at the settlement of *Tsarskoe Selo* ('The Tsar's Village', renamed *Detskoe Selo* – 'Childrens' Village' – in 1918, and finally, in 1937, 'Pushkin', after the great poet who attended its *lycée* as a boy). Both were constructed and opulently adorned in flamboyant rococo style by the Italian architect Bartolommeo Rastrelli (1700–71), who took much of his inspiration from the Palace of Versailles. Monumentally magnificent and awe-inspiringly impressive as these royal residences may be, it should be remembered that their construction – or more accurately *re*-construction, for the buildings were originally started before Elizabeth's accession – was commissioned at a time when the country's finances were in a state of near-bankruptcy, when there were massive tax arrears, when national trade and commerce were flagging, and when huge masses of the population were on the verge of famine (not that a halt to the building programme would have released any funds with which to feed the starving). Of course, senseless, selfish prodigality on the part of those in power at the cost of neglecting the public welfare is not peculiar to the Romanovs, and, indeed, may be regarded as a universal phenomenon not confined to any age or clime. But the present-day visitor to St Petersburg, bedazzled by Rastrelli's glittering baroque masterpieces, should bear in mind the degradation and suffering of the Russian people on whose continued oppression their rulers battened.

With regard to the nobility, Elizabeth continued the policies of Anna Ivanovna in fostering their interests and responding positively to – if not yet totally satisfying – their major concerns. These concerns centred on two simple objectives: first, to disentangle themselves from the life-long compulsory state service obligations imposed on them by Peter the Great; second, to increase their power over the serfs. These twin aims were the driving force behind the *dvoryanstvo*'s relations with the autocracy throughout the entire period 1725 to 1861, and led to the formation of a kind of corporate identity or 'class consciousness' of the nobility, whose ambitions, despite a number of concessions by the state, were not fully realised until Catherine the Great's landmark 'Charter to the Nobility' in 1785. It will be remembered that, as a reward for their support at the time of her accession, Anna had abolished the hated Entail Law, and established the officer Cadet Corps. As also mentioned above, in 1736, state service was reduced from life to 25 years, though on certain conditions, including the acquisition of a proper education and the more assiduous (and profitable) cultivation and management of their estates. A series of decrees throughout the 1740s and 1750s gave greater powers to the noble landlords in controlling the residual rights of the peasantry (for example, to marry freely, to engage in trade, to choose where to live), and in exercising almost unlimited seigneurial authority over the bodies and souls of their servile population. As mentioned earlier, in addition to the infliction of brutal corporal punishments, the landlord was also granted the power to exile uncooperative or unwanted serfs to Siberia. The landowner was then compensated by being relieved of the requirement to provide a commensurate number of military recruits. The legislation was intended as a measure to increase the rate of enforced colonisation in Siberia, but unscrupulous landlords often took advantage of its provisions to rid themselves of peasants who were not necessarily disobedient, but too old, infirm or otherwise unfit to work (and therefore unprofitable), thereby thwarting the aim of providing Siberia with a viable labour force. Added restrictions on the right of other sections of the population to own serfs meant in effect that, apart from the crown, the Church and the state, the private ownership of serfs remained the exclusive preserve of the nobility.

The increasingly oppressed peasantry did not, however, submit with total passivity to its fate, and the incidence of flight, depopulation and rebellion continued to be a serious problem, both for individual noblemen and for the government authorities. Flight from the land obviously led to loss of manpower, agricultural production and tax revenue, but the business of suppressing insurgencies, exacting reprisals and policing the affected areas was not only costly, but also fuelled further peasant resentment, which in turn led to renewed outbursts of opposition, anger and violence. Such violence was in fact endemic in the Russian countryside throughout the mid-eighteenth century, and may be regarded as evidence of continuing and simmering class warfare, though this did not boil over into regime-threatening proportions until the massive cossak and peasant rebellion led by Pugachëv during the reign of Catherine the Great (see Chapter 6).

As is by now clear, Elizabeth, unlike Peter I and Catherine II, took little personal interest in affairs of state, though she did intermittently attend a number of meetings of the Senate, which was now restored to something like the position it had formerly held under Peter. Its duties and activities were, however, hampered by the same kind of surveillance and meddling in its affairs by state officials, and also by the fact that certain important areas of governance were outside its jurisdiction, including such crucial matters as foreign and military affairs and internal security. The fact that the army, the navy, the policing system and other institutions fell beyond the Senate's remit meant that what was theoretically one of the highest organs of government was in effect powerless, its functions carried out by other bodies or individuals appointed or co-opted by the empress at her own caprice. A succession of highly placed personages, many of them serially enjoying not only the patronage but also the intimate favours of the empress, were placed in positions of authority, sometimes falling out of favour, sometimes elevated to higher and higher office. In this way, the constituted institutions of the state were replaced by the administrations of Elizabeth's close confidants, companions and bedmates. It was not, of course, the first or the last time in the history of Russia (or the history of many another country) that the serious conduct of government was to be embroiled with the sexual activities of its most eminent incumbents.

One of the reasons that the nobility successfully, albeit gradually, managed partly to disengage itself from its service obligations was the falling need of the state for its permanent military services, as a result of fairly long periods of peace, at least in comparison with Peter's constant warfare. However, the country did not escape entirely from the pressures, rivalries and shifting enmities and alliances among the European powers. Peter's victory over Sweden in the Great Northern War had ensured that Russia was bound to be a major actor on the wider European stage rather than engaging only with her immediate neighbours. At the start of her reign, Elizabeth found herself battling with her father's old Scandinavian enemy, but the brief war between Russia and Sweden (1741–43) took on nothing like the proportions of the earlier conflict, and was concluded in Russia's favour with the signing of the Treaty of Åbo, by which Russia obtained further territories on the Finnish Gulf. Between 1740 and 1748 Russia's major foreign preoccupation was her involvement in the War of the Austrian Succession, the details and diplomatic complications of which need not detain us here, since it resulted in no important gains or losses for Russia, and no change in her international status or prestige. Nor, despite the dispatch of Russian troops against Prussia in 1748, did Russia play any role in the ultimate peace negotiations, since she took no part in the actual fighting. Suffice it to say that, despite Russia's close involvement in the diplomatic intrigues surrounding the war, it did not constitute a major chapter in her military history.

More significant, but ultimately inconclusive, in terms of the outcome for Russia, was the country's participation in the Seven Years' War, which began with Prussia's invasion of Saxony in August 1756. The war must be understood principally as a struggle involving Russia, Prussia and Austria for the mastery of central Europe. France and Britain also had their own interests in the conflict, but were rather less concerned with the passage of events in continental Europe than with their further-flung overseas rivalries in North America, the West Indies and Asia. St Petersburg's involvement was also complicated by the fluctuating enthusiasms and favouritisms of influential Russian statesmen and courtiers, such as the anglophile Chancellor Count Aleksei Bestuzhev-Ryumin (1693–1766), his deputy Count Mikhail Vorontsov (1745–67), the three brothers Shuvalov, and yet another of Elizabeth's lovers and the commander-in-chief of Russia's armies in the closing stages of the war, Field Marshal Aleksandr Buturlin (1694–1767). Each of these powerful figures had his own personal agenda and international likes, dislikes and prejudices.

Muddying the waters still further was also the problem of the 'young court'. Using her royal prerogative of selecting her own successor under the law introduced by her father, Elizabeth picked out her nephew, Karl Peter Ulrich, Duke of Holstein-Gottorp, the future Emperor Peter III (r. 1761–2). Peter, as he was known in Russia, left his German duchy and settled in St Petersburg in 1742, aged 14, and was betrothed three years later to Princess Sophie Fredericka Augusta of Anhalt-Zerbst. Under her adopted Russian name of Yekaterina, and converted to the Russian Orthodox faith, this was the young lady to be better known to history as the Russian empress Catherine the Great, whose achievements form the subject of the following chapter. Peter's German origins and his strongly pro-Prussian sympathies made him the focus of attention for the minority of those in government circles who objected to Bestuzhev-Ryumin's policy of isolating Prussia, and forging stronger links with Britain. However, the surprise conclusion of an Anglo-Prussian alliance in 1756 prompted the formation of an anti-Prussian bloc made up of Russia, France and Austria – despite the understandable objections of the Grand Duke, later Emperor, Peter. In July 1757 Russian troops under the command of Field Marshal Stepan Apraksin invaded eastern Prussia, soundly defeating German forces at the battle of Gross-Jägendorf. Despite his victory, Apraksin failed to follow up his success, withdrew to winter in Poland, and was soon relieved of his command. His dismissal was quickly followed by that of Bestuzhev-Ryumin, who was replaced as Chancellor by Vorontsov. At this point, the empress suffered a severe illness, prompting expectation of her imminent demise and the succession of her pro-Prussian nephew,

Peter. Despite the more circumspect attitude towards Prussia of those in charge of Russia's foreign and military affairs, the war dragged on, with further Russian victories, but against the background of increasing apathy and disengagement of the other continental powers from the central European conflict. Finally, Elizabeth died on Christmas Day 1761, and the throne passed in orderly succession to nephew Peter. The new emperor immediately called a halt to the hostilities and, in a dramatic diplomatic volte-face, Russia concluded, first, an armistice, followed by a peace treaty, finishing in an alliance with Prussia, in what Florinsky describes as 'the disgraceful *dénouement* of Russia's participation in the Seven Years' War'.[7] Although Elizabeth had begun her reign with a declaration of her firm intent to rule in the spirit and manner of Peter the Great, in neither her foreign nor domestic policies can one detect any of the vision, commitment, energy and accomplishment of her ferocious father.

Cultural advances

Despite what may appear to be the rather disparaging conclusion of the previous section, it cannot be denied that in the fields of both the arts and the sciences, in literature, exploration and education, the middle third of the eighteenth century in Russia saw some modest progress in the country's cultural development. Under Elizabeth, the brutalities of Peter the Great, most horrifically exemplified in his slaughter of the *strel'tsy*, and the *grotesqueries* at the court of Anna Ivanovna, gave way to a slightly more refined and less savage conduct of public life. Notwithstanding the continuation – or even intensification – of serfdom, the spectacle of public floggings with lethal instruments of flagellation, the standard use of torture in legal proceedings, and the living death of the Siberian exile system, which annually swallowed thousands of victims into its icy maw, Russia, or at least sections of her privileged classes, did begin to reap the benefits of western learning and civilisation.

Graduating from the primary stages inaugurated by Peter the Great, members of the nobility began to familiarise themselves with foreign languages – increasingly French, which became virtually the lingua franca of polite society – to exhibit more decorum in their social activities and, in short, to enter into a period of apprenticeship in the literature, manners and culture of the west. Russian writers, poets, playwrights, grammarians, historians and satirists aped, emulated and aspired to the perfection of their foreign masters' skills, crafts and expertise in their chosen fields. Much of what was produced, it is true, was imitative, clumsy and lacking the sophistication of their exemplars, but then that is in the very nature of apprenticeship, a process through which trainees seek to achieve the same levels of accomplishment as their mentors and instructors.

At any rate during Elizabeth's reign the wide gulf between west European and Russian culture started to narrow, and a bridge – albeit somewhat shaky – began to be built which would ultimately lead to the magnificent, world-class achievements of Russian literature, music and other cultural genres in the nineteenth century. Four writer/scholars are worthy of particular attention: Antiokh Kantemir (1708–44), Vasilii Tredyakovskii (1703–69), Mikhail Lomonosov (1711–65) and Aleksandr Sumarokov (1717–77). Kantemir, a much travelled diplomat and polyglot scholar (he was Minister-Resident in London between 1730 and 1738, thence transferring to Paris), is best known for his satirical verses, published only after his death, in which he lampooned contemporary Russian mores, and caricatured the enemies of Enlightenment in a vigorous, vernacular Russian which made him, in D. S. Mirsky's words, 'the first deliberate and artistically conscious realist in Russian literature'.[8] Tredyakovskii, a man of humble, non-noble background from the provincial town of Astrakhan, exhibited in his own somewhat cumbrous verses none of the wit, sparkle and cosmopolitanism of Kantemir. He is better remembered as a translator and author of an erudite treatise on prosody and versification whose theories are still valued by modern literary historians.

Of an altogether different calibre is Mikhail Lomonosov, who is without doubt one of the towering intellectual geniuses of eighteenth-century Russia. Born the son of a peasant fisherman in arctic Russia near Arkhangelsk, he later studied at the prestigious 'Slavo-Græco-Latin Academy', at that time the leading academic institution in Moscow, and then at the German universities of Marburg and Freiburg. On his return to Russia in 1741 he was appointed assistant professor at the Academy of Sciences, established in St Petersburg by Peter the Great, and devoted his life to learning and scholarship in an astonishing range of academic disciplines. He was at the same time chemist, physicist, mathematician, poet, grammarian, philologist, mining engineer, rhetorician and educationist, and it is entirely fitting that Moscow University, Russia's first, founded in 1755, should bear his name and today display his statue. Aside from his pioneering work in the physical and practical sciences, Lomonosov's own poetic compositions, particularly his religious and panegyrical odes written in the fashionable classical mode, are not particularly inspiring, though the dexterity of his use of the high Slavonic literary style are models of their kind. It was in fact his work in classifying the various levels of 'high', 'middle' and 'low' levels of Russian and Church Slavonic vocabulary, appropriate to various literary genres, which laid the linguistic foundation for the development of Russian literary style. The ground-breaking lexicographical lessons learnt from Lomonosov's writings such as *Rhetoric*, his *Russian Grammar*, and *The Use of Sacred Books in the Russian Tongue* have justly earned him the title 'the father of the modern Russian language'. He died at the age of 54, worn out by a combination of his mental exertions and a ruinous addiction to alcohol, a not uncommon affliction in Russia.

Less of a polymath, but more prolific and popular in his literary output was Sumarokov, a nobleman of different temperament from that of Lomonosov, who was perhaps the first Russian *littérateur* to devote his life entirely to the pen. Best known for his classical dramas, he also dabbled in a variety of other genres, including fable, satire, song, journalism and literary criticism. Although the mid-eighteenth century can hardly be described as a golden or even silver age of Russian *belles-lettres*, at least there was a glimmering of some semi-precious nuggets which were clear indications of the rich veins of artistic achievement that were to be mined in the following century.

Not only in the field of literature was progress made during these years. Theatrical entertainment in the French classical manner became fashionable, and Sumarokov was appointed director of Russia's first permanent theatre in 1756. The foundation of Moscow University has already been mentioned, and in 1757 Elizabeth followed her father's example in his establishment of the Academy of Sciences by authorising the inauguration of the Imperial Academy of Arts in order to foster the development of painting, music, sculpture and architecture. Neither the university nor the academy immediately shone as great centres of learning, beset as they were by problems of both staffing and student recruitment, but the very fact of their existence is further evidence of the advances made in Russian culture at the time which were to be exponentially enhanced in the following century.

However, a truly great scientific undertaking also belongs to this period, which does stand out as one of the century's most outstanding achievements: the Great Northern Expedition (*Velikaya Severnaya ekspeditsiya*, 1733–43), also known as the Second Kamchatka Expedition (*Vtoraya Kamchatskaya ekspeditsiya*. (Peter the Great, it will be remembered, authorised the first, shortly before his death.) Some historians regard these great journeys of exploration as actually two stages of a single process and describe them jointly as the Siberian-Pacific Expedition (*Sibirsko-Tikhookeanskaya ekspeditsiya*), which is how they will be referred to in the following passages. They were in fact both under the direction of the same institution (the Admiralty), led, until his death in 1741, by the same seafaring explorer, Vitus Bering, and shared the same ambitious scientific objectives of charting, cataloguing, collecting and recording all that was humanly possible at that time about the geography, history, natural resources, native peoples, languages, economic potential, demography and general environment of that gigantic, almost permanently frozen, landmass stretching from the Urals to the Bering Strait, and even beyond. If one bears in mind the huge logistical difficulties in manning and equipping such a vast enterprise, the great distances to be covered, the cruel climate and the hostile terrain, as well as the frustrating bureaucratic and financial difficulties at the centre, it is truly amazing how remarkably successful was the ten-year mission, which must rate as one of the greatest expeditions of scientific discovery in all time. When it set off from St Petersburg in February 1734, Bering's wagon train consisted of 600 personnel, nine cartloads of scientific instruments, more than 200 academic books, and a caravan of pack-horses laden with paper, writing materials and provisions, including several casks of German wine, for which the expedition's botanist, Johann Georg Gmelin (1709–55) in particular had a well-developed taste.[9]

The achievements of the Siberian-Pacific Expedition were in no small measure due to the labours of two brilliant German scholars who were leading members of Bering's scientific staff: the oenophil naturalist, Gmelin, and the perhaps better-known Gerhard Friedrich

Müller (1705–83), whose prodigious labours as a cartographer, ethnographer, economic analyst, linguist, archivist and topographer extraordinaire were crowned with the appearance of his seminal, multi-volume work, 'Description of the Tsardom of Siberia' (*Opisanie Sibirskogo Tsarstva*), written between 1750 and 1752, though not published in its entirety until long after his death.[10] Müller also became editor of a newly established journal entitled 'Monthly Compositions' (*Ezhemesyachnyya sochineniya*), in which he published further materials about Siberia, and which became one of Russia's most popular, widely read and informative periodicals. In its pages, not only did the German scholar establish his position as Russia's, and possibly the world's, leading expert on everything Siberian, but also, in the words of Larry Black, provided 'an invaluable wellspring for the consolidation of the notion of Siberia as the most vital part of the "Russian Lands"'.[11] Whether the 'most vital' or not, certainly the value to the Romanov Empire of its huge north-Asian territories as a fabulously rich resource frontier was certainly well established by the mid-eighteenth century, and remains so to the present day.

Peter III

Emperor Peter III of Russia has had a lousy press. He is traditionally described as ugly, bad-tempered, pock-marked, infantile, pro-German, half-witted and usually drunk. While none of these alleged characteristics might automatically disqualify one from mounting the Russian throne, Peter certainly managed, during his brief occupancy, to alienate influential sections of the Russian court and the high nobility, as well as making himself utterly repugnant to his bride, Catherine, whom he married in 1745, though whether the union was ever properly consummated is a matter for speculation. In all likelihood it was, in the physical sense, but the young couple became rapidly estranged from each other, and found their erotic gratification with a succession of other paramours, as they were both being groomed in their own way as the royal couple at the 'young court' who would succeed Empress Elizabeth on her death.

Even the paternity of Catherine's son, the future emperor Paul, is in doubt, and some suppose the natural father to have been Catherine's then lover, a court chamberlain named Sergei Saltykov.

At all events, the baby prince was removed from his mother's care almost at birth and his upbringing superintended by the empress herself. The long-term results of this separation between Paul and his parents, particularly his mother, will be addressed in the following chapters. Despite the uncharitable manner in which Peter's character has been treated by later historians, there is little in his policies – except his passion for Prussian-style militarism – which suggests that he departed in any particularly damaging way from the paths trodden by his immediate predecessors. Indeed, the process of what has been described as the emancipation of the nobility from state service was given an extra dimension with the promulgation of Peter's 'Manifesto to the Nobility' in 1762. Under its terms, members of the *dvoryanstvo* were no longer compelled to perform military or bureaucratic service to the state, but were allowed to do so on a voluntary basis. They were, moreover, free to travel abroad at will and even enter the service of foreign states, provided, of course, that those states were not counted among Russia's enemies. Erring nobles could still be deprived of their estates, and were still subject to corporal punishment, which was naturally much resented, but there is no doubt that Peter's Manifesto was yet another step towards the total liberation of the nobility that was eventually to be granted by his successor. Further evidence of Peter's relatively liberal attitude is provided by the abolition of the internal security forces, the freeing of certain trade restrictions, the reduction of some indirect taxes, a measure of religious toleration for Old Believers, and a limited secularisation in the administration of ecclesiastical finances, which, however, not surprisingly incurred the displeasure of the Church.

Given this programme of moderate reform, the explanation for the eventual coup which threw Peter from office and ended in his murder in yet another palace conspiracy must be sought elsewhere. The only plausible answer is the unpopularity which the emperor brought on himself by his treatment of the military aristocracy, in particular the imperial guards regiments, whose officer class had enjoyed a degree of luxury and privilege during the reign of Elizabeth. Peter was something of a military martinet, who delighted in endlessly drilling his troops, insisted on rigorous attention to all military duties by all ranks, imposed Prussian-style uniforms, and generally interfered with the rather relaxed and pampered lifestyle of the senior echelons of the Russian army. From a strictly military point of view, the renewed insistence on discipline and efficiency was probably no bad thing, but in political terms it was disastrous. On the other hand, his wife, Catherine, had never spared herself in wooing the support of powerful court and military figures and had gained such a degree of popularity among influential courtiers, diplomats and officers as to make it unlikely that her ultimate bid for her husband's throne would meet any serious opposition.

Peter's unpopular intention to embark on a war with Denmark in July 1762 gave an opportunity for the plotters to strike. Supported by influential dignitaries, including her lover, Prince Grigorii Orlov (1734–83) and his four brothers, with the enthusiastic backing of the powerful Izmailovskii and Semënovskii guards regiments, and with the approval of the Orthodox hierarchy, Catherine was proclaimed Empress in the Kazan Cathedral in St Petersburg and straightaway proceeded to occupy the Winter Palace in the early hours of 27 July. On the following day, Peter, who was lurking with his mistress in his country residence at Oranienbaum, a short ride from the capital, was presented with the fait accompli of his own dethronement, which he appears to have accepted with fatalistic resignation and no attempt at resistance. The now deposed emperor was placed under house arrest and kept under guard on his estate at nearby Ropsha, where, on 6 August, he was smothered and strangled to death by Aleksei Orlov, the brother of Catherine's lover, Grigorii. While there is no evidence that Catherine connived in her husband's murder, it is doubtful that its likelihood would have caused her any qualms. As a woman, a foreigner and a usurper, with no dynastic links to the Romanovs other than through her joyless and fruitless marriage, she would obviously find it somewhat inconvenient to have her dethroned husband roaming at large as a possible rallying point for any potential opposition. Indeed, later pretenders to the crown would declare themselves to be the real Peter III, back to claim his rightful throne – the most notorious of them being Emelyan Pugachëv in 1773 (see Chapter 6). The official announcement of the overthrown monarch's demise attributed the cause of death to haemorrhoidal colic, though the true nature of his assassination was not revealed until 1881, when a letter from Orlov to Catherine, confessing the deadly deed, was made public. No great significance need be read into the slaying of Peter III. It was simply a matter of domestic and dynastic relationships and rivalries, with an admixture of foreign policy considerations resulting from Peter's unpopular pro-Prussian leanings, and the vaunting ambition of his scheming and adulterous wife.[12]

In the final analysis, Peter was merely the last in the rather pathetic procession of inadequate monarchs who occupied the Romanov throne between the death of Peter the Great and the accession of Catherine II. The period from 1725 to 1762 saw no outstanding domestic reforms from above, no widespread revolutionary movements from below, no major wars, and no world-standard cultural or artistic achievements. It was a rather desultory period in Russia's history, which is personified in the uninspiring roll call of her imperial rulers during those years who, it will be recalled, comprised one Lithuanian peasant woman, one teenaged youth, one suckling babe, two semi-literate nymphomaniacs and a drunken Holstein duke.

6 The age of Catherine the Great, 1762–1796

Empress Catherine II of Russia is, without serious opposition, the most redoubtable, outstanding and intriguing female in the political history of the Romanov Empire. From her relatively obscure origins as the daughter of a minor German princeling, Christian Augustus of Anhalt Zerbst, she rose to be one of the most powerful, admired and well-loved potentates in late eighteenth-century Europe. Only four years into her own reign, Empress Elizabeth, after trawling through the shoals of eligible aristocratic maidens in Europe in quest of a suitable wife for her chosen heir, Peter – whose sorry reign was described in the previous chapter – finally netted the 16-year-old Princess Sophia Augusta Fredericka, born at Stettin on 2 May 1729. She had no obvious qualifications for her role as consort of the future emperor of Russia, other than her reputedly pretty looks, her undoubted intelligence, her obvious compliability and an eye for the main chance. She was brought to St Petersburg, where she enthusiastically embraced the Russian Orthodox religion under her adopted Russian name of Yekaterina, learned the rudiments of the Russian language, and rather less enthusiastically embraced her bridegroom, Peter, in 1745. Whether the marriage was appropriately consummated can only be a matter of conjecture. However, the royal newlyweds were duly ensconced in a suitably appointed palace, where their household soon came to be dubbed the 'young court', and where they were prepared for the eventual succession. As mentioned above (Chapter 5), there was really no love to be lost between the pair from the start, and each of them quickly sought the comfort and sexual gratification of extra-marital partners. Healthy, energetic, well educated, ripe, robust and, above all, ambitious, the vivacious Catherine filled her hours of enforced leisure not only with satisfying her physical lust, but also in the more sedate pursuit of learning and widening her intellectual horizons, and became thoroughly au fait with the latest fruits of the European Enlightenment. Among her acquaintances and epistolary correspondents, both before and after she seized the throne, she numbered such luminaries as Voltaire, Diderot, Montesquieu and the brothers Melchior and Friedrich Grimm. As may be expected, she was also intimately involved in the various royal intrigues, political scheming, rumour-mongering and support-seeking machinations of the vying palace cliques which were an intrinsic feature of Elizabeth's court and her immediate entourage. Her relationship with Count Nikita Panin (1718–83 – later her foreign minister), the Orlov brothers (particularly Grigorii, who sired her illegitimate son, Aleksei, born in April 1762), and her wider popularity among officers of the guards regiments were to bear political fruit during the coup which finally deposed her serially cuckolded husband in July 1762.

The Legislative Commission and the *Nakaz*

It has already been pointed out that, on assuming the throne, Catherine had a triple handicap: her sex, her German origin and the decidedly dubious circumstances of her accession. However, with considerable determination, aplomb and the powerful personal backing of her favourites, the new *Imperatrix* immediately plunged into the business of acquainting herself with the state of her empire. Despite her intimacy with the comings and goings and ins and outs of high society in the capital, the young princess had actually led a fairly secluded, pampered existence, ignorant of life beyond the salons, soirées and seductions of St Petersburg's *beau monde*. She was far more familiar with the sophisticated cerebrations of the French *philosophes* and the sexual prowess of her paramours than with the wretched condition of the Russian people over which she now ruled. Consequently, she set off on a number of expeditions into the Russian provinces, attended meetings of the Senate, acquainted herself with the parlous position of the nation's finances, reviewed the fleet – which she pronounced was 'fit only for herring-fishing'[1] – and was made aware of the rebellious nature of the Russian countryside, which was in a state of almost permanent unrest, including the regular occurrence of heavily armed insurgency.

As a daughter of the Enlightenment, and now freshly equipped with at least an elementary understanding of the 'state of the nation', Catherine embarked on a twin project which she hoped would address some of the country's problems, of which she was now aware, and also establish a reputation for being a truly 'enlightened' monarch, thereby winning not only the approbation of her people, but also the acclaim of her European contemporaries. The first stage of the project was the compilation of a work of some erudition and perspicacity, but of rather muddled moral intent, which is usually referred to in English as her 'Great Instruction' (*Bol'shoi Nakaz*), promulgated and distributed among a limited readership in 1767. The second was the summoning of an elected Legislative Commission, which was intended to revise the state of Russia's laws and produce a new legal code in the spirit of, and guided by, the provisions of the said *Nakaz*. The latter is a complex and intriguing document, which is the only example of a ruling Russian monarch composing an extensive statement of his or her political, moral, legal and economic philosophy as the guiding principles of government. As Catherine's personal *profession de foi* the 'Instruction' has been variously hailed as an expression of her genuinely held enlightened ideals, an act of gross plagiarism, and an example of the lady's hypocrisy, duplicity and humbug. While seemingly contradictory, all three descriptions are to a greater or lesser extent correct. The 'Instruction' is not composed in the style of a philosophical treatise or continuous piece of political theory, but rather comprises a number of axioms, 526 articles in all, arranged originally in 20 chapters, much of the content culled from the published works of leading European thinkers. The author drew particularly heavily on Montesquieu's *De l'esprit des lois* ('The Spirit of the Laws', 1748), and the work of the progressive Italian jurist, Cesare Beccaria, *Dei delitti e delle pene* ('On Crime and Punishment'), published anonymously in 1764, just one year before Catherine started on her *Nakaz*.

The work contains chapters on the nature of monarchical power, the relationship between the citizen, the state and the law, jurisprudence, crime and punishment, demography and the 'propagation of the human species' (in the physiological preliminaries to which she was personally well experienced), commerce, social estates, education and religious toleration. Whether it was Catherine's initial intent for her 'Instruction' to act as a prescriptive manual for the delegates to the Legislative Commission is not clear. But if that *were* the intention, the deliberations of the delegates were somewhat circumscribed in their revision of the laws in 'conformity with Nature' and according to 'the situation and the circumstances of the people for whom they are instituted' (Article 5), by two bold and unequivocal declarations. Article 6 simply states, 'Russia is a European State', and Article 9, rather less pithily, reads, 'The Sovereign is absolute; for there is no other authority but that which centres in his single person that can act with a vigour proportionate to the extent of such a vast dominion.'[2] So – despite Russia's declared European identity, with all its implications for progress and modernity – given the absolute nature of Catherine's sovereignty, what chance was there of introducing new legislation, new institutions and new principles which would alter, diminish or affect her supreme autocratic power? It is true that she expressed: abhorrence of corporal punishment ('All punishments by which the human body might be maimed should be abolished', Article 96); an insistence on equality of all citizens before the Law (Article 34); a belief in the benefits of education (Chapter XIV); and a preference for the prevention, rather than the punishment, of crime by eliminating its social and economic causes (Article 240). However, in the same document she went on to proclaim the necessity of a 'fixed order of society … [with] some to govern and others to obey' (Article 250); and, on the matter of serfdom, alluded to the danger of 'suddenly and by legislative action creating a large number of emancipated slaves' (Article 260).[3] There is, therefore, little, if anything, in Catherine's *Nakaz* or her early legislative acts to suggest that she, as absolute autocrat, had any intention other than to rule absolutely and autocratically.

Nor did the deliberations and results of the Legislative Commission, which sat between 1767 and 1769, amount to anything of great moment. It is tempting at this point to invoke the old Roman proverb, immortalised by the poet Horace, about the great mountains in labour delivering only a tiny mouse.[4] However, in the case of Catherine's Commission, it was more a case of a small range of puny hillocks experiencing a phantom pregnancy. That said, it has to be conceded that the Commission, consisting of 526 elected or selected delegates, who gathered together over a period of 18 months in no fewer than 203 sessions, was probably the most representative, variegated, democratic and motley assemblage of citizens of any state, debating among themselves in orderly and seemingly sober fashion, to have been convened anywhere in the world to that date. The members were granted a modest stipend, travelling expenses and immunity from arrest, and were drawn from almost all classes of society, from the remote provinces, and included some of the most highly educated sections of the nobility (though, oddly, only one from the Church), representatives of government institutions; and merchants, alongside state peasants, cossak communities and ethnic minorities summoned together from all over the empire. The only class which was totally excluded, as may well be expected, was the privately owned serfs (i.e. the majority of the population). Admirable as Catherine's intentions might have been, it was, however, the sheer diversity of the interests represented in the Commission which prevented it from reaching any formal conclusions or formulating the projected new code of laws which was to replace the antiquated *Ulozhenie* of 1649 (see Chapter 3).

Apart from the problem of reconciling the differing needs of so many social, regional, economic and special-interest groups, the Commission really had its hands tied from the very outset by the incompatible nature of the aims it was required to fulfil and the guidelines within which it was supposed to operate. As Klyuchevskii has pointed out with his usual acumen:

> It [the Commission] was ordered to work according to three principles:
>
> 1) it must be guided by the Empress's *Nakaz*, which set forth the very latest ideas of west-European political literature;
> 2) it must be guided by currently operating Russian legislation, of which the majority of the members of the Commission had no knowledge;
> 3) it must be guided by the needs and wishes of the population.
>
> The deputies therefore fell amid three fires, and were forced to address themselves to a range of ideas and expectations of such a nature as was impossible not only to reconcile but also even to approximate one to another.[5]

In a sense, Klyuchevskii is stating the obvious, that the latest principles of the eighteenth-century European Enlightenment, the existing state of Russian legislation (which dated from mediaeval Muscovy, or even Mongol times) and the deeply felt, but widely differing, desires of the Russian population as a whole were impossible to squeeze together on a Procrustean bed of mutually agreed and compatible legal enactments. However, the surviving speeches, supplications and suggestions of many of the delegates do provide both an insight into the concerns of various strata of Russian society at the time, and also form the basis for some of Catherine's future legislation.[6] Be that as it may, the Empress soon lost interest in the Commission's exertions – preoccupied as she became in her war with Turkey and the question of Poland (see below) – and, although a number of 'sub-commissions' continued to convene until 1774, to all intents and purposes by 1769 the Commission had ceased to function as a viable or remotely effective consultative assembly. Not, of course, without its own intrinsic interest, Catherine's much vaunted Legislative Commission may be properly dismissed, to use Klyuchevskii's felicitous phraseology once again, as nothing more than 'an all-Russian ethnographical exhibition' (*vserossiiskaya etnograficheskaya vystavka*).[7]

While it is true that the Commission produced nothing of real substance, Catherine did address herself to various areas of domestic policy in the early years of her reign, which some historians still regard as an earnest of her progressive, liberal intentions. There was, however, no grand legislative programme of reform until the combined pressures of the nobility, on whose support the empress continued to rely, and the forces of popular revolt, which were suppressed only with much bloodshed, forced Catherine to take appropriate measures to appease the former and contain the latter. Among the initial steps which she did take, however, were the abandonment of some of Peter III's detested military reforms, and the establishment of a new Military Commission which would revise the administration, control and command of Russia's armed forces along lines that were more acceptable to the general staff. Also, after some initial concessions, Catherine continued her late, unlamented husband's policy of secularising the administration of church property, closed down a number of monasteries, and imprisoned the archbishop of Rostov for his temerity in openly condemning and anathematising the secular authorities for those actions. In 1763 Catherine authorised the foundation of a medical college and, in her genuine efforts to promote the health of the population, set an example by having herself and her son inoculated against smallpox by her English physician, Dr Thomas Dimsdale. Congratulating her on this prophylactic example, the elderly Voltaire wrote to Catherine in February 1769 that she had bravely 'been inoculated with less fuss than a nun taking an enema'. In the same letter, the renowned French sage of Ferney also exhorted her: 'In God's name, beat the Turks.'[8]

Foreign policy (i)

It has been suggested, not without some justification, that Catherine's claim to 'greatness' was a result more of her foreign than her domestic policies. It is to this area of her activities, particularly in relation to the old problems of Poland and the Ottoman Empire, that we now turn. Catherine's first minor triumph in her conduct of foreign affairs was her success, in league with King Frederick II of Prussia (Frederick the Great, r. 1740–86), in securing the accession of her former lover, the Polish aristocrat, Stanisław Poniatowski (1732–98) as the last king of Poland (r. 1764–95). The combination of his election to the Polish throne and his former intimacy with Catherine was to guarantee his ex-mistress a decisive influence in the internal affairs of Poland over the coming three decades. Russian influence, however, did not go without protest.

Among the archaic, semi-anarchical features of the intricate system of governance in Poland was the institution of an elective kingship, and the so-called *liberum veto*, a device by which any member of the *Sejm* (Diet, or Parliament) was able to veto any motion, proposition or legislation under discussion and cause the dissolution of the assembly. Moreover, individual members of the Polish nobility (*szlachta*), who comprised the membership of the Diet, had the right to form armed 'confederations' through which they might seek to achieve their aims by force of arms. This was a much-cherished privilege of the fiercely individualistic Polish nobles, who believed that it was not only their right, but indeed their duty, to protect personal freedom and overthrow an unjust monarch, even if they had elected him in the first place. One such league, the Confederation of Bar, was formed in 1768 in Ukraine, which called for an end to Russian meddling in Polish affairs, particularly with respect to the rights of non-Catholic 'dissidents', mainly Orthodox and Protestant, living in Poland. The Confederation also demanded the overthrow of the unpopular, pro-Russian puppet on the throne, Poniatowski. In fact the Confederation was not just anti-Russian, it was anti-royalist *tout court*. But Catherine was determined to maintain Russian dominance in Poland and smother any movements for reform by continuing to back the feeble monarchy, if necessary by armed intervention. Large numbers of Russian troops were already positioned in Poland, and in response to a formal request from the threatened government, embarked on a bitter and destructive four-year struggle with the confederates in order to crush the insurgency on Russia's own terms. Eventually, Catherine's involvement with Poland led directly to Russia's participation in that country's partition, the outcome of an agreement in which Catherine, Frederick of Prussia and Maria-Theresa of Austria put their royal heads together in an alliance which would ultimately wipe Poland, as an independent, sovereign state, off the map of Europe for nearly a century and a half. The first stage of this process was the signing of the partition treaties in 1772, their reluctant acceptance by the king and the Sejm in September 1773, and the dismemberment of Poland, which lost around one-third of its territory, divided out among the three east European powers.

Meanwhile, Turkey had been keeping a wary eye on developments in Poland, viewing Russia's increased influence there with some apprehensiveness. In the summer of 1768 detachments of Russian cossaks pursued Polish insurgents across the border into Turkish territory, thereby giving the sultan a *casus belli*, which prompted the declaration of war on Russia. After initial inconclusive skirmishes, the war gradually turned in Catherine's favour, her troops occupying the principalities of Moldavia and Walachia on the Danube, and the Crimean peninsula in the Black Sea. Her navy, despite its somewhat ramshackle condition, soundly defeated a fleet of Turkish vessels at the battle of Chesme in June 1770. The fruits of the naval victory were in fact insubstantial, but nevertheless celebrated with exaggerated triumphalism in St Petersburg. However, by 1772, despite Russia's military edge over Turkey, the economic and diplomatic strains of simultaneous warfare against the armies of the Porte and the confederates of Bar compelled Catherine, under pressure from Frederick of Prussia, to seek a settlement on both fronts. Having, as we have seen, temporarily settled the problem of Poland to her own advantage, Catherine was now able to concentrate on the continuing war with Turkey, which feared, with some justification, that a fate similar to that of Poland was being contemplated for her own possessions. Despite diplomatic pressures on her from Prussia, Austria and France, and already threatened internally by the outbreak of Pugachëv's rebellion (see below), she was nevertheless encouraged by the brilliant military successes in the south of General Aleksandr Suvorov (1730–1800), one of Russia's great martial heroes, to pursue the war to ultimate victory. Her obduracy was rewarded with the eventual signing of the Treaty of Kuçuk Kainardzi in July 1774, under the terms of which the exhausted Turkey ceded large areas of territory to Russia on the north coast of the Black Sea, and was forced to agree to the independence of the Crimea. Russia also acquired Azov 'in perpetuity', the opening up of the Bosphorus and the Dardanelles to Russian shipping, and certain rights over the interests of the sultan's Orthodox Christian subjects. Taken together, the Polish settlement and the terms agreed at Kuçuk Kainardzi must count, in both military and diplomatic terms, as a palpable victory for the Russian empress. She had set her indelible stamp on the conduct of international relations in eastern Europe and the Balkans. But she had now to turn her attention to deal with the domestic crisis that already menaced the internal stability of her realm.

The *Pugachëvshchina*[9]

Russia has a long, distinguished history of mass popular revolt against her ruling classes, stretching at least as far back as the Time of Troubles at the beginning of the seventeenth century (see Chapter 3). Apart from the countless, localised, minor insurgencies, protests and violent disturbances among isolated sections of the brutalised lower orders of society, which were endemic throughout Russia, on occasion these uprisings took on more sizeable and ominous proportions which posed a major direct threat to the established powers. It will be recalled that the large cossak and peasant rebellions led by Bolotnikov (1606), Razin (1669–71) and Bulavin (1707) – see Chapters 3 and 4 – had all in their various ways dramatically highlighted the tensions, grievances and suffering of the Russian people and caused widespread mayhem across large swathes of the Russian land, but had all been ferociously repressed and their ringleaders savagely punished. It will also be recalled that Russia had an equally long tradition of opportunistic 'pretenders' of one ilk or another claiming to be the rightful, 'just' tsar, and posing a challenge to the incumbent ruler's right to the throne. The appearance of these sometimes colourful, but equally curious and ephemeral characters had been a particularly common phenomenon during the Time of Troubles.[10] Later, the various succession crises of the mid-eighteenth century had also spawned a succession of ambitious would-be monarchs – though why anyone would wish to choose that particular career path, given the actuarial risks involved, is difficult to comprehend. These two traditions – popular revolt and regal pretence – came together in the notoriously flamboyant figure of Emelyan Ivanovich Pugachёv, renegade cossak, revolutionary and rabble-rouser *extraordinaire*.[11]

The early years of Pugachёv's career, as Don cossak, soldier in the Seven Years' and Russo-Turkish Wars, deserter, reputed Old Believer, prisoner, escapee and flagellated fugitive from officialdom need not detain us here. Suffice it to say that in 1773 he made his appearance among the Yaik river cossak host, which had recently suffered a number of indignities and curtailments of their traditional liberties, inflicted on them by the regional and central authorities, leaving them in a highly charged state of potential rebellion. Whether as a result of popular gullibility, disingenuousness or readiness to accept any pretext for revolt, the Yaik cossaks eagerly accepted Pugachёv's outrageous claim to be their rightful monarch, Peter III, who, he declared, had survived the dastardly plot to assassinate him (see Chapter 5), spent a dozen years on the run, and had now returned among them to restore their rights and redress their grievances by overthrowing the foreign usurper. (The fact that Peter himself was the bantling of a petty German prince was no doubt lost on them.) While his self-proclamation may stretch the credulity of the modern reader, it must be remembered that the phenomenon of false claimants to the throne was common in eighteenth-century Russia, and in any case no one on the remote river Yaik had ever seen the real Peter III in the flesh, or even in illustration. Hence, any lack of physical resemblance was not an issue. The stark facts were as follows. First, the southern cossaks were tinder-dry material for rebellious conflagration. Second, the central government was still enmeshed in a foreign war, and negligent of what appeared to be just another borderland brushfire. Third, apart from the cossaks, there were further widespread grievances among the common folk of Russia, who were clamouring for justice and retribution against their oppressors. Fourth, Pugachëv seemed to offer a real possibility for redress of their social, economic, religious and ethnic grudges. Fifth, despite the obscurity of his origins, he was a forceful personality who, by contemporary accounts, exuded great qualities of leadership, inspiration and powerful charisma in a highly volatile and potentially explosive environment. Finally, he responded to a primordial, almost messianic yearning among the common people for the appearance of a 'rightful', just ruler who would miraculously restore a mythical, lost golden age. The fact that he was a lowly cossak claiming to be tsar of Russia was neither here nor there. As one of his close accomplices remarked, 'It does not matter to us whether he is the sovereign or not. Out of mud one can make a prince.'[12]

On 17 September 1773, Pugachëv issued his first manifesto (written on his behalf, as he was himself illiterate) to the already mutinous Yaik cossaks, promising them absolution, water, land, money, lead, powder and grain, and marched with over 2000 followers on the frontier fortress town of Orenburg, taking other outposts en route and slaughtering their defenders. More and more disparate and disgruntled elements of Russian society – fugitive serfs, religious schismatics, foundry workers, vagrants, escaped convicts and exiles, local tribesmen (Bashkirs, Tatars, Kalmyks, Kirghiz and Kazakhs), bandits, army deserters and even dispossessed petty gentry – flocked to Pugachëv's banner. Many had genuine cause to take up arms against an oppressive state, while others no doubt simply clambered onto the bandwagon of a bellicose popular hero, revelling in the opportunity for revenge, rapine and retribution against the local ruling classes. However, the sheer heterogeneity of his motley supporters – ill-equipped, mutually antagonistic, unruly and disunited in their goals – did not bode well for the success of Pugachëv's audacious enterprise. Despite these inauspicious circumstances, it is astonishing how widely and rapidly the rebellion flared across the empire's southern marches, and how easily and mercilessly the local landlords and garrisons fell before the insurgent hordes. Rape, pillage, arson, lynch-law, discriminate slaughter and all kinds of atrocity were perpetrated by Pugachëv's rampant forerunners of the French *sans-culottes*.

Orenburg managed to withstand a six-month siege, while other outposts were overrun and huge expanses of the southern Volga regions and the central Urals came under Pugachëv's control. In July 1774, the administrative and commercial centre of the Volga area, Kazan, was sacked, torched and briefly occupied by Pugachëv's plunderers, until finally relieved by government forces under the command of Colonel I. I. Mikhelson. The razing of Kazan finally struck genuine fear in the heart of government, and the spread of the pretender's support throughout the cis-Uralian provinces of the empire provoked a real panic that Moscow, and even the distant capital of St Petersburg, were vulnerable to the insurgents' attack.

Isabel de Madariaga, one of the finest historians of Catherine's reign, has argued that the empress's policy vis-à-vis the enserfed peasants was not as harsh as it has traditionally been portrayed.[13] However, and despite Professor de Madariaga's arguments, there can be little doubt that, from the point of view of an 'average' serf, festering, semi-starving, cowering and fearing the lash and the military levy in the depths of the Russian countryside, there was every reason to rally to Pugachëv's call. The peasants *were* exploited, they *were* over-taxed, they *were* still subject to conscription, to corporal punishment, to religious persecution and to all the personal humiliations inherent in mediaeval feudalism. It is no surprise, therefore, that the peasant jacquerie which broke out in the summer of 1774, prompted by the cossaks' initial insurgence, represented the most dangerous threat to the stability of the Russian state since the Time of Troubles. Huge tracts of the empire's southern and central provinces were affected; up to three million people were caught up in the rampage; the ancient capital, Moscow, was menaced; local authorities, both military and civilian, seemed impotent in the face of the popular upsurge; and Catherine herself was finally forced to sit up and take serious notice of the man she had earlier contemptuously dismissed as '*le Marquis Pugacheff*'.

The devastation caused by the rebel forces, and the threat to Catherine's regime, was eventually brought to an end by a conjunction of circumstances. First, Pugachëv's own personal credibility and charisma were beginning to wear rather thin, and his authority was increasingly being questioned by members of his own entourage, whom the impostor had encouraged to ape the composition, titles and names of dignitaries of the imperial court, a charade which was patently unsustainable, and ultimately led to the pretender's betrayal. Second, the range of interests, mentioned above, of the variegated components of his followers, which included cossaks, serfs, non-Russian tribesmen, Urals miners and factory workers, brigands, penurious petty nobles, deserters, dissidents, vagabonds and simple villains, did not provide the raw material for any kind of concerted, coordinated or cohesive political action against the state, based on a united, coherent social and political programme. Third, despite Pugachëv's reputation as an able military commander, ultimately his ragtag-and-bobtail mob of untrained, undisciplined and under-armed troops were no match for the drilled soldiers, officers, regiments and generals of Catherine's regular army. In the initial stages of the uprising, Catherine's attention was focused on her foreign wars, but following the signing of the treaty of Kuçuk Kainardzi in July 1774, battle-hardened fighters, under the command of experienced commanders, returned from the Turkish front to face, and defeat, the domestic foe.

No match for Catherine's professional legions, Pugachëv's hordes were swiftly ground down and their leader finally betrayed, captured and handed over to an officer of the imperial guards. Pugachëv himself was placed in an iron cage and transported to Moscow, where he was imprisoned and subjected to a month-long intensive interrogation under the supervision of the notorious head of Catherine's security service, Stepan Sheshkovskii. Catherine's main concern was to ascertain whether *le Marquis Pugacheff* was the tool of some foreign conspiracy against her rule, but finally had to accept that he was exactly what he was – the figurehead of a vast and violent uprising of the empress's own subjects against her government's oppressive and dictatorial rule. After the long process of aggressive interrogation, Pugachëv and his immediate accomplices were finally condemned to death in a swift and secret trial conducted by a handful of civilian and religious dignitaries. On 10 January 1775, he was conveyed on a tumbrel from his dungeon in the Moscow Kremlin to Bolotnaya Square on the banks of the river Moskva, and before an audience of thousands of Muscovites, publicly beheaded and his body chopped into pieces. Jealous of her reputation in Europe for her magnanimity and compassion, the enlightened

'Semiramis of the North' had instructed that, in order to prevent unnecessary torment, Pugachëv's head should be severed first, before the executioners began their work in carving up the rest of his members and placing them on public display. The watching crowds were entertained by other acts of punitive butchery performed on Pugachëv's closest henchmen, which lasted for several hours and no doubt satiated the bloodlust of the Muscovite mob. Not content with this sanguinary spectacle of official vengeance, Catherine ordered the arrest, exile or execution of thousands of his supporters in the rebellious provinces. Members of his immediate family were imprisoned in perpetuity, one of his daughters dying in her dungeon as late as 1834. The village where Pugachëv was born was razed to the ground and its inhabitants forcibly relocated. The river Yaik was renamed as the Ural, as was the Yaik cossak host. By an imperial decree of 15 March 1775, all mention of the rebellion was consigned to 'eternal oblivion and profound silence'.[14] Finally, in order to encourage the process of writing Pugachëv out of history, Catherine issued a general amnesty to the surviving mutineers.

However, notwithstanding Catherine's attempts to expunge the memory of Pugachëv from the public mind, his spectre continued to haunt the corridors of the Winter Palace and scare the Romanov tsars out of their limited wits for the coming century. He and his peasant bands also served as a shining inspiration for generations of future Populist Russian revolutionaries. Not for nothing was Emelyan Pugachëv, alias Emperor Peter III, revered in Russian folk memory as the 'people's tsar'. Hobsbawmian 'social bandit', Russian Robin Hood writ large, or merely a vicious, vengeful plebeian upstart lusting for blood and power, Emelyan Pugachëv has left his indelible imprint on Russian history as both the archetypal embodiment of violent popular protest, and the ultimately unsuccessful, but unforgettable, nemesis of imperial hubris.[15]

Having finally dealt with the bogus reincarnation of her murdered husband, Catherine was now free to address herself to her legislative programme.

'Reactive legislation syndrome'

It is common practice for governments everywhere – in reaction to a national threat or crisis, whether real, perceived or concocted for immediate political purposes – to respond by rushing through a series of legislative measures which may at the same time be well meant and ill-conceived. Emergency acts, decrees and laws are on occasion promulgated in order to ensure that conditions and preventative or punitive measures are put in force which will obviate or occlude a recurrence of a similar situation or crisis. Hence the condition referred to here as 'reactive legislation syndrome'.[16] In the aftermath of the *Pugachëvshchina*, Catherine displayed all the classic symptoms of this pathological state, which she herself described as 'a new sickness called legislomania'.[17]

First, given that Pugachëv's rebellion had spread so rapidly and so far – partly as a result of the feebleness of Russia's provincial administration – the empress immediately embarked on a complete overhaul of local government bodies and practices throughout her dominion. This was finally brought into legislative effect with her decree on 'Institutions for the Governance of the Provinces' (*Uchrezhdeniya dlya upravleniya gubernii*), promulgated on 7 November 1775, barely ten months after Pugachëv's grisly public execution and dismemberment. This was a piece of law-making of which Catherine herself was the chief author, although, as with her great *Nakaz*, it drew heavily on the works of foreign luminaries, this time including the publication of the great English legal scholar and former Vinerian Professor of English Law at the University of Oxford, Sir William Blackstone (1723–80). Blackstone's renowned *Commentaries on the Laws of England,* originally published between 1765 and 1769, and released in French translation starting from 1774, had occupied Catherine's reading hours throughout the summer of 1775, while she drafted her proposed provincial reform. In this her aim was simply to 'streamline' the local administration of her empire and to give more executive authority to her appointed regional officials, while at the same time paying lip-service to the principle of elective participation in local government.

To begin with, the territorial-administrative map of the Romanov Empire created by Peter the Great was redrawn. Russia was now divided into not 12 but 50 provinces (*gubernii*), each with its own appointed governor-general and a team of local administrators. These local officials were both elected and appointed, though the elected officers were generally of a lower social status than the appointed ones, and exercised no independence or autonomy in the discharge of their functions. The result was the creation of a rather lowly esteemed provincial bureaucracy charged with the administration of public matters such as education, finance, policing, and medical and charitable work. Actual policy making was not within their remit. Despite the apparent attempt to devolve power as a means to greater efficiency, the centrally appointed higher provincial officials, in cahoots with the wealthier local landowning nobility, ensured that nothing like genuine regional self-government with popular involvement was achieved. However, the general framework of provincial administration, with some later minor alterations, was to remain in place until the revolutions of 1917, though the local government reforms of Alexander II (r. 1856–81) did bring about some significant, though limited, changes in the operation of public services and amenities (see Chapter 9).

A planned reform of municipal government was inaugurated with the promulgation of the Charter to the Towns in 1785, but despite the provisions of this legislation, including the election of city councils by members of the various categories of the urban population, in fact the governance of Russia's towns and cities remained firmly in the hands of appointed officials headed by the 'mayor' (*gorodnichii*) and his cronies. (The corruption, and also the obsequious submissiveness of small-town officialdom before the central authorities is hilariously lampooned in Nikolai Gogol's satirical comedy, 'The Government Inspector' (*Revizor*, 1836), described by Mirsky as 'doubtless the greatest play in the Russian language'.[18])

Catherine's attempts at streamlining provincial and municipal government were bedevilled by rampant corruption, scarcity of sufficient trained and educated personnel, lack of adequate funding, and an absence of any tradition or experience of corporate responsibility or public participation in the properly regulated conduct of civil affairs. Underlying all this, despite the empress's intellectual dalliance with the legal worthies of the west – notably Montesquieu, Beccaria and Blackstone – Russia had no proper tradition or the institutions of 'the rule of law' as understood and, with varying degrees of justice, practised in the west. Nor was there any concept in Russia of the separation of the powers – legislative, executive and judicial – which meant that the political authorities, the administrative agencies, powerful individuals and administrators of such questionable criminal and civil laws as existed were often indistinguishable. This in turn meant that corrupt bureaucrats, perpetrators of malfeasance in office and other abusers of their public position were more or less immune from any jurisprudential procedure, responsibility or retribution. In the final analysis, the governmental system presided over by Catherine, the great *legislatrix*, had no proper foundation in law. Klyuchevskii's conclusion is that Catherine's declared espousal of the principles of the European Enlightenment in implementing her domestic legislation was belied by her provincial reform which 'reeked (*pakhlo*) of the mediaeval, feudal order'.[19]

One of the side effects of the provincial reform was that many of the powers of the central government institutions – the colleges – established by Peter the Great (see Chapter 4) became redundant as their functions began to be taken over by local agencies. In this way, between 1780 and 1788, six of the original departments of state were piecemeal abolished, leaving only the army, the admiralty and foreign affairs as central government departments. Likewise, the already limited powers of the 'ruling' Senate were eroded under Catherine as most of the important policy-making decisions continued to be taken by herself, her favourites and her personally appointed minions. Ultimately, of course, it was the personal whim, caprice, conviction or mere fancy of the empress herself which dictated the conduct of all public affairs, whether in the realms of domestic or foreign policy.

That said, despite the apparent impregnability of her position, Catherine was still circumspect enough to comprehend that she still needed to maintain the support of the most powerful section of society, to whit the landowning nobility, the *dvoryanstvo*. It will be remembered that during the reigns of Anna and Elizabeth, the nobility had managed to secure for itself a gradual easing of the strict state service obligations imposed on them by Peter the Great. This had culminated in Peter III's Manifesto to the Nobility in 1762, the provisions of which were described in the previous chapter. Despite its newly won privileges, the noble estate was still not entirely free of its responsibilities vis-à-vis the state, and Catherine was to acknowledge her debt to their continuing support by providing the icing on the nobles' cake under the terms of her Charter to the Nobility (*Zhalovannaya gramota dvoryanstvu*) of 1785, issued on the same day, 21 April, as the Charter to the Towns. Its most important provisions were as follows: (i) confirmation of the nobles' absolute right to their immovable property and the serfs living thereon; (ii) exemption from the forfeiture of a noble's rank and title except by trial of his peers for recognised offences, the sentence to be confirmed by highest authority; (iii) immunity from corporal punishment, and exemption from personal taxation and military recruitment; (iv) ratification of the rights contained in Peter's Manifesto to travel abroad and enter the service of friendly foreign states; (v) permission for nobles to own factories and to exploit mineral resources on their estates; and (vi) the granting to members of the hereditary nobility the right to form corporations, each headed by an elected marshal of the nobility, which had certain regional administrative duties and which were allowed to petition the empress on matters of a purely local nature.[20]

Unlike the contents of the Great *Nakaz*, the Charter to the Nobility was not based on or infused with any philosophical, ethical or political principles. It merely spelled out the personal and corporate freedoms of members of the noble estate, transforming it from a class of compulsory state servitors into something approaching a full-fledged, privileged, leisured, land- and serf-owning aristocracy. However, the nobility failed to use its freedom to exercise any collective pressure on the autocracy to limit in any way the absolute powers of that institution. It was in fact the autocracy which guaranteed the rights and prerogatives of the nobility, in return for which the nobility – apart from isolated, individual aberrations – fully supported the autocracy in the exercise of its sovereign power. The reign of Catherine the Great has traditionally been regarded as the 'Golden Age of the Russian Nobility', and indeed the symbiotic relationship between the supreme autocrat and the thousands of local petty autocrats wielding extensive personal powers over their serfs and their estates was to remain intact as the cornerstone of the Russian political, social and economic order for the foreseeable future. To echo Klyuchevskii's words quoted above, despite educated society's familiarity with the intoxicating ideas of the European Enlightenment, Russia at the end of the eighteenth century remained an essentially feudal society based on the mediaeval institution of serfdom.

Indeed, rather than granting greater freedoms to her servile subjects, and – *pace* de Madariaga's 'reappraisal' of peasant policies referred to above – Catherine was responsible for extending and exacerbating the conditions of serfdom during her reign. This was the result of two major factors. First was the policy of introducing the system into newly conquered territories of the Russian Empire where it was previously either unknown or extinct; second, Catherine's regular practice of lavishing gifts of state-owned land, together with their peasant populations, as rewards for services rendered by her favourites and generals, thereby transforming at a stroke those peasants' status from that of state peasant – whose lot was rather less onerous – to that of privately owned serf. This practice was continued with even greater prodigality by her son and successor, Paul (see Chapter 7). According to Semevskii's calculations, based on official census materials, between 1762 and 1796 the male serf population of Russia and Siberia, excluding Ukraine, rose from 3.8 million to 5.7 million, around 53 per cent of the total male peasant population.[21] Overburdened with their feudal labour obligations, ignorant, tax-ridden, pox-ridden, subject to their master's or mistress's caprice and living in constant fear of conscription and the lash, it is small wonder that the peasantry proved to be such highly combustible material for the steppe-fire raised by Pugachëv. After that was finally extinguished, it was only by the use of superior military force, together with terrifying punitive practices that the imperial regime was able to contain the still potentially explosive forces of peasant revolt more or less in check during the next century. Apart from their internal duties, however, Catherine's armed forces were constantly deployed throughout her reign in the pursuit of her ambitious foreign goals. Before an examination of post-Pugachëv foreign policies, however, it is appropriate briefly to divert attention to what has variously been described as Catherine's 'favouritism', 'nymphomania' or plain 'lechery'.[22]

Passion and politics: Catherine's sex life

This section is not intended to pander to the prurient minded, but the notoriety of Catherine's sexual appetites, habits and exploits – particularly for a female of her supreme power and authority – makes it a legitimate subject for serious scholarly analysis. A perusal of the relevant literature severally indicates that Catherine granted her intimate physical favours to anything from a dozen-or-so to 300 lovers. The latter figure may be safely dismissed – the only source being a quotation attributed to the American actress Mae West, who portrayed the empress in a 1940s Broadway revue, suggestively entitled *Catherine Was Great*, during a two-hour performance.[23] There is, however, rigid historical evidence that Catherine both covertly and openly entertained a fair variety of courtiers, generals, officers, secretaries, nobles and confidants during her long and busy reign. There is, however, no reliable evidence to support malign gossip of a perverse predilection for equestrian bedroom amusements. Her studful of human partners seems to have been just about up to the task of satisfying her considerable libido.

The roll-call of the most favourite of the empress's favourites is well known: Sergei Saltykov (probable sire of the future emperor, Paul); Stanisław Poniatowski (subsequently king of Poland); Grigorii Orlov (main organiser of the conspiracy which brought Catherine to the throne); Alexander Vassilchikov (his, a brief and unsatisfying affair); Grigorii Potëmkin (Prince of Taurida and the major love of her life – see below); Pëtr Zavadovskii (her very personal secretary); Semën Zorich (Serbian army officer); Ivan Rimskii-Korsakov (military officer and ancestor of the famous composer, dumped by Catherine for bedding one of her ladies-in-waiting); Aleksandr Lanskoi (guards officer, doted on by Catherine, died of diphtheria in 1784, much to her distress); Aleksandr Yermolov (a short, unremarkable fling); Aleksandr Dmitriev-Mamonov (related to Potëmkin, survived a three-year stint, finally discharged for the same reason as Rimskii-Korsakov, though with several ladies-in-waiting); Platon Zubov (38 years younger than Catherine, her last known lover and later one of the plotters in the overthrow and murder of her son, Paul, in 1801 – see Chapter 7).

So, while still in her teens, and already married to the future emperor, Peter III, Catherine's affair with the young court chamberlain, Sergei Saltykov (1726–??), resulted, so evidence suggests, in the birth of another future emperor, Paul, who was immediately removed by Empress Elizabeth from Catherine's direct maternal nurture and supervision. In her 68th year, shortly before her death, she was still conducting her last, distinctly unplatonic, relationship with young Platon Zubov (1767–1822). Between times, as indicated above, she managed to fit in a sizeable platoon of ready, willing and able servitors, of some of whom she was genuinely enamoured, and others of whom she quickly tired and dismissed from their duties, though never apparently with malice or rancour, even when she herself had been deceived. Indeed, after their withdrawal from royal favours, most of them were handsomely rewarded with honours, titles, land and serfs in gracious recognition of past services rendered. Although it seems that, as the lady grew older, her lovers were progressively younger and less intelligent, one man in particular both dominated her passions and outdistanced his rivals for her affection for over two decades, even when their physical intimacy ceased. That man was Prince Grigorii Aleksandrovich Potëmkin (1739–91), brilliant general, clever diplomat, energetic lover, witty raconteur, monocular poseur – in fact, generously endowed in every respect, and in all probability Catherine's clandestine husband. If that probability were actually the case, the marriage was never made public knowledge. Most reputable modern western historians of Catherine's reign seem to agree on the firm likelihood of the union, as does Potëmkin's most recent biographer.[24]

The long-standing, passionate and at times tempestuous relationship between the empress and the prince – whom she addressed in their intimate correspondence variously as her 'Cossak', '*Giaour*', 'Tiger', 'Golden Cock' (*sic*), *mon époux* (i.e. 'husband'), and even, perhaps surprisingly, as 'my Pugachëv' – deserves some attention as it most dramatically illustrates the phenomenon of 'favouritism' and the close, mutual interrelationship between personal passion and public politics in Catherine's life. The great Soviet Marxist historian, Mikhail Pokrovskii, somewhere defined the word 'favourite' in this context as merely a euphemism for someone having regular sexual relations with the reigning monarch. While that is perfectly true, it is also the case that the shared intimacies, opinions, advice, confidences and pillow-talk exchanged between the ruler of a great empire and her current bedfellow might have enormous potential consequences in the formulation of political, economic, social and military policies. This was particularly so in Catherine's case in view of her penchant for selecting powerfully built, ambitious military figures as her ephemeral or more durable consorts.

To take some obvious cases: Sergei Saltykov, as already mentioned, was almost certainly the natural father of the future emperor Paul – Catherine's affair with the young courtier thus having direct dynastic consequences on the Romanov succession. Grigorii Orlov and his brother, Aleksei, were the prime movers in Catherine's bid for the throne in 1762 and also responsible for her husband's assassination (see Chapter 5). The repercussions of that murderous conspiracy, partly orchestrated by Catherine's then lover, can hardly be exaggerated, though it has to be said that, even without the sexual connection with Orlov, the coup would in all probability still have taken place. Orlov continued to be a major influence on the conduct of his lover's domestic and foreign policies over the next ten years or so until his repeated infidelities finally became too much for Catherine to endure. After briefly dabbling with Vassilchikov, whose input was minimal, the restless empress turned next to Potëmkin, without doubt the major political and physical influence in her public and private life.

Potëmkin was first introduced into Catherine's company in 1762, though it is not clear when they first became physically intimate. It was, however, some time early in 1774, when the 44-year-old Catherine, still emotionally distressed by the cooling of the former ardour between herself and Orlov, and now craving both carnal and intellectual satisfaction, summoned the recently promoted 34-year-old Lieutenant-General to return from military campaigning against the Turks to the court at St Petersburg. Ever since their first meeting, Potëmkin had nurtured an ambitious, and not-so-secret yearning for his empress's favours, and now, encouraged by the transparently coded message of availability contained in Catherine's letter, he hastened to the capital no doubt eager to match his exploits on the battlefield with equal bravura in the royal bedchamber where the pathway to power and influence lay open wide. There was, however, a brief period of rather bizarre, no-contact foreplay, during which Potëmkin rather melodramatically retired to a monastery until his inamorata, quickly tiring of the tedious dalliance, finally succumbed to what they both knew was the inevitable. Thus began a long, torrid and rapturous liaison during which the mutually infatuated couple held not only each other but also the destiny of the entire Russian Empire in their embrace. From then on, Potëmkin's career remained firmly on the up and up, he being constantly showered with ever more extravagant honours, promotions, titles and offices both on and off the field of battle, while spurring his mistress on with ever more grandiosely ambitious schemes for the military glory and territorial aggrandisement of the imperial realm of which he was soon co-regent in all but name.

Rapidly advancing from Lieutenant-General to General, on to Field Marshal and virtual Minister of War, Admiral of the Black Sea Fleet, Viceroy of the southern provinces, and His Most Serene Highness, Prince of Taurida, Potëmkin became the virtual master of Catherine's military and foreign policy. His most audacious imperial plan – the so-called 'Greek project' – was to inspire Catherine's ambition to defeat and oust the Ottoman Turks from Europe, restore the glories of the Byzantine Empire under her rule, and place her second grandson, significantly baptised as Constantine, on the throne of Constantinople. This over-ambitious project is discussed in the following section. As far as its major promoter is concerned, Potëmkin, despite his ultimate aim never materialising, continued to bask in Catherine's favour even after he had ceased to share her bed on a regular basis, and not only remained one of her closest confidants and advisers, but, according to rumour, also vicariously ensured that her sexual needs continued to be satisfied by occasionally participating in the selection and introduction of a number of her succeeding lovers (though de Madariaga dismisses this allegation as lacking evidential foundation). Thus, Potëmkin, possible pimp, and arguably the most powerful non-royal personage in the entire history of the Romanov Empire, remained at the centre of Catherine's affections and continued to guide her domestic, foreign and most personal affairs until his death in 1791, five years before that of the empress whose power and passions he had so dramatically and decisively shared for so long.

Of an altogether different and lesser calibre was the young man destined to be Catherine's latest and last lover, the imperial toyboy, Platon Aleksandrovich Zubov, his mistress's junior by nearly 40 years, to whom the most commonly applied epithets, apart from small, dark and handsome, include 'mediocre', 'dim-witted', 'shallow', 'vain' and 'ambitious'. It was doubtless his vanity and ambition which drove him to reconcile his own youthfulness with the advancing age of the now obese, fading and flatulent empress. With far less justification, the scheming upstart was granted almost as many honorific titles and offices as had been Potëmkin, Catherine's still-powerful soulmate, for whom Zubov entertained a genuine dislike and whose continuing influence over his elderly mistress he persistently manoeuvred to undermine. Also, like Potëmkin, he, too, sought to fire up the failing Catherine's still smouldering ambition for grand military adventures, trying to trump the prince's much-vaunted 'Greek project' with his own more fanciful 'Oriental project', which was as vacuous as it was vainglorious (see below). Catherine responded to his calculated attentions with a mixture of genuine affection, quasi-maternal indulgence and senescent coquetry. Contemporary accounts of the Zubov *affaire*, as well as Catherine's own drooling correspondence, even in her letters to Potëmkin, leave one with the almost grotesque, but also rather sad image of a fat old broiling fowl clucking besottedly over a post-pubescent peacock chick. Furthermore, Catherine's literally doting bounteousness in terms of the material rewards and lavish endowments bestowed upon her final favourite was no less of a drain on the imperial coffers than the generosity routinely extended to her previous paramours. Reference to this prodigal practice brings us to an evaluation of not only the financial, but also the political and moral ramifications of Catherine's apparently insatiable venereal appetite and the whole unsavoury phenomenon of 'favouritism'.

First, on the economic question, there is little doubt that the monarch's munificence in showering her lovers, both in and out of service, with vast estates, gold plate, jewellery, millions of rubles, sumptuous palaces and tens of thousands of peasant serfs proved to be an incalculable loss to the national exchequer. This regular practice led at the same time to the obscene enrichment of a handful of people, some of whom would otherwise be regarded as utter nonentities, and the continuing impoverishment and virtual enslavement of millions of Catherine's subjects who, of course, were in total ignorance of this shameless squandering of the national wealth on purely, or impurely, personal extravagances and in paying off superannuated companions of the royal bedchamber.

The situation was further compounded by the fabulously huge amounts from the country's treasury which were expended in pursuit of Catherine's military and territorial ambitions, often on the self-seeking advice of her current mating partner, and often in fulfilment of little more than a lust for martial glory and imperial aggrandisement at the added cost of spilling oceans of the people's blood. While in strictly military and political terms, Russia's triumphs may be counted as a series of foreign policy successes for the warrior queen, for her victorious generals and her scheming diplomats, on the higher scale of social and popular benefit, they were nothing short of a tragically unjustifiable waste of the nation's material and human resources. Nevertheless, while Catherine's ephemeral flirtations and more enduring amatory relationships did at times have a deep, dramatic impact on imperial policy-making, advantage-seeking or waging war, the strong-minded and iron-willed empress never allowed herself to be swayed or persuaded solely or merely by the urgings and importunities of whoever happened to be her current heart-throb.

Finally, the morality, immorality or amorality of Catherine's sexual exploits need to be judged or evaluated in their proper context, and in their peculiar historical, social and cultural setting. It must be borne in mind that here we are dealing with a robust, energetic, physically sensual woman with healthy bodily and natural emotional needs, living in a hothouse environment where court intrigues, dangerous liaisons, routine adultery, bed-hopping, partner-swapping and quotidian concupiscence were endemic. Although obviously in breach of a strictly Christian ethic of moral, marital or even extra-marital probity, in which the virtues of chastity, purity and fidelity are extolled, within the context of contemporary mores in St Petersburg high society, Catherine's behaviour was by no means either abnormal or excessive. Indeed, fornication and sexual promiscuity were almost *de rigueur* in that environment. But whether it were a passing peccadillo or a fiercely burning *grande passion*, an ardent, deeply heartfelt love or a one-night stand, for Catherine her public duty as mistress of her vast domain (whatever the actual cost to the public) always took precedence over her activities as the mistress of this, that or the other object of her current infatuation. Even when there was a more than usually close involvement, as in the case of Potëmkin in particular, she was always able to keep a proper balance between affairs of state and affairs of the heart. Nor, as will be seen in the following section, did Catherine neglect the finer things in the cultural, artistic and intellectual life of her country, although the benefits of her patronage in this respect were of course confined to the privileged elite of Russian society. She plunged herself with equal enthusiasm into the pleasures of the mind and the delights of the body. To borrow from the taxonomy of palæoanthropology, whether she were engaged in intellectual discourse with the finest minds of the European Enlightenment, or in rather less cerebral intercourse with some muscular guardsman,

Catherine proved to be equally as comfortable in the company of the most accomplished specimens of contemporary *Homo sapiens* as of the less sophisticated *Homo erectus*.

Libidinous, lascivious – even licentious – her behaviour certainly was, but there is little real evidence which lends credence to the more salacious legends of perverted practices or obscene orgies; of Potëmkin's plaster-cast phallus with which she consoled herself during his absences; of preliminary trials of her suitors' sexual stamina carried out by her ladies-in-waiting; or of nocturnal horse-play. Whether or not making an oblique allusion to Catherine's preferred *in coitu* posture, John Alexander is surely right, in his assessment of Catherine the Great's love life, to conclude that: 'A nymphomaniac she was not, but a normal person in an abnormal position.'[25]

Foreign policy (ii)

It has been noted above that, among Catherine's favourites, Grigorii Potëmkin played an especially dominant role in influencing the direction of her foreign policies and military affairs. As in the first decade or so of her reign, her twin major preoccupations in what may be called the post-Pugachëv period continued to be the questions of Turkey and Poland. Against the background of shifting alliances with the major European powers, during which Russia edged further away from Prussia while simultaneously drawing closer to Austria, the newly ascendant Potëmkin stoked the fires of Catherine's interest in expanding further southwards at the expense of the Ottoman Empire, which was already showing signs of internal debility. Russia's ambitions in this direction, as indicated above, were most grandiosely and romantically expressed in the 'Greek project', the main objects of which were as audacious as they were amorphous. It envisaged the total political reorganisation of the Balkans; the expulsion of the Turks from the European side of the Bosphorus; the re-establishment of a Byzantine mini-empire ruled over by Catherine's grandson, Constantine; the amalgamation of the Danubian principalities of Moldavia, Walachia and Bessarabia into an independent kingdom of Dacia, in all probability with Potëmkin as its monarch; the annexation of the Crimean peninsula and further encroachments on the northern coast of the Black Sea.

Until the turn of the decade, Catherine avoided embroilment in any major foreign conflicts, beyond playing a diplomatic role in settling the brief War of the Bavarian Succession (1778–9), and maintaining a judiciously non-aligned position during the American War of Independence (1775–83) through a policy of 'armed neutrality', by which Catherine displayed her equal distaste for American republicanism and King George III of England. It was clear to both Catherine and Potëmkin that even an attempt at realising the Greek project could not be contemplated without the cooperation or at least tacit support of Austria – which was eventually acquired as a result of the warming relationship between Catherine and the Austrian emperor, Joseph II, following the death of Maria Theresa in 1780. After much imperial sabre-rattling, Catherine made the first lunge in the south by the military and political occupation of the Crimea in 1783 and its formal incorporation into the Russian Empire. Austria nodded its approval; Britain, Prussia and France looked askance; Turkey was appalled; and the Crimean Tatars sullenly bowed to the inevitable. In Russia's newly expanded southern territories, Potëmkin acted with vice-regal powers to consolidate, settle and colonise the region, continuing the policies introduced by Catherine early in her reign of encouraging immigration, foreign settlement and the economic development of what became collectively known as 'New Russia'. A motley collection of Serbs, Swabians, and Scots, Armenians, Balts and Prussian Mennonites, farmers, merchants, artisans, breeders of merino sheep and viticulturalists helped to transform Catherine's southern domains into one of the most cosmopolitan and commercially successful regions of her empire.[26] The crust of success, was, however, only wafer-thin, and below the surface there continued to fester the age-old Russian problems of poverty, exploitation, ignorance, savagery and serfdom. The sparkling facade of Catherine's achievement which masked the misery of her people is nowhere better exemplified than in the infamous 'Potëmkin villages', or at least in the legends of such, which attended her grand tour of her southern possessions in 1787.

On 7 January of that year, Catherine – accompanied by a huge, sumptuously appointed entourage of coaches, sledges, horses, servants, soldiers, courtiers, ambassadors, princes, handmaids, and scores of other sundry officials and acolytes – set off from Tsarskoe Selo to embark on a spectacular, six-month expedition. The object of this elaborate and exhausting journey was not only to conduct a personal inspection of the southern empire, including her new Crimean prize, but also to make a grand imperial statement to the world – not least to the Turkish sultan – concerning the extent, the might and magnificence of the Semiramis of the North's enormous power in the south. Chief coordinator, choreographer and great panjandrum in charge of this royal pageant was of course His Serene Highness, Prince Grigorii Potëmkin, who spared nothing in the expenditure of money and manpower in providing his imperial mistress with a lavish extravaganza of brilliantly stage-managed spectacles and *mises en scène* designed to provide a dazzling illustration of the prosperity, the prowess and the permanence of Catherine's 'New Russia' and its grateful population. In Kiev and Kherson, amid the semi-oriental splendours of the Crimea's capital, Bakhchisarai, on the battlefield of Poltava, where Peter's famous victory over the Swedes in 1709 was re-enacted with a cast of thousands, and in countless towns and tiny villages *en route*, the empress was left in little doubt as to the seemingly limitless extent of her personal popularity and her imperial omnipotence.

Rumours soon became rife, however, that Potëmkin's elaborate displays were literally a façade, a fabricated ensemble of stage sets, prosperous-looking model villages with artificially contrived props representing a rustic scenario full of waving, happy, well-fed, gaily dressed peasants flocking to gawp and cheer at their beloved empress. The genuine rural squalor, the poverty, the hunger and the oppression of the enserfed masses were hidden from the empress's fleeting view by the sham cottage fronts and imported extras, rehearsed to impersonate the fictitiously fruitful peasant population of the 'Potëmkin village', a term that is now a byword for anything bogus, superficially masquerading as something wholesome and attractive, which is in reality shameful, unattractive or grim. Potëmkin's modern biographer, Simon Montefiore, ever reluctant to detract from the fawning adulation of his hero, raises some legitimate questions over the authenticity of the Potëmkin village, declaring that the mendacious stories of these mock edifices were a bigger sham than the purported originals.[27] However that may be, the fact that the allegations stuck, and are still given credence by reputable historians, is a token of the realisation that the ostentatious exhibitions, the mock battles, the costume dramas, all the gaudy displays of gross sensationalism which *were* staged by Potëmkin throughout Catherine's theatrical pilgrimage, were a far cry from the harsh reality and starkly drawn wretchedness of Catherine's Russia as experienced in the daily drudgery of her people. If Potëmkin's villages were a figment of his detractors' imagination, then equally fantastical was the looking-glass world of *ersatz* imperial splendour and military *braggadocio* which he constructed for his sovereign lady's delectation.

Catherine's journey, if nothing else, succeeded in flaunting her power in the face of the Sublime Porte and provided a direct provocation for the resumption of hostilities between the two rival powers. Shortly after Catherine's return to St Petersburg, Turkey in effect declared war by demanding the return of the Crimea, accusing Russia of violating the treaty of Kuçuk Kainardzi and imprisoning the Russian envoy, Ya. I. Bulgakov. Catherine's second war against Turkey lasted from the summer of 1787 until 1792. Hostilities were exacerbated by Sweden's declaration of war on Russia in 1788 in the hope of regaining lost territories while Catherine was otherwise engaged. The outbreak of the French Revolution in 1789, the death of Catherine's Austrian ally, Joseph II, in 1790, and the continuing reluctance of England and Prussia to become embroiled further complicated the situation. However, a rapid conclusion of the conflict with Sweden and a series of military successes against Turkish forces eventually resulted in peace negotiations culminating in the Treaty of Jassy which, after three years' fruitless warfare, merely restored the *status quo ante bellum* with no gain to either side. Potëmkin's fledgling Greek project had turned out to be a dead duck.

Catherine's hands were now free to deal with what remained of post-partition Poland, where a nationalist revolt against Russian rule had taken place in 1791. Having taken advantage of Catherine's preoccupation with Turkey and Sweden, and with the cautious approval of Prussia, in May 1791 the Polish *Sejm* adopted a new constitution, abolished the country's elective kingship and the controversial *liberum veto* (see above), and also cancelled the nobility's ancient right to form independent confederacies. Catherine regarded this independent action as no less than a manifestation of revolutionary Jacobinism sweeping eastwards from France, though it is difficult to see how the increased power of the throne and the corresponding curtailment of the powers of parliament could be so interpreted.

However, anxious to smother the spirit of Polish independence, Catherine dispatched her troops to meet this threat to Russian hegemony, and after a few weeks' fighting against disorganised opposition, crushed the 'revolutionary' Diet, restored the political status quo and embarked on negotiations with Prussia which led to the second partition of Poland in January 1793. Under its provisions, Russia acquired around 90,000 square miles of new territory with a population of over three million. Prussia received a much smaller share, Austria nothing, and the territory of Poland was more than halved. The ancient Catholic kingdom was on its way to extinction. The *coup de grâce* was delivered in 1794. Only weeks after the second partition, another, more determined, insurgency led by Tadeusz Kościuszko (1746–1817) – a veteran of the American War of Independence – broke out in Cracow in an act of national defiance. Despite spirited defence against superior Russian forces led by General Suvorov, Kościuszko's troops were finally defeated at the battle of Maciejowice. Warsaw was stormed amid much slaughter of the civilian population, Kościuszko was severely wounded and later arrested, thousands of insurgents were exiled to Siberia, and the third partition of Poland (3 January 1795, N. S.), which finally obliterated the country from the political map of Europe for over a century, was put into effect. The actual business of dismembering the old kingdom and doling out the spoils among Russia, Prussia and Austria was concluded in January 1797, after Catherine's death. It was, though, even in death, Catherine's own personal triumph. Her military successes against Turkey in the south, the annexation of the Crimea, the deployment of the powerful Black Sea fleet, the fortification of Sevastopol and the construction of the important commercial port and trading city of Odessa, had fallen short of the Greek project, but were nevertheless considerable achievements which were now matched by the establishment of Russia's political pre-eminence in eastern and central Europe for the foreseeable future.

The ageing empress's thirst for military glory was not yet slaked. Platon Zubov was to inspire his elderly mistress with one last fanciful fling, sometimes called the 'Oriental project'. In 1796, Russian troops and cossaks under the command of Zubov's one-legged younger brother, Valerian (then aged 24), set off to embark on the conquest of the Caucasus, Persia and all points east along the ancient trading route linking northern India with Constantinople. Simultaneously, Suvorov was scheduled to invade the Balkans from the north, while Catherine, then barely able to manage her bloated land-legs, was personally to lead the Black Sea fleet to attack Constantinople by sea. Fortunately, the ridiculous venture was nipped in the bud by the intervention of Catherine's own death in November 1796. Her successor, Paul, immediately recalled the legions, and Platon Zubov, his mother's final fancyman, fell into political disgrace and royal disfavour. Thus the triumphant military progress of the warrior queen ended in a preposterous farce orchestrated by a pair of over-ambitious noble pipsqueaks.

Judged in purely military and political terms, Catherine's foreign policies were marked by some spectacular achievements. The empire had been expanded by around 200,000 square miles and its population had almost doubled in size. The cost, however, in human lives lost and national resources squandered was hardly commensurate with the contentious gains. What Russia did gain in territory and tax-paying subjects of the crown was offset by the seething resentment and potentially revolutionary nationalist aspirations of the conquered peoples. This was especially so in the case of the Poles, who remained a constant thorn in the flesh of the Romanovs throughout the ensuing century, and who were responsible for some of the bloodiest uprisings against Russian rule in the wider revolutionary struggle against autocracy. And it was in the Crimea, won for the Russian Empire under Catherine, that she was to suffer a humiliating defeat at the hands of Turkey and her western allies, Britain and France, in the middle of the nineteenth century, thereby inaugurating a period of agonising internal change which was to lead ultimately to the empire's collapse. As was so often the case in the country's history, the aggrandisement of the Russian state under Catherine the Great brought no palpable benefit, no peace nor prosperity, to the Russian people who fought her wars.

Culture and the case of Aleksandr Radishchev

Culture

'Peter,' it has been said, 'gave Russia a body. Catherine gave her a soul.' What is presumably meant by this glib apophthegm is that while the former provided the physical power and material means for Russia to achieve her internationally recognised imperial status, the latter, while not neglecting matters corporeal, also went further by adorning her realm with the more cerebral – intellectual, cultural and spiritual – refinements of an enlightened, sophisticated civilisation. It is certainly true that Catherine was extremely conscious of her western heritage, and from an early age applied her own considerable intelligence to improving herself and her adopted nation in the pursuit of learning and what are often described as the finer things in life – the arts, sciences, philosophy and other areas of intellectual and creative activity. Catherine herself possessed a clever mind, a ready wit, native acumen and an ability to apply herself to rigorous intellectual discipline. She was a prodigious reader, a prolific writer, and was endowed with an aptitude for language learning, and a critical discernment for fine painting, literature, architecture and philosophical debate. She also appreciated the achievements of the physical, natural and medical sciences, and was a firm believer in the beneficial effects of a sound secular education, which she personally did a certain amount to encourage in others. She was well versed in the most recent fruits of the European Enlightenment, and both conversed and corresponded with the leading thinkers, writers and *philosophes* of the age. She was also of a naturally autocratic disposition, haughty, steely-willed and intemperate in resisting any form of opposition to her absolute will, and totally ruthless in her treatment of those with the temerity to challenge her authority. She therefore combined in her personality the twin attributes of enlightenment and of despotism, and the extent to which the one or the other was predominant in her psychological make-up and her public activities is a question that has been mulled over and over by her biographers and historians since the time of her reign. To a degree, the debate over Catherine's own peculiar brand of enlightened absolutism is rather otiose, not so much because it has been so often rehearsed and reiterated, but because the arguments one way or another really do little to shed more light on the unique nature of Catherine's character or the quality of her achievements.

In practical terms she did much to spread the ideas of the Enlightenment within the upper classes of Russian society, and this bore fruit in the published works of a clutch of poets, playwrights, prose authors, journalists, satirists, historians and other more or less accomplished literati, the polish of whose compositions was at least one step ahead of the artistic junior apprentices of mid-century, though not yet, by world standards, advancing much beyond the mediocre. Among the more notable were the following. The dramatist, Denis Fonvizin (1745–92), author of 'The Brigadier' (*Brigadir*), in which he lampooned the excessive francophilia of the nobility, and 'The Minor' (*Nedorosl'*), a scarcely veiled attack on the corrupting effects of serf ownership, eventually fell foul of censorship, but pointed the way for the later comedic *œuvre* of Nikolai Gogol. Gavrila Derzhavin (1743–1816), Catherine's unofficial 'poet laureate', was the foremost exponent of Russian classicism, and is considered by many to be the greatest poet of the eighteenth century. His favoured genre was the panegyrical ode, in which he extolled the virtues of his benefactress while gently mocking the foibles of her minions. Paradoxically, this disciplined student of his Greek and Roman exemplars (Anacreon, Horace) was also a bold, eclectic and inimitable iconoclast in his use of the Russian language. Indeed, it is a measure of his greatness that the inimitability of his linguistic anarchism meant that he left behind him no literary school which could emulate his unique style. He also held a number of minor bureaucratic posts and was very briefly Alexander I's Minister of Justice. Of lesser fame was Mikhail Kheraskov (1773–1807), a popular dabbler in various genres and styles, including a pair of historical epic poems cast in the Homeric mould, but possessing scant literary merit.

Prose authors of modest renown included Nikolai Karamzin (1766–1826), whose best known tear-jerker, 'Poor Liza' (*Bednaya Liza*), published in 1792, was a pioneer of the school of sentimentalism which paved the way for the later Russian romantics. Later turning from creative literature to historical research, Karamzin was the author of the monumental 'History of the Russian State' (*Istoriya Gosudarstva Rossiiskogo*) published in 12 volumes, 1816–29, which, while ultra-conservative in tone and in its own way a kind of prolix ode to autocracy, marked a new, professional, stage in the development of Russian historiography. Much more radical in his social and political views was the great satirical journalist, Nikolai Novikov (1744–1818), freemason, philanthropist, critic and amateur philosopher, whose literary and charitable civic activities eventually earned him a spell of imprisonment in the notorious Schlüsselburg fortress near St Petersburg, from where he was released and pardoned by the Emperor Paul immediately after his mother's death. Another author of note was the historian, Mikhail Shcherbatov (1733–90), though his chronicles of pre-Romanov Russia are less well known than his ethical treatise 'On the Decline of Morals in Russia' (*O povrezhdenii nravov v Rossiii*) in which he bitterly bemoaned the plummeting standards of public and private life in Russia since the reign of Peter the Great, reserving his greatest indignation for his condemnation of the appalling moral laxity which he believed characterised Catherine's regime. However, not so much in terms of literary accomplishment as in public notoriety and political fallout, without doubt the most famous *cause célèbre* of the period was the publication of an innocent-looking semi-fictional travelogue entitled 'Journey from St Petersburg to Moscow' (*Puteshestvie iz Peterburga v Moskvu*), written by Aleksandr Radishchev (1749–1802) and published in 1790. This seminal work and its author form the subject of the following section, but first it is necessary briefly to review Catherine's other contributions to the cultural life of her country.

Despite her genuinely held belief in the benefits of a sound education, Catherine's efforts to enhance the literacy and numeracy of her population by meaningful practical measures were negligible and of nugatory effect. Little, if anything, was done to encourage the education of the lower classes, and the opening of a handful of pedagogical institutions for the privileged sections of Russian society, such as the Smolnyi Institute, a kind of finishing school for young noblewomen, failed to create any spectacular efflorescence of real learning, even among the nation's elite. True, huge fortunes were spent on the construction and embellishment of gorgeous palaces and the acquisition of great collections of European art; elegant additions were made to the Winter Palace; Scottish and Italian architects, English gardeners, French and German designers, as well as native Russian masters, contributed to the beautification of the capital and its environs; and a wave Gallomania swept through the mansions of the nobility, as familiarity with the French language, Parisian fashions, and the falderals of Franco-European high society served as paltry substitutes for the genuine stuff of enlightenment and civilisation. No significant advances were made in indigenous painting, music, or the other plastic and performing arts.

Despite the derivative nature of Russia's cultural achievement during Catherine's reign, one outstanding, monumental artefact is worthy of special attention, which in its own peculiar fashion is a fitting symbol of the Catherinian age. This is the renowned equestrian statue of Peter the Great immortalised in Pushkin's famous poem (see Chapter 4) – commissioned by Catherine, designed and cast in bronze by the French sculptor Étienne Falconet (1716–91), and unveiled in 1782. The enormous horseman, mounted on a rearing charger, is set on a gigantic plinth of pink Finnish granite, facing westwards with right arm outstretched towards the waters of the Baltic and beyond to Europe. The figure is dressed in the robes of a conquering Roman emperor, a sword at its side, and its head crowned with the laurel wreath of military victory. The great hind hooves of the dynamic brazen steed are trampling down the sinuous coils of a fearsome serpent, representative of the rider's evil enemies, internal and external. On either side of the granite monolith is the apparently modest inscription, on one side in Russian, on the other in Latin, 'To Peter the First, Catherine the Second, 1782':

PETRO PRIMO
CATHARINA SECUNDA
MDCCLXXXII

There is no elaborate list of honorific titles, battles won, achievements made, no fancy scrolling, trumpeting cherubs or superfluous symbols of triumph. The symbolism and the triumphalism are explicit in both the statue and the inscription. It is a monument not simply to Peter, but also to Catherine herself, an unashamed piece of self-advertisement and narcissistic propaganda, establishing Catherine as the direct inheritor, torch-bearer and propagator of the Petrine traditions of military conquest, European civilisation, imperial grandeur and the greatness of Russia's power. But the apparent modesty of the dedication belies the egotistical message contained in its signature. By associating the greatness and the glory of her predecessor with her own achievements, Catherine was in effect composing her own epitaph and displaying her own hubris. The man who did more than anyone to expose and excoriate the nature of that hubris was Aleksandr Radishchev.

(ii) The case of Aleksandr Radishchev

Aleksandr Nikolaevich Radishchev was born into the family of the minor nobility and at age 13 was enrolled in the Imperial Corps of Pages, thereby gaining an opportunity to witness the comings and goings of court life at first hand.[28] In 1766 he and 11 other noble youths were selected to be sent to the University of Leipzig, where for five years he studied the thought of the contemporary European Enlightenment, jurisprudence, and also the classics, through which he developed an admiration for the democratic traditions of fifth-century BC Athens and the republican ideals of ancient Rome. After returning to St Petersburg, he was employed in various branches of the government bureaucracy. However, it was in his private literary activities – translations, commentaries and minor treatises – that he first displayed the adumbrations of those radical, independent social, moral and political views that were later to land him in such deep trouble with the authorities, not least the supreme authority of the empress herself.

The occasion, in 1790, was the publication on his private printing press of the seemingly innocuous account of a stagecoach journey undertaken by a fictitious traveller between the two Russian capitals. *Journey from St Petersburg to Moscow*, consciously modelled on Laurence Sterne's *Sentimental Journey through France and Italy* (1768), far from being a simple travelogue, turned out to be the publication bombshell of the age, though the reverberations of the explosion were confined to only a small portion of Russia's very tiny reading public. In any case, only 650 copies were printed, and only a fraction of those distributed. Radishchev himself destroyed the rest when the scandal broke. So what was it that made this travel journal such literary and political dynamite? Rather than being merely a collection of sketches and musings penned by the traveller to describe the various stop-offs and staging posts on his journey south (the names of which form the chapter titles), the book comprised an angry and compassionate philippic against the evils and abuses of the entire imperial social, administrative, economic and political system. Using a range of authorial devices – dreams, discovered documents, chance conversations, historical comments, personal apostrophes, and so on – Radishchev produced a trenchant, bitter and indignant denunciation of all that he considered wicked, inhuman and corrupt in Catherine's Russia. The system of military conscription, bureaucratic venality, malfeasance in office, prostitution, pornography and the licensed abuse of serf-girls, corporal punishment, military adventurism, the trade in false genealogies, clerical ignorance and corruption, superstition and censorship, slavery and sycophancy, fiscal maladministration, individual and collective despotism – in fact the whole rotten edifice of the entire tsarist social and political structure, based on the double outrage of serfdom and autocracy, came under the stinging lash of Radishchev's implacable invective.

In the chapter entitled *Gorodnya*, the author, after recounting a particularly heart-rending story of serf abuse, declares that his gaze penetrates through the veil of an entire century, and there, unless the government redresses the grievances and expunges the wickedness which he has described, he sees a vision of bloody popular revolt. In one of his most vitriolic tirades, Radishchev declaims:

> Oh! if the slaves, burdened with their heavy bonds, inflamed by their despair, were to shatter our heads, the heads of their inhuman masters, with the iron which obstructs their liberty, and redden their fields with our blood! What would the state lose thereby? Soon from among their midst would arise great men to replace the slaughtered generation. But they would be of another mind and have no right to oppress others. This is no dream. My vision pierces the dense curtain of time which veils the future from our eyes. I see through an entire century.[29]

No doubt there have been more lurid and incendiary visions of a coming revolution, but in the context of its place and time, this was pretty strong, and prophetic, stuff. Similar sentiments were also expressed in the 'Ode to Liberty' (*Vol'nost': Oda*) contained in a manuscript given to the traveller during his stopover at Tver. Within these stanzas, the shades of Samson, Brutus, William Tell, brave fighters against tyranny, are invoked; and Oliver Cromwell, though condemned as a criminal, is also extolled for setting an example to peoples down the generations on how to drag an unjust monarch to the block. George Washington is also glorified for leading the Americans out of colonial oppression, and the traveller's visit to Novgorod is used as an opportunity for him to hymn the virtues and the democratic traditions of the popular assembly (*veche*) of the mediaeval city-state.

When one remembers that Radishchev launched his literary missile at a time when Russia was at war with both Turkey and Sweden, under pressure from the rebellious Poles, and still mentally staggering from news of the storming of the Bastille less than one year earlier, Catherine's horrified indignation at the contents of her erstwhile protégé's diatribe may be readily appreciated, as she accused the author of being 'infected with the French madness', and condemned him as 'a rebel worse than Pugachëv'. To add personal insult to the general injury, in one scene Radishchev describes in almost perfect detail the court of Catherine herself, as the fairy *Istina* (Truth) reveals herself to a great potentate sitting on a splendid throne, surrounded in ostentatious luxury by obsequious courtiers, medallioned generals and richly apparelled grovelling sycophants. Once in the lifetime of every despot, *Istina* reveals the truth behind the glittering façade, and the great ruler witnesses the misery, the suffering, the spattered blood and splattered brains of the countless victims of his tyranny and his wars. The identification with Catherine's own court, her own entourage, and her own vainglorious hypocrisy is unmistakeable. Such was Catherine's fury that Radishchev was arrested, interrogated and condemned to be beheaded, the decapitation to take place, oddly, in the town of Nerchinsk in the far east of Siberia, close to the Chinese frontier. However, careful of her now somewhat tattered reputation for civilised standards and anxious to display her magnanimity, she chose to exercise clemency and instead sentenced Radishchev to ten years' exile in eastern Siberia, from which, like Kościuszko, he was recalled by Emperor Paul in 1801.

Radishchev has been called many things by his biographers and admirers: the first Russian radical, father of the Russian intelligentsia, the first repentant nobleman, founder of the Russian revolutionary tradition, a forefather of Bolshevism, a visionary, a democrat, a crank. What is certainly true is that Radishchev's aim in writing his book was not directly to *foment*, but to *prevent* a revolutionary conflagration. It was a warning to Catherine and the serf-owning nobility of the consequences of continuing to maintain the iniquitous and inhumane system over which they presided. He was not a political theorist or advocate of popular insurrection, but more of a humanitarian moralist, a sensitive son of the Enlightenment whose soul, in his own words 'was afflicted by the sufferings of mankind', and who felt a deep 'compassion for the misery of my fellow beings', and was severely punished by his empress for preaching in the spirit of those enlightened ideals to which she herself had once professed to subscribe. A question along the lines of 'Who posed the greater threat to the security of the Russian state, Pugachëv or Radishchev?' is sometimes asked in examination papers on Russian history. There is, of course no definitive answer to this question as to whether in the short or long term Radishchev's pen proved mightier than Pugachëv's sword, or, for that matter, the peasants' axe. What can confidently be averred is that so long as the forces of popular rebellion, personified by Pugachëv, remained isolated from and uninfluenced by the powers of intellectual critique and moral leadership in the tradition of Radishchev, then the Romanov regime remained relatively secure. When, however, Radishchev and Pugachëv metaphorically joined hands and forces in the early years of the twentieth century, the last Romanov would fall. Throughout the nineteenth century a continual battle raged between the tsarist government and the radical, later revolutionary, intelligentsia. By initially condemning Aleksandr Radishchev to death, it was Catherine who loosed the first warning salvo across the critical intelligentsia's bows. The final shots were fired by Bolshevik guards into the bodies of the last tsar and his family in 1918, in a town which, ironically, bore Catherine's name, Yekaterinburg.

Conclusion

As mentioned above, the question of Catherine the Great's sincerity in terms of her espousal of the humanitarian ideals of the Age of Reason, her adherence to progressive principles, when these are measured against her actual achievements, is a well-ploughed furrow. Was she a genuine daughter of the Enlightenment, a petticoat *philosophe* or a crowned hypocrite? Her shining reputation, founded on a mixture of diplomatic success, military victories, territorial expansion, the pursuit of civilised standards in public life, and a predilection for encouraging the cultural advancement of at least the educated classes of Russian society, is both dimmed and diminished by her cavalier disregard for the general welfare of the vast majority of the Russian people and her callous indifference to the interminably wretched circumstances in which they continued to live, fight and suffer, all for the greater glory of Catherine and the Russian state. Against the magnificent triumph of Russian arms and the cultural attainments of the Semiramis of the North and her *noblesse dorée*, must be set the primitiveness of the judicial system and the barbarity of the penal code, which still countenanced the use of public flogging and branding, torture, and the exile of thousands of innocent, shackled victims to the freezing hell of Siberian exile, what Victor Hugo – himself a political exile – described (in the French context) as *la guillotine sèche*. Her victories must also be seen against the backdrop of the abortive Legislative Commission, which utterly failed to promulgate any meaningful reform of the country's legal and administrative system, and the almost total lack of any success in widening educational opportunities for ordinary Russians, the great bulk of whom remained ignorant, illiterate and uncouth. The economy remained stagnant, and the exchequer drained by the insatiable demands of continuous and profitless warfare. In this latter respect, not even Russia's military superiority over Turkey succeeded in the ultimate aim of sweeping the Ottomans out of Europe, and the Polish settlement brought only a long legacy of anguish, both for the occupiers and the occupied – Russians, Poles and Jews alike, though in differing degrees of suffering. And the embryonic Russian intelligentsia, encouraged by Catherine to enhance its intellectual accomplishments and skills, was to turn its talents and its mental faculties into an increasingly vociferous movement of determined opposition to the whole autocratic structure of tsarism.

But in the final analysis, the greatest criticism must be reserved for Catherine's failure to grasp the nettle of serfdom, the most glaringly anachronistic and inhumane feature of the entire system. If anything, as noted above, it became even more deeply entrenched and more indefensible against any form of moral, practical or economic criticism. But it was to be over half a century before another ruler was forced by abysmal defeat in a major international war to address the problem which was actually at the root of that defeat (see Chapters 8 and 9). Catherine, like all major historical figures, must be judged against the values, standards and mores of her own time. But her activities, her successes and failures, her fame and her foibles must also be judged against the longer perspective of history. All in all, despite the adulation of her many admirers, including some eminent present-day historians of eighteenth-century Russia, it is difficult to find anything of sufficient worth in the policies of Catherine II to deserve the accolade of 'greatness'. The unwholesome amalgam of superficial sophistication, officially perpetrated atrocities and sheer human misery that were all features of Catherine's unhappy realm, rather than being designated as approximating to or departing from the concept of enlightened absolutism, would be more aptly described – as it was by Klyuchevskii – as 'civilized barbarism' (*tsivilizirovannoe varvarstvo*).[30]

Paul, Alexander I and the Decembrists, 1796–1825

The reign of Paul, 1796–1801

Catherine died of an apoplectic stroke on 6 November 1796 and was immediately succeeded by her son and heir, the Grand Duke Pavel Petrovich. The policies he pursued during his brief reign have traditionally been seen by historians as being partly motivated by a peevish desire to countermand those of his mother, from whom he was estranged as a child and with whom no strong bonds of filial affection were forged. Some evidence of this was his grisly decision to have the mortal remains of his murdered father exhumed and reinterred alongside Catherine's body. Rather happier was his order for the release from prison and exile of Kościuszko, Novikov and Radishchev. He spent his early adult life on his private estates at Gatchina and Pavlovsk, outside St Petersburg, banned from affairs of state and passing much of his time drilling his private army of soldiers, dressed, dragooned and disciplined according to the contemporary Prussian manner. This predilection for Prussian militarism was to be one of the causes of his eventual undoing. He is commonly portrayed as being physically unattractive, even ugly, and in temperament irascible, malicious, bullying, sadistic, and given to sudden fits of uncontrollable anger and playing cruel practical jokes. He was also a reputed alcoholic. He has, too, been somewhat fancifully described as a 'tsar-democrat', an oxymoron based on his allegedly pro-peasantry and anti-nobility policies. As will be seen, there is no evidence to support either the picture of Paul as a deranged, dypsomanic psychopath, or as a principled, progressive 'people's tsar'. Other than his Prussophilia, and a fanatical adherence to the principles of efficiency and centralisation, he had no particular guiding philosophy, and both his attitude towards serf ownership and his belief in the virtues of monarchical absolutism were firmly rooted in the tradition of his eighteenth-century predecessors. His imagination, too, was constantly haunted by the spectre of Pugachëv at the head of his cossak and peasant hordes, and the head of Louis XVI on the Paris scaffold.

Paul's accession coincided with a recrudescence of peasant violence, which, while never escalating into the proportions of another *Pugachëvshchina*, nevertheless in 1797 affected 32 out of the 41 provinces of European Russia. Baseless rumours were abroad that, following the 'emancipation of the nobility' from compulsory state service, the emancipation of the serfs from bondage would automatically follow, rumours which were encouraged by the fact that, for the first time, the servile classes were required to take the oath of allegiance to the new tsar, suggesting that the vestiges of real citizenship were being acknowledged. It was, however, a gratuitous gesture, as also was Paul's ambiguous later legislation banning the performance of *barshchina* (compulsory labour on the nobles' land) on Sundays and holy days, and limiting it to only three days per week. This had in any case been the law since the *Ulozhenie* of 1649, but it continued, as before, to be ignored in practice, as records of serf complaints and petitions attest. (Incidentally, the right of direct petition to the monarch, abolished by Catherine, was restored by her son.) However, following his mother's practice, Paul also continued to bestow large numbers of state peasants on those to whom he wished to grant favour, thereby reducing their status to that of the more intensively exploited privately owned serfs. If anything, Paul was, pro rata, even more munificent in this respect than Catherine. The latter dispensed three-quarters of a million 'souls' in this manner during her 34-year reign; Paul managed to give away half a million in less than five years. Ever mindful of Pugachëv, Paul hastened to deal with the peasant disturbances with ruthless efficiency, dispatching punitive expeditions into the countryside to reassert the authority of the landlords and the local authorities. His spurious reputation as the 'tsar-democrat' seems, therefore, to be unfounded. 'All things considered,' in Florinsky's words, 'there was little in the peasant policies of Paul to disturb the peace of mind of the most conservative serf owners.'[1]

Nevertheless, deteriorating relations between Paul and the landowning nobility are often seen as the major cause for his eventual downfall, although, as with the peasants, there is little in Paul's activities to suggest that he did anything to cause any significant alteration in the privileged status and economic security of the noble estate. Such reforms as he did introduce, however, were perceived as an attempt to reconstitute the principle of *service* as a prerequisite for the holding of noble rank, and it was this that caused the resentment. While the hard-won provisions of the 1785 Charter to the Nobility were never fully revoked, a number of apparent restrictions were put in place which chipped away tiny fragments from the gilded surface of the nobility's 'Golden Age'. These included such items as the imposition of a tax on the nobles' land; growing demands for more military service; the increasing practice of depriving errant nobles of their rank, thus removing their immunity from corporal punishment; and reinforcement of the restrictions on foreign travel already imposed by Catherine in the wake of the French Revolution. There were also some minor administrative changes which apparently, though not in actual practice, curtailed the powers of the nobility at local level. All these, on top of the unpopular military reforms discussed below, accelerated the rapid alienation of the *dvoryanstvo* from the person of the autocrat, if not yet from the principle of autocracy. That Radishchevan concept had to wait another quarter-century to attract wider support.

The fact that these seeming encroachments on the nobility's privileged position were carried out in the name of encouraging greater efficiency, and a less sloppy, more businesslike attitude to administrative, economic and military affairs, cut no ice with the members of Russia's ruling classes, which had become used to their rather pampered, even effete, existence under Catherine. Nowhere was Paul's drive for efficiency, discipline and cost-effectiveness more clearly seen than in his treatment of the military. The crucial role of the senior officer corps, in particular the regiments of the imperial guards, in the making and unmaking of the eighteenth-century monarchs is a matter of record. Only the accession of the infant Ivan VI in 1740 was accomplished without their intervention (see Chapter 5). During the reign of Catherine especially, Russia's military elite had come to regard itself, in fact with every justification, as occupying the very pinnacle of privilege, influence and authority in the empire – within the limits, of course, of the supreme imperial power wielded by the sovereign. The leisured, rather cavalier, laissez-faire complacency of the country's senior officer corps was given a sudden jolt by the new emperor's passion for punctilious uniformity and control.

Ruthless discipline was enforced throughout all ranks of the Russian armed forces, and no longer was the holding of an officer's commission a passport to leisure and pleasure. Prussian-style uniforms were introduced; regular and rigorous drilling took place; a definite hierarchy of rank and responsibility, command and control was imposed; and the exclusivity of the elite guards regiments was diluted somewhat by the inclusion in their ranks of officers from Paul's private Gatchina army. Strict financial accounting and elimination of frivolous expenditure were also brought into practice. Precision, drill, punctilious obedience, economy, lack of corruption, promotion strictly on merit, faultless attention to every jot and tittle of military rules and regulations, spit, polish and knee-jerk perfection were the order of the day. From a purely technical, military point of view the new regimen was successful in eliminating some of the laxer practices which had crept in during recent years, and in creating a slicker military machine. And it was this that the entrenched officer class resented, adding to the pool of discontent already spreading throughout the disgruntled nobility as a whole.

In the event, it was among the highest echelons of the military and bureaucratic hierarchy, joined by a number of disaffected individuals, such as Platon Zubov, with a personal axe to grind, that the fatal plot was hatched to depose Paul in favour of his eldest son, the popular Grand Duke Alekandr Pavlovich. It is ironic that the last of the Russian emperors to perish in a palace coup, true to the sanguinary and capricious traditions of the eighteenth-century succession, should have been the one who finally regularised the legislation for the hereditary accession to the Russian throne. Peter the Great's law, that every monarch should nominate his own successor – which had created such a muddle after his own death – was abolished and replaced with a straightforward law of succession enshrining the simple principle of male primogeniture within the Romanov family. (This is even more ironic when one considers that, given the doubts surrounding his paternity, Paul himself – and therefore all the succeeding tsars – may not have been of Romanov blood.) Among the chief movers in the conspiracy, apart from the obnoxious Zubov, were the then Vice Chancellor, Count Nikita Panin, a member of the powerful clan which had held many high offices of state under Catherine, and Count Pëtr Pahlen, military governor of St Petersburg. The extent of the heir apparent's own complicity in the machinations is a moot point. Alexander was certainly aware of his father's unpopularity among the aristocracy, and also made privy to the plan to depose him. Given the fate of earlier royal victims of court intrigue – and Alexander could not have been ignorant of the historical record – it seems unlikely that he was not alert to at least the possibility of his father's assassination during the proceedings. His ambiguous reaction to news of the deed when it was done is discussed in the following section. The coup took place on the night of 11 March 1801. Having previously composed an announcement of his abdication, the regicides gained admittance to the emperor's bedroom in the recently built and heavily fortified Mikhailovskii Castle in St Petersburg. There is some speculation as to whether the conspirators intended to murder him on the spot or at some later date, but in the event a scuffle took place during which Paul suffered a battering with a heavy snuff box, and was finally strangled with one of his own ceremonial sashes. Alexander's accession was announced, to the general satisfaction of the nobility, and the unconcern of the Russian people.

Whether Paul was any more malevolent or unbalanced than any of his predecessors is a matter for debate. If not totally mad, he was certainly much maligned as such, and also probably misunderstood by those who believed themselves to have suffered most under his regime, and who initially wrote the record of his rule. If the reign and regicide of Emperor Paul conformed to the eighteenth-century tradition of Russian political history as one of 'autocracy tempered by assassination', then the following century was to develop along a different, exponential trajectory of autocracy tempered by the forces of intellectual challenge, economic change and social revolt.

Alexander I – the 'enigmatic tsar', 1801–1825

Liberal promise

In many ways the reign of Alexander I may be regarded as a kind of watershed between eighteenth- and nineteenth-century Russia. Many of the traditions, practices and processes evident in the earlier period continued into the Alexandrine age and were brought to an end only by the dramatic events of December 1825 (see below). These events were to inaugurate a different pattern of political, social, economic and intellectual developments in the nineteenth century which came to an even more dramatic *dénouement* in the early years of the twentieth. The new tsar's complex reaction to his father's assassination was a mixture of grief, guilt, anguish, self-delusion and remorseful acknowledgement of his own complicity. This multi-layered, muddled response is in a sense symptomatic of the mystery that still surrounds the tantalising character of the ruler whose behaviour was to earn him such sobriquets as 'the enigmatic tsar' and 'the Sphinx of the north', an indication of his ambiguous, mercurial, double-edged, even duplicitous, nature. His notorious inscrutability has also led to charges of hypocrisy and of moral and intellectual dishonesty.

Without dabbling in the psychology of infancy or adolescence, some importance must be placed on the unsettlingly ambivalent effects of Alexander's curious upbringing and education. During his teens, he divided his time and attention between the dilettante intellectualism of his grandmother's court, under the tutelage of the Swiss republican Frédéric César La Harpe (1754–1838), and the more Spartan rigours and military routine of his father's regimental parade ground at Gatchina. La Harpe instilled in his rather languid pupil a familiarity with, and indeed a certain amount of enthusiasm for, the fruits of the European Enlightenment, including more than a passing respect for the revolutionary ideals of 'Liberty, Equality and Fraternity'. By contrast, in the barracks-like surroundings of Gatchina, Alexander made the acquaintance, and enjoyed the comradeship, of Aleksei Aleksandrovich Arakcheev (1769–1834), a stern military martinet and ultra-disciplinarian who was later to become Alexander's closest confidant and one of the major influences on his policies during the second half of his reign (see below). Throughout his enigmatic life, until his equally mysterious death, the tsar was to oscillate disconcertingly between the free-thinking liberalism of La Harpe and the reactionary regimentalism of Arakcheev, 'the corporal of Gatchina'.

The first few years of Alexander's reign are sometimes referred to as the period of the 'Secret Committee' (*neglasnyi komitet*), though in fact no 'committee' as such existed, and the term simply referred to a small coterie of Alexander's close friends and acquaintances, rich young aristocrats such as Counts Viktor Kochubei and Pavel

Stroganov, Nikolai Novosiltsev and the Polish Prince Adam Czatory-ski, all of whom enjoyed the emperor's enthusiasm for western culture, a professed, though flimsy, libertarianism, and a firm belief in the necessity of reform in Russia in the interests of progress and the common weal. Apart from being influenced by French radical-ism, they also entertained an admiration for the less intoxicating ideals and institutions of Britain's constitutional monarchy and its parliamentarianism. However, their intermittent, convivial and well-meaning discussions between 1801 and 1804 produced nothing like a coherent plan of action, and were bedevilled, despite their liberal froth, by a continuing belief in the dangers of serf emancipation and in the benefits of despotism, albeit the 'enlightened' variety. Nevertheless, what has been rather extravagantly described as a 'cascade' of minor legislation was enacted in the first flush of Alexander's early reforming zeal, none of which, however, did much to alter the essentially authoritarian and hierarchical nature of the autocratic order or its social and economic base.[2] These well-meant but ultimately empty innovations, which served to keep the more progressive-minded sections of educated society buoyed up with high expectations of greater things to come, form part of the histori-ographical legend which seeks artificially to divide Alexander's reign into a supposedly 'liberal' first half (1801–12) and a 'reactionary' second half (1812–25). The dichotomy is, however, a false one, as will be demonstrated.

Among the early changes introduced by Alexander, some were purely nominal while others were a more substantial indication of the new liberal, vaguely humanitarian spirit that appeared to be in the air after the hated military-style conformism and rigidity of Paul. In 1802 the old system of central government colleges, introduced by Peter I (see Chapter 4), and recently more or less ignored by Paul, was abolished and replaced by the establishment of eight ministries (*ministerstva*) – those of foreign affairs, war, navy, justice, internal affairs, finance, commerce, and education. The reform amounted to little more than a change in nomenclature, and one could be for-given for hardly noticing any difference in practice. Nor did the attempt to revivify the powers of the Ruling Senate introduce any substantial change. The ban on the import of foreign books and restrictions on foreign travel were lifted, censorship became rather more easy-going, and all the rights of the nobility as enshrined in

Catherine's Charter of 1785 were reinstated. The establishment of the Ministry of Education ('Public Enlightenment' – *Ministerstvo narod-nogo prosveshcheniya*) in 1802 was followed by the reorganisation of primary and secondary schools, and to the three existing universities of Moscow, Dorpat and Vilna were added those of Kazan (1804), Kharkov (1805) and St Petersburg (1819), though the lack of adequate resources and the paucity of appropriately qualified teaching staff rendered them largely ineffectual as pedagogical or research institutes for a considerable time. The actual number of students did, however, grow appreciably. In 1801 Radishchev was recalled from his Siberian exile, pardoned, and appointed by Alexander to membership of a special commission charged with working out the draft of a new code of laws. It is a sad indication of the returned exile's early disillusionment with the emptiness of the new regime's promise that in 1802 he committed suicide by taking poison. Also in 1801 the so-called Secret Expedition (*Tainaya ekspeditsiya*), a kind of political police organisation set up in 1762, was abolished, but after 1807 its functions continued to be discharged by a special security committee dealing with supervision of public law and order – another change in appearance without altering the substance. This was in effect the precursor of Nicholas I's more notorious 'Third Section' (see Chapter 8). Some amelioration in the harshness of judicial and penal procedures was introduced, including a ban on the application of judicial torture, and some typically ambiguous reforms in the Siberian exile system, which were virtually ignored by the authorities in charge of administering that pernicious institution. Thousands of convicted criminals and innocent victims exiled by administrative (i.e. extra-judicial) process continued to make the gruelling journey across the Urals every year. Not until 1822 did the Siberian reforms of Mikhail Speranskii bring any kind of rational order into the operation, though it still remained at the core of the tsarist penal system and continued to be used on a massive scale until the revolutions of 1917, as will be explained in a later chapter.

Far from a 'cascade' of substantial legislation, Alexander's enactments amounted to not much more than an insignificant dribble. Even less impressive was the pettifogging tinkering with the problem of serfdom. In 1801, the advertisement of serfs for sale without land was prohibited, as, in 1808, was the public auction of serfs under the hammer – though again the practice continued in both cases. As alluded to above, the serf owners' right to deliver their recalcitrant bondsmen for exile and hard labour in Siberia was curtailed, but the ambivalence of the wording of the relevant decrees did little to stem the tide of those so banished. Slightly more positive was the new law of 20 February 1803, clarified in 1807, which allowed individual serfs to purchase their freedom from their masters, obviously with the latter's consent. The cash price of the manumission varied enormously and could amount to several thousand rubles per individual male serf, and in any case this superficially liberal measure was taken advantage of by only a tiny proportion of the servile population. Between 1803 and 1825, only something like 35,000 serfs were allowed to purchase their freedom, out of a total peasant population of over 50 million. Despite its no doubt good intentions, the new legislation could hardly be regarded as the harbinger of a universal emancipation. Nor did the experimental liberation of the serfs *without land* in the Baltic provinces, introduced in a series of legislative acts between 1804 and 1816, prove successful, and led only to a renewed wave of agrarian disturbances and the impoverishment of the rural economy in those regions. Further experimentation in the field of agricultural organisation was undertaken in the infamous military-agrarian colonies established under the direct command of Alexander's reactionary adviser and disciplinarian extraordinaire, Aleksei Arakcheev. These hybrid communities – part villages, part barracks – were to become a sinister symbol of the quasi-dictatorial regime masterminded by Alexander's 'Grand Vizier' during the period following the Napoleonic invasion in 1812. Both the invasion and the later reaction associated with his name are dealt with in the following section. But before Arakcheev came to wield such pre-eminent authority in the decade or so before the emperor's death, another prominent statesman had begun to personify the allegedly more liberal side of Alexander's nature. That man was Mikhail Mikhailovich Speranskii (1772–1839).[3]

Born the son of a lowly village priest, Speranskii rose through the ranks of the civil service to become what has been described by a number of writers as the most brilliant bureaucrat of imperial Russia. By 1808, by dint of his remarkable abilities, enthusiasm and sparkling intelligence, as well as the patronage of Alexander's friend, Viktor Kochubei, he had already held a number of senior posts in the government bureaucracy, and in that year he was commissioned by the emperor to compose the draft of a Russian constitution. Alexander and the 'Secret Committee' had for some time flirted with constitutional ideas; indeed, both the Grand Duchy of Finland (annexed by Russia in 1808) and Poland were granted some kind of quasi-constitutional status, and, although being integral parts of the empire, enjoyed a greater degree of autonomy in administering their own internal affairs, laws, finance, local institutions, etc., than any other region of the empire, though in Poland's case this was to alter radically after the nationalist uprising in 1830 (see Chapter 8). Speranskii's project was finished and presented to Alexander in 1809, but its provisions, though considered, were never put into effect, nor even seriously contemplated when its practical implications – which were far too radical in the aftermath of the French Revolution – became clear. Perhaps the most interesting part of the document, which remained largely unknown and was not published *in toto* until 1905, is the preamble in which its author subjects the political and social structure of Russia to intense critical scrutiny, the tone of which, though not in the same words, echoes his declaration in a memorandum of 1802 that:

> I find in Russia only two classes: the slaves of the sovereign and the slaves of the landowners. The first are called free only in relation to the second, but there are no truly free persons in Russia except beggars and philosophers ... The interest of the nobility is that the peasants should be in their unlimited power; the interest of the peasants is that the nobility should be in the same degree of dependence on the throne. The nobles ... must base the freedom of their life entirely ... on the enslavement of the peasants.[4]

It would be difficult to find a more succinct appraisal of the serf/noble/crown relationship in Russia, though Speranskii's constitutional design did nothing to suggest how this particular form of slavery might be abolished, or how social relationships within the country might be secured on a more humane footing based on the rule of law. What it did was to advocate the separation of governmental powers – executive, legislative and judicial – within a monarchical system, and to recommend the setting up of a legislative State Assembly (*Gosudarstvennaya Duma*) with restricted powers, its representatives to be elected by indirect voting based on a high property qualification. No provision was made for the emancipation of the serfs, though Speranskii, as previously indicated, was personally in favour of such a measure. The only two items that were salvaged from the constitutional plan were (i) the establishment of an appointed State Council (*Gosudarstvennyi Sovet*), which had the power to initiate legislation but in no way limited the powers of the crown, and (ii) the reorganisation and supplementation of the central ministries. Such were the meagre results of Speranskii's carefully drafted project for a constitution which was already extremely modest and circumscribed in its conception, and in any case known only to a very narrow circle of the emperor's closest confidants. It *was* perhaps an honest attempt to introduce at least the beginning of some kind of constitutional structure, but ultimately it proved impossible to do that within an essentially feudal, autocratic system. One hundred years later the establishment of the State Duma in 1906 proved to be similarly incompatible with the preservation of Nicholas II's autocratic powers (see Chapter 11).

Speranskii's equally well-thought-out plans for fiscal reforms which sought to address the parlous state of the country's finances likewise found no favour within the establishment, and over the next two years their author found himself increasingly marginalised in court and government circles. His meteoric rise from provincial obscurity had attracted a good deal of resentment, jealousy and personal enmity, and in 1812 an influential clique of ill-wishers, including Arakcheev and the conservative historian Karamzin (see Chapter 6) conspired to have Speranskii removed from office and banished in disgrace to Siberia. Apart from personal animosities, the underlying cause of Speranskii's fall from grace was the basic incompatibility between the practical possibility of actually implementing his constitutional plans, and the shallow, shifting nature of Alexander's commitment to genuine reform.

1812

Speranskii's downfall occurred at the time of his country's greatest test, in the form of the invasion of Napoleon's *Grande Armée* on 12

June (24 June N.S.) 1812. The Gallomania which had gripped Russian high society throughout most of Catherine's reign had been transformed into official Francophobia after the storming of the Bastille, the execution of Louis XVI and the other hapless victims of Madame Guillotine. The only things originating in France that were now welcome in Russia were fleeing French émigrés. Emperor Paul continued his mother's anti-French policies but, after Napoleon's nomination as First Consul of France following the revolution of 18th Brumaire 1799, Paul made overtures to the new leader of what he now saw as a counter-revolutionary French government in an effort to form some sort of alliance, or at least a rapprochement. Paul's terms proved unacceptable to Napoleon, and relations continued to deteriorate, as did those with Britain, much to the dismay of Russia's largely Anglophile elite. The dismay was deepened by Paul's launch of an ill-advised military campaign against British possessions in India, which was, mercifully, cancelled on his death in 1801. Alexander favoured a close alliance with Britain, but also kept his options open by signing a treaty of friendship with France in October 1801, despite the latter being at war with Britain. Russia also maintained close relations with Prussia and Austria, a further indication of Alexander's apparently even-handed policy of maintaining peace with all parties – that is, a policy that was at the same time both dextrous and sinister. In the event, Alexander's support for both Austria and Prussia involved her in military operations against the French, which led eventually to Napoleon's capture of Vienna and Berlin, and to the defeat of Russia's armies at the battle of Austerlitz, which Alexander personally witnessed, in December 1805. Russian troops fled in disarray, leaving over 25,000 dead, wounded and captured. Over the next two years it became clear to both the Russian and the French rulers (Napoleon had been declared hereditary Emperor of France in 1804) that some sort of concordat was necessary to both countries, in Napoleon's case so that he could concentrate on his war with the British, and in Alexander's chiefly because Russia's finances and military capabilities were in no fit state for him to contemplate the possibility of further hostilities. Consequently, the emperors met on a decorated raft on the river Niemen on 22 June 1807, and on 22 July signed the Treaty of Tilsit, under the terms of which, apart from the rulers agreeing to carve up various European territories between them, Russia was to mediate between Britain and France, and, failing a satisfactory outcome, would declare war on Britain. France, for its part, undertook to intervene between Russia and Turkey, who had been at war since mid-October 1806. Tilsit was a no-hoper from the start, particularly from Russia's viewpoint. It threatened the country's involvement in a costly war against Britain; it allowed Napoleon to consolidate his control over eastern Europe, including Poland; it led Russia into an unnecessary war with Sweden; and it was massively unpopular among Russia's ruling classes, which had grown to regard Napoleon as a bogeyman and a creature of the French Revolution who would, given the chance, emancipate the Russian serfs. In a sense the Treaty of Tilsit may be seen as a kind of precursor of the infamous Molotov–Ribbentrop *Pakt* between Nazi Germany and Stalin's Russia in 1939, which delayed Hitler's invasion of the Soviet Union for two years. In the case of Tilsit, it was to be another five years before Napoleon, after an interval during which both sides steadily built up their forces along Russia's western border, threw his troops across the Niemen and invaded the territory of the Russian Empire. The cadet from Corsica did not even have the courtesy to declare war – a precedent to be followed by the corporal from Braunau in July 1941.

La Grande Armée of half a million men, only a third of them French, faced three Russian armies collectively less than half that size under the command of generals Barclay de Tolly, Bagration and Tormasov. Russia's response – though it had little choice – was one of rapid retreat far into the country's vast hinterland, sucking the invaders deeper and deeper into the country's interior and waiting for their extended lines of supply and communications, the rough and roadless terrain, and the ravages of the Russian winter to take their toll. Meeting little resistance, therefore, Napoleon's forces swiftly advanced across present-day Belarus and took Smolensk on 6 (18, N.S.) August. Alexander himself had sensibly followed wise advice and departed from the front for the capital where he was to remain for the duration, refusing to entertain for one moment the thought of surrender. Promising, if necessary, to retreat as far as Kamchatka, Siberia's remote far eastern peninsula, the emperor obdurately echoed the defiant words of Count Fëdor Rostopchin (1723–1826), Governor General of Moscow and author of anti-French propaganda *feuilletons*, that: 'The empire has two powerful defenders in its vastness and its climate … The emperor of Russia will always be formidable in Moscow, terrible in Kazan, and invincible in Tobolsk.'[5]

Following the fall of Smolensk, Barclay de Tolly was fired, and replaced as commander-in-chief by the elderly, one-eyed General Count Mikhail Kutuzov (1745–1813) who, though a popular choice, had the unfortunate reputation in some circles of being hesitant, indecisive and even a coward. This was based on his reliance on the Fabian tactics of delay and refusal to engage the enemy in pitched battle for as long as possible, much to the frustration of his more gung-ho subordinates and critics. However, faced with the possibility of having to abandon Moscow without a fight, the cautious Kutuzov was finally forced by bellicose public opinion to give open battle to Napoleon's forces at the village of Borodino about 70 miles west of Moscow, a short distance by Russian standards. The outcome of the battle, fought on 26 August (7 September, N.S.) was indecisive and resulted in dreadful casualties and heavy losses on both sides. It is nevertheless regarded as one of the most glorious pages in the chronicles of Russia's military history, a symbol of the valiant resistance of the Russian people against an arrogant foe. Kutuzov (appointed Field Marshal on 31 August), true to his own delaying tactics, succeeded in interrupting Napoleon's progress to the ancient capital, but was unable to prevent it. One week after the mutual slaughter of Borodino, Bonaparte's troops finally entered Moscow on 2 (14, N.S.) September.

However, rather than entering in triumph over a cowed and conquered population, they entered a silent, abandoned city which was almost totally deserted. Moreover, on the evening of the occupation, a series of mysterious fires broke out which resulted in a general conflagration, destroying three-quarters of the city. The fire was probably started deliberately by the evacuating Muscovites on the orders of the governor-general, Rostopchin. Despite the devastation, Napoleon established his headquarters in the mediaeval Kremlin, stabled his horses in the ancient cathedrals, and demanded Alexander's surrender. The latter, however, scornfully and determinedly rejected the French overtures, as well as the criticisms of the more faint-hearted in his own camp who believed enough was enough, and that – after Smolensk, Borodino and Moscow – St Petersburg itself now lay virtually at the invaders' feet. In the end it was Alexander's stubborn resolve and steadfast will which won the month-long stand-off between the two emperors. Thousands of miles from home, deep in hostile territory, his soldiers underfed, faced with fierce patriotic resistance, and in the initial stages of the savage Russian winter, Napoleon was finally forced to abandon his prize and begin the long, arduous and agonising retreat from Moscow, his desperate and demoralised troops murderously harried by the freezing cold and the daredevil *razzias* of Russian partisan guerrilla bands as well as detachments of the regular army and the people's *opolchenie* (civilian militia). The rout was not an entirely one-sided affair, and Russian casualties almost matched those of the once grand army during its ignominious withdrawal. The French had been more than decimated since the initial invasion only five months earlier. Out of an original strength of nearly half a million, barely 27,000 survived. Proportionately heavy Russian losses resulted from disease, death and desertion.

The controversy surrounding Kutuzov's tactics on the eve of Borodino also bedevilled the French retreat. The Field Marshal continued to refuse to engage in a set-piece battle, contenting himself with the harrying tactics mentioned above. His personal aim was simply to see the disappearance of the French emperor and his men from Russian soil. But Alexander and some of his immediate entourage were bent on the total annihilation of the French armies, and the humiliation and capture of their chief. The fact that Kutuzov's strategy finally allowed Napoleon to escape beyond the frontier, thereby condemning Europe to another two years' bloody warfare, was immediately blamed on the hesitant commander, who himself died in 1813, never to see his old enemy meet his Waterloo. He has, however, received due posthumous recognition as one of Russia's outstanding military heroes, a monument now standing to his immortal memory on the field of Borodino.

The victory over Napoleon, celebrated in Russian history as the first 'Great Patriotic War' (the second was that against Hitler's Germany, 1941–45), has received national acclaim in the country's art, literature and music, most famously in Vereshchagin's memorable and moving battle paintings representing the people's struggle against the invader, Tolstoi's mammoth epic novel, *War and Peace*, and Chaikovskii's rumbustious pyrotechnical masterpiece, *The 1812 Overture*. Immediate and later interpretations of the triumph have varied from hailing it as the victory of legitimate autocracy over an upstart scion of the French Revolution, to lauding it as an expression of the Russian masses' defiance and titanic struggle against external domination – a 'democratic' people's war over the forces of foreign imperialism. Certainly Russia's crucial role in the ultimate defeat of Napoleon Bonaparte placed Alexander I at the peak of his international prestige, but internally the sweet fruits of victory were to turn increasingly bitter during the more obviously illiberal second half of his reign, which was marked by resentment, disillusion and despair at the reactionary policies of Alexander's right-hand man, Count Arakcheev, who was to lend his name to the period: the *Arakcheevshchina*.

The *Arakcheevshchina*

As mentioned earlier in this chapter, it is difficult to give much credence to the dubious contention that the reign of Alexander – 'Alexander the Blessed' (*Blagoslovennyi*), as he later became known – can conveniently be bisected into 'liberal' and 'reactionary' halves. The flimsy edifice of superficial reform constructed in the first heady years of his rule was underlaid with a basic and abiding conservatism that vitiated any genuine potential benefits, and the life of the country remained largely unchanged. It is nevertheless the case that, both in his domestic and foreign policies, this fundamental conservatism was more obviously displayed and more rigorously implemented during the decade or so after the six-month wonder of Napoleon's invasion and defeat. It was also suffused, again both at home and abroad, with Alexander's oddly eclectic brand of militant religiosity and perverse pietism which contained elements of mysticism, Orthodox traditionalism, Quakerism, œcumenicalism and evangelicalism which – by the very nature of the beast – defies rational analysis. It was in this spirit of whatever it was that Alexander approached his new self-appointed role as both saviour of Europe and mouthpiece of the Almighty. The appropriately dubbed Holy Alliance was signed into existence in September 1815 by all the European powers save Britain (whose Foreign Secretary, Viscount Castlereagh, famously dismissed it as a piece of 'sublime mysticism and nonsense'), Turkey and the Vatican. But it was, in the eyes of Alexander – its principal mover – not only a diplomatic device to secure the restoration and preservation of legitimate monarchies in

Europe, but also a guarantee of traditional Christianity as the guiding principle of the new international order, blessed by God Himself. This poisonous mixture of political conservatism and religious zeal (sadly, a not unknown phenomenon among political leaders even in the early years of the twenty-first century) was equally conspicuous in Alexander's attitude to the conduct of affairs within his own domain.

Although they were well acquainted with each other as early as the reign of Paul, the relationship between Alexander and Count Aleksei Arakcheev took on a greater significance in the period 1812–25. As noted above, so all-pervasive did the latter's influence appear to be, that this stage of Alexander's rule is traditionally known as the *Arakcheevshchina*, rather than the *Aleksandrovshchina*. Despite the fact that Arakcheev was reputed to be personally opposed to the scheme, the setting up of the system of 'military colonies' under his draconian regime has become something of a symbol for the reactionary nature of Alexander's later years as a whole.

The basic idea behind the project was inspired in the emperor during a visit in 1810 to Arakcheev's private estate at Gruzino, near Novgorod, where he ran his affairs, his properties and his peasants in the way he knew best – that is to say, as a military machine. The neatness, the discipline, order, efficiency and profitability of the Gruzino model, with its platoons of well-drilled serfs, so impressed Alexander that he determined to emulate the example by setting up a whole network of similar establishments on crown estates in the western borderlands of the empire. The communities were isolated from the rest of society, their populations divided into so-called 'active' and 'settled' battalions, who spent half their time in the fields and half on the parade ground. Alternately tilling and drilling, the peasant soldiers were to be self-sufficient in agricultural production, financially proficient in their economy, and militarily efficient in defence of the fatherland. In reality, they endured the worst hardships and most onerous burdens of the enserfed peasant and the conscript soldier, subject to fierce discipline, unremitting toil and the robotic routine of their barnyard barracks. Even the schoolchildren were dressed in soldiers' uniform and subjected to strict military discipline. The right-wing American historian, Richard Pipes, typically attempts to portray these colonies as an example of the liberal, reforming side of

Alexander's nature, and quotes the approval of the institution voiced by the French ambassador to St Petersburg as 'a purely philanthropic idea'.[6] Unlike Pipes or the French ambassador, public opinion at the time was in general rather less enthusiastic about the experiment. Progressive-minded intellectuals were naturally disapproving, while conservative private landowners regarded the colonies with suspicion as potential seed-beds of revolt – and, indeed, a series of rebellions during the 1820s was a prelude to their eventual closure by Tsar Nicholas I in 1831. Even that most austere of monarchs, renowned far and wide for his own predilection for military discipline and efficiency, disapproved of them. And most disapproving of all, of course, was the hapless, militarised peasantry itself, half soldier, half serf, simultaneously suffering the miseries of each existence.

Beyond the regimented confines of these artificial communities, it is surprising how little the life of the average nobleman, peasant, cleric, courtier, officer, merchant or menial altered during the reign of Alexander the Blessed.[7] Certainly the serf population was not to be blessed with the promise of its freedom, despite the commissioning and even drafting of a number of schemes as to how this might be effected, one of them drawn up by none other than Arakcheev himself. Further, the prospect of a constitutional government – notwithstanding Alexander's declaration that the constitution granted to Poland in 1815 would eventually be extended throughout the empire – likewise ran into the sands. Russian letters under Alexander saw the first stirrings of a literary movement in which the early genius of Aleksandr Pushkin burst into flower. But even he, the father of modern Russian literature, fell foul of the government for penning some politically inflammatory juvenilia and was banished to the south of Russia – Bessarabia, Odessa, the Caucasus – before finally being allowed back to the capital in 1827. Already he had published a number of romantic poems, small in compass but great in literary value, including 'The Prisoner of the Caucasus' (*Kavkazskii plennik*, 1821), 'The Fountain of Bakhchisarai' (*Bakhchisaraiskii fontan*, 1822), 'The Gypsies' (*Tsygany*, 1824), and the historical drama set in the Time of Troubles, *Boris Godunov* (1825) – later transformed into the well-known opera by Modest Musorgskii, premiered in 1874. He had also written the first two chapters of his famous novel in verse, 'Eugene Onegin' (*Yevgenii Onegin*, 1823–30) which set the tone for the great realistic prose novels of the mid-century, and is widely regarded as one of the greatest masterpieces of Russian literature. It is better known in the west in its operatic rendition, composed by Chaikovskii and first performed in 1879.[8]

The radical temper of some of Pushkin's youthful verses (not counting his regular forays into bawdy) is in some ways a reflection of the critical turn in the thinking of many young intellectuals of the day, a turn that was hardly likely to appeal to Alexander's new, post-1812 authoritarianism. More members of Russia's fledgling intelligentsia were joining together in semi-clandestine circles, many of them influenced by Freemasonry, and beginning to raise challenging voices against the prevailing religious and political orthodoxy. While not abandoning all aspects of his recent mystical phase, in the early 1820s Alexander began to come under the influence of the fiercely reactionary, obscurantist senior cleric, Archimandrite Foty (Photius), who frowned on the emperor's earlier spiritual flirtations. It was partly under his influence that Alexander introduced, in 1822, a ban on all secret societies, and also conducted a purge of the universities of St Petersburg and Kazan. Disaffection and discontent were even rife in the armed services, and not just among the conscript common soldiery. In 1820, a mutiny in the crack Semënovskii Guards in St Petersburg, protesting against conditions of service and voicing grievances which were not without wider social and political implications, led to the regiment's dispersal and transfer to the provinces. This revolt among the officers of a highly prestigious regiment of the imperial guards was an ominous adumbration of one of the most celebrated manifestations of opposition to the Romanov autocracy in the history of nineteenth-century Russia, and one which was to mark the beginnings of the Russian revolutionary movement. That occasion was the military revolt of 14 December 1825.

The Decembrist débâcle

The curious set of events which took place in St Petersburg's Senate Square on the morning of 14 December 1825 is usually referred to in the historiography as the Decembrist revolt, the Decembrist uprising, rebellion, insurgency, mutiny or some other such term chosen from the lexicon of popular sedition, and has been hailed in at least one account as 'The First Russian Revolution'.[9] However, in view of the miserable failure of the movement to achieve a single one of its confused objectives, and the ignominious rout and retribution inflicted on its participants, it is difficult to see how it can be termed in any other way than as a fiasco, in fact as the 'December débâcle'. However that may be, it is difficult to avoid the traditional usage, and the conventional terminology will therefore be employed on occasion in the pages that follow.

After Napoleon's departure from Russia, Alexander's decision to pursue his armies across Europe meant that hundreds of well-educated, open-minded, wide-eyed young Russian army officers were able to experience at first hand the attractions of life in post-revolutionary Europe – the freer intellectual atmosphere and the less restricted social ambience offered by Paris even under the Bourbon restoration, when compared with the more repressive environment of autocratic, Orthodox Russia. Yet on returning home, these young men were met, not by a continuation of the reforming promise of Alexander's early years, but by the more oppressive conservatism of the *Arakcheevshchina*. With their enthusiasm for progressive change in their own country undiminished, indeed whetted by their foreign experiences, it was with a mixture of disillusionment and determination that, turning to their own devices, many of them began to combine together in the private debating circles and philanthropic societies mentioned above. One of these, the Union of Salvation (*Soyuz spaseniya*), founded in 1816, was to be the first of a number of groupings which were eventually to develop into what may be generically described as the Decembrist movement. Little more needs to be said about this tiny organisation – probably with around a mere 20 members – than its terse entry in a recent Russian encyclopaedia:

> First secret political organization of the Decembrists, 1816–17. Founders: A. N. and N. M. Muravëv, S. P. Trubetskoi, M. I. and S. I. Muravëv-Apostol, I. D. Yakushkin, M. S. Lunin, M. N. Novikov, F. P. Shakovskoi, P. I. Pestel. Aim: abolition of serfdom and the creation of a constitutional monarchy by means of a military coup (*perevorot*). Conspiratorial (*zagovorshchicheskii*) in character. Organizational weakness and disagreements

between members led to its self-dissolution and creation of the Union of Welfare (*Soyuz blago-denstviya*).[10]

The latter was larger in composition – maybe 200 members – but its aims were only slightly less amorphous than those of its predecessor. Its leadership also comprised more or less the same personnel, though the society was geographically more widely spread, with branches in Moscow, Tulchin and Kishinëv. The Union of Welfare was also similarly divided both programmatically and tactically, but at least it agreed on the two basic objectives of abolishing both serfdom and autocracy. More practically it sought to create a climate of opinion favourable to its aims by engaging in publicistic and prop-aganda activities. At a meeting of the Union's executive board in 1820, one of its more radical members, Colonel Pavel Pestel (1793–1826), succeeded in persuading the majority to support a policy of republicanism as part of its political platform, rather than the more moderate aim of securing a constitutional monarchy. He was unsuccessful, however, in gaining support for the assassination of the tsar as a necessary part of the coup to overthrow autocracy. The idea of regicide was too strong meat for the plotters to stomach, and was eventually dropped. The fact that it was mooted, however, is both a hangover from the tactics of the eighteenth-century palace revolutions, including the murder of Alexander's father as recently as 1801, and also a foretaste of the revolutionary plans which led to the assassination of his nephew, Alexander II, in 1881. In the event, the Union of Welfare went the same way as the Union of Salvation, though in this case its more radical members, including Pestel, refused to accept the dissolution, and in 1821 reconstituted the organisation in the south – where he was stationed with his regiment – under the name of the Southern Society (*Yuzhnoe obshchestvo*). Its immediate political aim was unequivocally stated as, 'by decisive revolutionary means to overthrow the throne and in extreme neces-sity to kill all persons who might represent invincible obstacles'.[11] Thereafter a republican form of government was to be established. In 1822 a northern branch of the Decembrist movement was revived, more moderate in its objectives and calling itself, not very imagina-tively, the Northern Society (*Severnoe obshchestvo*). The geographical divide between the Northern Society in St Petersburg and the

Southern Society in Ukraine is symbolic of the ideological and tactical differences between the two organisations. A comparison of their respective programmes will illustrate the divergence.

In the capital, Nikita Muravëv (1795–1843), a veteran of the French campaigns and one of the original founders of the Union of Salvation, produced an unfinished constitutional project, which bore some similarities with Speranskii's earlier draft constitution back in 1809. Briefly, its main proposals were as follows: (i) introduction of full basic civil rights – freedom of speech, press, assembly, religious belief, and so on; (ii) equality of all before the law and trial by jury; (iii) emancipation of the serfs, though no detailed recommendations were offered as to how and on what terms this might be accomplished other than the distribution of small plots of land to tenant farmers; (iv) the granting of political rights – that is, the right to stand and to vote in elections to a national legislative body, the bicameral People's Assembly (*Narodnoe veche*); (v) the franchise to be determined on the basis of a graduated property qualification, which guaranteed that political power would remain in the hands of the wealthiest citizens (not unlike the contemporaneous situation in Great Britain); (vi) the replacement of absolute autocracy by an hereditary constitutional monarchy; (vii) the establishment of a federal system of government, consciously replicating the model of the United States. The actual process by which these revolutionary changes were to be accomplished was not spelled out, though obviously the notion of regicide was dismissed.

In the south, Pestel rejected Muravëv's ideas as nothing more than a plan for a constitutional plutocracy, 'a terrible aristocracy of wealth',[12] and considered that a federal structure of government would harm the unity of the state and cause internal divisions which could lead to civil war. (The federated states of America were, of course, to follow exactly this path only 40 years later.) Pestel had already drawn up his own riposte to Muravëv's half-hearted scheme in a set of much more radical proposals contained in his 'Russian Justice' (or 'Russian Truth' – *Russkaya Pravda*). The major items on *its* agenda were: (i) the setting up of a centralised, unified republican state, one and indivisible, with one central government, one language and one religion; (ii) the introduction of universal adult male suffrage; (iii) the elimination of all social distinctions based on wealth; (iv) the total abolition of serfdom, to be replaced by an ingenious, though complicated, system for the redistribution of the land; (v) the Russification – that is, total ethnic assimilation – of all non-Russian peoples, with special arrangements made for Catholic Poland and for the Jews, who were to be 'assisted' to leave Russia and establish an independent homeland somewhere in Asia Minor (on the territory of the Ottoman Empire); (vi) the revolution to be carried out by means of a quick military coup which would involve the execution of the monarch and the destruction of the royal family by a trained terrorist *garde perdue*; (vii) the *Putsch* would be followed by the introduction of an eight- to ten-year military-style dictatorship during which, however, full civil liberties would be guaranteed – though this provision was somewhat vitiated by a proposed ban on all independent societies, whether overt or secret, and the maintenance of a special political police force to eliminate subversion.[13]

Pestel's *Russkaya Pravda* is a singular mixture of political, social, legal, economic and racial views and recommendations which has led to him being variously, and contradictorily, described as a Jacobin, a socialist before socialism, a Bonapartist, a revolutionary democrat, a leveller, an authoritarian, a utopian, a *laissez-faire* liberal, a *petit-bourgeois*, and a communist. The completion of the document was in fact interrupted by its author's own execution in 1826, but it is impossible to believe that its provisions could ever have been put into effect. They were internally contradictory, over-ambitious, impractical, unrealistic and, although rational in conception, totally unrealisable in implementation. Pestel did, however, give careful consideration to the paramount problem of a post-emancipation land settlement which combined the egalitarian principle of providing each citizen with a land entitlement granted from the nationalised public land fund, while at the same time allowing for the growth of private enterprise, property development, and – in a word – capitalism, agrarian, mercantile and industrial. The most unsavoury aspects of Pestel's version of a brave new world, apart from the unnecessary preliminary of massacring the clan Romanov, were his racialism and religious bigotry, his proposed ban on independent clubs and societies, and the institution of a political police organisation.

Another 'Decembrist' organisation based in the south was the Society of the United Slavs (*Obshchestvo soedinënnykh slavyan*), similarly Pestelian in its views, but with the added aim of bringing about a confederation of all the Slavic peoples, an idea to be taken up later by the Panslavist movement (see Chapter 9). The United Slavs joined forces with the Southern Society in 1825.

Although no precise plans were laid, a provisional date for some kind of revolt was tentatively set for the spring of 1826. However, whatever action was being contemplated, it was precipitated by the unexpected death of Alexander on 19 November 1825 in the southern town of Taganrog. News of his demise arrived in the capital only on 27 November, thereby causing a succession crisis which created a three-week interregnum before the accession of the next monarch was announced. Both the circumstances of Alexander's death and the nature of the dynastic confusion require some comment. Without going into unnecessary detail, it is sufficient to note that, shortly after Alexander died, rumours began to circulate that he was not in fact dead at all, but, weary of the cares of office and still prone to religious delusions, had decided to abandon his throne, fake his own death, substituting the body of a common soldier in the coffin, and disappear to lead the life of a wandering holy man. Attention later centred particularly on one Fëdor Kuzmich, a peripatetic recluse who died in Siberia in 1864, and who was believed by some to be the real Alexander. The emperor's own oft-expressed wish to retire from public life, certain irregularities surrounding the autopsy and cause of death, the fact that his corpse was not displayed in an open coffin, as Orthodox ritual requires, and a number of other fortuitous factors helped to fuel the rumours. However, similar legends are not uncommon (Jesus, Hitler and Elvis Presley spring to mind), and there is nothing of real substance to suggest anything other than that Tsar Alexander the Blessed, who suffered in any case from poor health, did indeed contract a fever and go the way of all flesh – even beatified flesh – while on an extended visit to the Black Sea coast region on 19 November 1825. But a mystery which still remains unexplained is the fact that when his tomb in St Petersburg's Peter and Paul Cathedral was opened later in the century, it was found to be empty.[14]

The dynastic muddle caused by Alexander's death, faked or not, was the result of the decision, taken by the heir apparent, Grand Duke Constantine, to renounce his right to the throne in 1822. Alexander had no male offspring. Therefore, formally next in line to the throne, according to his father's law on the succession, was Constantine, who did not particularly relish the prospect of kingship, and in any case had forfeited his royal inheritance by entering into a morganatic marriage with a Polish noblewoman of non-royal blood, the Countess Grudzinska. Accordingly, the throne was scheduled to pass to the next youngest brother, Grand Duke Nicholas, in a secret deal that was drafted by the archbishop of Moscow, Filaret, and known only to a handful of dignitaries. The arrangement was not made public, the oath of fealty to Constantine was duly taken by official institutions and personages, including Nicholas, and even a ruble coin of the realm was minted, bearing the putative Emperor Constantine's profile and the date, 1825. (Only two examples of this numismatic rarity have survived.)[15] To all intents and purposes, the reign of a new Romanov tsar had begun. Constantine, however, refused to make a public declaration of his 'pre-abdication' and, instead of either him or Nicholas, it was confusion that reigned for a period of three weeks. Eventually, alarmed by rumours that some kind of resistance to his accession was in the offing, and exasperated by his older brother's procrastinations, Nicholas – an unpopular, authoritarian figure – cut the Gordian knot, issuing orders that his own accession should be formally announced and that a new oath of allegiance, to himself, should be administered on 14 December.

Taking advantage of the dynastic hiatus, the Decembrist leaders in the capital decided to seize the opportunity and stage their ill-prepared rebellion in defiance of Nicholas's accession. Labouring under the naive delusion that a show of strength by mutinous troops under the command of seditious middle-ranking officers would force Nicholas to back down, persuade the Senate to appoint a provisional government and convene a constituent assembly, the conspirators made their fateful move. In the early hours of the day, a contingent of bewildered soldiers, about 3000 strong, was marched into Senate Square, and there, in the shadow of Peter the Great's imperious figure on its huge bronze steed, they took their stand, nominally mutinous, but in fact leaderless, orderless and ultimately clueless as to what they were actually doing there in the first place. There is a story, maybe apocryphal, that, when encouraged to voice their opposition to Nicholas and raise the cry for 'Constantine and a Constitution (*Konstantin i Konstitutsiya*)!', many of the mutineers thought they were actually calling for Constantine and his Polish wife. In the ensuing mêlée, one of the protesting officers, a lieutenant Pëtr Kakhovskii, loosed off a shot which fatally wounded the Governor-General of St Petersburg, Count Miladorovich, who was attempting to persuade the immobile and uncomprehending insurgents to withdraw. The man who had been designated as leader of the rebellion, Prince Sergei Trubetskoi, in an act of last-minute funk sought refuge in the Austrian Embassy and failed even to make an appearance, as did several other prominent plotters. To his credit, Nicholas did try to end the confrontation by peaceful persuasion, sending a number of emissaries to plead with the troops. But towards the end of the afternoon, when the crowds of onlooking civilians threatened to join the reluctant rebels, even pelting loyal officials with logs and stones, the new emperor was forced to take the first crucial decision of his reign and order artillery pieces to be brought into action. Thereupon, four cannon were loaded with grapeshot and commenced their deadly fusillade directly into the crowd. Within minutes the square was cleared, leaving over 70 dead and many more wounded, the snow red with blood. Others were trampled to death in the headlong flight, while yet more drowned as they plunged through the ice – shattered by cannon shot – while attempting to flee across the frozen river Neva. Nicholas had won the day. The Decembrist revolt had been turned into the December débâcle.

Another military insurrection in the south, led by Lieutenant-Colonel Sergei Muravëv-Apostol was easily crushed by loyal troops at the beginning of January. By then, Nicholas had already set up a commission of inquiry into the whole affair which investigated the activities of over 500 arrested suspects. After a hearing before a hastily convened special tribunal, of the 121 arraigned men, five of the ringleaders were condemned to be publicly quartered, 31 to be beheaded, and the remainder to various terms of penal servitude, hard labour and settlement in Siberia. The sentence, delivered by a 'kangaroo court' with no legal status (and two of whose members had been complicit in the murder of the emperor Paul), was immediately commuted from quartering to hanging, and from decapitation to hard labour and exile. The five executions – of Pavel Pestel, who had been arrested on the eve of the rebellion, Sergei Muravëv-Apostol and Mikhail Bestuzhev-Ryumin, who had led the revolt in the south, Pëtr Kakhovskii, who had shot Milarodovich, and the poet, Kondratii Ryleev, perhaps the most radical leader of the Northern Society – were rather clumsily carried out in the early hours of 13 July 1826, much to the horror and dismay of educated society. The rest began their long terms of penal servitude in Siberia, regarded by many as a living death. It is perhaps ironic that the man who did most to expedite the smooth operation of the sentencing tribunal was the returned exile, now back in imperial favour, Mikhail Speranskii, whose own constitutional project, drawn up at the behest of Alexander I, was so similar to that composed by the now exiled Nikita Muravëv, and who, while governor of Siberia, had drafted the reforms which had completely overhauled the exile system and brought to it a measure of order and efficiency.

It is sometimes asked why the Decembrist revolt failed. The question should really be: did it ever stand the remotest chance of success? The answer must surely be an unequivocal 'No'. Many reasons have been adduced to support such a negative response. There was a lack of determined leadership and a chronic failure to agree over basic aims and objectives. The Decembrists were determined that the revolt should take the form of an elite military *Putsch*, and that there should on no account be any involvement of the masses. Their motives derived from a muddled amalgam of patriotism, idealism, rationalism and romanticism, humanism, liberalism, constitutionalism and republicanism. But they were devoid of the total commitment, determination and ruthlessness of the dedicated, professional, full-time revolutionary. (Pestel, with his insistence on discipline and organisation, was perhaps the nearest they had to this, and is remembered for it as the first representative of Russian 'Jacobinism'.) Their aims, it has been said, were those of men born too early; their methods those of men born too late. They were dilettante rebels; intellectuals in uniform; the quintessence of what Lenin was to call the 'gentry revolutionaries' (*dvoryanskie revolyutsionery*) with no real guts to carry through the adventure – for such it was – which they had set in motion. All these explanations are true, but subsidiary to the main point. The real underlying reason for the failure of the Decembrist revolt is that they were attempting to engineer a revolution *in the absence of a revolutionary situation*. When the conspirators decided to take to the streets there was no national emergency, no economic crisis, no breakdown of the social order, no mass disaffection, and no son of Pugachëv rampaging through the Russian countryside. In fact, there was none of the objective circumstances in place that usually constitute the preconditions for a successful revolution, as there were in 1917. There was merely a hiccup over the royal succession.

But although it failed – maybe *because* it failed – the Decembrist revolt can properly be regarded as marking the start of the nineteenth-century revolutionary movement. It is of major historical importance for a whole number of reasons. First, it was the first attempt in Russian history to transform an intellectual critique of the system of autocracy – a trail already blazed by Radishchev – into an organised (if badly organised) opposition movement and mount a physical challenge to that form of government. Second, it demonstrated that some of the most highly educated, privileged and principled members of Russian society – young, enlightened noblemen, mid-ranking military officers who had fought for their country and were unflinchingly patriotic – were prepared to launch an attempt, however half-baked, to overthrow the regime which they had served, and to replace it with a more humane, progressive and just system of government, if necessary by violent means. Third, by doing this they provided an inspiration for later generations of radical critics and opponents of the tsarist autocracy, many of whom – indeed most of whom – traced their intellectual ancestry back to the example of the Decembrists. Fourth, as a result of their execution and exile, they came to be regarded as martyrs, who, while they could not by any stretch of the imagination be described as fanatics, nevertheless acted in the knowledge of what the consequences of their action might be should it fail, and were prepared to pay the price. Finally, while their revolt combined features of intellectual opposition in the Radishchev mode, together with the mid-eighteenth-century traditions of the military coup, it failed absolutely to take account of, or in any way involve, the Russian *narod* – the people – in its calculations. Indeed, beyond inciting a regiment or two of soldiers at the eleventh hour, it did everything possible to exclude them, which contributed to the rebels' ultimate failure. Future generations of Russian revolutionaries would learn from that lesson and go on to develop theories and take practical action which saw the transformation and regeneration of Russia as being achievable *only* with and through the full, direct participation of the masses. This was particularly true of the later revolutionary Populists (*narodniki*) and the Russian Marxists (see Chapters 9 and 10).

It was, therefore, amid these portentous and dramatic circumstances, which contained elements of both tragedy and farce, that there began the reign of Emperor Nicholas I, 'the Iron Tsar'.

8 The *Nikolaevshchina*, 1825–1855

The rout of the Decembrists and the inauspicious circumstances of Nicholas I's accession ushered in what is traditionally considered to be one of the most reactionary and authoritarian regimes in the history of nineteenth-century Russia. The eminent Soviet historian, A. E. Presniakov, writing in 1925, entitled his book on Nicholas's reign 'The Apogee of Autocracy' (*Apogei samoderzhaviya*),[1] suggesting that there is a qualitative difference in the degree of absolutism wielded by Nicholas than that of any of his predecessors or successors. If the word 'apogee', borrowed figuratively from astronomy, signifies the highest point in a particular trajectory, then it follows that there must be other, lower or less distant points. It is the purpose of this chapter to test whether Nicholas's reign deserves Presniakov's superlative designation or not.

The apogee of autocracy

As has been demonstrated in previous chapters, it is in the very essence of autocratic government that the personality of an individual autocrat will affect, modify or colour the nature of the regime over which he or she presides. Such had always been the sheer extent of the power exercised by both the Muscovite and the post-Petrine tsars, all of whom held total sway over their subjects, and whose word was literally law, that the individual foibles, preferences, opinions, kinks and caprices of each ruler were bound to have a direct, palpable effect on the character of their rule. Sovereigns of a stern, cruel or tyrannous disposition do not habitually go in for liberal reforms; nor do those of a gentler, more considerate and compassionate nature usually earn their reputation by imposing a reign of bloody terror. Theoretically, all the rulers of Russia were invested with the same amount of absolute power. It was the manner in which they exercised that power which differentiated them, though only to a limited degree. There is no such thing as the moderate application of the thumbscrew.

Even before he was eventually proclaimed Emperor and Autocrat of All Russia, Grand Duke Nikolai Pavlovich was well known for his severity, lack of humour and imagination, fondness for strict military discipline and a corresponding distaste for intellectual pursuits. His 'paradomania' and punctilious attention to pettifogging detail, like that of his father, was much influenced by the Prussian military tradition. (His wife, incidentally, the Empress Mariya Fëdorovna, was originally Princess Charlotte of Prussia, daughter of King Friedrich Wilhelm III.) It was also part of an ethos which turned the army that had defeated Napoleon into squadrons of synchronised marching automata. Nicholas's infatuation with the army provided this 'drill sergeant on the throne' with the guiding philosophy for the administration and governance of his country and people, of whom he regarded himself as the divinely appointed *Kommandant*. (Though when asked, were he not emperor of Russia, what he would have preferred to be, he promptly replied, 'a drummer' – *barabanshchik*). He saw the Russian Empire rather as an enormous barracks, rigidly hierarchical and despotically controlled. At the top, the tsar ruled through a huge, more or less efficient general staff of bureaucrats, civil servants, policemen, clergymen and spies. Almost the entire senior personnel was recruited from the ranks of the land- and serf-owning nobility, the *dvoryanstvo*, whose members ranged in wealth from the fabulously rich aristocracy down to the almost impoverished petty provincial squires, some of whom were reduced to tilling their own land. His ministers were usually military generals, though none of them had seen any action in the field, and within his own personal entourage he preferred the company of Teutonic Baltic barons rather than native Russian noblemen, whose frail allegiance had been exposed during the Decembrist affair. (Nicholas's own blood was about 90 per cent German in any case. The poet Pushkin was fond of demonstrating this by pouring a measure of wine, symbolising the pure Russian blood of Peter the Great, and then diluting it with glass after glass of water, which represented the German parentage of so many of his successors.)

Apart from the other official estates (*sosloviya*) – the clergy, the merchantry and the *meshchane* (roughly, the urban class, e.g. artisans, small traders and other '*petit-bourgeois*') – the rest of the population, comprising approximately 90 per cent, consisted of the peasantry, numbering some 45 million and divided roughly equally into state peasants and privately owned serfs (*krepostnye lyudi*), who were the personal property of their lords, the *pomeshchiki*. (The origins, nature and obligations of the various estates are discussed in Chapter 1.) The whole of the peasantry, whether state or privately owned, remained sunk in a vast mire of ignorance, superstition and periodic famine. The majority adhered faithfully to the official Orthodox Church, whose doctrines they only faintly understood, and also espoused a naive brand of misplaced loyalty to the throne, an institution which was remote from their everyday existence and comprehension. This remoteness of both crown and altar from the daily grind of the common people is encapsulated in the rhyming Russian folk expression – 'God's on high, and the tsar is far away' (phonetically pronounced, *Bok vysok, i tsar' dalyok*). Killer diseases such as cholera, typhoid, smallpox and syphilis were pandemic, and the servile population was also continually plagued by the twin horrors of corporal punishment and military conscription. The frequent outbreaks of dissent, protest and opposition were always mercilessly suppressed. One of Nicholas's many appellations was 'the cudgel', and his myrmidons were unsparing in its use. He did, however, formally abolish the use of the dreaded knout in 1848, magnanimously substituting it with the three-thonged leather lash (*plet'*), and the number of convicts exiled to Siberia actually declined during his reign from over 11,000 in 1826 to 7500 in 1855, partially, no doubt, as a consequence of Speranskii's reform of the exile system in 1822.[2]

Nicholas himself was personally aware of the problems of serfdom, even condemning it as 'an evil', and in fact appointed no fewer than nine separate secret commissions to investigate the possibility of abolishing it. However, after balancing the pros and cons, he finally decided that on the whole the disadvantages of abolition outweighed the advantages, and virtually nothing was done. In 1842 the law of 1803 allowing individual owners to manumit their own peasants, at a price, was confirmed and extended, though its provisions were, again, little used, and in 1844 the *pomeshchiki* were empowered to free their household serfs (i.e. domestic servants and other menial staff of the nobleman's residence) – though without land. Otherwise, the system stayed intact. The state peasants fared rather better, and in 1838 the Minister of State Domains, Count P. D. Kiselëv (1788–1872) introduced reforming legislation which to a certain extent lightened their burden, improved their economic situation, eased their tax obligation, and extended educational and welfare provisions in their communities. These measures, however, did little to assuage the peasants' discontent with their lot, and outbreaks of unrest continued to be a regular feature of the rural scene. The explosive nature of these frequent disturbances was not lost on the government, to the extent that the serf problem was once famously described by one of Nicholas's highly placed officials as 'a powder keg' beneath the throne.

It is sometimes suggested that the dictatorial nature of Nicholas's style of government was simply a reaction to the Decembrist conspiracy. There is, however, little in his character to suggest that, even without that particular scare, the pattern of his rule would not have been marked by the same harshness, severity and obscurantism as was in fact the case. However, the events of 14 December certainly increased the emperor's morbid suspicion of further possible opposition, and confirmed him in his resolve to stamp out all traces of heterodoxy, independent thought and activity, dissent and disorder from his domain. There was in fact to be no departure during his watch from the principles of what later came to be called the theory of 'Official Nationalism' (*ofitsial'naya narodnost'*), first enunciated by Nicholas's Minister of Education, Count Sergei Uvarov (1785–1855), in 1833. The kernel of the doctrine was the tripartite formula of 'Orthodoxy, Autocracy and Nationalism' (*Pravoslavie, samoderzhavie, narodnost'*). These 'Three Articles' of the Nikolaevan faith were in reality imperial government gobbledegook for the reactionary principles of intellectual paralysis, political quietism and Great Russian chauvinism, which remained in effect the official ideology of the Romanov regime until the revolutions of 1917.

To uphold 'Orthodoxy', Uvarov – who had declared that his task as Minister of Education was 'to multiply as much as possible the number of intellectual dams' – meant simply to worship unquestioningly in the faith and ritual of the Russian Orthodox Church. Not to do so – to query, criticise or reject the teachings of the Church of Holy Russia – was not only heretical and an act of apostasy, but also tantamount to treason or *lèse majesté* (in so far as the tsar, as well as being appointed to his position by the Almighty, was also head of the Church). To be a loyal Russian was to be an Orthodox Christian. Some other religious affiliations were tolerated, but particularly abhorrent were members of schismatic 'Orthodox' sects, such as the Old Believers, and materialist, agnostic or atheist intellectuals who profaned both God and the tsar.

The second, and therefore the central, icon on the triptych of Official Nationalism was 'Autocracy'. The Orthodox tsar was the anointed sovereign of all Russia, whose secular power was of divine provenance and could not be challenged. The emperor's person was sacrosanct, his word was law, and his (or her) power was literally boundless (*bezgranichnaya*). Any act of political, moral, philosophical, individual, collective or organisational opposition to the principle of autocracy or the person of the autocrat was the most heinous crime in the Criminal Code. To entertain or advocate such un-Russian concepts as liberalism, constitutionalism, republicanism, parliamentarianism, democracy, socialism, representative government or participatory politics was in itself proof of treason against the Russian state, and would be punished accordingly – as the treatment of the Decembrists had already demonstrated.

Finally, *narodnost'*: this untranslatable term has been variously rendered into English as 'nationalism' (which is preferred here), 'nationality', 'nationhood', 'patriotism' and even 'nationism'. None of these adequately captures the sense of the Russian original, though the German word *Volkgeist* ('spirit of the people') comes closer to it. In his scholarly analysis of Official Nationalism, the American Russian émigré historian, Nicholas Riasanovsky, posits two distinct, though related, interpretations of *narodnost'*, one of which he calls the 'dynastic', and the other the 'romantic'.[3] By 'dynastic' he suggests that *narodnost'* signifies a patriotic loyalty to the state of Russia as embodied in the All-Russian Empire (*Rossiiskaya Imperiya*) and the Romanov dynasty. To display fealty to the Russian state and the Russian emperor was to demonstrate one's 'Russianness', one's 'nationality'. To do otherwise was, therefore, 'un-Russian'. This, according to the loyalists and royalists, was the essence of good, honest *narodnost'*. (One is reminded at this point of the McCarthyite campaign in the USA in the early 1950s against what were alleged to be 'un-American activities'.) The 'romantic' interpretation points to a devotion to the Russian *narod*, to Russian peasant traditions, to Russian folklore, the demotic Russian language, Russian popular institutions and common virtues as being in some way superior to those of other nationalities or alien traditions. At its best, this 'romantic' interpretation of Russian *narodnost'* is innocuous, emotional, communally bonding and 'folksy'. At its worst, it is culturally divisive, dangerously jingoistic, and ultimately encourages racialism and xenophobia. The sinister synthesis of patriotism, the people, and the person of the nation's leader contained in Uvarov's mantra is frighteningly redolent of the Nazi slogan, *Ein Volk, ein Reich, ein Führer!*

So much for the theory. But how did Nicholas set about ensuring that these three cherished principles were observed in practice? The most powerful weapon in his armoury of surveillance and control of the population was the 'Third Section of His Majesty's Personal Chancery'. Established in July 1826, barely six months after the Decembrist revolt, this extra-governmental department was one of a series of similar organs introduced to supervise and administer various areas of the nation's affairs, personally and directly responsible to the sovereign alone, and bypassing the 'proper' institutions such as the central ministries, councils and Senate. Nicholas was always a 'hands-on' ruler, wishing to be personally involved in the business of the day, prone to making sudden, unannounced tours of inspection, and taking off-the-cuff, on-the-spot decisions without recourse to established procedure, often wasting time on individual, trivial cases which prevented him from seeing the forest for the leaves. To facilitate this modus operandi, between 1826 and 1843 he set up six 'sections' of his own chancery, which dealt with specific areas of administration such as state lands, law-codification, educational institutions, the civil service and one for the governance of Transcaucasia. But overshadowing them all, and every other facet of the nation's life, was the sinister Third Section. This was in effect the headquarters and the nerve centre of the entire coercive system, the operational heart of the embryonic police state, and the direct ancestor of Stalin's NKVD.

Like other police organisations, the Third Section had a uniformed and an un-uniformed branch. The former – the corps of gendarmes – was spread throughout five quasi-military districts of the empire and was responsible for the overt maintenance of law and public order through the investigation of political subversion rather than common crime, which came within the remit of the 'ordinary' police force. The commander of each region reported directly to the head of the Third Section, the first of which was Count Aleksandr Benkendorff (1783–1844) an apparently affable ex-cavalry general who suffered from mild amnesia and was a personal friend of the tsar, to whom he, in turn, reported (though reputedly visibly blanching each time he did so). Covert operations were carried out by an undercover network of plain-clothes security agents, hired informers, stool-pigeons, sleuths and sneaks. According to the wording of the decree establishing the Third Section, the chief objects of its attention and inquiries were religious sectarians, forgers and foreigners. In addition, it was responsible for the supervision of all people already under police surveillance, for places of confinement, and for the exile of 'harmful persons'. In a literally 'catch-all' clause the agency was also instructed to furnish: 'Reports on all events, without exception.' Although its full-time senior professional staff was relatively small in number, maybe 40 or so, the Third Section, through its active agents, soon developed into a vast self-reproducing organism which penetrated, codified and sought to control every area and institution in the nation's life, including the royal palaces. It was in fact a huge internal intelligence operation directed by the tsar at the thoughts and activities, hearts and minds of the many millions of his own subjects. It was outside and above the law, answerable to Nicholas alone, and often dispensing its own arbitrary 'justice' and retribution. As such, it became the main organ of what Pipes describes as the 'prototype' of the modern police state.[4] As yet, however, it obviously did not possess the sophisticated electronic equipment and computerised means to develop along the lines of the totalitarian regimes of more recent times. It had the will, it had the organisation, it even had an ideology. All it lacked was the technology.

If the Third Section was above the law, at least the law itself received proper codification under Nicholas. Mikhail Speranskii, fresh from masterminding the trial of the Decembrists, was placed in charge of the Second Section of His Majesty's Chancery, charged with the task of bringing together, editing and publishing the entire corpus of laws, decrees and *ukazy* which had been enacted since the *Ulozhenie* of 1649 (see Chapter 3). The mammoth, multi-volume edition, 51 tomes in all, was published in 1833 – a remarkable accomplishment – under the title 'The Complete Collection of the Laws of The Russian Empire' (*Polnoe sobranie zakonov Rossiiskoi Imperii*), which systematised the entire legal and constitutional history of Russia over the past two centuries. As such, it is of inestimable value to the historical researcher. In addition, the criminal law of the country was also brought into regular order with the publication of Russia's first comprehensive Criminal Code in 1845, completed under the editorship of D. N. Bludov, following Speranskii's death in 1839. As well as common criminal offences, political crimes were also dealt with in two major chapters defining and detailing the appropriate action to be taken in the case of 'felonies against the government' (Chapter 3) and 'felonies against the system of administration' (Chapter 4), which, writes Pipes, together 'constitute a veritable constitutional charter of an authoritarian regime'.[5] Yet despite the existence of the new penal statutes, the actual administration and implementation of the duly codified laws remained arbitrary, convoluted and staggeringly corrupt. Not until 1864 was any purposeful attempt made to bring some semblance of justice into Russia's judicial system (see Chapter 9).

Not surprisingly, the rather lax censorship regulations that existed under Alexander I were considerably tightened up, and a grotesquely large number of committees were instituted to scrutinise, bowdlerise and sanitise all written works submitted for publication on the government-licensed press. The supreme censor was, of course, Nicholas himself, who, for instance, having allowed the return of Pushkin to St Petersburg society in 1827, made it a condition of his rehabilitation that everything he wrote must be submitted for the emperor's personal scrutiny before receiving the official imprimatur. One result of this was that Pushkin's marvellous poem, *The Bronze Horseman*, already referred to elsewhere in this book (Chapter 4), was not published until 1837, after Pushkin's death, and then only with Nicholas's amendments which Pushkin had himself refused to incorporate while he was alive. (Pushkin was killed in a duel to protect his wife's honour in January 1837.) The full, unexpurgated version was not published until after the Bolshevik Revolution in 1917. Most notorious of all the censorship organs was the so-called Buturlin Committee, after its first chairman, Count D. P. Buturlin (1790–1849), who in 1848 inaugurated what has been described as the 'reign of censorship terror' which lasted until 1855 – 'the gloomy septennium' (*mrachnoe semiletie*). Those whose job it was to wield the blue pencil were themselves often only half-literate, and stories of the absurdities committed in the name of preserving the purity and 'political correctness' of the written word during Nicholas's reign are legion. Similarly plentiful are the instances of journals closed, editors exiled, books banned, and authors arrested or forced to exercise a self-denying ordinance on venturing into print for fear of the censor's or, worse, the Third Section's wrath.

In view of this formidable army of military martinets, paid informers, secret policemen, semi-educated censors and black-robed archimandrites, it is quite astonishing, and even somewhat paradoxical, just how much intellectual, literary and cultural activity survived, indeed flourished, in the insalubrious atmosphere of the *Nikolaevshchina*. This was particularly so during the 'remarkable decade' of the 1840s, which in this context encompasses the years from 1836 to 1848.[6]

The remarkable decade: Westernisers and Slavophils

Chaadaev's *Philosophical Letter*[7]

The intellectual history, so to speak, of Nicholas's reign may be conveniently, if rather arbitrarily, divided into three periods: 1826–36, 1836–48 and 1848–55. During the first, post-Decembrist decade, intellectual thought and activity in Russia were driven, in the words of Martin Malia, 'not so much underground as into the stratosphere'.[8] Highly cultured malcontents of the day found in Nicholas's empire no respectable outlet for their talents, and inhabited a kind of socio-intellectual limbo between the idealism of their aspirations and the philistinism of the Third Section. Viewed from one angle they were the rump-end of the glittering, sophisticated youth of Alexander I's reign, the generation which had spawned Speranskii, Pushkin and Pestel. Looked at from another angle, they formed the nucleus of the radical intelligentsia which was soon to swell into such an explosive force in Russian history.

For the time being, however, their revolt was purely cerebral. Lacking any practical channels for their energy, intelligent and sensitive youths of their day plunged into an orgy of introspective inquiry and metaphysical speculation, or else soared into a cloud-cuckoo-land of abstract concepts, ethereal notions and hazy, narcotic visions. It was the age of the dreamer and the 'superfluous man', both familiar 'types' in the literature of the day. This does not mean that they were simply 'dropouts'. They did not retire to their garrets or languish on their couches because they were inherently bored, indolent or craven. On the contrary, their endless inquiries and their ceaseless philosophising were imbued with a feverish singleness of purpose which in a more stimulating environment would have been less emptily dissipated, but which set its stamp on the obsessive mentality of the intelligentsia for the next 100 years.

In 1836 they were brought down to earth with a jolt by the publication of an article in the journal, 'The Telescope' (*Teleskop*), written by a familiar figure in St Petersburg's intellectual circles and close friend of Pushkin, Pëtr Chaadaev (1794–1856). The article was in epistolary form, and entitled *Philosophical Letter to a Lady*. In style it is somewhat turgid, circumlocutory and abstruse, which perhaps explains why the censor, too ignorant to 'decipher' its real meaning, nodded it through for publication. The use of a term from the world of cryptography is here deliberate, as the controversial writers of the time had developed a kind of literary code in which to convey their message. Known as the 'Æsopean language' (*Ezopov yazyk*) – that is, the language of allusion, allegory and periphrasis as used in fabulistic literature – it was designed to mask the meaning and bamboozle the bureaucrats. While Chaadaev did not quite employ this device in his *Letter*, his choice of language obviously had a similar effect, and the piece was duly printed. But the capital's literati and cognoscenti were not as easily duped, and the work's appearance caused an immediate furore. Copies of the journal were impounded, *The Telescope* was banned, its editor was exiled and Chaadaev was himself arrested, pronounced insane, confined under house arrest and subjected to periodic examination by a military doctor. However, the great socialist thinker, Aleksandr Herzen, was later to describe its contents as 'a pistol shot in the dead of night', and its detonation was to signal the start of one of the most intense and pivotal debates in Russia's entire intellectual history.

Just three years after Uvarov had expounded his 'theory' of Official Nationalism, with all that that implied in terms of the excellence, incomparability and essential paramountcy of all things Russian, as described above, Chaadaev regaled his reading public with the explicit (not even Æsopean) proposition that Russia was a blank page in the history of mankind and had added nothing to the sum total of human progress. In grand rhetorical, if repetitive, style, he asks:

> Where are our wise men, where are our philosophers? ... Placed between two divisions of the world, between the East and the West, resting one elbow on China and the other on Germany, we ought to combine in ourselves the two great principles of human intelligence, imagination and reason, and fuse in our civilization the history of all parts of the globe. ... [But] we are alone in the world, we have given nothing to the world. ... We have produced nothing for the benefit of mankind ... not one great thought has emerged from our midst ...[9]

and so on, and so on. Elsewhere, having extolled the western traditions of justice, right, order and rational thought, he went on to declare that, 'we all lack a certain assurance, a certain method in our thinking, a certain logic. The syllogism of the West is unknown to us.'[10]

Where Russia went wrong, Chaadaev added, was in taking its Christianity from what he regards as the corrupt source of 'wretched Byzantium', thereby missing out on the great civilising and unifying experiences of the west such as the Renaissance, Latin and Roman law. In their place Russia's past was merely the history of territorial expansion, despotism and servitude. This was strong stuff indeed for the champions of Russian 'Orthodoxy, Autocracy and Nationalism'. Little wonder they thought he was mad. And perhaps they were right. No one but a lunatic would dare to utter such unpatriotic, blasphemous and treacherous thoughts in the Russia of Nicholas, Official Nationalism and the Third Section. Even Chaadaev himself – once described as a 'Decembrist turned mystic' – appeared to acknowledge this in a later retraction, written in 1837 and entitled 'Apology of a Madman' (*Apologie d'un fou*), though there are grounds for doubting the sincerity of his explanation.[11]

Beyond the intrinsic value of Chaadaev's letter as an exposition of his own philosophy of history, it also acted more importantly as a catalyst in the process of intellectual fermentation among Russia's emerging intelligentsia which would split its members into two opposing camps, known ever since as the 'Westernisers' and the 'Slavophils'.

Westernisers and Slavophils

The 'remarkable decade' of the 1840s was dominated in the intellectual life of the country by the great jousting contest between the pro-western admirers of Chaadaev's critique of Russia's backwardness and semi-barbarism, and those who were appalled by his condemnation of Russia's Orthodox Christian heritage and the character of the Russian *narod*. The former came to be called the 'Westernisers', or, in Russian, *zapadniki*, from the geographical term *zapad*, the West. The latter were called the 'Slavophils' – *slavyanofily* – that is, lovers of all things Slavonic. Both terms were misnomers.

Zapadnik, a word which has derogatory undertones, implies an excessive, unquestioning adulation of all things western, or more precisely, west European, and a rejection of everything Russian. But apart from the difficulty of defining 'the West' or 'Europe' in the first place, the Westernisers were equally as devoted to Russia as were their opponents, but believed that the country could move forward only along more civilised, just and humane lines by learning from the west, in particular from her respect for individual liberty, her secular science and her law. Their idol was Peter the Great, who had forced Russia to march out of its Muscovite mediaevalism into the modern world. The time had come for the country to resume that march forward. The Slavophils, on the other hand, considered Peter to be at the twisted root of Russia's problems. He it was who had destroyed the organic unity of Russia's past by his brutal introduction of foreign ideas and alien practices. While some of them admired certain features of European culture, and all of them were well versed in it, they saw an earnest of Russia's future greatness in the vanished virtues of a largely imaginary ancient Muscovy, which they wished to revivify.

Neither the Westernisers nor the Slavophils were of uniform complexion, but the latter were, by the very nature of their philosophy, with its emphasis on community and collegiality, of a more homogeneous nature than the more individualistic, more variegated Europeanists. It was suggested above that 'Slavophil' is a misnomer. It would be more accurate, if more long-winded, to describe them as 'romantic, Orthodox, nationalist Russophils'. The best known of their circle were: Aleksei Khomyakov (1804–60); the brothers Ivan and Pëtr Kireevskii (1806–56; 1808–56); two more brothers, Konstantin and Ivan Aksakov (1817–60; 1823–86), the sons of the writer, Sergei Aksakov; and Yurii Samarin (1819–76). All were comfortably-off landowners, some of them related by blood or marriage, all highly educated, and based in the Moscow region – in fact a rather cosy, close-knit circle of fellow-savants, an intimacy which is in a sense reflected in their shared ideas. Each, though, had his own particular specialism.

Khomyakov was their most eminent theologian, or rather religious philosopher, but was also more tuned in to the practical implications of his belief in the primacy of Orthodox traditions and popular institutions such as the village commune. He developed and was the leading proponent of the concept of *sobornost'*, another untranslatable term which is usually given in English as 'conciliarity' – that is, the essential, spiritual communality and organic 'oneness' of the Russian people, bound together in the faith and unity of the Orthodox Church. Moreover, it was only the Orthodox Church which had preserved the original integrity and wholeness of early, pre-schismatic Christianity before the western church introduced the *filioque* cause into the creed,[12] and began its steady descent into scholasticism, rationalism, Protestantism, materialism and atheism. By applying his theories of spiritual distinctiveness Khomyakov went on to identify two essentially different 'types' in mankind. These he rather quaintly called the 'Kushite' (from the biblical word for Ethiopia, the 'land of Kush'), and the 'Iranian'. 'Kushitism', which he believed characterised pagan societies, Ancient Rome, Roman Catholicism and European civilisation in general, was based on the principles of coercion, conquest, hierarchy, reason and the imposition of law, whereas 'Iranianism' was distinguished by freedom, faith, voluntarism, community and, above all, *sobornost'*. It was axiomatic to Khomyakov that the Iranian principle pervaded the Slavic peoples and that 'the spirit of Slavdom (and therefore of Iranianism) was expressed in its purest form in the Russian people'.[13] (Catholic Poland – 'the Judas of Slavdom' – was, of course an exception.)

Of the Kireevskii brothers, the elder, Ivan, was the early Slavophils' leading publicist. Originally an ardent admirer of western civilisation, he underwent a religious crisis out of which he emerged as a firm believer in the innate superiority of Russia over the West as a result of the unsullied nature of its Orthodox Christian faith which had preserved its spiritual integrity intact, as opposed to the nation-states of Europe, which had been created by conquest, ruined by Roman Catholicism and destroyed by individualistic particularism. The 'rotten West' (*gniloi zapad*) was riven by social atomisation and the class struggle; 'Holy Russia' was bound together by *sobornost'*. His brother Pëtr was well known as a folklorist whose researches and published anthologies of songs, stories, legends and saws gathered together and preserved in written form the collective oral wisdom of the simple Russian *narod* which was at the heart of the Slavophils' social philosophy. Their *political* ideology, in so far as it can be called one, was given its clearest, but also its most questionable, exposition by the elder of the Aksakov brothers, Konstantin, in a later memorandum presented to Nicholas's successor, Alexander II, in 1855. His basic message was that the Russian people was *a*political, and that it had no 'lust for power'. He states:

> Proof of this is to be found in the beginnings of our history, when the Russians *of their own free will* [emphasis added] invited foreigners to Rule over them – the Varangians, Ryurik and his brothers. Even more telling proof is to be seen in the Russia of 1612 [*sic* – it was actually 1613], when … even as they had done in 862, the people called on others to rule over them; they chose a tsar and, having wholly entrusted their fate to him, they peaceably laid down their arms and returned to their homes.[14]

This palpable nonsense about what were admittedly important turning points in Russia's past conveniently ignored the centuries of bloodshed through which the country waded in the early centuries of its history, and presents a distorted image of the supposedly submissive, irenic nature of the Russian people. Elsewhere he went on:

> Without wishing to *rule*, our people wish to *live* [original emphasis] … without seeking political freedom, they seek moral freedom, the freedom of the spirit, communal freedom – life in society within the confines of the people … Hence we need a sovereign, a monarch. Only a monarch's power can be absolute. Only under an absolute monarchy can the people draw a line between itself and the state.

And finally, amazingly:

> … the people do not meddle in governmental or administrative matters; the state, for its part, does not meddle in the life and ways of the people, does not force them to live according to its rules.[15]

One *is* forced to wonder whether Aksakov knew of the existence of 51 volumes of *The Complete Collection of the Laws of the Russian Empire*, or indeed anything at all about the real nature of his country's history!

Together with the publicistic and journalistic activities of the younger Ivan, the combined efforts of the Aksakov brothers helped to popularise Slavophil ideas, though in Ivan's case, he was responsible for developing a debased form of their ideology which appealed to ignorance, anti-Semitism and xenophobia for its support. All the Slavophils believed passionately in the freedom of the individual, which could be achieved, however, only within the community. They were thus staunch supporters of the abolition of serfdom, and it was Yurii Samarin who, of all the original Slavophils of the 1840s, did most by his practical personal participation in the work of the drafting committee which worked out the terms of the actual emancipation settlement of 1861, to ensure that the rural commune, the *obshchina* or *mir*, was preserved as the bedrock of peasant life. In this way the Slavophils' romantic vision of the spiritual uniqueness and blissful social 'togetherness' of the traditional peasants' commune became translated into official, legislative fact.

It may appear that some of the Slavophils' teaching, with its emphasis on the spiritual supremacy of Orthodoxy, its belief in the necessity of absolute autocracy, and its support for national virtues and traditions as preserved in the Russian peasant commune, came alarmingly close to the theory of Official Nationalism. However, their critique of the Petrine state – which they regarded as over-militarised, over-bureaucratised and over-Germanised – their support for peasant emancipation and freedom of the press, their opposition to capital and corporal punishment, and the simple fact that their ideas were a manifestation of independent thought – which Nicholas was determined to eliminate – made them just as much a target of the government's animosity as the more obviously anti-tsarist out-pourings and activities of the Westernisers and other free-thinkers.

To summarise, Slavophilism was essentially a religious phenomenon, a major tenet of which pointed to the existence of a spiritual, almost anthropological, divide between Slavdom and individualistic, egotistical, belligerent western man, obsessed with private property, evincing a solipsistic neglect of the common good, and relying on a set of coercive written laws to protect his spurious freedom. Europe was in fact decadent, moribund and putrescent – hence the frequent charges aimed against the 'rotten West'. Slavophils also extolled the benefits of monarchical government, but berated the Russian state as created by the monarchical will of Peter the Great, who they believed had ravished the virgin purity of immaculate, Orthodox Russia and destroyed its organic unity. In a romantic vision which ignored reality, they sought to repair the ruptured hymen of Russian history by advocating a return to the largely mythologised Muscovite past. But the basic flaw at the heart of Slavophilism – lambasted by the Westernisers for its fundamental religiosity and its sophistical advocacy of autocracy – was the contradiction between their paradoxical attempt to reconcile the oecumenical, genuinely 'catholic' nature of pristine Christianity, with their ideas of Russia's uniqueness, exclusiveness and superiority. In a curious way, this prefigures the later contradiction between classical Marxism's internationalist vision of the victory of universal, worldwide Communism, and Stalin's narrow nationalistic doctrine of building 'Socialism in One Country'.

Turning now to the Westernisers, one cannot so easily identify a single, unifying set of principles, as was the case with the Slavophils. Inspired by the individualism of the West, which they, unlike the Slavophils, regarded as a virtue, their own individual views covered a wide spectrum from the romantic conservatism of Chaadaev, derived from his admiration for mediaeval, Catholic Europe, through the liberal constitutionalism and legalism of T. N. Granovskii (1813–55), Professor of History at Moscow University, the rather more right-wing jurist, B. N. Chicherin (1828–1904), and assorted *littérateurs* such as P. V. Annenkov (1812–87), V. P. Botkin (1811–69) and the celebrated novelist Ivan Turgenev (1818–83). Though their views differed from one to another, they all favoured the emancipation of the serfs, the introduction of a constitutional form of government, the observation of full civil rights and a vague, woolly admiration for 'European values', whatever they might be. On the left wing of the spectrum, and rather more significant in their longer term historical impact, stood Mikhail Bakunin (1814–76), Vissarion Belinskii (1811–48), and 'the father of Russian socialism', Aleksandr Herzen (1812–70).[16]

Bakunin, who is perhaps better known in the West as one of the leading ideologues of European anarchism, was also a pioneer of western-inspired radicalism during the late 1830s and early 1840s. He studied for a time at the University of Berlin, where he became familiar with the currently fashionable philosophy of Hegel and the 'left Hegelians' such as Feuerbach. From the latter he learned of the revolutionary implications of Hegel's dialectical method of reasoning, and underwent the conversion from 'abstract philosopher' to 'abstract revolutionary'.[17] It was Bakunin who, on his return to Russia, was largely responsible for disseminating knowledge of Hegelianism in the celebrated, semi-clandestine discussion circles which flourished at Moscow University at the time. These circles (*kruzhki* – sing. *kruzhok*) were hotbeds of intellectual ferment and passionate debate in the unfavourable climate of Nicholas's Russia. They were later described by Herzen, one of their leading lights, as 'islands of freedom in a sea of tyranny', and by the Third Section as 'gangs of liberal bandits'.[18] Bakunin was an habitué of the circle originally led by the popular young idealist, N. V. Stankevich (1813–40), and it was here and in the more politically orientated *kruzhok* led by Herzen that the dialectic of Hegel became transformed into what the latter called 'the algebra of revolution'.

Between 1844 and 1851, Bakunin was back in Europe throwing himself into the maelstrom of radical ideas and rebellious activity which finally exploded into the national revolts of 1848, 'the year of revolutions'. Among other causes, he briefly espoused a primitive form of what later in the century developed into the Panslavist movement (see Chapter 9), and also displayed a distinct anti-Germanism ('St Petersburg', he once said, 'is in reality a camouflaged German') which was later to manifest itself in his personal dislike of and ideological rivalry with Karl Marx, a dispute which partly led to the dissolution of the first International Workingmen's Association in 1876. He had already established a reputation for revolutionary *Schadenfreude* by his essay of 1842 entitled 'Reaction in Germany', in which he declared that 'the passion (*die Lust*) for destruction is also a creative passion', and this was soon to mature into the fully developed anarchism and anti-statism of his later years. (His later activities do not really concern us here, but it is worth recording that, after leaping from one barricade to another in revolutionary Europe in 1848 [Paris, Prague, Dresden], he was finally arrested by the Austrian-Hungarian police, imprisoned, and extradited in 1851 to Russia where he was gaoled in the SS Peter and Paul fortress before being exiled to Siberia in 1857. He escaped from Siberia in 1861 and eventually returned via Japan and the USA to Europe, where he became one of the leading ideologists of the Russian revolutionary Populist movement in the 1870s – see Chapter 9.) Always an ardent believer in individual freedom and the revolutionary instincts of the masses, Bakunin remains one of the giants of both Russian and European revolutionary thought.

Less flamboyant and lacking the personal magnetism of Bakunin, but with his own special importance in the history of Russian radicalism, is Vissarion Belinskii. Although a formidable social and political thinker, it was as a literary critic that he made his biggest impact, though in the context of nineteenth-century Russia it is difficult to disentangle literary and social criticism. Writers of the time who had even a scintilla of social conscience were beginning to emerge from their romantic youth and to compose increasingly authentic portrayals of present-day Russian reality. Until the alarm call of Chaadaev's *Letter*, as mentioned above, they had sated themselves on a diet of German idealistic philosophy and romantic poetry, the works of Schiller and Schelling, Schlegel and Hegel. But now they began to descend from the intoxicating higher regions of abstract intellection with their anguished apostrophes about Truth, Beauty, Love and the 'Beautiful Soul' (Schiller's *die schöne Seele*), to the more fetid climate of Nikolaevan Russia, bringing to bear the same enthusiasm they had applied to metaphysics on the social, moral and political problems of the day. It was Belinskii more than anyone else who guided Russian literature along the path of 'critical realism'. In his view of things, it was the sacred duty of the writer to turn his muse to a critique of the 'accursed questions' (*proklyatye voprosy*) which plagued the country – the problems of serfdom, oppression, political freedom, corporal punishment and tyranny. *Ars gratia artis* was no longer sufficient: art must be used in the service of humanity and its basic needs.

Belinskii went through a number of intellectual phases, shedding his early romanticism and surviving a period of 'reconciliation with reality' which he briefly espoused in the early 1840s, influenced by Hegel's dictum that 'all that is real is rational, and all that is rational is real', before he embraced what he called 'socialism', or rather 'the social spirit' (*sotsial'nost'*). By this he meant not a socio-economic system based on the common ownership of the means of production and distribution – a Marxian concept – but an almost utopian belief in total human freedom and the brotherhood of all mankind. This happy state, he came increasingly to believe, would be achieved only by revolutionary change, if necessary by violent revolution. In a letter to Botkin he ranted: 'People are so stupid that you have to drag them to happiness. And, in any case, what is the blood of thousands in comparison to the humiliation and suffering of millions?'[19] Although it would be going too far to describe Belinskii as a 'revolutionary socialist' – as he has been by Soviet eulogists – the passion, the anger and extremism of his hatred for Nicholas I's oppressive tyranny, the terrible fury which imbued his invective, and the mesmerising influence he exerted on the moral and literary commitment of the intelligentsia ensured his status both in the pantheon of Russia's most famous rebels, and in the rogues' gallery of the Russian secret police. 'Furious Vissarion', as he was known, died of consumption – which had plagued nearly his whole life – in St Petersburg in 1848, thereby, in the words of the head of the Third Section, 'robbing the Schlüsselburg fortress of its prey'.[20] Before his premature death, however, he managed to pen his final burning philippic, the famous 'Letter to Gogol' (*Pis'mo k Gogol'yu*).

The occasion was the publication, in 1847, of Nikolai Gogol's grotesque, sanctimonious gallimaufry of perverted, pietistic platitudes entitled 'Selected Passages from Correspondence with Friends' (*Vybrannye mesta iz perepiski s druz'yami*). Its long-winded title captures the flatulent prolixity and pomposity of its contents, which are little more than a bombastic encomium to social inequality, the moral efficacy of corporal punishment, the unchallengeable wisdom of the Orthodox hierarchy, fear as the basis of family life and, in short, all the evil appurtenances of the police state, as encapsulated in the malign principles of Orthodoxy, Autocracy and Nationalism. Even the Slavophils were shocked, but Belinskii was incandescent. Having earlier lauded and encouraged Gogol as a brilliant exemplar of the school of 'critical realism', as the author of 'The Government Inspector' (*Revizor*), which ridicules the inanities and boorishness of provincial officialdom, and the hilariously funny 'Dead Souls' (*Mërtvye dushi*), Gogol's masterpiece in which the wickedness of serfdom is stripped bare in all its pathetic, tragic ugliness, Belinskii reacted to the book as one would to a particularly nasty personal insult. Addressing Gogol as 'Advocate of the knout, apostle of ignorance and reactionary mysticism, eulogist of Tatar customs', he asks:

> What are you doing? … That you tie in your ideas with the Orthodox Church I can well understand – it has always been the champion of the knout and the toady of despotism: but why bring in Christ? What do you think he has in common with any Church, particularly the Orthodox Church? He was the first to teach men the ideals of liberty, equality and fraternity, and He illustrated and proved the truth of His teaching by His martyrdom. But it was man's salvation only until a Church was organised around it, based on the principle of orthodoxy … the Church which is an enemy and persecutor of brotherhood among men … You say the Russian people are the most religious in the world. A lie! … The Russian only speaks the name of God while scratching his arse …

In an earlier passage, Belinskii declared that:

> The most topical and urgent questions in Russia today are the abolition of serfdom, the repeal of corporal punishment, and the strictest application of at least those laws which are already on the books.[21]

Belinskii's *Letter* was a searing, bitter tirade which was not only his last testament, but also a statement, written with a pen dipped in vitriol, of the increasingly militant temper of the younger, tougher intelligentsia that was soon to emerge out of the oppression of the *Nikolaevshchina*.

Different again in both temperament and achievement from his rebellious comrades, though no less of a rebel himself, was Aleksandr Herzen, perhaps the most prolific, influential and celebrated of the radical intellectuals of the 'remarkable decade'. Born out of wedlock in 1812, the son of a wealthy nobleman and a German Lutheran mother, the young Aleksandr Ivanovich was present in 1826 at a service in one of the Kremlin cathedrals to give thanks for the suppression of the Decembrist revolt and, by implication, the execution of its leaders. The precocious youth was appalled by the macabre ceremony, and later swore an adolescent oath, along with his cousin, Nikolai Ogarëv (1813–77), to dedicate their lives to avenging the martyrs of 14 December. And that, in effect, is just what they both did. At Moscow University, Herzen was the leader of one of the famous *kruzhki*, reckoned to be the one which was most clearly political in its concerns and orientation, and also the one that was most vociferous in its opposition to the circle of the Slavophils. Though he later denied being influenced by the German idealists, he was certainly an avid student of Schiller and Schelling, and later persuaded of the revolutionary implications of Hegelianism. But it was his close study of contemporary French socialist thinkers such as St Simon, along with some alleged indiscretions contained in an intercepted personal letter, which brought him to the attention of the secret police, and in 1834, aged 22, he was arrested, imprisoned, interrogated (with the civility appropriate to his social status) and exiled to the remote province of Perm as a 'free-thinker'. He was later transferred to Vyatka, where he married an illegitimate cousin,

Natalya, with whom he was passionately in love, but who was to bring him such anguish in later years through her affair with his male cousin, Nikolai Ogarëv. As far as romance was concerned, Herzen and his relatives certainly believed in keeping things in the family. In 1840, he returned to Moscow, where he immersed himself in the serious study of Hegel and soon afterwards moved to St Petersburg, where once more he fell foul of the police and received another short spell of exile. Eventually he was permitted to reside in Moscow, under police surveillance, until 1847 when he used his connections (and his considerable inherited wealth) to gain permission to travel abroad. He left Russia in January 1847, never to return.

Herzen's early biography has been given in a certain amount of detail because his experiences and his intellectual journey were in some ways typical of the young, radically minded, gentry intelligentsia of the 1840s, and because of the legacy of those years in his future philosophical and political development. His personal experiences, his brushes with the police, his student activities, his familiarity with what were regarded as dangerously seditious foreign ideas, his admiration for the secular thought and the individual freedoms of the West, his years in exile and the frustration at being the perpetual object of official snoopery – all of this instilled in him a passionate hatred of Nicholas's regime and caused in him an inexorable emotional and intellectual drift, rather than lurch, towards the idea of revolution. Herzen's writings of the 1840s contain frequent references to the concept of 'rebirth', 'renewal', 'renaissance' and the equivalent Greek term 'palingenesis', which he constantly reiterated. He set off on his expedition to Europe in the high expectation that there he would find further inspiration, this time at first hand, in translating the revolutionary ideas of such gurus of the left as Fourier, Proudhon and Blanc into concrete action to bring about fundamental change to the social and political order of his wretched homeland. He was to be sadly disillusioned. In Paris in particular, cradle of the great revolution, capital of the land of *liberté, égalité, fraternité*, he was rapidly appalled by the philistinism, the commercialism, the money-grubbing greed of '*les grénouilles à paraplui*' – the detested bourgeoisie whose depressing triumph he witnessed on the streets of Paris in 1848. Eugene Lampert perfectly sums up Herzen's horror of the banal values and the repellent mindlessness of the French middle classes in the following passage, which could well have come from Herzen's own pen:

> He looked, sickened, at the infinite cosiness of the *bourgeois*' rounded up thoughts, feelings and actions, of his hermetically bottled art and learning, of his culture for its own sake, of self-sufficient little decencies and indecencies, of artful dilemmas and moral questions felicitously answered. He saw the turbid pleasures and secret vices of the *bourgeois*, who enjoyed no freedom even in evil, who never wasted a thing but kept a budget of his pleasures … who was senile of heart and mind, hedged round by the constricted virtues of egotism, thrift and the family instinct, and crawling with principles like a corpse with maggots.[22]

As a result of his disillusionment with what his Slavophil opponents had derided as the 'rotten West', aggravated by the devastating discovery of Natalya's adultery, not only with Ogarëv, but also with the egocentric German poetaster, Georg Herweg, Herzen made two important shifts in his life. First, he moved physically from Paris to London. And, second, he made an emotional and psychological migration from the Europe of his dreams back to his beloved Russia and to the Russian people. It was, however, a migration only in the mind, for he spent the rest of his life in one European city or another constantly working for the consummation of his revolutionary aspirations in his homeland. In doing so, he arrived at a kind of synthesis, in the grand Hegelian manner, of his earlier Westernism with some aspects of the Slavophilism which he had so much despised. This transition, which led to the 'birth of Russian socialism', is dealt with in the following chapter.[23]

After the revolutionary events in Europe in 1848, Nicholas continued his reactionary policies with increased vigilance and rigour behind an 'iron curtain' of conformity and control. University syllabuses were revised to exclude subversive subjects from the syllabus; cultural contacts with the west were severed; Belinskii had died; Bakunin languished in a foreign gaol; Herzen had quitted

Russia for good; the Slavophils retired to their estates; the 'circles' at Moscow University were dissolved in Nicolaic acid. In St Petersburg, in 1849, members of a clandestine discussion group, known as the *Petrashevtsy*, after their leader, Mikhail Butashevich-Petrashevskii (1821–66), which met every Friday evening at his apartment in order to discuss the ideas, chiefly, of French socialist thinkers, were raided and arrested by the police on suspicion of plotting an insurrection. One of their number, N. A. Speshnev, may have harboured such conspiratorial designs, but the majority gathered merely to debate the thoughts of such people as St Simon, Proudhon, Blanc, and especially Fourier, whose plans for the establishment of self-sufficient, self-administering agrarian communities, called 'phalansteries', had attracted considerable attention. After a cursory investigation by a special commission, 20 of the *Petrashevtsy*, including Petrashevskii, Speshnev and the young writer, Fëdor Dostoevskii (1821–81), were sentenced to death by firing squad, and 51 to various terms of hard labour and exile. Three of the condemned men were already wearing their white execution gowns, tied to the stake and waiting for the order to fire when, at the very last moment, and right on cue, a proclamation was read out commuting the sentence to penal servitude in Siberia. With this grim, melodramatic charade, the 'remarkable decade' was at an end.

The 1840s were not, however, remarkable just for the ferment of social and political thought, as exemplified by the Westerniser/ Slavophil controversy. The heightened social consciousness of the Russian intelligentsia is also illustrated in the literature of the day. The works of Mikhail Lermontov (1814–41), Nikolai Gogol (1809–52), Ivan Turgenev (1818–83), Nikolai Nekrasov (1821–77) and Fëdor Dostoevskii, among others, accurately mirror the mood of the 1840s and highlight in their *belles-lettres* the concerns of its most sensitive representatives. (One excludes, obviously, Gogol's pernicious *Selected Passages*, mentioned above.) In such works as Lermontov's 'Hero of our Time' (*Geroi nashego vremeni*, 1840), Gogol's 'Dead Souls' (*Mërtvye dushi*, 1842) and 'The Overcoat' (*Shinel'*, 1843), Turgenev's 'A Huntsman's Sketches' (*Zapiski okhotnika*, 1843–4), Dostoevskii's 'Poor Folk' (*Bednye lyudi*, 1845) and 'The Double' (*Dvoinik*, 1846), and Herzen's 'Who is Guilty?' (*Kto vinovat?*, 1847), the 'long short story' (*povest'*) and the realistic prose novel had taken on a new confidence, a new maturity. No longer the exclusive preserve of the dandified nobility, the portrait gallery of Russian literature began to lose something of its exclusive gentility and open its doors to the people, admitting alongside alienated aristocrats and 'superfluous men' (*lishnye lyudi*), impoverished artists, petty clerks, peasants, Germans, junkies, tailors and tarts – 'The Lower Depths' of Russian society, as later described in Maksim Gorkii's play (*Na dne*, 1902). The method was now purposefully realistic and the mode necessarily critical. The settings were authentic, and the characters were recognisably Russian, grappling with Russian problems. Under the guiding influence of Belinskii, literature, like the intelligentsia, was coming of age, and with adulthood came a sharpened sense of social responsibility. The best of the novels, plays and stories were suffused with a spirit of intense humanism, a concern for the feelings and sufferings of other individuals and for the predicament of Russian society. Man, and not a disembodied ideal, was now the measure of all things. The 'Insulted and the Injured', to borrow the title of Dostoevskii's later novel (*Unizhennye i oskorblënnye*, 1861) had now found a voice. From now on Russian literature, and with it the Russian intelligentsia, would remain *engagée*, morally and socially committed. And it was during the remarkable decade of the 1840s, at the height of the *Nikolaevshchina*, that it made that commitment and delineated both the extent and the quality of its involvement with Russian reality.

When Dostoevskii returned in 1859 from the charnel house of Siberian imprisonment and exile, what he later called 'The House of the Dead',[24] Russia had survived the 'gloomy septennium' of Nicholas's final years, the 'crowned drummer-boy' was dead, a new generation of intelligentsia had taken the stage, and most critically, the new tsar, Alexander II, his government and the whole nation were getting to grips with the repercussions of their first major defeat in international war since the battle of Narva in 1700. How did Russia become involved in the Crimean War, and why did she lose it?

Foreign policy and the Crimean War

If Nicholas was known for his domestic policies as the 'drill-sergeant on the throne', abroad he was regarded as the 'Gendarme of Europe', officiously policing the maintenance of legitimate order throughout the continent in the spirit of the Holy Alliance. From his accession in

1825 until the outbreak of the Crimean War, he pursued a vigorous, even aggressive, foreign policy in which his two major preoccupations were: first, that of ensuring the peace, stability and permanence of the legitimate monarchies of Europe and in general preserving the imperial status quo as established by the Treaty of Vienna of 1815; and, second, the so-called 'Eastern question' – that is, the same question that exercised the other major continental powers and Great Britain, of how to conduct relations with the declining Ottoman Empire, which Nicholas himself described as 'the sick man of Europe'.

On the first matter, Nicholas demonstrated his granite determination to crush all forms of actual or potential revolt against the imperial system by dealing with a crisis within his own realm, which in a sense lay halfway between domestic and foreign policy. That was the brutal military suppression of the Polish uprising of 1830. It will be remembered that after the third partition of Poland in 1795, Russia had swallowed up most of the ancient kingdom in its own capacious maw. In 1815, Alexander had granted what was now officially known as the Congress Kingdom of Poland a comparatively liberal constitution which gave the elected Diet a fair amount of autonomy in administering its own internal affairs. It even had its own army, observed the Napoleonic Code in legal matters, and established the University of Warsaw in 1816 and the national Polish Bank in 1828. The relatively benign governance of Alexander, however, was to end with the accession of his younger brother in 1825. 'Constitutionally' unfitted to the role of a constitutional monarch, to whom the very term was anathema, Nicholas soon began to meddle in the operation of the Polish army, police and judicial system, while the agents of his Third Section regularly prosecuted suspected subversives, in flagrant contravention of the 1815 settlement. Against the background of the July Revolution in Paris and the declaration of Belgian independence, internal tensions within Poland were exacerbated by the abortive attempt to assassinate Nicholas's brother, Constantine, Viceroy of Poland, in November 1830, and the decision of the Diet to dethrone Nicholas. However, the Polish nationalists were split by squabbles between left and right and, after a few weeks' stand-off, Nicholas, despairing of successful negotiations, finally invaded the Congress Kingdom in February 1831. Although Russian military victory did not come easily, eventually Warsaw was taken, the constitution was suspended, the Diet dissolved, and summary field courts-martial condemned 80,000 insurgent Poles to penal servitude and perpetual banishment to Siberia. General Ivan Paskevich, 'the butcher of Warsaw', was appointed as virtual military dictator, any further pretence at constitutionalism was abandoned, and a determined campaign of Russification, aimed at the Polish language, Polish schools and the Polish Church was introduced, which attempted to bring the country into line with the rest of Nicholas's unhappy empire. The 'Iron Tsar' had made his point with an iron fist.

Nicholas's natural fear of liberalism, democracy and the nationalist aspirations of all subject peoples was reinforced by the European revolutions of 1848. To the tsar in the Winter Palace it seemed that barricades were being thrown up across the entire continent, threatening to destroy what may be termed the *status quo post-bellum* which followed the defeat of Napoleon and the peace of Vienna. Moreover, the popular insurrections, which took place in the same year as Karl Marx and Friedrich Engels published their *Manifesto of the Communist Party*, displayed 'a distinct proletarian and socialist character'.[25] Marx had opened his seminal pamphlet with the famous warning, 'A spectre is haunting Europe – the spectre of Communism', and Nicholas was determined to take all necessary measures to ensure that the spectre did not float through the great wall of changelessness which he had erected along the western borders of his empire. He was not, however, averse to crossing those borders in the opposite direction, if by doing so he could exorcise the spirit of revolution before it took on flesh and thrived. His willingness to rescue the Bourbon monarchy in 1830 had come to nothing, but in 1849 he eagerly accepted the invitation of the Austrian Government to step in to help suppress the nationalist Hungarian revolt led by Lajos Kossuth (1802–94). Russia's military intervention under General Paskevich was decisive, and in August 1849 the Magyars' cause for independence from Hapsburg rule was lost, the Hungarian army laid down its arms, Kossuth fled to Turkey, and 13 Hungarian generals were executed, a terrible vengeance which even Nicholas, the hangman of the Decembrists, thought excessive.

If the emperor's determination to uphold legitimism in Europe was unshakable, in the case of Turkey he found himself impaled on the horns of a dilemma. Russia's ambitions vis-à-vis the sick man of

Europe had long historical antecedents. But with the latter's strength failing fast, and his power over his non-Turkish subject peoples increasingly challenged – by Greece, Egypt and the Balkan Slavs – Russia was torn between its declared policy of supporting the integrity of *all* 'legitimate' empires, including the Ottoman version, and taking advantage of Turkey's malaise in order to extend Russia's power in the Balkans and the Middle East. By encouraging the centrifugal forces of the various national independence movements, one half of Nicholas's advisers saw an opportunity to complete his grandmother's unaccomplished 'Greek project' (see Chapter 6), while the other half foresaw the dangers of expansionism and the resulting head-on confrontation with the other great powers, particularly Britain and France, in the eastern Mediterranean. The western governments for their part entertained no illusions about the predatory pretensions of Russia on the Bosphorus and beyond. London especially believed it was Russia's firm intent to establish its power in the Balkans, and Nicholas's periodic declarations of indifference to Turkey's future cut no ice with the largely Russophobic British. For the time being, Nicholas resisted the temptation to go to the assistance of the sultan's Orthodox Slavonic subjects, a disruptive policy which would in any case have sat uneasily on the shoulders of the monarch who had crushed the Poles in 1830, and was soon to be instrumental in doing the same to the Hungarians in 1849.

That is not to say that Nicholas steered clear of any military activity to the south. Hostilities with Persia in 1826 to 1828 led to considerable Russian gains in Transcaucasia and the right to maintain a fleet in the Caspian Sea under the terms of the Treaty of Turkmanchai (February 1828). In the following year further conflict with Turkey was brought to an end by the Treaty of Adrianople (September 1829) by which Russia took further territory in the Transcaucasus, including the eastern littoral of the Black Sea with ports at Sukhumi, Poti and Batumi. Russia also acquired a protectorate over the Danubian principalities of Moldavia and Walachia, and rights of merchant passage through the Bosphorus. Western alarm at these encroachments on Turkish power was reinforced by the signing of the Treaty of Unkiar-Skelessi between St Petersburg and Constantinople in July 1833. The very generous terms which Russia received, including virtually total control over the Bosphorus and the Black Sea, and what was interpreted as a military alliance between the two empires, were a reward for Nicholas's support for Sultan Mahmud in bringing to an end the revolt of Mehemet Ali, pasha of Egypt, in quest of his country's independence from Ottoman rule. It appeared that Nicholas had freed himself from the horns of his dilemma, adroitly exchanging them for the extension of Russian influence on the Golden Horn while at the same time preserving the Ottoman Empire more or less intact. In 1839, following the so-called 'second Mehemet Ali crisis', Russia was forced to accept a sharing of interests in Turkish affairs, and consequently signed the Straits Convention of 13 July 1841 (N.S.) along with Britain, Austria, Prussia and, belatedly, France. This in effect confirmed Russian gains at Kuçuk Kainardzi and Adrianople, and cancelled Unkiar-Skellesi. Russia's influence in the area was now shared among the five great powers.

Despite this apparent dilution of her international authority, Russia still managed to maintain an image of superiority and invincibility, yet continued to be loathed by all liberal, progressive opinion in Europe as the incarnation of despotism, reaction and the worst form of imperialism. Nicholas was still 'Gendarme of Europe'. It was, however, partly an over-estimation of Russia's diplomatic clout and military strength, both by herself and by her potential enemies, that was to lead to the outbreak of major international war in the Crimea in 1853.

The ostensible *casus belli* was the so-called dispute over 'the keys to the Holy Places'. Put simply, in what the British Government dismissed as 'a churchwarden's quarrel', Orthodox Russia and Catholic France had long been at loggerheads with each other and with Muslim Turkey over who should have the right to control the Christian shrines in Jerusalem and elsewhere in Palestine (then part of the Ottoman Empire), including the Church of the Nativity in Bethlehem. Obviously much more was at stake than the guardianship of a bunch of keys and the location of a piece of Christian mythology. Reasons of national power and prestige, commercial interests, clashes of leading personalities, military ambitions, and the whole course of British, French, Russian and Turkish relations over the previous 70 years were involved. The upshot was, when the sultan decided to hand over the keys to the Catholic French at a time coinciding with the establishment of the Second French Empire under Louis Bonaparte, Russia sought to assert its own case by claiming special privileges in protecting the rights of *all* Orthodox subjects of the Sultan, and backed up its demands by sending in troops to occupy the Danubian principalities in June 1853. As yet there was no declaration of war. There were, however, loud diplomatic protests from Britain, France, Prussia and Austria (which Nicholas regarded as an act of gross ingratitude on Austria's part, following his own role in suppressing the Hungarian revolt against Vienna in 1849), but for a while a peaceful solution to the impasse continued to be sought. By October, these efforts had come to nought, Nicholas still feeling himself powerful enough to defy what was building up into a formidable anti-Russian coalition. Finally, on 4 October 1853 (N.S.*), Turkey, backed up by a token display of British and French naval presence on the Bosphorus, declared war on the Russian Empire, issuing Nicholas with an ultimatum to evacuate his troops from Moldavia and Walachia.

As yet there was no direct military intervention by the two western powers, but the situation changed dramatically after the so-called 'massacre of Sinope'. What occurred was the sinking by the Russian navy under the command of P. S. (later Admiral) Nakhimov, of a squadron of the Turkish Black Sea fleet while still at anchor in the harbour of Sinope. Although, given the Turkish declaration of war of 4 October, this may be regarded as a legitimate act of war, it was greeted by a huge public outcry in Britain and France and at the end of December their joint naval forces received orders to take control over the Black Sea. Nicholas refused to respond to a further ultimatum to pull out his forces from the Danubian principalities, and consequently found himself committed to full-scale war against the combined forces of Britain, France and Turkey. Prussia and Austria remained in what may be termed a state of 'armed neutrality', though in fact this favoured the allies rather than Russia by keeping many of the latter's forces tied down along the Austrian frontier. More troops and shipping were tied down in the north in order to protect Russia from possible attacks in the Baltic region. In fact British naval superiority was demonstrated with attacks on Russian territory as far apart as the Finnish coast, Solovetskii in the Arctic north, and the Kamchatka peninsula in the remote far east.

---

* Hereafter, all dates relating to diplomatic and military activities during the war are given according to New Style.

But it quickly became clear that the main theatre was to be in the south, specifically in the Crimea. This is not the place to give a blow-by-blow, battle-by-battle account of the campaign, but a number of the major engagements deserve at least a mention. In September 1854 a joint French/British expeditionary force of over 60,000 men landed on the Crimean coast and headed cross-country for the major garrison port of Sevastopol. Their advance was checked by the Russians at the river Alma on 20 September, at what was to be the first major encounter of the war. Losses were heavy on both sides, but the Russians were forced to fall back on the poorly defended town. The allies had hopes for a quick surrender following a combined naval and land attack. However, commander Nakhimov ordered the sinking of part of the Russian fleet across the approaches to the harbour, thereby frustrating a close naval bombardment by the allies, and compelling them to dig in for what turned out to be a lengthy siege of the garrison from the south by land. The combination of Nakhimov's obstructive seaward stratagem, the rapid construction of a circle of solid defensive emplacements around the town, the onset of a bitter winter for which the allies were unprepared, and the fierce, dogged resistance of the defending Russians resulted in a siege lasting over 11 months which, though ending in Russian defeat, is nevertheless regarded as one of the most heroic chapters in the country's military history. First-hand experience of the siege also provided one of the young Russian officers present, Lev Tolstoi, with battleground material which he turned into literary form in his 'Sevastopol Stories' (*Sevastopol'skie rasskazy*, 1855), published in the leading literary journal, 'The Contemporary' (*Sovremennik*), while the siege was actually still in progress. It also gave him both the military and literary experience which was later to bear magnificent fruit in his celebrated novel *War and Peace* (1869). Twice at the beginning of the campaign, the Russians tried to raise the siege, first at the battle of Balaklava, famous for the disastrous charge of the British Light Brigade (25 October) and, second, at the battle of Inkerman (5 November), both ending in a Russian rout. Not that everything went well for the allies. Throughout the campaign, they were plagued not only by death in battle, but also by disease, especially cholera, atrocious weather conditions, massive supply problems, ineptitude and personal rivalries within the high command, foolish military decisions and indecisiveness on the part of both French and British officialdom. Eventually, with both sides exhausted and decimated by the conflict and amid intensive diplomatic pressures – including the threat of possible Austrian military intervention on the allies' side – Sevastopol fell on 9 September 1855. Nicholas did not live to see the final collapse of his cherished army and the ignominious defeat of Russia's much-vaunted, but also overrated, military power on which he had lavished so much devotion and fanatical attention. He had died on 18 February, almost certainly of natural causes, though rumours circulated that, unable to bear to witness the final throes of his country's looming defeat, he took his own life, the victim of 'civic grief' (*grazhdanskaya skorb*'). There is little to support the truth of these rumours, though it is the opinion of Presniakov that, 'If Nicholas I did not end his life by suicide, he had every reason for doing so.'[26]

The incoming tsar, Alexander II, immediately agreed to peace negotiations which resulted in the signing of the Treaty of Paris on 30 March 1856. It was a bitterly humiliating, though not a disastrous, defeat. No Russian territory was occupied by a victorious foreign power, no ground was ceded, the government remained in place, and the major feature of the settlement which affected the country both militarily and economically was the naval neutralisation of the Black Sea – meaning that Russia was banned from maintaining a fleet there, thus affecting her southern trade through the Bosphorus. The securing of the repeal of the 'Black Sea clauses' of the Treaty of Paris was to be the mainspring of Russia's foreign policy for the next two decades. But the major impact of Russia's defeat in the Crimean War was felt not so much on the international stage as at home.

To use a well-worn cliché, the Russian colossus had been revealed as having feet of clay. Internationally, the country, though still very important, was to remain a second-rate, or maybe a one-and-a-half-rate, diplomatic and military power until the battle of Stalingrad in 1943. Internally, the essential weaknesses and backwardness of Russia's social and economic structure had been rawly exposed. Technologically, too, Russia was way behind the west. One of the major factors in her defeat was the woefully inadequate transport and communications system, described in Chapter 1. Road and rail facilities just did not exist to enable large quantities of men and material to be transported over large distances with sufficient speed. Fighting on her own territory, it took longer for Russia to get her troops and guns to the front than it did France and Britain by sea from their Channel ports. Her military equipment was also outdated, her weapons obsolete and her navy still under sail with wooden bottoms, while the metal-clad western battleships were powered by steam. (Some vessels of Russia's in-shore fleet still comprised antique galleys, propelled by conscript oarsmen!) But, above all, it was the economic and social system based on the iniquitous and untenable system of serfdom which was seen by all, or almost all, to be desperately in need of a total overhaul.

The Crimean War has been described as an ideological conflict between liberal, progressive, bourgeois Europe, and the despotic, backward, almost mediaeval empire of Nicholas I – ultimately a victory of the industrialised, capitalist west over serf-bound, feudal Russia. It is ironic that the tsar who inherited a mighty empire still basking in the glow of the victory over Napoleon, the tsar who was almost maniacally obsessed with military efficiency and power, whose name was a byword for ruthless authoritarianism, was to preside over the ruinous defeat of his own legions, on his own ground, in the agony of Sevastopol. However, Presniakov's judgement, quoted at the beginning of this chapter, that Nicholas's reign represented the 'Apogee of Autocracy', does not really stand up to close scrutiny when his activities are measured against those of his equally autocratic, dogmatic and domineering forebears and successors. That was in the very nature of tsarist absolutism, irrespective of who occupied the Winter Palace.

But the last word must go to one of Nicholas's own civilian army of censors, the distinguished academic and critic, A. V. Nikitenko, who ruefully declared: 'The main shortcoming of the reign of Nikolai Pavlovich consisted in the fact that it was all a mistake.'[27]

9 Reform, revolutionary populism and regicide, 1855–1881

Just over halfway through the nineteenth century, Emperor Alexander II came to the Russian throne at a time when most of the countries of Europe were already well advanced in the process of industrialisation and the development of capitalism. Although the word 'capitalism' did not gain international currency until the 1860s, it had already by that time become the foundation for a society which believed that economic growth rested on competitive private enterprise, and in which a 'triumphant bourgeoisie' derived its material prosperity through exploitation of the cheap labour of the working classes – what Marx termed the 'proletariat'.[1] It provided the infrastructure of a Europe that was criss-crossed by thousands of miles of railway track, marked by great mills and manufactories, coal pits and quarries, mechanised mass-production plants, and rapidly burgeoning centres of an equally rapidly growing urban population. Russia, meanwhile, recently defeated in the Crimea by the industrial might of the west, remained an economically and technologically retarded, and therefore feeble, giant whose progress into modernity was impeded by what Soviet historians regularly referred to as the 'remnants of feudalism' (*ostatki feodalizma*). The two most obvious features of this state of retarded development were the political system of autocracy and the socio-economic system of serfdom. After the trauma epitomised by the fall of Sevastopol in 1855, it was clear to all but those whose mental capacities were as retarded as the economy that, in order for the country to regain its international reputation and prestige, in order to compete effectively with its European rivals, Russia must undergo a radical reform of its economic, social and political order. As the abolition of autocracy was out of the question (autocracy being a God-given trust, and therefore part of the divinely appointed order), then the abolition of serfdom had to be considered as at least a practical possibility. However distasteful or dangerous, it was with this in mind that, shortly after the signing of the Treaty of Paris in 1856, the incoming tsar addressed the members of the Moscow nobility with a memorable short speech in which he first publicly raised the issue. Although a copy of the original text does not survive, there are three extant variants of what was said, one of which is quoted here in full:

> There are rumours abroad that I wish to grant the peasants their freedom; this is unjust (*nespraved-livo*), and you may say so to everyone to right and left; but a feeling of hostility between the peasants and the landlords does, unfortunately, exist, and this has already resulted in several instances of insubordination to the landlords. I am convinced that sooner or later we must come to it (*k etomu priiti*). I believe that you, too, are of the same opinion as I; consequently, it is far better that this should come about from above, rather than from below.[2]

The emancipation of the serfs

As will no doubt be noticed, Alexander was still at this point pretty vague about his intentions. When, for instance, he said 'we must come to it', to what did 'it' actually refer? To the abolition of serfdom? To recognising the problem of serfdom? Or to thinking about the abolition of serfdom? Or all three? The last is surely the correct answer. But at the same time, the emperor wishes to scotch any rumours that such a thing was on his mind in the first place! These are mealy-mouthed, weasel words at best, but of one thing he *was* certain: that in view of the peasant-*pomeshchik* hostility, coyly referred to as 'several instances of insubordination' (no doubt referring to the no fewer than 674 peasant uprisings throughout the provinces officially recorded during the reign of Nicholas I), any initiative in the direction of emancipation should come from the government and not from the people – top-down, not bottom-up. It is, of course, inconceivable that Alexander would be unaware of the high state of tension existing in the Russian countryside, and the equally high levels of anticipation among progressive-minded members of society, following the Crimean débâcle and the consequent 'rumours' of emancipation that he was so anxious to quash. Mention has been made in the previous chapter of one government official's reference to the peasant 'powder keg beneath the throne', and both police records and the memoir literature of the time abound with allusions to rural unrest, popular discontent, and violent expressions of peasant grievances, including the routine murder of landlords. There are, too, ominously frequent references to the shades of Stenka Razin and Emelyan Pugachëv …

One literary image offering the prospect of the common people taking matters into their own hands was provided by the angry young journalist and literary critic, Nikolai Dobrolyubov (1836–61), in a review article entitled 'What is Oblomovism?' (*Chto takoe Oblomovshchina?*), published in *The Contemporary* in 1859. The review was of the novel by Ivan Goncharov (1812–91), *Oblomov* (1859), in which the eponymous hero, a fairly wealthy, slothful, self-indulgent, useless, witless and superficially harmless absentee landlord, is portrayed as the epitome of the moribund, parasitical serf-owning nobility. His badly-run estate, Oblomovka, which he has not stirred himself to visit for years, is also presented by the author as a kind of microcosm of, or allegory for, the whole of serf-owning Russia, of which, of course, Dobrolyubov is fiercely critical, and 'Oblomovism', or *Oblomovshchina*, a wasting disease which infects the entire serf-owning class. Some way into the article the critic recounts a fable of a tribe of people lost in a dense jungle out of which they can find no path. A few self-appointed leaders have the bright idea of climbing a tree from the branches of which they can spy out which way the road lies. They discover nothing of help, but get used to their lofty perch and even find some tasty fruit on which to feed themselves. Eventually the disoriented, suffering crowd below, despairing of guidance from those above, lose their patience and begin to hack, chop and slash their own way out of the deadly forest. In doing so, they bring crashing down the trees on which their leaders sit, destroying them in the process. The allegory is unmistakeable: it is time for the Russian masses to ignore the useless assurances and noble sentiments of those from whom they once sought guidance – the intellectuals, the wise men and the 'superflu-ous men' of the 1840s, the Oblomovs of the world – time to take their axes and carve their way out of the jungle by their own exertions. 'The time', insists Dobrolyubov, 'for social activity has arrived.'[3] For 'social activity' read 'revolutionary activity', but by that the author does not mean simply wanton, mindless violence, but conscious, practical action of every kind on behalf of and in the name of the people in order to achieve a better world. If that involved violence, then so be it. But it was in order to avoid that threat of 'social activity' in the shape of popular violence that Alexander determined on his path of emancipation 'from above'.

It should not be thought, however, that the new ruler, whose accession had been greeted with some relief after the stultifying uni-formity and oppression of the *Nikolaevshchina*, embarked on his project with any enthusiasm, nor out of any altruistic desire for an improvement in the lot of the Russian *narod*. He has been variously described as more liberal, more humane and more compassionate than his stern, unbending father; in place of the 'drill-sergeant on the throne' came the 'Tsar Reformer', the 'Tsar Liberator', pupil of the reforming bureaucrat, Mikhail Speranskii, and the romantic poet, Vasilii Zhukovskii. True, he did demonstrate a degree of compassion in granting an amnesty to the surviving exiled Decembrists, along with many of the Polish insurrectionists of 1830 and the *Petrashevtsy*, and also in closing down Nicholas's few remaining military colonies (see Chapter 8). But it was fear, not philanthropy, which forced him on a path that was essential for the economic and political survival of the empire. The emancipation, when it took place, was the result of a combination of pressures – economic, moral, social and military – and an exercise in political expediency undertaken by an autocratic monarch who, before coming to the throne, had been a resolute anti-abolitionist and had no real stomach for the enterprise.

The economic arguments against the continuance of serfdom were well known and thrown into stark relief by the defeat in the Crimea. If Russia were to modernise and embark on the process of large-scale industrial development, then it was essential that the mediaeval constraints of serfdom be removed to allow for the growth of free enterprise, capitalist relationships and a geographically mobile labour force. On the question of the morality of serfdom, the more enlightened members of Russian society had long found the system to be repugnant and incompatible with the ethical and humanitarian standards of a civilised country. (It may be noted *en passant* that autocratic Russia peacefully abolished serfdom in 1861, four years before negro slavery was abolished in the 'democratic' United States following a bloody civil war.) The social pressures of continuous peasant uprisings and the threat of another *Pugachëvshchina* have already been mentioned. The question of a *military* explanation for the decision to abolish serfdom is less often explored, but has been thoroughly and persuasively argued by the American historian, Alfred J. Rieber.[4]

According to Rieber's theorem, the catastrophe in the Crimea had demonstrated the parlous state of Russia's armed forces, which were in desperate need of reorganisation, re-equipment and reform. The maintenance of a huge peacetime standing army was no longer a viable option. Not only was it costly beyond the nation's means, it was also both inefficient and inadequate for the needs of modern warfare. What was required in particular was a different system of recruitment and service, whereby conscripts would spend fewer years on active duty, followed by a period on reserve, during which they were subject to instant call-up in a national emergency. Added to this, a thoroughly updated structure of command, communication and control was needed, together with better training and education of recruits, modern weaponry appropriate to the demands of the age of mechanised warfare, and improved conditions of service, which were then of an almost punitive nature. However, so long as the horrors of serfdom remained, shorter periods of active military service were a dangerous proposition. On completing their time with the colours, each year thousands upon thousands of demobilised peasant soldiers, highly disciplined and trained in the use of modern weaponry, many of them with battlefield experience, would return home to villages still suffering the impositions of mediaeval-style bondage. In such circumstances, any future peasant insurgencies might well consist, not of an unruly, scythe-brandishing mob, but of phalanges of well-trained, disciplined fighters. In other words, the modernisation of the military was incompatible with the maintenance of serfdom. *Ergo*, for the sake of both external and internal security, serfdom must be abolished. QED.

While Rieber may be accused of overstating his case, the military factor in establishing any hierarchy of causes behind the decision to abolish serfdom must figure very prominently. (And, of course, it is a well-established fact that the role of deserting, demobilised or disaffected soldiers during the October 1917 Revolution and the ensuing Civil War was crucial to the Bolsheviks' victory (see Chapter 12).) In sum, it was a combination of all the objective factors mentioned above, rather than his own generosity of soul, which impelled the reluctant Alexander towards his inevitable decision. That said, however, once he had set his mind to the enterprise, he did throw all the weight of his 'boundless' imperial authority behind the task of seeing it through to fruition, and to overcome the procrastination, opposition and filibustering of those backwoodsmen, both among the nobility and in the administration, who remained adamant in their objection to any alteration in the traditional order, however anachronistic.

Something has already been said about the history and organisation of the serf-owning system in Russia (see Chapter 1). Suffice it to reiterate here that at the time of emancipation the Russian peasantry, numbering some 53 million souls, still accounted for almost 90 per cent of the population, of which roughly half were privately owned *pomeshchik* serfs, the majority of the remainder consisting of state peasants whose conditions had been marginally improved under Kiselëv's legislation of 1838 (see Chapter 8). The vast majority were organised into rural communes, whose elders – that is, patriarchal heads of individual households – in consultation with the landowner or his bailiff, controlled every feature and facet of the peasants' existence. In addition to their feudal labour obligation to work their owners' land (*barshchina*) or pay a quit-rent (*obrok*), they were still subject to Peter the Great's despised poll tax, savage corporal punishments, military conscription by the state and, in the case of schismatic sects, religious discrimination and persecution. They were also liable to be exiled to Siberia, more or less at their owner's whim, separated from their families, and sold like cattle. They were used to pay off gambling debts, gifted as marriage dowries, and young peasant girls were sexually abused as a matter of course. (Russia's much-revered national poet, the egregious Aleksandr Pushkin, casually fathered a child on one of his father's serf wenches.) In sum, short of inflicting capital punishment, a landlord (or landlady for that matter) could dispose of his human property as he would dispose of the rest of his goods and chattels.

Advertisements such as the following (though dating from 1797) appeared regularly in newspapers right up to the time of emancipation:

> For sale, well behaved menial craftsmen: two tailors, a cobbler, a cook, a wheelwright and two coachmen. Price on request ... Also for sale, three young racehorses, one stallion, two geldings and a pack of hounds.

> An officer has for sale a 16-year-old girl, formerly belonging to a poor house. She can knit, sew, iron, starch and dress a lady. She has a comely figure and a pretty face.[5]

The poet, Nikolai Nekrasov (1821–77), writing in 1848, described in rhyming stanzas the flogging with the knout of a young peasant girl in one of St Petersburg's public squares, identifying his own muse with the girl's silent suffering.[6] (That was in the same year that Nicholas I prohibited the use of the knout.) Richard Pipes typically attempts to play down the brutality of the landowners' treatment of their peasants by making light of the sadistic activities of a late-eighteenth-century landlady, Darya Saltykova, who notoriously tortured her own serfs, sometimes to death. In his airy opinion, 'She tells us as much about imperial Russia as does Jack the Ripper about Victorian London.' But Pipes misses the obvious point that Jack the Ripper's serial murders (which actually tell us quite a lot about Victorian London) were acts of criminal violence that shocked the whole country, whereas Saltykova's behaviour, however abhorrent, was not even technically illegal.[7]

It is not necessary to dwell here on the details of the complex bureaucratic process through which Alexander's veiled intentions, as announced in his speech of 30 March 1856 (quoted above) finally became law in the form of the 'Manifesto' and 'Statute on Peasants Released from Serf Dependence' on 19 February 1861.[8] It is, however, important to note that the negotiations and deliberations of the various drafting committees and editorial bodies should not be seen as a kind of contest fought between progressive bureaucrats on the one hand and reactionary landowners on the other. There were pro- and anti-abolitionists in both camps, but the latter, however vehemently they opposed the whole idea of ending serfdom, were not only clearly flying in the face of enlightened public opinion, but were also handicapped in their objections by the tsar's own new-found commitment to the undertaking. But while formulating their proposals, all of those involved were forced to accept that (a) the serfs *would* receive their freedom, and (b) they would also receive land. It was also explicitly understood, however, that when the statutes were finally promulgated it would be the interests of the *landlords*, not of the peasants, that would be paramount. Alexander had made that much unambiguously clear in a speech to the State Council on 28 February 1861, when he announced: 'I hope, gentlemen, that when you have examined the projects put before you, you will be convinced that everything that it was possible to do to protect the interests of the landowners – has been done'.[9] It is worth noting that the Russian word *vygody* (sing. *vygoda*), translated here as 'interests', can also mean 'benefits', 'gains' or 'profits'. But any one of them would accurately reflect Alexander's intent. Moreover, if the good councillors should discover anything in the proposals to the contrary, they were invited to make any amendments they thought fit.

Though the Manifesto and Statute were promulgated on 19 February, they were not formally announced in public until 5 March – that is, until such time as the government felt satisfied that it had taken all necessary precautions – such as deploying extra police and military in the provinces and ordering exceptionally large quantities of whips and canes to be supplied to the local authorities – to ensure that any popular manifestations of disapproval or disappointment with the terms of the edict would be dealt with appropriately. In fact the Manifesto, composed by the reactionary Metropolitan of the Orthodox Church, Filaret, was couched in such a pompous, pietistic and patronising style as to have a soporific rather than inflammatory effect on its audience when its contents were duly intoned in churches throughout the heavily garrisoned countryside. Similarly, the Statute consisted of a long series of convoluted clauses, sub-clauses and legalistic codicils which seem to have been deliberately designed *not* to be understood by the illiterate, uneducated peasants whose lives were being affected. Indeed, so circumlocutory was the terminology that not even did the straightforward words 'freedom', 'liberation' or 'emancipation' (*osvobozhdenie*) appear in the text. In vain, too, did the peasants wait to hear their own word for freedom – *volya* – uttered amid the official verbiage. In fact, even the very mention of *volya* on the lips of a humble information-seeker could be followed by terrible retribution. One poor fellow, a lowly janitor, was awarded 230 stokes of the lash for suggesting that, 'freedom (*volya*) has been granted, that's for sure, because they don't allow you to talk about it'.[10]

The main provisions of the legislation were as follows. First, the serfs were granted their technical, legal freedom – that is, they were no longer the private property of their masters and were at liberty to trade, marry, litigate and acquire property. Second – and this was sorely resented – there was to be an initial period of 'temporary obligation', during which peasants continued to perform some of the duties pertaining to their former serf status while the amount of land they were eventually to be allotted was calculated by local officials in consultation with the landlords. When the local 'norms' – that is, the agreed acreages to be distributed – had been established and agreed on, the peasants were then required to begin paying for the land they had been allotted through a series of 'redemption payments', whereby they reimbursed the government with the money paid by the latter to the landowners to compensate them for the loss of land disbursed to the peasants. It was a kind of extended mortgage arrangement, under the terms of which the newly liberated serfs were forced to pay for land which they had previously worked free of charge, and which they believed was theirs by God-given right in any case. Moreover, the amount the peasants were compelled to pay for their allotments, often of poor quality land, was massively higher than the current market value of the property. The level of the repayments was calculated at an interest rate of 6 per cent over 49 years. This inflated cost to the peasants in fact represented a 'hidden' compensation to the landowners for the loss, not only of their land, but of their free servile labour, for which they would now have to pay wages. In this way, too, a form of rudimentary capitalism was beginning to creep into the rural economy. So high were the redemption payments set that peasant communities often fell into arrears, thereby attracting a financial penalty, which then extended the period of repayment at a higher rate, which led to further default … and so on. When all added together, it has been calculated that, had it not been for the intervention of more climacteric events in the early twentieth century, the Russian peasants – or their descendants – would have been paying off their 'mortgages' well into the 1950s.

A central feature of the settlement was that, although technically free men, the peasants were still organised within, and legally bound to, their village commune. In legal parlance this institution was designated as the 'rural community' (*sel'skoe obshchestvo*), more commonly called the *obshchina*, and referred to by the peasants themselves as the *mir*. Here, the terms are used interchangeably, but it is no coincidence that the peasant word – *mir* (spelt in the pre-1918 Russian Cyrillic мiръ; the homophone *mir*, meaning 'peace', is spelt миръ) is the same as the Russian word for 'world', and there are hundreds of popular expressions and folk aphorisms which indicate the total identification of the individual peasant with his commune, which was for him literally his *world*, life outwith and without which was unimaginable.[11] The post-emancipation commune wielded extensive powers over its individual members, both of an economic and a quasi-judicial nature, as well as regulating personal relationships among them. Taxes, redemption payments and other imposts were communally gathered and paid; in areas where land was periodically redistributed among the peasants rather than being held in hereditary tenure, the *mir* was responsible for the adjudication and reallocation of land allotments among the individual households within the commune; no peasant could leave the community without the permission of the village elder (*starosta*) or board of elders; and the commune was also empowered (a power 'inherited', as it were, from their previous masters) to banish its wayward or obstreperous members to exile in Siberia, or, indeed, to refuse to accept back into the community those who had committed some felony for which they had already been punished by the courts. In which case, they, too, ended up in Siberia. In the second half of the nineteenth century just over 50 per cent of all people exiled to Siberia were sent there by 'administrative order' (*v administrativnom poryadke*), and of these, over 90 per cent by order of their community, either for 'bad behaviour' (*za porochnoe povedenie*) or for 'non-acceptance after punishment' (*neprinyatie posle nakazaniya*).[12]

Even the most intimate personal relationships involved communal assistance or intervention. A father-in-law, for instance, was customarily entitled to have sexual relations with his daughter-in-law during his son's absence – on military service, in prison, or working (with the commune's permission) beyond the confines of the village – a practice called *snokhachestvo* (from *snokha*, a daughter-in-law). It was also not unknown for marriages, usually arranged by an old crone who was the village matchmaker (*svat*), to be actually consummated in full view of the assembled villagers. This was not so much an act of collective voyeurism as of genuine public-spiritedness. Such was the degree of communal cooperation on these occasions that, if the groom were unable to carry out his marital duties under public gaze, one of his more considerate older male relatives would rise to the occasion and chivalrously fill his place.[13] Peasants could still be flogged, and were indeed still subject to different, harsher, forms of punishment than the privileged classes of society, under the provision enshrined in the Russian Penal Code that all are unequal before the law. Military conscription, payment of the poll tax (until 1887), and other forms of obligation from which other social categories were exempt, were still in force.

In other words, the peasantry did not enjoy equal status with the other estates in Russian society. It still remained a separate 'caste', with its own internal structures, officials, procedures, code of conduct, vocabulary, world-view, economic arrangements and punitive powers. Moreover, the retention of the Slavophils' much-beloved *obshchina* as an officially recognised institution, although firmly rooted in Russian tradition, meant in effect that the peasant had merely traded bondage to the serf-owner for bondage to the *mir*. Lack of capital investment, rural impoverishment (of noble landowners as well as their former serfs), periodic reallocation of land, primitive agricultural techniques, crippling financial burdens and impediments to mobility meant that the agrarian sector of the Russian economy more or less stagnated for the next 40 years.

In terms of popular protest, too, the countryside – after a short-lived and rapidly extinguished burst of activity in the immediate post-emancipation period – remained relatively quiescent. Among the 2000-odd flare-ups which did occur between 1861 and 1863, triggered by the disillusionment over the legislation, but all of them brutally suppressed with a medley of mass floggings, executions and deportations, perhaps the most notorious was the 'Bezdna massacre' on 12 April 1861. Bezdna was a small village in the Kazan province, where a literate peasant by the name of Ivan Petrov, attempting to 'interpret' the exact meaning of the emancipation statutes in order to enlighten his less learned fellow villagers, claimed to have discovered that the tsar had indeed granted them real *volya*, and urged them to take over the fields. Thousands of peasants flocked to the village and, when ordered to disperse and hand over the publicly proclaimed herald of freedom to the military authorities, refused to do so. Thereupon, the military commander, General A. S. Apraksin, ordered his troops to fire at will into the crowd surrounding Petrov's cottage. Nearly 500 peasants were slaughtered; Petrov was arrested and executed by firing squad; several peasants each received a whipping; and a distinguished young professor of theology at Kazan University, Afanasii Shchapov (1831–76), was imprisoned and later sacked from his academic post for delivering a eulogy at the requiem ceremony held to honour Bezdna's dead. Apraksin was awarded the imperial order of St Vladimir.[14]

However, by 1864 the rural disturbances had more or less died down and the remainder of the nineteenth century was comparatively free of serious agrarian unrest, which may be explained by a number of factors. First, after the initial outbursts, which were caused mainly by the fact that the bewildered peasants simply did not understand the complexities of the legislation, the majority settled down, as it were, to adjust to their new situation, however wretched, as technically free citizens. Second, the speed and ferocity with which incidents such as the Bezdna scandal were dealt with, including floggings and shootings, obviously had the desired effect of discouraging any repeat performances. Third, within the confines of the communal system, there were limited opportunities for the more enterprising – or unscrupulous – peasants to take advantage of the emerging new economic order to increase their landholdings and better themselves. This led later in the century to the development of a small sub-class of relatively wealthy peasants, derogatorily referred to as *kulaki* (sing. *kulak* – literally, a 'fist') or, less commonly, *miroedy* ('commune eaters'). Fourth, the reduction in the term of military service by virtue of the army reforms of 1874, and the abolition of the poll tax in 1887 both lightened peasant burdens to some extent. Fifth, the improvement in educational, medical and welfare provision as a result of the local government reforms of 1864 (see below) meant that, in some respects at least, rural conditions in post-emancipation Russia were marginally more tolerable than under serfdom. Finally, the abolition of the seigneurial rights of the serf-owners over their peasants removed the immediate object of peasant hostility, which had traditionally been vented on their noble masters.

The emancipation of the Russian serfs in 1861 has been variously described as the greatest single act of legislation in the country's entire history, and also as not worth the paper it was written on. It was certainly a major piece of social engineering which, more than anything else, symbolised Russia's gradual, and belated, transition from mediaeval feudalism to a more modern set of social and economic relationships which Marxists would say bore all the hallmarks of embryonic capitalism. However, the imperfections and continuing inequalities inherent in the emancipation settlement meant that peasant Russia continued to suffer acute and long-term hardship, discrimination, land hunger and widespread poverty, which was to lead to the peasant wars of the early twentieth century and contribute so much to the revolutionary upheavals of 1917. But now that the old administrative and judicial superstructure of the serf-owning system had been abolished, something was needed to replace it. It was to this business which the government now turned.

The major reforms

The wording of this section's heading has been deliberately chosen to describe the administrative changes introduced by Alexander II during the 1860s and 1870s, rather than the more familiar appellation of 'the *great* reforms', used, for instance, as the title of W. Bruce Lincoln's helpful book on the subject.[15] That is because the use of the adjective 'great' already implies some kind of pre-judicial accolade and degree of superlative excellence which may not be appropriate to a final dispassionate evaluation of the noun which it qualifies. However, the 'programme' of local government, judicial, financial, cultural and military reforms inaugurated during the reign of the 'Tsar Liberator' undoubtedly had widespread ramifications for the development of Russian society in the last decades of the nineteenth century that may certainly be regarded as of 'major' significance, though not necessarily 'great' in what they achieved.

Following the loss of the *pomeshchiki*'s seigneurial power over their former bondsmen, the government was faced with the necessity of constructing some new form of local government organisation and judicial institutions to replace the old feudal practices which had existed under serfdom. Accordingly, legislation was drafted which, commencing in 1864, established unprecedented new organs of local self-government in the countryside called *zemstva* (sing. *zemstvo*) – that is, rural councils. These were set up at both district (*uezd*) and provincial (*guberniya*) levels, their members being chosen by three electoral colleges – local landowners, town dwellers, and members of rural communes – and comprising three 'elements'. These were: first, the elected councillors, the representatives of their respective constituencies, who convened annually to discuss and decide on policy issues; second, the permanent, paid officials or civil servants of the councils, the *zemstva* bureaucracy whose job it was to administer and implement policy; and finally, the 'third element' of the *zemstva*, consisting of the councils' qualified, professional employees such as doctors, schoolteachers, lawyers, agronomists, veterinarians, and other technical experts who actually carried out the day-to-day work in those areas of public welfare for which the *zemstva* had responsibility. Among those responsibilities their most important functions were the staffing of educational institutions, provision of medical care – both clinical and prophylactic – light engineering works such as maintenance of roads and bridges, fire-fighting, upkeep of prisons, asylums and orphanages, promotion of local industry, poor relief, and help and advice with agricultural problems. In 1870 similar organs of municipal local government called *dumy* (sing. *duma*) were set up in towns and cities. Their structure, organisation and responsibilities were roughly the same as their rural equivalents, though with more emphasis on local economic activity.

Although a positive move in terms of granting a degree of limited autonomy to the local authorities, both the *zemstva* and the *dumy* suffered from a number of restrictions on their activities. In the first place, their introduction was not universal throughout the empire. They were established in a piecemeal, incremental fashion, which for instance excluded the whole of Siberia, and in 1914, on the eve of the First World War, extended to only 43 of the 70 provinces of the Russian Empire. Second, the actual electoral system left much to be desired. Suffrage was based on property qualifications, and, although this was common practice elsewhere in Europe, these were pitched so high as to guarantee that an overwhelming preponderance of the *zemstva*'s elected membership was drawn from the landowning nobility and the very wealthy urban classes. Despite some peasant representation, local affairs were still, after serf emancipation, very much in the hands of the local nobility. Financially, too, the rural and urban councils were very restricted in the amount of room they had to manoeuvre. They had a certain amount of authority to raise local taxes – a kind of rating system – but this only scratched the surface of their monetary difficulties, and both town and countryside remained largely dependent on central government for the majority of their funding; and, as is usually the case in these matters, he who paid the balalaika player called the tune. Similarly, the maintenance of law and order, and the policing of the provinces remained the direct responsibility of the Ministry for Internal Affairs and the central Department of Police (the latter a department of the former, set up in 1883). There was nothing like a regional, or even metropolitan, police authority.

Notwithstanding these drawbacks, the *zemstva* and the municipal *dumy* were remarkably successful in promoting welfare and providing public service in the areas where they existed. By all the usual indices in matters such as health, hygiene, literacy levels, mortality and longevity rates, environmental issues and similar concerns, those towns and villages in which the local councils were up and, if not running, then visibly moving forward at a steady pace, enjoyed much higher standards than those without. That is not to say that the poorer sections of Russian society in *zemstvo*-controlled localities were universally happy, healthy and highly educated. On the contrary, the regular outbreak of epidemics, periodic famines, abysmal literacy levels, orphanhood, distressingly high infant mortality rates, alcoholism, general squalor and violent crime remained part of the routine experience of millions of Russia's lower classes, *zemstvo* or no *zemstvo*.

Nevertheless, some real progress *was* made, and in two other respects the local councils did have a positive effect. In the first place, they provided fora for members of society to gain some experience of participatory politics, albeit at local level, and it is no surprise that many of the leading members of Russia's moderate, 'liberal' national political parties in the early years of the twentieth century – the Constitutional Democrats, the 'Octobrists' and others (see Chapter 11) – cut their teeth and flexed their infant muscles in the political nursery of the rural *zemstvo* or the municipal *duma*. These institutions also provided an opportunity for members of the intelligentsia, through their professional activities as the 'third element' of the *zemstva* both to serve and gain first-hand experience of the Russian *narod*. During the revolutionary events of the 1870s, discussed in the following section, the radical, educated youth of the day tried to stir the masses to engage in direct revolutionary action, but found that their subversive seed fell on stony ground. But the new professional and economic opportunities which opened up in the post-emancipation era meant that the intelligentsia did not necessarily count revolution or rebellion among the 'three Rs' which they brought to the people. Instead of iron in the soul or fire in the belly, they carried schoolbooks in their hands and stethoscopes round their necks. At last there was some real communication between the intelligentsia and the *narod*, between the rural practitioner and his patients. And yet this new level of personal communication was not without revolutionary implications. The village schoolmarms, solicitors and physicians did not just teach, litigate and heal, they also *talked* to the trusting peasants, and in this way progressive ideas began to penetrate and be articulated in areas where hitherto there had been only suspicion, ignorance and outbursts of elemental, uncomprehending fury. It was this gradual intellectual osmosis, as much as the propaganda and agitation of professional revolutionaries, that encouraged the process of social and political fermentation which built up into such an explosive head in the revolutionary events of 1905.

The next major area of reform to be considered is that of the judicial system. Before the emancipation of the serfs, the administration of what could only loosely be described as 'justice' was notoriously inefficient, long-winded, socially discriminatory and appallingly corrupt. Trials were usually held *in camera*, written evidence was rarely used, witnesses were regularly suborned, judges often had no legal training, suspects had no formal representation, *habeas corpus* was unknown – many suspects spending years in prison unaware of the charge, and the wheels of procedure churned around so slowly that they seemed to be stuck in a *perpetuum immobile* of legal ineptitude and farce. (When the accused Decembrists were brought before the special tribunal to hear their sentences, they were not even aware that they had been on trial; they had merely been interrogated in their cells!) In a laudable attempt to remedy these lamentable deficiencies, in 1864 a new judicial system was introduced, which for the first time in Russian history strove to incorporate some of the west-European concepts, principles and procedures of 'the rule of law'. These included: trial by jury; equality before the law; proper training and irremovability of judges (except for malfeasance in office); the establishment of a professional bar; open courts and public reporting of trials; and the separation of the judiciary from the legislature and executive (though it would be foolish to believe that the last two did not influence the first). A bi-cameral juridical structure was established, with lower, magistrates', courts to try lesser felonies, and the higher 'crown' courts where crimes of a more serious nature were heard with an adversarial system of prosecution and defence attorneys pleading their cases before judge and jury. Jurists were chosen, as in the west, according to property qualification, which may be thought, as also in the west, to be prejudicial to the interests of the less well-off members of society, who were barred by virtue of their poverty from participating in the business of deliberating the guilt or innocence of their fellow citizens. For both the higher and the lower courts a proper appellate system, based on the French *cours de cassation*, was introduced.

As in the case of the *zemstva*, the new judicial arrangements and institutions were a distinct advance on the inequitable and labyrinthine procedures which they in part replaced. Similarly, however, they were not without their imperfections, both in intent and execution. One of the major imperfections was the institution of the 'township' or 'parish' (*volost'*) courts which dealt with cases involving peasants only – the adjudicators were also peasants – and which had a set of different operations as well as different punish-ments, including corporal punishment, from those employed in the regular courts. These 'peasants only' tribunals put a rather large dent in the concept of the equality of all citizens before the law. Also, the new judicial bodies were slow in the appearing, the first ones being established in St Petersburg and Moscow only, in 1866. And, again like the *zemstva*, they were never introduced throughout the whole country. Moreover, the police still enjoyed extensive powers of arrest and punishment without trial of persons deemed to be socially or politically undesirable, and popular disturbances were 'administratively' dealt with by extempore floggings as an almost routine matter. These arbitrary police powers were greatly extended following the assassination of the tsar in 1881 (see below and Chapter 10). As time went by, more and more cases were removed from the jurisdiction of the newly established regular courts and placed before special tribunals or ad hoc bureaucratic bodies for adjudication. This was particularly so in cases involving offences against the state. Finally, the new-fangled judicial system did not sit easily with the institution of absolute autocracy and Russia's long tradition of administration by arbitrary decision. Notions of modern jurisprudence were extremely slow in penetrating both the official and popular consciousness, and were only just beginning to take proper shape before the whole concept of legality, along with class-based judicial procedures, was thrown into disarray during the revolutions of 1917. Nevertheless, however flawed, the reformed judicial system did go some way to meet standards of impartial justice, and the new institutions also became a forensic arena for the public voicing of non-conformist and critical opinion. Members of the newly established legal profession acted as a kind of buffer between the people and the state, and many of them, like the *zemstvo* councillors, were later to play a prominent part in anti-government, even revolutionary, political activity. One needs hardly to be reminded that Aleksandr Kerenskii, Prime Minister of the last Provisional Government in 1917, and Vladimir Lenin, leader of the Bolshevik Party, were both trained lawyers.

The local government and judicial reforms were the most important of the post-emancipation administrative and institutional changes which affected most areas of Russian life during this period. In addition, reforms of the secondary and higher educational system, relaxation of the censorship regulations, new developments in public and private finance, commerce and communications (for example, banks, stock markets, railways), and a thorough overhaul of the organisation, training, recruiting and equipment of the armed forces were all symptomatic of the transition through which Russia was slowly groping its hesitant way from a semi-feudal to something approaching a modern capitalist society. The military reform, like all the rest, was an ambiguous process. The permanent, standing army was reduced in size, and conscription was abbreviated to a period of 15 years, six of them with the colours, and nine on reserve; corporal punishment was abolished, except in penal battalions; modern weaponry, consistent with the industrial age, was introduced; *all* classes of society were liable for the draft, though generous exemptions or postponements, based on educational qualifications, were easily secured – this obviously benefiting the privileged classes; training methods were streamlined; and an enlightened programme of compulsory education for the conscript troops was introduced which contributed to a modest increase in popular literacy rates; finally, military service was no longer regarded as a penal institution – that is, it was no longer available for the criminal courts to prescribe as a punishment. Despite these measures, however, the common soldier's lot was not a happy one, and it was becoming increasingly clear by the early years of the twentieth century that the regime could no longer count on the unswerving and unquestioning loyalty or reliability of its armed forces either in international war or in maintaining domestic order. When faced with the acid test of major modern warfare, against Japan in 1904–05, and against Germany and Austria-Hungary in the First World War, Russia's armies, the largest in the world, were still found wanting.

Faced with the shock of defeat in the Crimea, the Russian government had reluctantly tried to face up to the challenges of the modern world by inaugurating this cautious process of change and transformation. There was, however, no plan behind the reforms. They were conceived, enacted and administered in a clumsy, piecemeal fashion in response to economic and social pressures by officials who in many cases were downright opposed to them. Ignored by the radicals as meaningless, condemned by the conservatives as dangerous, and forced on the people by the agents of monarchical absolutism, Alexander's reforms satisfied no one but the bureaucrats who designed them. However, in the final analysis, the entire undertaking, which was in many ways both unavoidable and incomplete, was vitiated by the very simple fact that the government was attempting, with varying degrees of success or failure, to reform just about every area of Russian life, *without reforming itself.* The absolutist autocracy remained, and the Romanov regime was ultimately to be hoist with this petard of its own unique design. Therefore, rather than satisfying the public with its institutional innovations and structural alterations, it is perhaps not paradoxical that the period of the mistakenly named 'great' reforms should also have witnessed the beginnings of a spectacular new phase in the history of the Russian revolutionary movement.

Revolutionary Populism[16]

The few years on either side of the emancipation of the serfs – between, say, 1857 and 1864 – have been described by Soviet scholars as Russia's 'first revolutionary situation'. Indeed, during the 1960s and 1970s a whole series of academic works was published in Moscow devoted to its study,[17] though most western historians deny that any such crisis occurred. However, the indisputable fact that a revolution did not occur does not prove *ex post facto* that a revolutionary situation did not exist. While it is not suggested here that one *did*, there is sufficient evidence of manifest popular discontent, expressed in mass outbreaks of anger and disillusionment; of organised opposition to the government by disaffected intellectuals; of revolutionary sentiment articulated in newspapers, journals, pamphlets and works of creative literature; of nationalist feelings against Russian imperialism; of significant student unrest; and of the heightened awareness and state of alert on the part of the security services, to suggest that the government was experiencing, if not a full-blown revolutionary situation, then at least a palpable 'crisis of autocracy' (*krizis samoderzhaviya*) about which so much has been written.

Taking popular discontent first, sufficient has already been said to demonstrate that both before and after the emancipation, the peasantry had been expressing, often in violent manner, at first their impatience and frustration during the agonising build-up to the edict, and then their disappointment, bewilderment and exasperation when its virtually incomprehensible contents were announced. The Bezdna massacre was only the most notorious of thousands of similar clashes in many provinces of European Russia which provide a clear barometrical reading of the peasants' threatening mood. Hence the apprehensive tone of Alexander's famous speech in 1856. Hence the constant invocations of Razin and Pugachëv.

On the intellectual front, a new mood was also visible, and audible, among the ranks of the increasingly militant intelligentsia. (On the origins and meaning of the term intelligentsia, see Chapter 1.) Rebellious youth now emerged from the salon and prepared to take to the streets. A new kind of *intelligent* appeared, hard, tough, intransigent and revolutionary. To borrow from the title of Turgenev's novel 'Fathers and Children' (*Ottsy i deti*, 1862), these were the radical, materialist sons, the nihilists and 'men of the sixties' (*shestidesyatniki*), who engaged in patricidal polemics with their liberal, aristocratic fathers, the generation of the 1840s. The fathers in most cases denied parental responsibility for their rebellious brood, but the angry young men of the 1860s had unmistakably sprung from the idealistic soil of the 1840s, a soil sown with the wild oats and dragon's teeth of the 'remarkable decade'. An organisational, if ineffectual, manifestation of the new determination to engage in practical action was the appearance, in 1861, of Russia's first consciously revolutionary political society since the Decembrists. Calling itself 'Land and Liberty' (*Zemlya i volya*), it took its name from an article written by Aleksandr Herzen's cousin and comrade, Nikolai Ogarëv and other co-authors. Published in Herzen's London-based newspaper, 'The Bell' (*Kolokol*), on 1 July 1861, and entitled 'What do the People Want?' (*Chto nuzhno narodu?*), its first line answered the question with the words: 'It is very simple: what the people want is land and liberty.'[18] One cannot but note that this blunt statement of the people's needs was written just four months after the government believed it had granted 'the people' precisely that.

However that may be, 'Land and Liberty' from then onwards became the slogan and the battle-cry of Russian revolutionary Populism (*narodnichestvo*), which was to be the major preoccupation of the radical left over the next two decades. Although Populism does not present a uniform, homogeneous set of beliefs or doctrines, the various strands which make up its fabric are sufficiently coherent for it to entitle its adherents (*narodniki*) to be regarded as a 'movement', in the same, rather amorphous way in which the Decembrists were a movement. The first Land and Liberty (there was to be a second, formed in 1876) had no specific programme beyond the ideals and principles contained in Ogarëv's piece. It was at best a shadowy organisation, with no disciplined membership and no properly formulated plan of action; it was more a loose congeries of like-minded individuals who had a vague notion of harnessing the intellectual and organisational leadership of the intelligentsia to the collective power of the *narod* in order to achieve the genuine land and freedom for the masses, out of which they had been cheated by the bogus emancipation of 1861. Nevertheless, its short-lived appearance, which ended around 1864, was symptomatic of the highly charged atmosphere of the time.

That atmosphere was also captured in the written word. From his London exile, Herzen and his *The Bell* were a constant thorn in the flesh of the St Petersburg authorities with their insistent criticisms and excoriations of the continuing hypocrisy, bumbledom and injustice of Alexander's government. The paper was widely, though clandestinely, circulated inside Russia, and is even said to have regularly been read by the tsar himself. At the same time, in St Petersburg the men of the 1860s found their most popular mouthpiece and sounding board in the radical literary-political journal, 'The Contemporary' (*Sovremennik*), owned by the civic poet, Nikolai Nekrasov, and edited by the coryphaeus of the revolutionary left, Nikolai Chernyshevskii (1828–89), and his literary editor, Dobrolyubov. If Herzen was a thorn in the flesh, Dobrolyubov in particular attacked the government's hide like a furious gadfly, drawing blood with every bite of his venomous invective, at least until his untimely death in 1861. In his literary critiques of Goncharov's 'Oblomov', the playwright Ostrovskii's 'Thunderstorm' (*Groza*, 1860) and Turgenev's novel, 'On the Eve' (*Nakanune*, 1860), he not only vilified the iniquities of the regime, but also eagerly looked forward to the day when his generation, then 'on the eve' of momentous events, would see the light of a genuine revolutionary dawn (the title of his review of Ostrovskii's drama is 'A Ray of Light in the Kingdom of Darkness', and of Turgenev's novel, 'When will the Real Day Come?').

Apart from journalism and *belles-lettres*, the most strident articulation of the temper of at least the more radical end of the political spectrum is to be found in the many flyers, *feuilletons*, incendiary pamphlets and proclamations that were broadcast around this time, which has led to its being somewhat extravagantly called the 'era of manifestoes'. The first of these to appear in July 1861, entitled 'The Great Russian' (*Velikorus*), was not directed at any specific audience and put forward no clear political line, other than a general appeal for genuine reform and a criticism of the inadequate terms of the emancipation. It did not, however, call for a revolutionary solution. A more explicit document was an appeal addressed directly at the youth of the day (it was in fact called 'To the Young Generation' (*K molodomu pokoleniyu*)), written by Nikolai Shelgunov and Mikhail

Mikhailov, and released in May 1862. It attacked the autocracy, criticised the emancipation and appealed to the 'young generation' to form revolutionary cells and incite the peasantry to rebellion. The authors were soon arrested by the police, imprisoned and exiled by administrative order, thus providing the Third Section with its first political victims since the emancipation. Although 'To the Young Generation' was not squeamish in its advocacy of violence, in an altogether different league of sanguinary anticipation was another, more notorious, proclamation, also with its accent on youth, entitled 'Young Russia' (*Molodaya Rossiya*, 1862), the work of a 19-year-old student called Pëtr Zaichnevskii (1842–96). Despite the violent tone of its rather adolescent rhetoric, 'Young Russia' did set out a coherent programme of social and political objectives which envisaged the slaughter of the entire 'Imperial party'. Summoning the people to their axes, it called for the ruling classes ('the foul swine') to be mercilessly cut down 'in the squares, in their homes, in the narrow alleys of the towns and the broad streets of the capital, in the villages and hamlets'. It also clearly identified the problem of the relationship between the revolutionary intelligentsia and the *narod*, a problem which Zaichnevskii tackled by proclaiming that the revolutionary masses must be led by a disciplined, centralised party organisation which would, moreover, form a post-revolutionary dictatorship to supervise the introduction of the new social and political institutions.[19] Among these, Zaichnevskii's insistence on the paramount role of the peasant commune places him squarely in the populist tradition, but his advocacy of an elite leadership for the revolution makes his manifesto one of the first voicings of that tendency in Russian political thought that is usually referred to as 'Jacobinism' – that is, the belief that a popular rising must be organised and led by a centralised, revolutionary vanguard. Many commentators and critics have seen the views of Lenin on party organisation and discipline as the culmination of this Jacobinist tradition (see Chapter 10). As far as the 'era of manifestoes' is concerned, these inflammatory proclamations were yet one more of the ingredients in the 'crisis of autocracy' in the aftermath of emancipation.

Another was the Polish uprising of 1863. Nicholas I's dictatorial regime had failed to smother the still glowing embers of Polish nationalism, and the country continued to burn with anti-Russian hatred in the years following his death. In 1861 several hundred Poles had been killed, wounded or arrested during the suppression of a number of protests and demonstrations, but nationalist emotions could not easily be contained. Ultimately, in January 1863, a self-appointed anti-government 'Central National Committee' declared the country to be in a state of insurrection, but it was an insurgency that was doomed to failure almost before it started. The opposition to Russian rule was disunited in its objectives, split between the so-called 'Reds' and 'Whites', received little international support, was bereft of effective leadership and faced the largest regular army on the continent. Against all the odds, what amounted to a poorly equipped guerrilla campaign managed to hold out for 16 months before finally being crushed, its leaders hanged and thousands more Poles deported to Siberia. Poland was once more brought to Russia's heel and forced to submit to her tyrannical suzerainty for another half-century.

Meanwhile, within Russia itself, the mood of youthful protest was evident at the universities of St Petersburg, Moscow and Kazan, where, in 1861 and 1862, students had staged a series of demonstrations in which protests against student poverty, poor accommodation, police interference in academic affairs, antiquated syllabuses and poor professorial guidance were mixed with political demands which reflected the appeals contained in the incendiary manifestoes referred to above. And incendiarism of the real sort occurred in 1862 when a number of mysterious fires which broke out in St Petersburg was linked by the police to radical groups, thereby further increasing levels of tension in the capital.

While in quantitative terms all these manifestations of public disquiet and forthright opposition to the regime may not have added up to a revolutionary situation that was on the verge of making the qualitative transformation into genuine revolution *per se*, they were nevertheless symptomatic of the widespread and deeply felt popular dissatisfaction that constantly threatened to escalate to even more critical proportions. And it was in the midst of this crisis-ridden period of public and official uncertainty that the main outlines of the Populist ideology began to take shape.

Whatever their individual or group differences – and there were many – the *narodniki* all shared a common vision of the destruction of the tsarist social and political order and its replacement by an agrarian-socialist society based on the collectivist traditions and institution of the village commune. All of them insisted, too, that a purely Russian path of social and economic development must be trodden that would avoid the potholes and pitfalls of western capitalism. The *obshchina*, they believed, was a guarantee that this could be achieved. Generally acknowledged to be the father of Russian Populism was Aleksandr Herzen. After his bitter disillusionment with bourgeois Europe after 1848 (see Chapter 8), this erstwhile radical Westerniser began to draw inspiration from some of the Slavophils' views, especially their idealisation of the innate collectivism of the peasant commune, and saw in this the kernel of a future socialist society in Russia that would avoid the process of proletarianisation and pauperisation which was a feature of the capitalist mode of production. It was Herzen's amalgam of his earlier admiration for western socialist theory and his discovery of the Russian peasants' 'natural socialism' that represented the first stage in the history of Russian *narodnichestvo*.

The next stage in the development of revolutionary Populism was dominated by a man of altogether different character, Nikolai Chernyshevskii, already mentioned as editor of *The Contemporary*. According to Venturi: 'Herzen created Populism; Chernyshevsky was its politician.'[20] A man of more plebeian origins than Herzen – the 'gentry revolutionary' – Chernyshevskii was a typical product of the post-Crimean generation of the intelligentsia, young men and women of no fixed rank in society, the rootless, *déclassés* radicals who in Russian were known as *raznochintsy* (sing. *raznochinets* – literally 'people of various rank'). Vissarion Belinskii was perhaps the archetype of this breed. But Chernyshevskii, a natural scholar and what Lampert describes as 'a phenomenon of precocious erudition',[21] brought to bear a more academic, dispassionate and ascetic approach than had the men of the '40s to the pressing economic, social and political issues of the day. His appreciation of the value of the peasant commune as the embryo of a future socialist society was based, not on romantic notions of spiritual *sobornost'*, like the Slavophils', but on firmer historical and economic grounds. It was by a process of rational deduction and scientific calculation, typical of the *raznochinets* mentality, rather than from a veneration of some collective Arcadian idyll, that Chernyshevskii argued for his own more sober vision of his country's socialist potential. That potential could not be realised, however, without a struggle, indeed without a *class struggle*, and, although no Marxist, Chernyshevskii welcomed the inevitable challenge from 'the [most] numerous and lowest class – the peasants, wage-earners and artisans':

> We welcome the oppression of one class by another, for it will lead to a struggle, and then the oppressed will know who is oppressing them in the present order of things and that another order is possible in which there will be no oppressed … Far better anarchy from below than from above.[22]

Nor did he delude himself that the struggle would be non-violent. An anonymous article which appeared in 1859, if not written by Chernyshevskii himself, is certainly redolent of his views at the time: 'Only the peasants' axes can save us. Nothing apart from these axes is any use … Summon Russia to arms!'[23]

Chernyshevskii was arrested by agents of the Third Section in 1862. In 1864, after two years' imprisonment in the SS Peter and Paul fortress, he was convicted – on spurious charges, backed up with forged evidence – of inciting revolution, and sentenced to 'civil execution', hard labour and perpetual exile to Siberia.[24] This, together with the disappearance of *Zemlya i volya*, the suppression of the Polish revolt, the imprisonment and exile of the manifesto-mongers, and the dying down of peasant unrest, marks the end of Russia's 'first revolutionary situation', if that indeed is what it was.

After two years' relative lull in revolutionary activity, the next dramatic incident to take place was the attempted assassination of the tsar on 4 April 1866. The perpetrator was a young man named Dmitrii Karakozov (1840–66) who was a member of a splinter group (calling itself rather melodramatically 'Hell' (*Ad*)) from a tiny revolutionary cell known simply as 'The Organization' (*Organizatsiya*), led by his cousin, Nikolai Ishutin (1840–79). Acting solely on his own initiative, Karakozov first composed a document which was part-manifesto, part-explanation for his action, then travelled from Moscow to St Petersburg and fired a pistol shot at the tsar while the latter was taking a public stroll in the Summer Gardens, not far from the Winter Palace. Someone in the crowd of 'royal watchers' deflected the would-be assassin's aim, the bullet missed its target, Karakozov was arrested, cruelly interrogated and publicly hanged.

Ishutin and the rest of his 'Organization' were exiled to Siberia. Such was the public shock and outrage at the attempted murder of the 'Tsar Liberator' that the government and police had little difficulty in gaining popular support for inaugurating an intensive crackdown on known or suspected subversives, agitators, 'nihilists' and other enemies of the state, in a campaign generally known as the 'White Terror'.

Over the next few years, there was a further pause in overt revolutionary activity, though a few individual, isolated instances of politically motivated violence did occur, one of the most notorious being the celebrated 'Nechaev affair'. Sergei Nechaev (1847–82) was a young revolutionary zealot, fanatical almost to the point of infantile dementia, who in 1869 organised the murder of Ivan Ivanov, one of his comrades in a fictitious revolutionary cell, in order to seal the collective guilt and loyalty of the other cell members. Nechaev fled abroad, but was later arrested and returned to Russia where he was condemned to imprisonment in perpetual solitary confinement. Ivanov's murder, which caused a public scandal at the time, provided the germ of the plot for Dostoevskii's novel, 'The Devils' (*Besy*, 1872), in which the character of Pëtr Verkhovenskii is closely modelled on that of 'the unmentionable Nechaev'.[25] During the years of the White Terror, many young students and intellectuals, in order to escape arrest and possible exile, left Russia for Switzerland where they continued their studies, and where the ideology of Populism developed along different theoretical lines. The three major tendencies were associated with the ideas of Pëtr Lavrov (1823–1900), Mikhail Bakunin and Pëtr Tkachëv (1844–86).

Lavrov, who had been associated with the first Land and Liberty organisation, believed that it was the task of the intelligentsia to engage itself in a programme of education, preparation and propaganda which would gradually raise the level of its own, and the people's, political consciousness to the point where they, the people, would rise, overthrow the state and establish a socialist society. In his 'Historical Letters' (*Istoricheskie pis'ma*), published between 1868 and 1869, he spoke of the moral debt of the 'penitent gentry' to the Russian *narod*, and of the need to redeem their debt by dedicating themselves to the service of the people – but only when they themselves were fully prepared. Lavrov's, therefore, was a 'preparationist' approach to popular revolution, revolution which began in the classroom. More urgently, and more influentially, Bakunin passionately believed that there was nothing that the intellgentsia could teach the *narod*. 'The Russian people,' he said in a memorable phrase, 'is revolutionary by instinct and socialist by nature.' Invoking the spirit of Pugachëv, Bakunin scorned the idea that it was the intelligentsia's job to indoctrinate the people. On the contrary, he put his faith in the spontaneous peasant insurrection – the *bunt*. If the intelligentsia had any role, it was simply that of helping the peasants to coordinate their local rebellions into a nationwide revolution that would destroy the state, thus leaving the people free to organise themselves into a federation of autonomous, self-governing communes. 'We must not act as schoolmaster for the people,' he said, 'but we must lead them to revolt.' And if for Lavrov the revolution commenced in the schoolroom, for Bakunin it began in the fields. Leading the people to revolt was also a central feature of Tkachëv's philosophy. Unlike the anti-authoritarian, anarchist Bakunin, however, Tkachëv produced the most fully articulated expression of the 'Jacobinist' tendency which had appeared in Zaichnevskii's 'Young Russia', and even earlier in the strategy of the Decembrist, Pestel. With an impatience that is exemplified in the title of his journal, 'The Tocsin' (*Nabat*), Tkachëv urged the intelligentsia to *organise* itself for revolutionary action and form a vanguard which must lead the masses in both the destruction of the old order and the construction of the new, thereby displaying an emphasis on centralised leadership which foreshadowed the essence of Lenin's later revolutionary views on party hegemony.

As an indirect result of a fusion of Lavrovism and Bakuninism, of the return of many of their young acolytes from their Swiss universities back to Russia, and of the heightened public awareness of the appalling plight of Russia's exploited peasants and workers, as revealed in V. (N). Bervi-Flerovskii's book, *The Condition of the Working Class in Russia* (1869),[26] in the 'mad summer' of 1874 an amazing event took place. Without leadership, without organisation and without planning, thousands of young intellectuals, both men and women, left their homes, universities and jobs, joining in a mass spontaneous movement, almost a crusade, to spread the socialist gospel throughout the Russian countryside. This was the famous 'going to the people' (*khozhdenie v narod*). There was no immediate signal for the exodus. It represented a curious mixture of semi-digested socialist ideals, genuine sympathy for the sufferings of the common people and sheer youthful enthusiasm, and was infused with an almost missionary zeal. The whole affair was a miserable fiasco. Many became disillusioned by the sullen, conservative and unresponsive nature of the peasants themselves; others succumbed to diseases which were endemic in Russian rural areas; some were actually detained by the suspicious peasants and handed over by their officials to the police for speaking 'against God and the Tsar'.[27] Hundreds were imprisoned and later put on public trial in St Petersburg. The intelligentsia had 'gone to the people' to immolate themselves on the altar of peasant socialism. The people had sent them back. Nothing illustrated more clearly and tragically the continuing gulf that separated Russia's educated classes from the *narod*.

The failure of the 'movement to the people' actually to move the people forced the revolutionaries to take stock and reconsider both the strategy and tactics of their war against the government. From Lavrovist propaganda techniques and Bakuninist agitation, there was now a definite shift towards the Tkachëvian tactics of organisation and leadership. In 1876 a second Land and Liberty (*Zemlya i volya*) party was founded, dedicated to raising the revolutionary stakes through a carefully planned campaign of clandestine activities aimed at the 'disorganisation' of the state. Its members trained themselves in a programme of conspiratorial subterfuge, which contained all the cloak-and-dagger stuff of both espionage and sabotage. Secret presses, safe houses, infiltration, disguises, false papers and identities, home-made explosives, invisible ink and gaol breaks became the stock-in-trade of the new revolutionary underground. The use of increasingly more violent methods eventually caused a crisis within *Zemlya i volya*, which came to a head over the specific question of terror. The policy of armed resistance to arrest and consequent shoot-outs with police and prison guards soon escalated into pre-emptive assassination attempts on police officers, local officials and eventually senior government dignitaries.

The practice of organised terror began in the south of Russia, but soon spread to the capital in 1878 with the attempt of Vera Zasulich (1849–1919) on the life of General F. F. Trepov, governor of St Petersburg, in revenge for ordering the fatal flogging of one of her imprisoned comrades. As the terror attacks multiplied, even claiming a victim in General N. V. Mezentsov, head of the Third Section, who was stabbed to death in broad daylight, so did the authorities step up the number of arrests and executions, which in turn were met with more terrorist reprisals. This vicious circle was not only costly in terms of money and personnel, but some members of Land and Liberty were beginning to question the political effectiveness of individual terror as a revolutionary weapon, rejecting it as an expensive and ideologically unsupportable diversion from the pristine Populist aim of arousing mass revolution. Eventually the issue was formally raised at a meeting of the party's executive committee, which resulted in a split into two new bodies: one, the opponents of terror, led by Georgii Plekhanov (1856–1918), calling itself 'Black Repartition' (*Chërnyi peredel*); the other, the terrorist group called 'The People's Will' (*Narodnaya volya*). On 26 August 1879, the executive committee of *Narodnaya volya* formally condemned Alexander II to death, solemnising their intent by adopting as their slogan the famous oath of the Ancient Roman orator, Cato, '*Delanda est Carthago!*' They spent the next two years attempting to execute their sentence, and the tsar.

Lack of space precludes a detailed account of the many failed attempts on the emperor's life. They tried blowing up the imperial train as it carried the tsar back to St Petersburg from holidaying in the Crimea. But they got the wrong train and succeeded only in blowing up a coachload of jam destined for the royal pantries. They tried planting a bomb under the main banqueting hall in the Winter Palace, primed by its maker, Stepan Khalturin, to go off as the tsar sat down to dine. It exploded dead on time, the banqueting hall was wrecked, 11 people were killed and 36 injured. The tsar was not among them: a visiting foreign dignitary had delayed him on his way to dinner. Another royal escape, but the fact that the terrorists had managed to plant an explosive device right in the heart of the royal household – shortly after the brazen fatal stabbing of the chief of the secret police – was something of a psychological victory for the *Narodnaya volya*, and part of a relentless campaign of 'propaganda by deeds'. They tried several other potentially deadly stratagems until eventually, on 1 March 1881, the terrorists finally got their man.

The organiser of the final, fatal plot was Andrei Zhelyabov (1850–81), the only Populist leader to be born a serf. He was, in fact, already in prison on the fateful day, and the last details of the assassination were supervised by his mistress, Sofiya Perovskaya (1854–81), whose father had earlier been governor of St Petersburg.

The conspirators had planned to detonate a landmine placed beneath the road along which the tsar's coach regularly passed, but a last-minute change of itinerary meant that the device was never activated. 'Plan B', however, was. As Alexander's entourage passed along the Catherine canal on its way back to the Winter Palace after attending a military ceremony, a hand-grenade was tossed by a young man called Nikolai Rysakov, blowing off the back of the royal carriage. Unhurt, the tsar insisted on alighting in order to confront his would-be killer, assuming him to be a Pole. At that point, what nowadays would be called a 'suicide bomber' stepped forward and dropped his explosive at the emperor's feet, mortally wounding both the tsar and himself. The police succeeded in rounding up the rest of the plotters, and after a three-day trial, six of them, including the two lovers, Zhelyabov and Perovskaya, were sentenced to death. One of them, Gezya Helfman, was reprieved when it was revealed that she was pregnant. The rest were publicly hanged on 3 April.

The killing of the Tsar Liberator and the execution of the regicides did not, however, mark the end of revolutionary Populism, and although its intellectual influence diminished somewhat in the century's two closing decades, it was to revive spectacularly in the early twentieth century in its theoretical, organisational, and even terrorist guises (see Chapter 11). In political terms, Alexander's assassination was both futile and counter-productive, ushering in, as it did, a period of oppressive government reaction during the reign of his successor, Alexander III, whose reputation for bigotry, illiberality and heavy-handed police methods rivalled that of his grandfather, Nicholas I. Before examining the so-called 'era of petty deeds' over which he presided, a few words need to be said about the conduct of Russia's foreign policy following her humiliation in the Crimea.

Foreign policy

As mentioned in the foregoing chapter, the main driving force behind Russian foreign policy in Europe after the signing of the Treaty of Paris in 1856 was the unrelenting effort to bring about the cancellation of the 'Black Sea clauses' of the agreement, whereby Russia was denied naval rights in the Black Sea and the Bosphorus, thus dealing a severe body-blow to her southern maritime trade.

Russia's exertions were eventually rewarded with the abrogation of the Black Sea clauses being agreed by the major European powers at the Convention of London in 1871. In fact, Russia had already unilaterally repudiated those provisions of the Treaty of Paris to which she objected, a *démarche* which had caused varying degrees of consternation in the foreign chanceries of Europe. But their eventual endorsement of Russia's action, with the consequence that both she and Turkey could resume peacetime naval operations in the Black Sea, the Bosphorus and the Dardenelles, was an indication that Russia was beginning to regain some of the international status lost in the Crimea. Prussia's weighty support for Russia in these negotiations was not unconnected with Russia's pro-Prussian stand in the Franco-Prussian War which ended in victory for Prussia, closely followed by the unification of Germany, both of which also occurred in 1871. This new Russo-German concordat was expanded to include Austria-Hungary by the formation of the unofficial 'Three Emperors' League' in 1873, which was little more than a re-affirmation of the pre-Crimean principles of the Holy Alliance. Moreover, despite the superficial cordiality of the Slavo-Teutonic entente, the establishment of a unified German Empire as a powerful new factor in central and east European affairs contained a latent threat to Russian interests which manifested itself in the Bulgarian crisis of 1885–87 and exploded in the outbreak of the First World War in August 1914.

At the other end of the Romanovs' vast empire, Alexander was more successful in expanding Russia's territories and establishing her military, diplomatic and commercial power in northern Asia. By the treaties of Aigun (1858) and Peking (1860), Russia acquired huge tracts of land from China along the left bank of the river Amur and the area between the Amur-Ussuri region and the sea of Japan. Through a mixture of quiet diplomacy, softly-softly annexations, subtle settlement and sheer good fortune – largely as a result of the far-sighted and skilful policies of Count Nikolai Muravëv-Amurskii (1809–81), Governor-General of Eastern Siberia, Russia gained possessions in the Far East, which were larger than the territory of France and Germany combined, without spilling a drop of blood. Her permanent presence on the 'eastern Bosphorus' was marked by the founding of the settlement and naval base – home to Russia's Pacific fleet – of Vladivostok ('Lord of the East') in 1860, elevated to city status in 1880. It was in recognition of his exploits in the Amur region, that Muravëv was awarded the hyphenated honorific of 'Amurskii'. Also in the same part of the world, in 1875 Japan relinquished her claim to the large island of Sakhalin, which was soon to gain notoriety as the final circle of punishment in the penal hell of the Siberian exile system.[28] Further north, across the Bering Strait, Russia had already divested herself of her no-longer-profitable possessions in North America by selling off the territory of Alaska in 1867 to the United States for the paltry sum of 7,200,000 gold dollars, which James Gibson has helpfully informed us works out at 'two cents an acre'.[29] Notwithstanding this far northern truncation, during Alexander II's reign, 37,000 square miles of Asian territory were added to the Russian Empire. If no blood was spilt during the annexation of the Amur and Ussuri districts, minor rivers of it flowed in the arid regions of Central Asia, which were subjected to a seemingly inexorable process of Russian imperial subjugation during the 1860s and 1870s. This confrontation between Orthodox Russia and the Muslim peoples of the steppes, deserts and mountains of inner Asia was in some ways a continuation of the age-old battle between the two civilisations, though in the mid-nineteenth century the advantage was to lie very definitely with the militarily superior Slavs. The suppression of the largely Turkic tribesmen and khanates of Bukhara, Khiva and Kokand was accompanied by the standard atrocities which are a well established feature of any colonial experience, and their once independent, though mutually hostile entities – comprising the present-day Uzbek, Kirgiz and Turkmen republics – were absorbed into the new administrative unit of Russian Turkestan, with its centre at Tashkent. The territorial expansion of the Russian Empire to the borders of Afghanistan became a constant source of alarm and concern to the interests of the British Raj in India.

Ever since the earliest years of its history, relations between Russia and Constantinople, whether under Byzantine or Ottoman rule, had been bedevilled by mutual antagonism and mistrust, aggravated by religious hostility, and punctuated by regular outbreaks of open warfare. Most recently, Turkey, in coalition with Britain and France, had been on the winning side in the Crimean War, but this did not mean that Russia's chastening experience in that conflict in any way diminished her interest in the affairs of her southern neighbour. During the reign of Alexander II this interest was stimulated by the increasingly vociferous role played in Russian politics by the Panslavist movement. Panslavism was an ambiguous phenomenon, linked with the classical Slavophilism of the 1840s, which now adopted a more assertive, indeed often belligerent, attitude in relation to Russia's position vis-à-vis the Slavonic, particularly the Orthodox Slavonic, subjects of the Turkish sultan. In its most extreme form the more militant wing of Panslavism envisaged a grand, fraternal union of all the Slavonic peoples, liberated from Ottoman and Hapsburg imperialism, under the paternalistic hegemony of the Orthodox Russian tsar. Of course, such a grandiose vision overlooked the fact that this would merely mean swapping one brand of imperialism for another, and also blithely ignored the widely diverging historical, cultural, linguistic and religious differences that had divided the eastern, western and southern Slavs over many centuries. Warsaw and Prague both owed more to Europe than to Muscovy, and a large proportion of the Slavonic peoples owed more to Catholic Rome than Orthodox Byzantium.

Moreover, the Slavonic peoples of the Balkans struggling for independence from foreign oppression could hardly find comfort in Russia's recent treatment of her fellow Slavs in Poland. St Petersburg's record in this respect was scarcely one of benevolent fraternalism, however tricked out in the rhetoric of spurious traditional kinship. If the Poles and the Russians are part of the same extended family, the kindest that can be said of it is that it is a somewhat dysfunctional one. Despite this ethnic, religious and military antagonism among the Slavs, Russian Panslavists saw it as their sacred mission to support the liberation movements of their Balkan brethren wherever and whenever an opportunity presented itself. It was partly as a result of these pressures, with which influential members of the government were in sympathy, that Russia found herself once more at war with Turkey in 1877. The ostensible cause was the brutal Turkish suppression of the Bulgarian uprising of 1876, but the underlying motive was really the pursuit of more influence and, if possible, territory, in the region. Fanned by the winds of the Panslavists' increasing clamour for war, which found a surprising resonance among the Russian public of most political persuasions, the flames of ancient Russo-Turkish enmity flared once more as Russia's troops, including many enthusiastic, idealistic volunteers, went to the aid of their valiant Bulgarian, Serbian and Bosnian brothers. After facing stiff Turkish resistance at the battle for the fortress of Plevna, Russia finally forced the sultan to agree to the Treaty of San Stefano (3 March 1878, N.S.), whereby Russia acquired considerable territory; Serbia, Montenegro and Rumania gained their independence; and an extended Bulgaria, although also nominally independent, remained very firmly in the Russian 'sphere of influence'. The other European powers, however, looked askance at Russia's growing power in the Balkans, and threw the Treaty of San Stefano out of the window at the Congress of Berlin, convened by Bismarck in July 1878. Under the revised arrangements, to which Russia was compelled to accede, not only was her influence in the area much reduced, but she had also to accept that in wider diplomatic terms, at the end of Alexander II's reign – despite her huge territorial gains in central and northern Asia – she remained as much a minor player in the international power game as she had been at its start.

That situation was to continue to be the case during the reign of the succeeding emperor, Alexander III, to which we now turn.

Reaction, industrialisation and Russian Marxism, 1881–1904

The terrorist bomb which blew Alexander II's body apart on 1 March 1881 also destroyed any possibility of implementing tentative plans for the establishment of some kind of representative body to advise on central government decision-making. In response to the wave of political assassinations and other 'disorganising' activities which swept the country from 1876, the tsar had declared a state of emergency, divided the country into military-type governor-generalships, and appointed as Minister for Internal Affairs with quasi-dictatorial powers Count Mikhail Loris-Melikov (1825–88), a hero of the Turkish War. Loris-Melikov exercised his brief virtual dictatorship by using the iron fist/velvet glove technique of cracking down ruthlessly on the revolutionaries while granting a number of concessions to the more progressive elements of public opinion, which, while being critical of terrorist outrages, were also unhappy at many aspects of government policy. Such measures as *were* taken, such as loosening the censorship, abolishing the Third Section – or, rather, re-naming it as the Department of Police – and advocating more public participation in national policy-making made hardly any impression on the course of events. However, a set of very modest proposals for legislative changes which would have allowed representatives of the rural *zemstva* and urban councils to scrutinise and advise on legislative bills before they went before the State Council for ratification, was privately approved by the tsar, but never implemented, as a direct result of his assassination. It was this project, sometimes extravagantly described as Loris-Melikov's 'constitution', that was unceremoniously, even contemptuously, scrapped by his son and successor, Alexander III, immediately on his ascending the throne. The possibility of further steps, however hesitant, in the direction of anything with even the faintest whiff of constitutional government around it was now out of the question. As Pipes puts it: 'The terrorists could not have been more effective in scuttling political reform had they been on the police payroll.'[1] (In fact several *were* on the police payroll.) Needless to say, Loris-Melikov had no alternative but to resign. He was replaced by Count Nikolai Ignatev (1832–1908), also a hero of the Turkish War and the central Asian campaigns, and a rabid Panslavist. Despite his reactionary opinions, he in turn was replaced by a man of even more ultra-conservative views, Count Dmitrii Tolstoi (1823–89), Alexander II's former Minister of Education and one-time Procurator of the Holy Synod. That particularly influential position, virtually that of 'Minister of Religion' and chief lay official of the Orthodox Church, was now held by a man who was as renowned for his erudition as for his extreme obscurantism, virulent Russian nationalism of the most offensive kind, anti-Semitism and a patho- logical loathing of everything that deviated from the antediluvian principles of Official Nationalism – Konstantin Pobedonostsev (1827–1907). Along with the influential extreme right-wing journal- ist, Mikhail Katkov (1818–87), it was this grisly *troika* – Pobedonostsev, Tolstoi and Katkov – who were the chief demiurges of Alexander's retrogressive programme of counter-reform and the major inspiration for the 'era of petty deeds'.

Petty deeds

The first casualty of the counter-reform was the miscalled Loris- Melikov 'constitution', which was not so much killed off as stillborn. Anything smacking of liberalism, democratic participation, consti- tutionalism or parliamentarianism was anathema to the tsar and his terrible trio. Pobedonostsev was the most vociferously colourful in articulating their views. Even before Alexander II's murder, he described those highly placed people who were toying with the idea of a constitution as 'half-wits and perverted apes', and condemned parliamentary government and 'the principle that all power issues from the people' as the 'great falsehood of our time'. Democracy, trial by jury, secular education, scientific materialism, non-Orthodox reli- gions, public opinion, Jews, a free press, free-thinking, free anything that did not conform to the tenets of Orthodoxy, Autocracy and Nationalism – all came under the lash of his vituperative scorn. 'It is terrible,' he remarked, 'to think of our condition if destiny had sent us a fatal gift – an All-Russian Parliament! But that will never be.'[2] Sadly, as the failure of the later Duma experiment was to confirm, he was right (see Chapter 11).

While the emperor himself preferred to spend most of his time in the safety of his highly fortified estate at Gatchina, as what Marx described as 'a prisoner of war of the revolution',[3] his government departments and the police were given extensive new arbitrary powers to deal with more or less anything or anyone they deemed to be a threat, or even potential threat, to the security of the state. In the 'Statute on Measures for the Preservation of Political Order and Social Tranquillity' (14 August 1881), and the 'Statute on Police Surveillance' (12 March 1882), officials of the Department of Police were empowered to declare any area of the empire where they suspected subversive activity to be taking place to be in a state of either 'reinforced' or 'extraordinary' security (*usilennaya* or *chrezvychainaya okhrana*).[4] In what was now virtually a police dictatorship, its operatives and agents were able to search, arrest, detain, interrogate, imprison or exile to Siberia for indefinite periods those who had committed, who were thought likely to commit, who knew or were related to anyone they suspected might be likely to commit, 'acts against the imperial form of government'. Such 'untrustworthy' (*neblagonadëzhnye*) persons could be held incommunicado, with no rights to inform relatives or have access to legal representation or recourse to *habeas corpus*. Even if no crime were proved to have been perpetrated or planned, the suspect could be administratively banished for either a stipulated or indefinite period. While in exile, usually in Siberia, they remained under constant police surveillance (*podnadzornye*), were confined to a designated locality, and were banned from a whole range of activities, employments and professional positions. Teachers could not teach, doctors could not practise medicine, and all kinds of personal literary, artistic, recreational and social activities were subject to police scrutiny.

George Kennan, who studied the workings of the Siberian exile system at first hand during the 1880s, gives many harrowing accounts of the indignities, and worse, suffered by perfectly innocent victims of official caprice while serving out their banishment orders. While it is true that political exiles comprised only a tiny percentage of the total exile population (around 1 per cent), and the conditions in which they lived varied enormously from the relatively tolerable (if spartan) to the downright insufferable, the whole history of political exile to Siberia in the late nineteenth century is replete with horror stories which illustrate the inanity, vindictiveness and sheer bloody-mindedness of the police and exile authorities, which drove many of their victims to the point of madness or suicide.[5] In many respects, the Siberian exile system, both political and criminal, represented a microcosm of Alexander's entire administration.[6] Although the new legislation was supposedly intended to be a temporary measure, in force for only three years, it was in fact triennially renewed until 1917 and, in Lenin's words, became 'the *de facto* constitution of Russia'.

Apart from official government reaction, one particularly disconcerting example of the conservative backlash following Alexander II's assassination was the formation of a sinister body of loyal aristocrats calling itself the 'Sacred Host' (*Svyashchënnaya druzhina*), a relatively small organisation supported by a larger company called the 'Volunteer Guard' (*Dobrovolnaya okhrana*), which launched a rampantly pro-monarchist, militant Christian campaign directed, with police connivance, against radicals, dissenters and other 'enemies of the state', often using the same methods of subversion and propaganda as employed by the revolutionaries who formed their quarry. However ardent their fierce, patriotic monarchism, the organisation was nevertheless an example of public spontaneity which could not be tolerated in the new mood of centralised authoritarianism, and it soon went into involuntary liquidation. Despite its short-lived existence, the 'Sacred Host' and its cohorts provided an unsavoury foretaste of the vicious depredations of the gangs of proto-fascist thugs, known as the 'Black Hundreds' (*chernosotentsy*), who, under the aegis of right-wing political organisations such as the 'Union of the Russian People' (*Soyuz russkogo naroda*), operated during and after the revolutionary events of 1905, brutally attacking students, left-wing intellectuals, labour leaders, liberal politicians and Jews (see Chapter 11).

Mention of Russia's Jewish community (referred to by the Interior Minister, Tolstoi, as the 'Hebrew leprosy')[7] raises the whole fraught question of the rampant racism and chauvinistic nationalism, including virulent anti-Semitism, which was one of the most deeply abhorrent features of Alexander's government policy, and, unfortunately, of his own personal philosophy. According to data provided by the Soviet historian, E. A. Lutskii, persecution of national culture was enforced during Alexander's reign in all ethnic minority areas. For example, in Ukraine in 1883 the publication of all works in the Ukrainian language was forbidden, including translated scientific texts and books of a political nature. In the following year, 1884, all theatres in five Ukrainian provinces were closed. In Poland, the Polish National Bank was shut down and a programme of intense Russification carried out in Polish schools. The teaching of almost all subjects in the Polish language was banned, the only exceptions being the Catholic religion and the Polish language! Naturally the Poles' atavistic hatred of Russia, mentioned in the previous chapter, was exacerbated by this senseless campaign, which not only nurtured the continuing growth of a vigorous Polish nationalism, but also turned many of the country's intelligentsia towards other forms of revolutionary theory and practice, including Marxist socialism. In Finland, various inroads were made into the remnants of the national constitution, and the indigenous peoples of the Caucasus, the Volga regions and Central Asia continued to be subjected to various forms of colonial exploitation. Popular uprisings against the yoke of Russian imperialism were mercilessly suppressed in Guriya, western Georgia, in 1892, in Bashkiria in 1884, in the Uzbek district of Fergana and in Armenia in 1886, and in Tashkent in 1892.[8]

The policy of Russification, carried out under the mindless, meaningless slogan of 'Russia for the Russians!' (*Rossiya dlya russkikh!*), was directed against all national minorities throughout the empire, not excluding the tiny, primitive aboriginal peoples of Siberia and the Far East. But it was the Jews – traditional whipping boys of good Christian folk throughout the ages – who bore the brunt of Alexander, Pobedonostsev & Co.'s institutionalised corporate racism. In this case the slogan was 'Beat the Yids! – Save Russia!' (*Bei zhidov! – Spasi Rossiyu!*). Unfortunately, official attitudes vis-à-vis the Jews found considerable popular resonance among traditionally anti-Semitic elements in the poorer classes of Russian society, who associated them not only with the killing of Jesus (a perception assiduously encouraged by Pobedonostsev) but with usurious and extortive financial practices. The fact that Gezya Helfman, the pregnant regicide condemned to, and reprieved from, hanging after Alexander II's murder, was a Jewess, did nothing to help their cause, and in the spring and summer of 1881 a campaign of particularly nasty pogroms, involving arson, looting, rape and murder, was carried out in Yelizavetgrad, Kiev, Odessa, Pereyaslavl, Borispol and Nezhin. The fact that these barbaric attacks were concentrated in Ukraine does not indicate that the Ukrainians were any more vicious or anti-Semitic than the Russians: it was simply that it was in Ukraine that the largest populations of Jews were settled. In 1882, in addition to discriminatory restrictions already in place, there was promulgated a set of 'Temporary Regulations' further curtailing Jewish 'rights'. Even within the 'Pale of Settlement' Jews were forbidden to acquire immoveable property and to live in purely rural areas, thus 'ghettoising' them even more in the larger towns and villages. Of these towns, in 1887 Rostov-on-Don and Taganrog were removed from the Pale, and in 1891 Jewish artisans were debarred from residence in Moscow, over 17,000 of them being forcibly deported from the old capital. A *numerus clausus* was imposed on the number of young Jewish people allowed into primary, secondary and higher education, and certain professions had a quota of Jewish members placed on them. During the 1890s, only one Jew was admitted to the legal profession. In 1894 they were prohibited from voting in local elections, and in 1894 were refused the right to hold a licence to sell alcohol, the trade in which became a state monopoly, thereby depriving Jewish innkeepers of a regular, and lucrative, income.

While anti-Semitism was not confined to Russia, it was out of the campaign of official and unofficial Jew-baiting within the borders of the Russian Empire during Alexander III's reign that two important political consequences were to flow. First, in proportional terms, the revolutionary movement contained a higher number of Jewish activists than other ethnic groups. They had, of course, multiple grievances as a result of their race, their religion, their occupations, and their social and fiscal status. Perhaps surprisingly, despite endemic peasant anti-Semitism, there had been many Jews among the pro-peasant *narodniki* revolutionaries. But it was within the largely urban and factory-based Marxist social-democratic movement that they played a prominent role, both in the leadership (Deutsch (Deich), Bronstein/Trotskii, Tsederbaum/Martov, Radomyslskii/Zinovev, Vallach/Litvinov, Helphand/Parvus *et al.*), and in the rank and file. For example, the 'General Union of Jewish Workers in Poland and Russia', usually referred to as the *Bund*, was the largest workers' socialist organisation within the Russian Social Democratic Workers' Party (*Rossiiskaya sotsial-demokraticheskaya rabochaya partiya* (RSDRP), see below), and fielded three out of the nine delegates assembled at the party's first 'congress' in 1898. Second, it was from the persecution of late nineteenth-century Russian Jewry that the Zionist movement emerged, seeking an independent, separate Jewish national homeland, either in America or the Middle East. The movement attracted more international recognition in the early twentieth century and was horrifically boosted by the Nazi Holocaust, leading ultimately to the founding of the state of Israel in 1948, thus shifting a problem born of centuries of east and west European anti-Semitism onto the lap of the Palestinian Arabs.

As will be seen, the emergence of national liberation movements against Russia's colonial policies played a leading role in the eventual disintegration of the empire. And it was largely Alexander III's xenophobic, racist and often brutal treatment of the non-Russian peoples of his domain that exacerbated their resentment against St Petersburg, and increased their determination to free themselves from tsarist oppression. It is, moreover, a telling indication of the government's cavalier and insensitive attitude to the emperor's non-Russian subjects that, despite their accounting for 60 per cent of the empire's population, and despite the heterogeneity of their composition, needs and cultures, neither the tsarist regime, nor, indeed, the Provisional Governments which replaced it in 1917, ever thought it necessary to appoint a minister with special responsibility for the non-Russian nationalities of the polyglot empire. In fact, it was not until after the October 1917 Revolution that the new socialist government, recognising the crucial importance of the nationalities question, appointed the Georgian Bolshevik, Iosif Dzhugashvili/Stalin, as the country's first Commissar (i.e. Minister) for Nationalities.

The short-sighted policy of Russification was, of course, simply part of the new administration's drive towards greater uniformity and centralised control, after what Pobedonostsev regarded as the dangerous liberalism of the previous emperor, despite his having had a part in the framing of Alexander II's judicial reforms. Apart from the nationalities, attempts were made to reimpose the leaden hand of central government in all those areas of the empire's affairs where a degree of local or institutional particularism had been allowed to creep in. Of course, the re-enserfment of the peasantry was virtually inconceivable, but in the governance of rural areas the power of the local nobility, never entirely lost, was reasserted through a number of measures which adjusted the regulations concerning membership and organisation of the *zemstva* and of the local peasant institutions even more in the *dvoryanstvo*'s favour. At the same time, however, the central administration increased its control over the provincial nobility itself, most notably by the creation of a new category of official, the 'Land Captain' (*zemskii nachal'nik*) in 1889. These new officers, who were appointed by, and directly responsible to, the Minister for Internal Affairs, were required to be members of the local hereditary nobility and owners of considerable property, to have spent a certain amount of time in government service, and to have reached a specified educational standard. The powers of the *zemskii nachal'nik* were extensive, and enabled him to disregard, override or overturn all agenda and decisions of, and even elections to, district and village assemblies. Even the verdicts of the local courts could be countermanded by the noble appointee of the central Interior Ministry, and he could also impose fines on local peasant officials without the irritating inconvenience of going through any judicial procedure. It would be wrong to say that the power of local authorities had been taken away, as they did not have much of that in the first place, but by these counter-reforms the government had re-established the class principle (*soslovnyi printsip*), or what has been described as a state of 'semi-serfdom' (*polu-krepostnichestnoi poryadok*), in the countryside.[9]

In the field of education, in which opportunities had been considerably widened during Alexander II's reign, his successor sought to re-affirm – as he did in local government – the hierarchical system which, except in rare cases, confined certain levels of education to specific social classes or estates. Put very simply, children of the lowest orders of society were restricted to primary education, admittance to secondary education operated on a quota system, and higher education was open only to the privileged upper classes. Putting it even more crudely, the new Minister of Education, I. D. Delyanov (1818–97), circulated a memorandum to all secondary schools in June 1887, which read in part as follows:

Concerned for an improvement in the composition of secondary-school pupils, I consider it essential to limit entry to these institutions only to those who are in the care and charge of people able to afford a satisfactory guarantee of proper domestic surveillance, and of the provision of the conditions necessary for academic study. Accordingly, in strict observation of this rule, all establishments of secondary education are to cease the intake of children of coachmen, domestic servants, cooks, washerwomen, small shopkeepers and other similar persons, whose children … should emphatically not be taken out of the social environment to which they belong, thereby … leading to disrespect for their parents, dissatisfaction with their way of life, and resentment against the existing and, by the very nature of things, inevitable inequality in the distribution of property.[10]

This objectionable document, known in pedagogical circles as the 'cooks' kids' memorandum' (*tsirkulyar o kukharkinykh detyakh*), at least demonstrated the government's awareness of the connection between a proper education and the development of social and political consciousness, which was, of course, for the regime a consummation devoutly to be discouraged. Needless to say, under Pobedonostsev's malevolent gaze, the Orthodox Church had a large say in the composition of the primary school curriculum, in which the efforts of dedicated village schoolteachers to raise literacy and numeracy levels among peasant children were somewhat offset by the church schools' concentration on church singing, religious indoctrination and the reading of Old Church Slavonic texts; though one could argue that a regular diet of such pious pabulum was as likely to fuel an attitude of rebellion as of religious conformity. (There was, in fact a strong tradition in Russia of sons of the cloth and Orthodox seminarists turning to revolution: Chernyshevskii, Dobrolyubov and Dzhugashvili/Stalin immediately come to mind.) The abolition of university autonomy in 1884, the raising of higher education fees, and the reintroduction of preliminary censorship in 1882 all conspired to ensure that the government of counter-reform kept the intelligent youth of the day on very tight leading strings.

That is not to say that the combined efforts of the Holy Synod and the Department of Police, with all their paraphernalia of surveillance, suppression and strict control, were totally successful in extinguishing the spirit of independent thought and radical opposition to Alexander's authoritarian regime. Despite what was said earlier about the relative quiescence of the Russian countryside following the brief flurry of disturbances in the aftermath of emancipation, it was not the case that the peasantry was entirely torpid during the final decades of the century. A report compiled by the Department of Police in June 1888, using what it admits are incomplete data, provides a detailed statistical breakdown of the figures for agrarian unrest (*besporyadki, volneniya*) throughout all provinces of the empire for the period between January 1881 and May 1888. According to its calculations, during that period, 332 instances of mass disturbance (i.e. involving crowds of people – '*skopom, tolpoyu*') took place in 61 out of 92 provinces and districts (excluding Finland), including 9 out of 12 of the central European provinces in which there were 43 disturbances, or 12.9 per cent of the overall total. The main cause of the disturbances was land disputes between peasant communities and local landowners, and they ranged in seriousness from illegal grazing of cattle and illicit tree-felling to acts of mass violence involving the use of both primitive weapons (sticks, stones, mattocks) and firearms. In 214 recorded cases, acts of violence including criminal assaults on property and persons were reported – that is, 14.4 per cent of the total. In 51 cases, military forces were deployed to suppress the disturbances. These outbreaks hardly added up to another *Pugachëvshchina*, and were nothing on the scale of the 'years of the "Red Cockerel"' (see Chapter 11), but the information in the police report is nevertheless a clear indication of the widespread, lingering discontent of the empire's peasantry (not only Russians, but also Polish, Ukrainian, Baltic, Central Asian and others) at the continuing inequality of the agrarian situation in which ten million peasant households shared 73 million *desyatiny* of land (one *desyatina* = 1.09 hectares or 2.7 acres), while 62 million *desyatiny* of the best land were owned by just 28,000 noble landlords.[11]

The hanging of Alexander II's assassins in 1881 and the subsequent purge of the *Narodnaya volya*, along with the reinforced police powers, did much to dampen the ardour of the revolutionary Populists during the 1880s and 1890s, but that did not mean that Populism as both an active and intellectual force disappeared altogether. At the theoretical level, writers and thinkers such as V. P. Vorontsov (1847–1918) and N. F. Danielson (1844–1918) developed their views on the non-capitalist development of Russia and argued for a socialist ownership of the means of production based on the peasant commune and the workers' cooperative (*artel'*). This school of thought came to be called 'Legal Populism'. Populism of the 'illegal' variety, while hardly thriving, managed to survive in isolated cells and conspiratorial groups that still had their hearts and minds set on bringing about revolutionary change, if necessary by violent means. One of these tiny organisations, calling itself the 'Terrorist Fraction of the People's Will' (*Terroristicheskaya fraktsiya Narodnoi voli*), attempted to mark the sixth anniversary of the assassination of Alexander II by hatching a plot to deal in similar fashion with his son. The first of March 1887, however, turned out to be the day, not of another regicide, but of the conspirators' arrest, followed by their interrogation and secret trial. On 8 May five of them were hanged in the Schlüsselburg fortress, among them Aleksandr Ulyanov (1866–87), elder brother of the future Bolshevik leader, Vladimir Ulyanov/Lenin. In light of the future Marxist, as opposed to Populist, direction of Lenin's thoughts, it is interesting to note that his brother Aleksandr, although implicated in a Populist revolutionary terrorist plot, was also already advocating propaganda and agitation among Russia's industrial proletariat, rather than the peasantry, as a way forward to bringing about revolution. Indeed, the growing size and strength of the workers' movement and embryonic illegal labour organisations were beginning to give more food for thought to the radical intelligentsia, many of whom were turning more and more to the revolutionary theories of Karl Marx and Friedrich Engels against the background of Russia's first gradual, then rapid, industrialisation.

Hugh Seton-Watson indulgently sums up the unspectacular achievements of the 'era of petty deeds' as follows:

> The main characteristics of the last two decades
> of the [nineteenth] century ... are stagnation in

agriculture, progress in industry, retrogression in education, russification of the non-Russian half of the empire's population, and an overall attitude of nostalgic, obscurantist, and narrowly bureaucratic paternalism.[12]

He could well have considered adding a word or two about the government's success in muzzling opposition, turning back the administrative clock in local government, stifling initiative, persecuting religious sectarians, implicitly condoning pogroms, encouraging economic policies which actively promoted famine, and transforming the country into the nearest thing to a modern totalitarian police state.

Industrialisation

Amid the all-pervading gloom, apathy and stagnant mediocrity of the period, which was admirably captured at the time in the atmospheric moodiness of Anton Chekhov's short stories, the one area of national life in which Seton-Watson allows there was some progress was in the growth of industry. The great lurch forward was to occur only during the early years of the reign of Nicholas II (r. 1894–1917), the last of the Romanov tsars, and under the administration of (later Count) Sergei Witte (1849–1915), Minister of Finance from 1893 to 1903. But the infrastructure of the 'Witte system', described below, had been gradually laid down during the 1880s and early 1890s, before his incumbency. As mentioned at the beginning of the previous chapter, Russia entered the second half of the nineteenth century in a state of retarded economic development, in comparison with industrialised Europe. Although there were no doubt other countries where levels of general poverty and technological development were as low or lower, it was the great yawning gap between Russia's vast reservoirs of natural resources and manpower on the one hand, and the actual levels of industrial output on the other, which placed her, by most indices of economic performance, somewhere near the bottom of the league table of European, indeed world, powers.

It has been pointed out by a number of historians that the terms of the emancipation of the serfs in 1861, although prompted partly

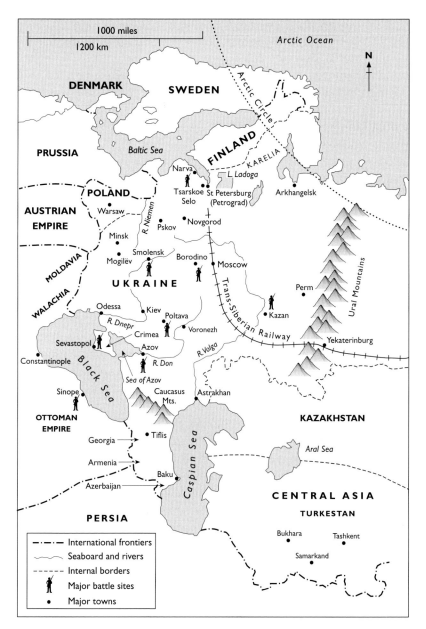

3 European Russia: late nineteenth and early twentieth centuries

by economic factors (see Chapter 10), in fact contained within them the very constraints which impeded, rather than encouraged, economic modernisation. Most importantly, the heavy financial burdens imposed on the peasants by direct and indirect taxation and payment of redemption dues ensured that the rural estate was kept in a state of continuing – in some cases increased – impoverishment, a situation which failed to generate the demand for consumer goods which would stimulate industrial production. The lack of a mass internal market is thus a major retarding factor. Another is the fact that the serfs were given their freedom – in any case limited – on a collective rather than an individual basis, thereby tying them to the village commune, which was reluctant to see the departure of its revenue-raising and communal tax-paying members. Able-bodied young peasants were therefore unable to leave the village in sufficiently large numbers to create the mobile mass labour force necessary to provide industrial manpower. Russia thus lacked both the financial and human capital essential for industrial development on a significant scale. It was not until the state, on Witte's insistence, belatedly took the political decision to intervene with policies designed to reverse this situation that any genuine progress was able to take place.

However, some important developments did occur during the 1880s which provided a skeletal framework around which the more substantial, concrete achievements of Russia's later industrial revolution could be built. The growth of a money-based economy during the transition period from feudal to capitalist relationships meant that Russia had to develop the financial institutions and communication networks which were essential to the running of a modern economic system. The establishment of banks, share dealing, joint stock companies and railway networks, as well as the steady incremental growth of factories and foundries with their attendant workforces, were all symptomatic of the birth pangs of a new economic order. (It is significant in this context that Russian creative literature, both prose and poetry, reflected this transition, as the theme of money, cash-flow, debt, the intricacies of banking, railway construction, labour relations and related issues found their way into the plots and concerns of the major characters. One wonders, for instance, how Tolstoi would have disposed of Anna Karenina had it not been for the existence of the Moscow–St Petersburg mainline.)

Table 10.1 illustrates the growth in output in three key industrial sectors – coal, iron and textiles – from the eve of emancipation until Witte's appointment as Minister of Finance in 1893, the year preceding Alexander III's death.

Table 10.1 *Industrial output in selected areas, 1860–1894*[13]

Years	Coal production	Pig-iron production	Cotton consumption
	in million *puds*: 1 *pud* = 16.38 kg or 36 lb)		
1860–64	21.8	18.1	(not given)
1870–74	61.9	22.9	3.7
1880–84	225.4	29.2	7.8
1890–94	434.3	66.9	10.1

The absence of figures for cotton consumption for 1860–64 is explained by the interruption of imports of raw cotton from the United States as a result of the American Civil War, and is an example of the way in which Russia's economic performance was very much linked with fluctuations on the international market, and with the international situation in general. Demand for arms and other military material in times of international tension or war, for instance, is obviously a major factor.

Another major factor in industrial development was railway construction, which expanded tremendously in the half-century following the Crimean War, which had done so much to expose the grotesque inadequacies of Russia's internal transport system. This growth was not remarkable in itself, and is part of any process of industrialisation in the nineteenth century, as, indeed, in the twentieth. However, even if one discounts the enormous boost given by the construction of the Trans-Siberian Railway (see below), the expansion of Russia's railroad network was obviously key to economic progress. It was, of course, a two-way process, as the building of industrially strategic railways linked up sources of valuable raw materials, which then needed transporting to manufacturing centres, which in turn stimulated the demand for more natural resources such as iron and coal in order to build and fuel more railways. The construction of a rail link between the Donbass coalfields and the iron-ore deposits in the Krivoi Rog area of Ukraine are an obvious example of this. Railroads connecting grain-growing areas with large population centres and ports of export were another major stimulus. Between 1860 and 1890 Russia's railway network increased from 1400 kilometres of track to around 30,000. Annual average construction rates are shown in Table 10.2.

Table 10.2   *Annual average railway construction, 1861–95*[14]

Years	Kilometres
1861–65	443
1866–70	1378
1871–75	1660
1876–80	767
1881–85	632
1886–90	914
1891–95	1292

Great strides in railway construction notwithstanding, the fastest-growing sector of the Russian economy was the oil industry, located in Georgia on the western littoral of the Caspian Sea, with its head-quarters at Baku. Massive investment by such internationally famous firms as the Nobel brothers and the Rothschilds boosted oil extraction, refinement and distribution so that, by the end of the century, the country's internal market was entirely self-sufficient in petroleum products and even began to outstrip the United States on the international market. Between 1885 and 1913 (the eve of the First World War) Russian oil production almost trebled, from 153 million *pud*s to almost 570 million.

Impressive as Russia's industrial development may have been in the 1880s, though with a modesty appropriate to the 'era of petty deeds', it was the elevation to the Ministry of Finance of Sergei Witte in 1893 which detonated the 'big boom' that marked the country's turn-of-the-century industrial revolution. However, a complex inter-play of economic, social and political factors linked to that revolution was to have the unlooked-for result that Russia's industrial 'remarkable decade', 1894–1904, finished off with a revolutionary 'boom' of a different sort in the tumultuous events of 1905 (see Chapter 11). In quantitative terms, as has been shown, the economy, or at least its industrial sector, had been gradually growing during Alexander III's reign, but the qualitative shift which turned industrial development into industrial revolution was brought about by Witte's success in persuading the government of the new tsar, Nicholas II, that, with a continuing shortfall in the amount of private capital, technical and managerial know-how and available labour power, it required direct state intervention in order to ensure that the necessary financial and human resources for investment would be generated. In other words, the process of what Marx called 'primary capitalist accumulation', which had played a major role in England's industrial revolution, and the financial backing of the big banks, which had helped to payroll Germany's, were just not available in Russia's case, and had to be substituted with a policy of government *dirigisme*. As Alexander II had inaugurated the abolition of feudal serfdom 'from above', so did the government of his grandson adopt a 'top-down' approach to the problem of completing, or at least accelerating, the process of capitalist development.

The main features of the 'Witte system' were as follows: the paramount role taken by the government in overall planning and finance; emphasis on capital (heavy) goods rather than consumer (light) goods industries; massive taxation increases imposed on an already over-burdened and penurious peasantry; a continuation of the policy of the former finance minister, A. I. Vyshnegradskii (1831–95) of 'export and starve' – that is, forcing the peasants to sell their grain for export while leaving no reserves to offset harvest failures and domestic famine; encouragement of huge foreign investment by offering high interest rates backed up by stabilising the ruble and placing it on the international gold standard, and lucrative profits guaranteed by low labour costs and an apparently stable political environment; and high concentration of production in key geographical locations – St Petersburg, Moscow, Ukraine, the Urals and the Baku oilfields – and in large factory units, over one-third of the industrial labour force in 1900 being located in enterprises employing more than a thousand workers, very high by contemporary European standards. The result of this was that during the period of Witte's tenure at the Ministry of Finance Russia's industrial growth rate was more than 8 per cent per annum, a remarkable achievement even taking into account the original low base line. During the decade 1887 to 1897 alone, the total value of industrial production in Russia rose from 1300 million to almost 3000 million rubles, excluding oil production. In the same period the number of industrial workers nearly trebled to around three million. At the centre of Witte's industrial expansion lay the railway construction industry, and the centrepiece of that was the building of the 7000-kilometre Trans-Siberian Railway linking the networks of central European Russia with Vladivostok and the Pacific coast. The enormous demands of this mammoth engineering project on the metallurgical and coal industries played a crucial role in the whole industrialisation process, and its completion, around 1901, with the consequent fall-off in government orders, contributed much to the economic slump which followed Witte's 'boom'.[15] At the turn of the century, from being at the bottom end of the league table of industrialised nations, Russia ranked third, fourth or fifth, according to sector, behind Britain, Germany and the USA.

The economic downside of Russia's industrial success was, of course, the relative neglect of agriculture. The second half of the nineteenth century had seen more than a doubling of Russia's total population from around 60 million in 1861 to 125 million at the time of the 1897 census. The reasons for this are many, which include – despite the rural disturbances mentioned above – a *relatively* more stable agrarian situation following the emancipation of the serfs; better health care and medical provision as a result of the activities of the physicians, nurses, midwives and other clinical personnel employed by the local *zemstva*; the lack of engagement in major international war (at least not on the scale of the Napoleonic or Crimean Wars) with the obvious consequence of many thousands fewer deaths in battle; improved hygiene; reduction in the length of military service, which meant that more virile young men of child-fathering age were around in the villages, thereby increasing the rate of natural procreation – with obvious exponential effects. And, finally, it is a well-established demographical and anthropological fact that peasant cultures tend to favour the creation of large families, a multiplicity of progeny being regarded not so much as more mouths to feed as more pairs of hands to work, and under the system of redistributional tenure linked to household size, additional land for them to work on.

While the size of the agrarian population increased, the amount of land available for the peasants to farm did not. It is true that the proportion of agricultural land owned by the peasantry had grown from about one-sixth at the time of emancipation, to slightly more than a half at the turn of the century, but it must be remembered that the 'rural estate' accounted for about 90 per cent of the total population. This glaring disproportion in landownership naturally led to what is usually referred to as 'land hunger' in the European provinces of the empire where the bulk of population was concentrated, which was barely offset as yet by the tiny flow of emigration to new agricultural settlement in Siberia. And this, more than anything else, accounts for the simmering rural tension noted above and for the recrudescence of more widespread violent unrest during the peasant wars of 1902–07 (see Chapter 11). Despite the abolition of the poll tax in May 1885 (effective from 1 January 1887), continuing high levels of direct and indirect taxation, including huge tariffs on essential items such as kerosene, vodka and sugar (yes, vodka *was* an 'essential item' in the peasants' way of life), as well as the inordinately costly redemption payments, all added to the peasants' store of understandable grievances against a government which seemed to them to be fleecing the peasantry in order to pay for industrial development, the benefits of which were little felt or appreciated in the land- and food-hungry villages. It is also worth noting as an indicator of the generally poverty-stricken and insalubrious environment in which the peasants existed, that, despite improved health care – particularly in those regions served by *zemstva* doctors and paramedics – at the end of the century a large proportion of army recruits from the peasant class were turned down as medically unfit for military service. Even more telling are the mournful statistics concerning mortality and morbidity rates in the rural provinces, which demonstrate that the incidence of the six most common killer diseases – smallpox, typhus, measles, scarlet fever, whooping cough and diphtheria – was alarmingly higher than in other European countries (twice that in Germany, three times that in England, and four times higher than in Holland and Ireland). More distressing still is the infant mortality rate: in the 1890s 57.4 per cent of all deaths in the whole country were of children below the age of five, and in some provinces even more (the figure for Perm *guberniya* in 1881 was 79.5 per cent). This is attributable to difficulties during labour and childbirth, and also to inadequate nutrition in infancy, which itself is an indicator of nursing mothers' own poor health. And finally, average life expectancy in Russia at the end of the nineteenth century was for males 27.25 years, and for females 29.38 (corresponding figures elsewhere are: France – 43.5 years, England – 45.25 and Switzerland – the grand old age of 50).[16] Squalid living conditions, lack of public sanitation, almost non-existent use of soap, inadequate sewage disposal, alcoholism, suicide, venereal disease and violent crime all added to the grim toll.

Living conditions among the urban working class were of a disturbingly similar wretched quality, with overcrowding, shared facilities, public and private squalor, and a more densely concentrated incidence of all the problems mentioned above. Such wonders of the modern age as electricity, efficient sanitation, adequate medical assistance, street lighting, clean water and other public amenities scarcely touched the lives of Russia's urban poor. On the other hand, at least some of the benefits of modern technology had penetrated the towns, some of which were growing into recognisable modern cities, whereas the overall picture of the Russian countryside remained little changed from the Middle Ages. The mediaeval system of strip farming and three-field crop rotation, animal and even human draught power, lack of modern machinery, wooden tools, labour-intensive working routines, disincentives to investment connected to the system of redistributional land tenure, and what many regarded as the dead hand of the village commune – all of these antiquated practices and institutions ensured that at the beginning of the twentieth century 90 per cent of the population of the largest empire in the world, and one of the planet's leading industrial powers, were still living, working, suffering and praying in conditions which would have been not unfamiliar to a traveller in seventeenth-century Muscovy.

Among Russia's still relatively tiny educated elite, at least among its more progressive-minded elements, the glaring contradictions, the huge social and economic inequalities, and the seemingly irreconcilable conflict between the westernised upper classes of Russian society and the peasant and proletarian masses, were still a matter of intellectual Angst, and a subject which merited both their theoretical and practical concern. Whereas in the middle of the nineteenth century their attention had been focused almost exclusively on the plight of the peasantry, the increasingly rapid industrialisation and urbanisation processes towards the end of the century had caused many members of the Russian intelligentsia to become more and more attracted to the social, economic and revolutionary theories of

Karl Marx and Friedrich Engels, who predicted that the contradictions of capitalism and the class struggle between the proletariat and the bourgeoisie, rather than the 'idiocy of rural life', would bring about a socialist revolution. It is against the background of continuing political reaction under the last two tsars, the industrial revolution of the 'Witte system', and the irrefutable evidence of growing capitalist relationships in the closing years of the nineteenth and the opening years of the twentieth century that the origins of Russian Marxism have to be traced.

Russian Marxism and the birth of Bolshevism[17]

A foreign journalist composing a snapshot description of Russian political parties at any time between 1905 and 1914 would probably have given only a passing mention to the tiny Bolshevik Party, or, more properly until 1912, the Bolshevik faction of the Russian Social-Democratic Workers' Party. However, the momentous events of 1917 which eventually brought that party to overall political power in Russia, forming a revolutionary government whose descendants would rule the Soviet Union for most of the twentieth century, turning it into a world super-power, suggest that its somewhat obscure origins deserve more than a 'passing mention' in the present study. The Populist revolutionaries of the 1860s and 1870s had failed to bring about a revolution. Neither did the Bolsheviks directly bring about the revolution which caused the overthrow of the tsarist regime in February 1917. That was doomed to collapse in any case (see Chapter 12). However, Russian Populism and Russian Marxism were both such important phenomena in the historical struggle of opposition against autocracy that it would be remiss not to afford them equal attention.

In 1883 four ex-Populists, one of them a former terrorist, gathered together in Geneva and founded the first self-styled Russian Marxist revolutionary group. They were: Georgii Plekhanov (1856–1918), Pavel Akselrod (1850–1928), Lev Deutsch (1855–1941) and Vera Zasulich (1849–1919), the lady who had taken a pot-shot at the Governor of St Petersburg in 1876 and was later acquitted at her trial (see Chapter 9). They called themselves the 'Group for the Liberation of Labour' (*Gruppa osvobozhdeniya truda*) and set themselves three objectives, which were, in good Marxist fashion, a mixture of theory and praxis. First, they set about a serious analysis of economic, social and political conditions in Russia in the light of, and guided by, Marx's revolutionary theories, which they believed were applicable to their own country. Second, they committed themselves to the task of spreading knowledge of Marxism more widely inside Russia itself through a programme of propaganda and agitation – the difference between them, as formulated by Plekhanov, being that *propaganda* consists of the careful putting over of a large, complex set of interrelated ideas to a small group of people (for example, in a seminar), whereas *agitation* involves the putting over of a small, immediately comprehensible and effective set of objectives to a large gathering of people (for instance, at a mass meeting of strikers by the factory gates). (The distinction was later to be the cause of some internal friction within the movement.) And, third, they vowed to establish a Russian Marxist socialist party, dedicated to bringing about a proletarian-socialist revolution in their homeland.

All three tasks presented considerable difficulty. In the first place, Marx's and Engels' ideas were based on a study of the political economy of the advanced industrialised countries of western Europe, the political and social superstructure of which was that of 'bourgeois democracy' based on the economic infrastructure of industrial capitalism. Russia, on the other hand, in the early 1880s, was still an autocratic state, with no political freedom or democratic institutions, no politically conscious middle class (bourgeoisie), and only a relatively tiny, undeveloped industrial working class (proletariat). In Marx's political scenario, he envisaged that the victorious proletarian-socialist revolution would take place in a socio-economic system of advanced industrial capitalist relationships. It seemed inappropriate, therefore, to think in terms of a proletarian revolution in Russia, when the country had not yet fully shaken off the remnants of feudalism. Second, at the practical level, the absence of a free press, the lack of a parliamentary forum for open political debate, the ubiquitous operations of the secret police (popularly referred to as the *Okhrana* or *Okhranka*), and the arrest, imprisonment, exile or voluntary emigration of Russian radical activists meant that the revolutionary opposition was for the time being fragmented, ineffectual and bereft of any recognisable organisation or leadership.

The Populists had, of course, argued that Russia could 'skip' the capitalist phase of development and proceed, by revolutionary means, straight from feudalism to socialism, based on the organisation of the peasant commune and the workers' cooperative. In his introduction to the second Russian edition of his *Communist Manifesto* (1882), even Marx himself had not discounted the idea that in certain circumstances the Russian *obshchina* 'may serve as the starting point for communist development'.[18] But during the 1880s Plekhanov in particular, afterwards known as the 'father of Russian Marxism', tackled the theoretical issues separating Populists and Marxists in his 'Socialism and the Political Struggle' (*Sotsializm i politicheskaya bor'ba*, 1883) and 'Our Differences' (*Nashi razno-glasiya*, 1885). In these, particularly in the latter, he argued that Russia had already embarked on the capitalist road, that both factories and factory workers were increasing in number, that the peasant commune was disintegrating and that the Russian proletariat would play the vanguard role in the inevitable revolution. His theory of 'proletarian hegemony in the bourgeois-democratic revolution' was later to give way to Lenin's view of the Party as the 'vanguard of the proletariat', discussed below. Plekhanov was right about Russia's growing industrial labour force, and during the 1890s there sprang up an increasing number of workers' organisations, embryonic, illegal trade unions, Marxist discussion circles, and other groups which conducted both agitation and propaganda, and helped to organise strikes in major industrial centres. On the first Sunday in May 1891 the St Petersburg-based 'Social-Democratic Society', organised by an engineering student, M. I. Brusnev (1864–1937), but consisting entirely of factory workers, celebrated the first socialist Mayday festival (*maëvka*) in Russia. It was a modest affair, consisting of only about 80 workers – several of whom made speeches which they had written themselves – but it was nevertheless, taken together with the increased regularity of industrial strikes, a significant pointer to the future development of organised labour in the country.[19]

In 1898 an attempt was made to weld these various cells, unions and regional organisations into a single, united Marxist revolutionary workers' party. This step was taken in the Belorussian town of Minsk, where the first congress took place in that year of the Russian Social-Democratic Worker's Party, forerunner of the Communist

Party of the Soviet Union.[20] 'Congress' is perhaps too dignified a term to describe the brief gathering of only nine 'delegates', which was in any case quickly broken up by *Okhrana* agents who arrested some of the participants, including two of the elected three-man 'Central Committee'. However, the congress did have time to issue a manifesto, drawn up by the economist, Pëtr Struve (1870–1944). (Then a Marxist, he was later to shift ever further to the right of the political spectrum, ending up on the side of the counter-revolutionary 'White' forces during the Russian Civil War.) The main theme of the manifesto, taking its cue from Plekhanov, was that of the proletariat's leading role in the revolutionary struggle. In practical terms, other than actually meeting, electing a Central Committee, issuing the manifesto and getting itself dispersed by the secret police, the newly founded 'Party' achieved little of great moment, and existed in name only until the next, more decisive, but divisive, second congress, which gathered first in Brussels then in London, in July 1903.

It was during the interval between the first and second congresses that a crucial role in the infant Party's internal history began to be played by a young Marxist lawyer by the name of Vladimir Ilyich Ulyanov (1870–1924), better known by his pseudonym, Lenin. It was his elder brother, Aleksandr, who had been hanged for complicity in the plot to kill Alexander III in 1886. Brother of an executed would-be regicide was not the most socially convenient thing to be in late tsarist Russia, but despite this handicap, and in recognition of his brilliant school record and armed with a glowing reference from his headmaster, one Fëdor Kerenskii (father of Aleksandr Kerenskii (1881–1970) whose Provisional Government Lenin's Bolsheviks were to overthrow in the October 1917 Revolution), he was duly admitted to read Law at the University of Kazan under close supervision – police, rather than professorial. Expelled in 1887 for attending a student demonstration, he later graduated as an external student, with top honours, from the Faculty of Jurisprudence of the University of St Petersburg. He practised for a while as an attorney in Samara, and in 1893 moved to St Petersburg where, two years later, he helped found the 'Union of Struggle for the Liberation of the Working Class'. His legal work and his political activities soon brought him once more to the attention of the police, and in 1887 he was sentenced to three years' exile at the village of Shushenskoe in western Siberia. While forcibly residing there in conditions of relatively comfortable austerity (which in any case suited his rather ascetic nature), his enthusiasm for the revolutionary struggle and the Marxist cause remained undiminished and, in 1899, under the *nom de plume* of Vladimir Ilyin, he published a major study of the breakdown of Russia's rural economy entitled 'The Development of Capitalism in Russia' (*Razvitie kapitalizma v Rossii*), still a significant work of scholarship on the subject. At the same time he was becoming increasingly perturbed by certain tendencies within both European and Russian social-democracy. First, he was alarmed at the 'revisionist' theories of the German social democrat, Eduard Bernstein (1850–1932), who suggested that the transition from capitalism to socialism could be achieved without a workers' revolution. Second, he bitterly attacked those in Russia who argued that the Party should concentrate the workers' attention on the immediate *economic* struggle against capitalism as a means of raising proletarian political consciousness. Lenin was later to develop these ideas in his 1902 pamphlet, 'What is to be Done?' (*Chto delat'?*), in which he argued that this dangerous trend of 'economism' would allow the workers to develop simply a trade union consciousness, and mere 'trade-unionism – *Nur-Gewerkschaftlerei* – means the ideological enslavement of the workers to the bourgeoisie'.[21] According to Lenin, it was the Party's task '*to divert* the working class movement from this spontaneous trade-union striving', and guide them in the vital *political* struggle to overthrow tsarism.

Lenin left Siberia in 1900 and travelled to Europe, where, along with Plekhanov and others, he founded a new revolutionary newspaper called 'The Spark' (*Iskra*), through the underground circulation of which he intended to fight the 'economist heresy', and develop a strong, organised party network. In *What is to be Done?*, his arguments against 'economism', 'spontaneity' and what he called 'tailism' (*ekonomizm, stiikhinost'* and *khvostizm*) were elaborated still further. In this seminal booklet he further ridiculed the idea that the working class could spontaneously and 'exclusively by its own efforts' develop anything other than a trade union consciousness. He also coined the contemptuous term 'tailism' – from the word 'tail' (*khvost'*) – to describe those who wished to drag along at the tail of the workers' movement, rather than lead it.[22] Rather than being at the rear, it was the role of the Party to be 'the vanguard of the proletariat', 'a Party of a new type', proletarian in content, political in its activity, and revolutionary in its aim. It was above all Lenin's uncompromising stand on party discipline, leadership and organisation, taken in *What is to be Done?*, that was to cause the fateful schism within the Party at its second congress in 1903.

Out of the 51 votes assembled at that meeting, there was a rough division into those who supported Lenin's *Iskra* group, the so-called 'hards' – already in a majority – and those including the Jewish *Bund*'s five delegates and supporters of the vaguely 'economist' trend – the 'softs'. An item-by-item, motion-by-motion rehearsal of the congress's convoluted proceedings would be tedious, but a small number of what appeared to be merely nit-picking disagreements emerged which were to determine the political history of Russia for almost a century. The first sign of a real split occurred over an item on the criteria to be adopted for party membership. Lenin's hitherto close comrade, Yulii Martov (1873–1932), proposed that, in order to qualify for membership, one must, first, accept the party programme; second, support the party 'by material means' (for example, by regular payment of membership fee); and, third, be prepared to work under the direction of one of the party organisations. Lenin agreed with the first two points, but objected to the third. In his formulation, a party member must work '*in*' one of the party organisations. This slight variation in wording, at first glance merely a semantic quibble over prepositions, in fact exposed two widely differing views as to what type of party there should be. The one (Martov's) envisaged a broad church of sympathetic supporters prepared to render 'personal cooperation' with party organisations. The other (Lenin's) implied a narrower, disciplined party of fully committed, dedicated activists. What was basically at issue was whether party members should be amateurs or professionals. Lenin lost the vote. His supporters now in a minority, conference proceeded to next business. At about this point, a motion proposing the autonomy within the Party of the Jewish *Bund* was heavily defeated, at which the *Bund* delegates marched out, leaving five supporters fewer for Martov. Further withdrawals by representatives of a pro-'economist' faction also meant that Lenin was fortuitously beginning to claw back his numerical majority. When a later agendum concerning the composition of leading party organs and committees was put to the ballot, Lenin's proposal for a smaller, more centralised structure won the vote by 24 to nil. His opponents had all abstained. But Lenin, armed with just 24 of the 51 votes originally assembled at the start of the congress, in a superb tactical move of political onomatology dubbed his supporters the 'majority-ites'. The Russian word for 'majority' is *bolshinstvo* – hence *bolsheviki*. His opponents, led by Martov, were henceforth lumbered with the humiliating label of *mensheviki* – the 'minority-ites'. Despite the fact that Lenin was soon to lose his temporary numerical superiority, the new appellations stuck. Although the words were at first used only in inverted commas, Bolshevism and the Bolsheviks had been born, and now entered the political vocabulary of the world.

Although that world was little disturbed by the febrile and arcane deliberations of a bunch of refractory Russian leftists gathered together in a small Congregational chapel in Shoreditch, the second congress of the Russian Social-Democratic Workers' Party in 1903 set in motion a course of events which was eventually to have global ramifications. However, over the next two years, while the Bolsheviks, Mensheviks and other assorted Russian Marxists conducted their fractional rivalries and feverishly polemicised about the nature, timing and organisation of the Russian Revolution, events inside Russia itself were steadily building up their own revolutionary momentum, a momentum which was to climax, significantly, among the striking workers of St Petersburg in January 1905.

11 1905 and the sham constitution, 1904–1914

Concentration at the end of the previous chapter on the rise of the Social-Democratic movement should not convey the impression that heightened political activity in Russia at the turn of the century was confined to the Marxists alone. In 1901, the left-wing writer, Maksim Gorkii (1868–1936), published a poem entitled 'The Stormy Petrel' (*Burevestnik*). The symbolism of the seabird heralding the coming revolutionary storm was unmistakeable, and the journal in which it appeared was closed down. Poet, petrel and police were all equally sensitive to the highly charged atmosphere at the time, which would require only a small barometrical disturbance to unleash the tempest.

Before the storm

In the same year that Gorkii's poem appeared, after two years of serious unrest in Russian universities, a former student named Pëtr Karpovich assassinated the Minister of Education, N. P. Bogolepov (1847–1901). Also in 1901, the still glowing embers of revolutionary Populism were fanned into flame by the creation in Kharkov of the Party of Socialist-Revolutionaries (*Sotsialistov-revolyutsionerov partiya* – SRP, or the SRs), co-founded by Viktor Chernov (1873–1952), grandson of a serf, and one of neo-Populism's leading theorists. He crossed swords with the Marxists by asserting that the interests of the workers and peasants were identical, and that both should unite against autocracy in the struggle to achieve the 'socialisation' of the land – that is, its redistribution among those who worked it, based on common ownership of property. The SRP, whose full programme was not in fact adopted until November 1905, also revived Populism's terrorist tradition by forming a number of 'fighting squads' (*boevye otryady*), which were to carry out a number of spectacular assassinations over the next few years, starting with that of Bogolepov, and including, in 1904, the Minister for Internal Affairs and Chief of the Corps of Gendarmes, V. P. von Plehve (1846–1904), and, in 1911, the Prime Minister, P. A. Stolypin (b. 1862).

The rash of terrorist attacks was not confined to prominent government ministers: the victims included royalty and hundreds of major and minor public officials, whose deaths were avenged by an almost equal number of executions. According to an official source, between 1905 and 1909 alone there were 2828 terrorist assassinations and 3332 woundings. During the same period, 4579 perpetrators were sentenced to death and 2365 actually executed.[1] In quite a few cases, including that of Stolypin, it was not always clear whether the assassin was acting in his (or her) role of Socialist-Revolutionary terrorist, or carrying out the orders of the secret police, in so far as many of them were in fact double agents working both sides of the political street. Russia's murky, cloak-and-dagger underworld of internal espionage and counter-espionage, sabotage and counter-sabotage, was full of these duplicitous and dangerous figures, now tossing a bomb at a government officer, now reporting mission accomplished to their *Okhrana* controller. The most notorious of these was Yevno Azef (1869–1918), head of the SRs' fighting detachment, *grand provocateur* and police agent, betrayer of many of his comrades, and organiser of the murder of his boss, von Plehve, in 1904. (He was exposed in 1908 and fled to Germany, where he died in 1918.[2])

Political opposition to the autocracy was not, however, the monopoly of the extreme left. After the accession of Nicholas II in 1894, *zemstvo* politicians began to flex the flaccid muscles of Russian liberalism and revive their calls for a constitution. The new tsar, in a speech probably written by his former tutor, Konstantin Pobedonostsev (see Chapter 10), dismissed these as 'senseless dreams', and vowed to fulfil his sacred duties as autocrat 'as firmly and unflinchingly as my late, unforgettable father'. Nicholas, however, was temperamentally unsuited to the task. By nature he was a rather weak, wishy-washy character, totally unprepared for kingship, of limited intellect, but possessing a stubborn anachronistic vision of the divine provenance of his exalted office, which he saw more in terms of a mediaeval-style theocracy, than of a modern, late nineteenth- or twentieth-century monarchy. Uncomfortable in the company of people of superior intelligence, he was also openly anti-Semitic. He was happiest in the bosom of his family, surrounded by his adoring, neurotic wife, Alexandra (born Princess Alix of Hesse-Darmstadt in 1872, granddaughter of the British Queen Victoria) and his five children, and regarded affairs of state, which the Almighty had placed upon his unwilling shoulders, not only as a burden to be borne with Christian fortitude, but as an unwelcome intrusion into his domestic tranquillity. His inaugural speech did not bode well for the moderate reformists' aspirations, but then neither did Nicholas's reign get off to a very auspicious start, as hundreds of his subjects were crushed to death at a mass celebration of his coronation at the Khodynka Field on the outskirts of Moscow in May 1896. (On the same evening the recently married Nicholas and his new bride danced blithely together at a lavish ball given by the French Ambassador.)

Despite the imperial rebuff to the liberal cause, at the turn of the century representatives of the *zemstva* and members of certain professional societies attempted to provide some organisational shape to Russia's emerging 'liberal' movement, and in 1904 founded the 'Union of Liberation' (*Soyuz Osvobozhdeniya*), a body which opposed revolution, but called for the end of autocracy and the establishment of constitutional government based on democratic institutions and the rule of law. In order to promote their campaign, around 50 society banquets were held in the winter of 1904, the first on the fortieth anniversary of the judicial reform of 1864 (see Chapter 9) and attended by scores of representatives of the country's liberal professional elite. Speeches were made, corks popped and toasts raised to constitutionalism, justice, democracy and other worthy causes in what was a rather tastelessly self-indulgent form of political lobbying. These occasions were publicly reported, but the police turned a deaf ear to the anti-government sentiments expressed, no doubt less concerned with the popping of corks and the gaseous emissions of liberal politicians than with the more lethal explosions of terrorist bombs.

Perhaps even more dramatically symptomatic of the malaise of discontent which seemed to be spreading throughout society was the recrudescence of violent agrarian unrest, which escalated in some provinces into the proportions of a peasant war, though in no case did anything take place on quite the scale of the *jacqueries* of the seventeenth and eighteenth centuries. Nevertheless, the regular sight of flames leaping from burning manor houses into the night sky, resembling a rooster's crimson comb, caused this particular period of Russia's agrarian history (1902–07) to be known as 'the years of the Red Cockerel', only brought to an end by Prime Minister Pëtr Stolypin's combination of dreadful retribution and incipient reform (see below). As in the past, these disturbances, which engulfed the central provinces, black earth regions, Poland, Ukraine and Georgia, ranged from acts of civil disobedience, illicit use of pasture and woodland and assaults on local officials, to the torching of noble piles and the lynching of landlords. Thousands of peasants were punished by arbitrary floggings, shootings sanctioned by field courts-martial and arrest and exile, all of which served only to aggravate an already critical situation.

Peasant protest in the fields was matched by proletarian unrest in the factories. The number of officially recorded industrial strikers escalated from 17,000 in 1894 to around 90,000 in 1904. That is not a large percentage of the total of around three million workers, but there is no doubt about the alarm with which the government regarded the increasing militancy of organised labour, to which it responded with a mixture of concessions, police-organised trade unions and brutal oppression. The no doubt honourable efforts of the Board of Factory Inspectors to improve working and living conditions were somewhat soured by the routine deployment of mounted cossaks armed with whips to deal with striking workers' demonstrations, a practice which was hardly conducive to amicable management/shop-floor relations. In order to deflect workers' legitimate grievances into less threatening, less disruptive and more easily controllable directions, the chief of the Moscow *Okhrana*, S. V. Zubatov (1863–1917) obtained permission to undertake an experiment in what came to be known as 'police trade-unionism' or 'police socialism'.[3] The idea was to take the revolutionary wind out of the workers' sails by providing official channels through which to listen to complaints, organise mutual benevolent societies, involve workers' leaders in civic responsibilities and sponsor communal leisure activities. Initially the ploy succeeded to some extent in diluting the influence of socialist propaganda and agitation, but it also provided the workers with experience of self-organisation and mass mobilisation, which, particularly in the Jewish Pale, threatened to get out of hand and turn on the authorities. And in any case, in order to appeal to the workers, these organisations had to offer something radical in terms of labour rights, which often acted against the interests of owners and management. In 1903, in most areas the Zubatov experiment was quickly abandoned or scaled down. Zubatov himself was dismissed and sent into provincial exile. Only in the capital was a type of attenuated 'Zubatovism' (*Zubatovshchina*) revived in the activities of the 'Assembly of St Petersburg Factory Workers', formed on the initiative of one Father Georgii Gapon (1870–1906), a 35-year-old Orthodox priest and police informer. Out of the discredited *Zubatovschina* sprang the equally suspect *Gaponovshchina*, out of which in turn, through a tragic set of events, there occurred the massacre of 'Bloody Sunday', which summoned up the great whirlwind of 1905.

Dress rehearsal for revolution

Encouraged by his Minister for Internal Affairs, von Plehve, to divert public attention away from domestic problems by engaging in a 'short, swift, victorious war', in January 1904 Nicholas II declared war on the rising Asiatic power of Japan. This followed the Japanese's sudden sinking of the majority of Russia's Pacific fleet while it lay at anchor in the leased naval base of Port Arthur, a Korean concession hundreds of miles away from Russian naval headquarters at Vladivostok. The scuttling of the Pacific fleet meant that the war was to be fought on land, at least until reinforcements could be dispatched from the Baltic, the Black Sea fleet being forbidden to navigate the Bosphorus in times of war under the terms of the Straits Convention of 1871 (see Chapter 9). Naturally it was not only domestic considerations that led to the opening of hostilities between the two Far Eastern powers. The government of Alexander III had by and large eschewed participation in any major international imbroglios during his reign, with the result that – apart from a brief, inglorious involvement in the complex Bulgarian crisis of 1885–86 – the country enjoyed a period of relative peace and stability in the conduct of its foreign affairs. In the Far East, Russian diplomacy had managed to consolidate the gains made by Muravëv-Amurskii (see Chapter 9), until, that is, her imperial ambitions in Manchuria clashed with those of Japan in the first years of the new century. As she had done before the Crimean War, Russia seriously underestimated the strength of her potential enemy, and indeed regarded the Japanese with a certain amount of racialist contempt. Nicholas's own Nippophobia was hardly dispelled by a sword attack on him by a deranged young Japanese policeman during a trip to the Far East in 1891. The arrogance of the tsar, who insisted on referring to the Japanese as *makaki* – 'little monkeys' – was to meet with a devastating comeuppance when the Russian bear was ultimately defeated by its smaller allegedly simian foe. The outburst of irrational, jingoistic enthusiasm with which the Russian public greeted the outbreak of hostilities was very short-lived, and soon gave way to sustained opposition to a war which was being ineptly and disastrously fought for a cause which no one understood, somewhere 10,000 miles from St Petersburg on the other side of the planet.

Back in St Petersburg itself, continuing popular discontent, now compounded by anti-war feelings, was to reach a flash point on Sunday 9 January 1905. Very briefly, the facts are as follows. In December 1904, four members of Father Gapon's 'Assembly of St Petersburg Factory Workers' were sacked from their jobs at the huge Putilov ironworks. This provoked a sympathetic strike in support of their reinstatement. When the demand was rejected, on the honourable principle of 'one out – all out!' the strike spread across the capital, involving up to 150,000 workers. Soon, political as well as economic grievances began to be voiced, but both management and government refused to budge. In an attempt to defuse the situation, Gapon hit on the naive idea of marching in peaceful procession on the Winter Palace, and there presenting the tsar with a humble petition listing his aggrieved but loyal subjects' demands. With what the organisers believed was official permission, in the early hours of Sunday 9 January thousands of unarmed workers, accompanied by their families and carrying hastily assembled sacred icons, patriotic slogans and portraits of former tsars, began to converge on Palace Square in front of the Winter Palace. Nicholas, however, rather than deigning to receive them, was cosily ensconced with his wife and children in their summer palace at Tsarskoe Selo. Instead, they were met with police and military barricades, mounted uhlans and cossaks armed with sabres, whips and guns. At Troitskaya Square, en route to the Palace, guards of the Pavlovskii regiment fired several

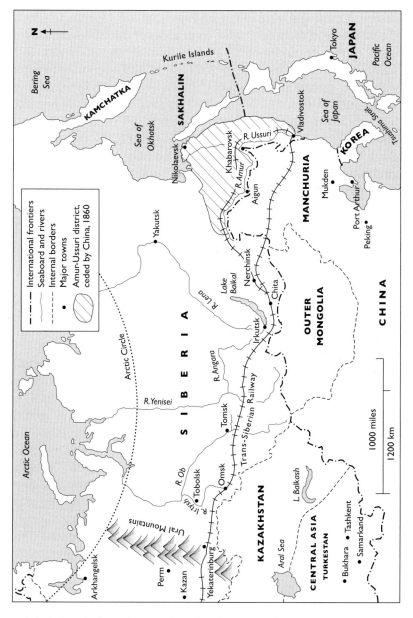

4 Asiatic Russia: late nineteenth and early twentieth centuries

volleys into the marchers, leaving around 150 dead and wounded. Then pandemonium broke loose. More shots were fired, the barricades were overrun and cossaks charged the crowd, which now rushed, lemming-like, to its fate on Palace Square. More regiments of the tsar were at the ready: three companies of the Pavlovskii Guard, eight of the crack Preobrazhenskii, four of the Chevalier, four squadrons of the Horse Guard, 200 cossaks and, according to some witnesses, several artillery pieces.[4] Incensed by news of other massacres such as the one on Troitskaya Square, the angry demonstrators refused to disperse, even when advanced on by troops with bayonets fixed and charged at by the cavalry. Finally, the order was given to open fire and the deadly fusillade began. Throughout the afternoon and evening, guards and cossaks swept through the streets firing indiscriminately into what had turned from a religious procession into a furious and embittered mob. When a semblance of order was restored, bullet-riddled, hacked down corpses lay everywhere in the blood-drenched snow. Exactly how many has never been firmly established. The ludicrously low initial government estimate was 76 dead and 233 wounded. The British *Daily Mail* sensationally reported 30,000 casualties.[5] Other foreign press reports, particularly the French, were even more exaggerated, but whatever the actual numbers, the effects were the same, at home and abroad. The butchery of Bloody Sunday shocked the world.

In Russia itself the revulsion following the carnage rapidly engulfed the whole nation, impelling it to widespread manifestations of grief and popular indignation against the guilty tsar. In Sablinsky's words: 'The working class of St Petersburg was revolutionized overnight, and the battle line between the workers and the autocracy had been drawn.'[6] In one fell swoop, the *tsar-batyushka* – the 'little father tsar' – had been for ever transformed into 'Nicholas the Bloody', the only Russian ruler to have such a disapprobatory epithet attached to his name since Ivan the Terrible. During the next few weeks more than half a million workers were on strike throughout the empire – more than in the whole of the previous decade. But it was no longer just the factory proletariat that was expressing its outrage. The middle classes, the professional organisations, the intelligentsia, the national minorities and the peasantry – in fact the whole of Russian society – was joining in the national clamour for atonement and reform. Nicholas himself reacted to the crisis with the pusillanimity that was the hallmark of his feeble and ineffectual nature. The mild-mannered Prince Svyatopolk-Mirskii was replaced as Minister for Internal Affairs by A. G. Bulygin (1851–1919), a safe bureaucrat who could be trusted to implement the emperor's will, whatever that might be, and Major-General D. F. Trepov (1855–1906) – son of the General Trepov whom Vera Zasulich had attempted to assassinate in 1876 – a man with the reputation of an unflinching disciplinarian, was made military governor of St Petersburg. In late January the tsar agreed to meet a carefully vetted delegation of hand-picked workers at Tsarskoe Selo. With a crass insensitivity, which belied his allegedly sensitive character, he merely chided them for being led astray by wicked men, and urged them, with God's blessing, to return to their honest labours. Needless to say, they were unimpressed, but were in any case prevented from returning to their labours as result of being ostracised by their outraged fellow workers.

In early February two events occurred which galvanised the tsar into taking something resembling action. On the Far Eastern front, Russian troops were bogged down in the disastrous battle of Mukden, in which they were to lose 90,000 men, the prelude to their ultimate defeat. In Moscow, on 4 February, the tsar's uncle, Grand Duke Sergei Aleksandrovich, was killed by a Socialist-Revolutionary assassin's bomb, a grim reminder of the royal family's unpopularity. Finally impressed with the urgency of the situation by these two disasters, Nicholas ordered Bulygin to draft legislation which would lead to the election of a representative, consultative assembly. Only two months previously, such a gesture by the Sovereign Emperor and Autocrat of All Russia would have been considered quite unthinkable, but now it was a woefully inadequate response to the new public mood which would now be satisfied with nothing less than a programme of full civil and political rights, universal suffrage and nationwide elections to a constituent assembly with full legislative powers. This became the accepted policy of the newly founded liberal 'Union of Unions', the 'Peasants' Union' and the conference of *zemstva* representatives in May.

By now unrest had spread to the villages and, ominously, to the armed forces. All over Russia the flames of the 'red cockerel' once more lit the sky. By and large the regime could still rely on the loyalty of its troops to crush the outbreaks of civil disobedience, but the spirit of mutiny was abroad and beginning to haunt even the barrack rooms and the lower decks. Two incidents took place in early summer which typified what Florinsky describes as the Russian navy's 'almost unrelieved record [in 1904–05] of futility and disaster'.[7] On 27 May, after a seven-month voyage around the world from the Finnish Gulf to the Sea of Japan, almost the entire Baltic fleet was sent to the bottom of the Tsushima Strait by Admiral Togo's superior forces in an engagement which lasted only a few hours. (The start of the Baltic fleet's journey had been marked by an incident which contained elements of tragedy and farce, but which underlined the combination of ignorance and incompetence that was a feature of Russia's naval command. While making a night-time crossing over the Dogger Bank in the North Sea, the Russian flagship, the *Suvorov*, opened fire on two of its own craft, believing them to be patrolling Japanese torpedo boats! Unfortunately, a small fleet of British trawlers, just out of Hull, was caught in the fire, resulting in the sinking of one of the ships and the drowning of two English fishermen.[8] Naturally, British public opinion was outraged at the 'Dogger Bank Incident', and demanded a punitive war on Russia, which was averted only by Russia's agreeing to pay reparations for the calamitous bungle.)

A month later the crew of the celebrated battleship *Potëmkin*, flagship of the bottled-up Black Sea fleet, rose up in protest against the putrid state of the ship's meat, but, after the shooting of one of their spokesman, the situation swiftly escalated into a full-blown mutiny in which the vessel was taken over by its crew, seven of her officers were killed and the red flag was hoisted on her mast. She then steamed into harbour at Odessa where the mutineers were joined in solidarity by thousands of townspeople, who came to pay their respects to the dead sailor. The people of Odessa were already in a state of rebellion against the local authorities, just one of the many manifestations of civic turmoil which now gripped the entire country. When the mourning sailors and citizens refused to disperse, troops were ordered to fire at random into the gathered crowd, resulting in between 2000 and 3000 deaths, more people than in St Petersburg on Bloody Sunday. The mutiny soon petered out, but it became known as the most notorious of the hundreds of instances of military mutinies which occurred from the Baltic to the Pacific during 1905. Research by John Bushnell has shown that the political disaffection of the Russian armed forces in 1905 was in fact far more widespread than has traditionally been supposed – providing ominous portents for the events of 1917.[9]

The disturbances were not confined to the central parts of the country, but swept through the empire from Vyborg to Vladivostok. In both Poland and Finland there were strikes, demonstrations, mass revolts and a clamour of calls for national independence. In Riga, 200 protesting workers were mown down in the streets by Russian military gunfire. Similar stories of civic unrest met by bloody repression poured in from all corners of Russia's enormous landmass. In short, the whole empire was in uproar, with both Russians and non-Russians alike united in their defiance and denunciation of the government of the Russian tsar. By now the only civilian support the government could rely on was provided by the ultra-nationalist gangs of the 'Black Hundreds' and their associated bully boys operating under the banner of the Union of the Russian People. These forerunners of the Nazi Brownshirts took advantage of the turmoil to indulge in their brutal, patriotic practices of Jew-baiting and beating up striking workers, students and left-wing activists. In Odessa, still smarting from the massacre following the *Potëmkin* mutiny, over 500 Jews were slaughtered in a three-day pogrom, and in Tomsk 200 people attending an anti-government meeting were burned to death when Black Hundred hooligans torched the building in which they were gathered. These vile attacks had both the tacit and open support not only of the police and government officials but of the tsar himself. (In December, the shamelessly anti-Semitic and generally xenophobic Nicholas graciously accepted the presentation of the honorary insignia of the Union of the Russian People at a public reception.)

The sinking of the Baltic fleet in the Tsushima Strait was the final straw which broke the back of Russia's military effort in the Far East, and in June, through the good offices of the United States' President, Theodore Roosevelt, she was forced to enter peace negotiations. These were concluded by the signing of the Treaty of Portsmouth (5 September 1905), under the terms of which Russia ceded considerable territory in the Far East, including the southern half of the island of Sakhalin. (The concessions were in fact rather less than the Japanese expected, given the scale of their victory, but they were forced to accept under US and British pressure.) Against this background of civil ferment and military humiliation, on 6 August Bulygin was ordered to publish details of the constitutional plan promised in

February. However, amid the explosive fireworks of this most traumatic of Russian social upheavals since the Time of Troubles (see Chapter 3), Bulygin's document turned out to be a damp squib. Hedged around as it was by so many territorial, electoral, financial, social and legislative restrictions, it was ludicrously inadequate to meet the political exigencies of the day. It was, accordingly, ignored by the public as at best an irrelevance, at worst an insult.

By the end of September events had reached a new fever pitch, and once more the impetus for the upsurge was provided by the industrial workers. At first, printers and bakers in Moscow refused to print or bake. They were joined by workers in other vital sectors of industry, rapidly precipitating a general strike which paralysed communications, isolated the capital and brought the administration of the whole country grinding to a standstill. A prominent role was played by the railway workers of Moscow, nerve centre of the nation's communications system, soon to be followed by telegraph operators, typographical workers, and other vital transmission belts of its economic and political life. Non-industrial institutions, including schools, hospitals, pharmacies, theatres and the courts of law closed down as the seemingly helpless regime floundered in the face of that most formidable weapon in the arsenal of civil confrontation, the political general strike.

There was, however, no concerted leadership nor organisational structure to the movement. The revolutionary parties, no less than the government, had been caught off guard by the speed and scope of events since Bloody Sunday, with most of their leaders exiled or abroad, and riven by internal rivalries and doctrinal wrangling. There was some broad consensus over ultimate objectives, but no grand plan or coordinated programme of action or reform. The Great October Strike was simply a powerful, spontaneous expression of the whole people's pent-up anger and frustration at the political paraplegia of an intellectually and administratively bankrupt regime. An important by-product of the general strike was the formation of a democratically elected workers' 'parliament' in the capital which represented the interests of the strikers and enjoyed the support of most of the revolutionary parties. This was the short-lived 'St Petersburg *Soviet* [Council] of Workers' Deputies', an institution that was to play a crucial role in Russia's future history and add a new word to the political vocabulary of the world. The publication of its first news bulletin, called *Izvestiya* ('News'), on 17 October coincided with the promulgation of a fresh imperial decree which, in an apparent effort to satisfy at least more liberal public opinion, promised full civil rights, an extension of the franchise, and immediate elections to a State Duma (parliament) with full legislative powers. Despite the concessions, the tsar was known to be unenthusiastic, the revolutionary parties remained sceptical and, far from settling the disturbances, the promulgation of the 'October manifesto' marked the beginning of one of the most violent phases of the revolutionary period since Bloody Sunday.

Throughout November a new tide of strikes, peasant risings, nationalist agitation and military mutinies convinced the tsar that his October concessions needed to be tempered with the heat of repression. The errant country needed finally to be brought to heel. Accordingly, having just pledged the introduction of full civil rights, Nicholas took immediate counter-insurgency action. Punitive expeditions were dispatched into the countryside to flog the peasants into docility; police and workers clashed in open, armed confrontation; strikes were met with lockouts; vicious pogroms terrorised the Jewish Pale, while troops and gendarmes implemented Trepov's callous command, 'Fire no blanks and spare no bullets.' Finally, on 3 December, the headquarters of the St Petersburg Soviet were surrounded and its leaders arrested, later to be tried and exiled to Siberia. Among them was its co-president and foremost tribune, the maverick young Jewish Social-Democrat activist, Lev Davidovich Bronstein (1879–1940), better known as Trotskii. The so-called 'Days of Freedom' were over, but one last desperate act in the drama of 1905 was yet to be played. In Moscow, the Bolshevik-dominated Soviet's call for another general strike led to an armed uprising and days of bitter street warfare. Until mid-December, the ancient capital was in effect in the throes of a violent civil war. Many hundreds died in the fighting or were summarily shot after street courts martial. Thousands more were arrested and driven into exile. Only after the deployment of regiments of elite guards from St Petersburg and a heavy artillery bombardment, which reduced the working-class district of Presnya to smouldering ruins, was the insurgency crushed and the revolutionary energies of the population curbed.

The suppression of the Moscow uprising marked the end of the immediate revolutionary situation, although relative calm did not return to the countryside for another two years. The convulsions of 1905 cannot, however, despite common usage, be described as a 'revolution' in the full sense of the term, which is why its substantive use has been avoided in the present section. Both Lenin and Trotskii at one time or another preferred to describe what happened in Russia in 1905 as a 'dress rehearsal' for revolution, the full performance of which was not to take place until 1917. The theatrical image is not, of course, quite accurate, as in 1917 history was to rewrite the ending, and the victors of 1905 became the vanquished. However, at both performances, as it were, the same dramatis personae were on stage, reading from a similar script and using the same props against a backdrop of defeat in international war, and supported by a cast of millions. A tragic drama it certainly was; a revolution it was not. After 1905, there was no real devolution of political power, which still rested in the hands of an irresolute emperor and his appointed ministers. There was no radical redistribution of property and no realignment of the hierarchical class structure of society. The principles of Orthodoxy, Autocracy and Nationalism still provided the regime with its ideological bedrock. The traditional institutions of the state – bureaucracy, church, military and police – continued to function unaltered. And the Romanov Empire remained – bruised, but unbroken.

However, in issuing the October manifesto, Nicholas the Bloody had been forced by irresistible popular pressure to concede the principle of representative participation in the nation's legislative processes. Whether the ensuing 'constitutional experiment' was a success, a failure, or simply a bodged laboratory trial, has now to be determined. But what is clear from the very beginning is that most of the guinea pigs were unhappy with the arrangements.

The 'constitutional experiment'

Between 1906 and 1917, having survived its first major confrontation with the revolutionary masses since the Pugachëv rebellion, the imperial government entered into a period of uneasy and ambiguous experimentation with quasi-constitutional politics. Although the October 1905 manifesto stated that 'no law shall become effective without confirmation by the State Duma', Article 4 of the new Fundamental Laws of the Russian Empire, published on 23 April

1906, declared: 'To the All-Russian Emperor belongs supreme autocratic power.' Some historians have tried to make something of the fact that the article omitted the adjective 'unlimited', which had appeared before the word 'autocratic' in previous definitions of the emperor's power, implying that power was in some way now 'limited'. This is patent nonsense. The formulation 'unlimited autocratic power' was in any case a tautology, since 'autocratic' power is by definition 'unlimited'. The omission was therefore quite gratuitous. Furthermore, Article 9 stated that without the emperor's ratification, 'no legislative act may come into force', and Article 87 allowed him to rule by decree without the Duma's approval in emergency circumstances when the Duma was not in session. Since the tsar was also empowered, under Article 105, to dissolve the Duma whenever he wished, it is clear that the power of the autocracy to legislate at will, unencumbered by the opposition of the elected chamber, was legally guaranteed. The Sovereign Emperor also possessed 'supreme administrative power'; was the 'supreme leader of all foreign relations'; was invested with 'supreme command over all land and sea forces of the Russian state'; had the sole power to appoint and dismiss government ministers, and to 'declare war, conclude peace, and negotiate treaties with foreign states'; and, moreover, had the absolute right to overturn the verdicts and sentences of the courts of law.[10] So much for the separation of the powers.

Given the accumulation of these formidable legislative, executive, supra-judicial and military powers in the hands of the Sovereign Emperor and All-Russian Autocrat, one may be forgiven for dismissing the whole concept of constitutional government under these circumstances as utterly absurd. The very juxtaposition of the words 'constitutional' and 'autocracy' is a political oxymoron and a gross violation of language, whether English or Russian. In effect, the Fundamental Laws legally invested the tsar with the autocratic right to tear up the Fundamental Laws. Much as he might have liked on occasion to exercise that prerogative, Nicholas Romanov did not possess the gumption to do so. He did, however, dismiss both the First and the Second Dumas, temporarily suspended the Third, and prorogued the Fourth.

Under the new, post-1905 arrangements, there were in fact two legislative houses: the lower chamber, the State Duma, consisting of around 500 members elected, though on an unequal franchise, from all classes of society; and the upper chamber, the State Council, comprising an equal proportion of elected and appointed representatives of the major social, religious, educational and financial institutions. (Though often maligned as merely a tool of the autocracy, the State Council was in fact a far more representative body of men than the British House of Lords, which was forced to abandon the hereditary principle only in the year 1999, and which still has no elected members.) Candidates from the newly legalised political parties, which spanned the ideological spectrum from ultra-right to extreme left, were elected for a five-year parliamentary session, though in fact only the conservative Third Duma lasted its entire span (1907–12), and even that had, on a couple of occasions, to be suspended while the government forced through legislation in its absence. Ignoring for the moment a number of insignificant fringe groupings and independent candidates, the main political parties of the day were as follows (moving from left to right).

- **Russian Social-Democratic Workers' Party (RSDRP):** Marxist revolutionary party founded in 1898; split into two main factions at its second congress (1903 – see Chapter 10), known as Bolsheviks and Mensheviks. The **Bolsheviks** emphasised discipline, centralisation and organisation, and advocated the leading role of the proletariat (led by the Party) in the overthrow of autocracy. After 1905, its leading figure, Vladimir Lenin, argued for a peasant/proletarian alliance in the bourgeois-democratic revolution. The **Mensheviks**, led by Yulii Martov, believed that the bourgeoisie and the liberal parties would create a democratic form of government after the collapse of autocracy, and the party should therefore cooperate with them, rather than the peasantry, in legal oppositional activity.

- **Party of Socialist-Revolutionaries (SRP, SRs):** Neo-populist revolutionary party, founded in 1901, led by Viktor Chernov. Advocated the 'socialisation' of the land and the public ownership of the means of production. Its 'Maximalist' wing resorted to the use of individual terror in the revolutionary struggle.

- **Labour Group (Trudoviki):** Non-revolutionary fraction of SR party made up of peasant and intelligentsia Duma delegates. They had no formal programme but supported the nationalisation of non-peasant land, the establishment of a constituent assembly, a minimum wage and an eight-hour working day. They tended to back the Constitutional Democrats in Duma debates.

- **Party of Popular Freedom, or Constitutional Democrats (Kadets):** Main centre liberal party; programme based on western parliamentarianism; led by the historian, Pavel Milyukov (1859–1943). Its chief objectives were the introduction of a constitutional monarchical, parliamentary system of government, full civil rights, compulsory take-over and redistribution of large private estates – though with compensation – and legal settlement of labour disputes.

- **Union of 17th October (Octobrists):** Right of centre, 'conservative' party, basing its programme solely on the provisions of the October 1905 manifesto (see above). Its membership and main support came from wealthy landowners and industrialists. Leaders included Aleksandr Guchkov (1862–1936), president of the Third Duma. The Octobrists shared some policies with the Kadets, but on the whole disapproved of them as being too radical. They also opposed any concession to workers' or peasants' demands.

- **Union of the Russian People:** Extreme right-wing, proto-fascist party espousing monarchism, chauvinism and anti-Semitism; leaders included Vladimir Purishkevich (1870–1920), a wealthy landowner and one of the conspirators in the plot to kill Grigrorii Rasputin (see Chapter 12). It promoted violent attacks on left-wing elements and organised anti-Jewish pogroms through its street-fighting gangs, known as the 'Black Hundreds' (see above).

There were also a number of nationalist (for example, Ukrainian, Polish, Georgian, Muslim) parties.

The elections to the First Duma (April 1906) were boycotted by both the Bolsheviks and the SRs. That, together with a miserable performance by the far right, ensured a 'radical centre' majority of its 448 delegates, 153 seats going to the Kadets and 107 to the Trudoviks. The next largest grouping (60 seats) went to an assortment of non-Russian nationalist parties. From the outset, it was clear that the composition of the Duma – which had a large number of peasant delegates – was far too radical in its demands, particularly on the land question, and in July an excuse was devised by the government to dissolve it. In protest, a large number of the dispersed delegates, including 120 Kadets, travelled to Vyborg on the outskirts of the capital and issued an illegal appeal calling on the citizens of Russia to refuse to pay taxes or submit to military conscription. For this, the signatories were sentenced to three months' imprisonment and disenfranchised, which meant that the Kadets were denuded of their most active leaders. (Milyukov was neither a Duma deputy nor a co-signatory, and was therefore not involved.)

This meant that when the Second Duma convened after elections in February 1907, the centre was much diminished, but the overall membership was even more radicalised. The extreme left parties (Bolsheviks, Mensheviks and SRs, all of which had lifted their boycott) together fielded 103 deputies, the Trudoviks 98, and the Kadets 92. The Octobrists, on the right of centre, also managed to increase their share of the seats from 17 to 42.[11] Once again government and Duma were set on a collision course. The tough new prime minister, Pëtr Stolypin, who had survived an assassination attempt in August, was in no mood to powwow with the left-leaning Duma politicians, and so, temporarily thwarted by the Duma's failure to ratify a piece of agrarian legislation brought in under Article 87 of the 'constitution' while the Duma was not in session, he fabricated evidence of a Social-Democrat plot to assassinate the tsar. When the delegates refused to waive the SD members' immunity from arrest, Stolypin simply abolished the Second Duma (2 June 1907), had the Social Democrat delegates arrested and exiled to Siberia, and immediately (and illegally) introduced an emergency law (again under Article 87) drastically altering the franchise regulations in favour of the wealthier classes of society. Such flagrant tampering with the electoral procedures was explicitly forbidden in the Fundamental Laws, and Stolypin's action may therefore properly be designated as a *coup d'état* – that is, 'an illegal or violent act carried out by the ruling state power'.[12]

The result was that when the delegates took their seats in the Third Duma in November 1907, it was a much more conservative, malleable and compliant body than the first two, one on which the government could, by and large, confidently rely obediently to ratify and rubber-stamp its policies. When, on occasion, even this poodle parliament had to be temporarily prorogued, its members always faithfully resumed their seats without remonstrance. Dominated by the Octobrists and the government-financed extreme right, the

Third Duma ran its full term from November 1907 to June 1912. During that period it scrutinised around 2500 government proposals, of which it ratified 2200, though most of these were of only slender import – what has been described as 'legislative *vermicelli*'.[13] Although the Octobrists lost seats in the Fourth Duma (down from 154 to 95), this was offset by the increased strength of the right-wing Nationalist Fraction, a militantly monarchist, chauvinist grouping with strong links to Panslavist circles and the Orthodox Church. So great, however, did the unpopularity of the tsar, the royal family and the government become during the years of the Fourth Duma, that even this conservative assembly became a focus of opposition to official policies. This was particularly the case with regard to the Rasputin scandal and Russia's role in the First World War, as will be seen in the final chapter.

The odds were stacked against the success of the 'constitutional experiment' from the very outset. Nicolas II was a ruler who believed unswervingly in the divine provenance of his earthly power; a man who admired – above all his Romanov forebears – not the powerful Peter I, Catherine II or Nicholas I, but the seventeenth-century theocracy of Aleksei, 'the most quiet tsar' (see Chapter 3). He was also the 'supreme' legislator and administrator with no stomach, or head, for government or politics, who hated the very idea of representative government or constitutional politics. Although he was fortunate enough to enjoy the service of a few competent ministers – Witte and Stolypin in particular – most of his senior officials, personally appointed on his own questionable judgement, were obsequious nonentities at best, dotards, fools or villains at worst, and totally out of tune with the needs of the twentieth-century world. He lived in a fur-lined cocoon of mediaevalism, religiosity and uxorious sentimentalism, and his limited mental capacities could cope with little that was more taxing than the pious, patriotic platitudes of Official Nationalism as dinned into his head by the pernicious genius of Pobedonostsev. The tsar and his ministers did everything in their considerable power to prevent the success of the trial run with constitutionalism. One could even go so far as to say that the whole enterprise was not merely bodged by maladroit agents, but deliberately sabotaged by a maleficent administration. In the final analysis it proved impossible to reconcile modern government forms, ideas and institutions with the mentality, traditions and procedures of the Middle Ages.

The Stolypin reaction

Pëtr Arkadeevich Stolypin has been described as 'the last effective statesman of imperial Russia'. In many ways he was a typically Russian character, a man who combined a fine intelligence with ruthless brutality, and undeviating loyalty to his tsar with a keen appreciation of the need for progress and reform. He was at the same time imbued with traditional values and in tune with the demands of the modern age. As Governor of Saratov *guberniya* between 1904 and 1906, he earned a deserved reputation for the severity, even savagery, with which he suppressed the peasant uprisings within his jurisdiction during the years of the 'red cockerel'. And as Minister for Internal Affairs and then Prime Minister (1906–11), so mercilessly did he stamp down on the terrorist activities of, mainly, the Socialist-Revolutionaries, that the number of executions that took place under his administration earned the hangman's noose the nickname of the 'Stolypin necktie' (*stolypinskii galstuk*). But it is for his attempts to introduce a radical reform of the rural economy that he is best remembered.

The unsatisfactory nature of the agrarian situation and the stagnation of the rural sector of the Russian economy at the end of the nineteenth century, and the inflammatory events at the start of the twentieth, have been described above. As a result of his own experiences in the Saratov region, Stolypin understood that simply crushing the peasants without addressing the fundamental causes of their often violently expressed grievances was not enough. Accordingly, starting in 1906, right at the beginning of his premiership, he introduced a series of measures which he hoped would finally tackle and eradicate some of the worst injustices and hangovers from the inequitable emancipation settlement of 1861 (see Chapter 9). Despite widespread and abject poverty, a significant proportion of the peasantry had managed to make a success out of their agricultural activities and had developed into a kind of rural upper class of relatively rich farmers, the *kulaki*. In an exercise in what may be termed *Realökonomie*, it was on these – what Stolypin described as 'the sturdy and the strong', rather than on the poverty-stricken and the weak – that he was to place his wager for a significant improvement in the state of Russian agriculture. The main features of the reform were: (i) abolition of redemption payments; (ii) consolidation of scattered land strips; (iii) phasing out of repartitional tenure and redistribution of allotments; (iv) the right to 'opt out' of the *obshchina*; (v) the consequent establishment of individual farm-steads; (vi) strengthening and widening of the powers of the State Peasant Bank; and (vii) massive increase in government subsidies to encourage peasant migration to and settlement in Siberia. Its chief objectives were the elimination of peasant land-hunger while at the same time preserving intact the estates of the landowning nobility, intensification of peasant agriculture on the basis of private owner-ship of the land, and an increase in the marketability of peasant produce.

Despite some progressive features, the legislation was incredi-bly complex in its detail and equally cumbersome, long-winded and bureaucratic in its implementation. By 1913 only 1.3 million out of 5 million applications for consolidation and hereditary tenure of indi-vidual farms had been dealt with, though by the end of 1915, the proportion had risen to just over half of all allotment land. It is of course possible that the figure might have improved further had it not been for the outbreak of the Great War. Emigration from European Russia and Ukraine to the fertile agricultural regions of south-west Siberia, where there was arable and pasture land in abundance, had been going on since the late nineteenth century. But the removal of remaining government restrictions on internal move-ment, the piecemeal breakdown of the commune system, the completion of the Trans-Siberian railroad, and positive financial incentives to migrate increased the numbers of those crossing the Urals in the first two decades of the twentieth century into what Donald Treadgold reckons was the second greatest wave of human resettlement in recent history, outnumbered only by the huge transatlantic migration from Europe to the United States and Canada during the same period.[14] Between 1896 and 1914, peaking during the years of Stolypin's reform, more than four million peasant settlers arrived in Siberia and turned it into one of the empire's major agricultural regions, dairy farming and butter manufacture being particularly important factors in the region's economy. Cereal pro-duction also increased enormously in Siberia, more than doubling its sown acreage in some districts.[15]

It is certainly the case that Stolypin made a genuine, honest effort to alleviate the plight and increase the productivity of Russian agriculture, and that it probably needed, as he himself suggested, a good 20 years for his reform to show any great effect. Whether the latter observation is true will never be known, as the process was to be interrupted by the far more cataclysmic events of war and revolution. But the wager on the 'sturdy and the strong', though making the rich peasants richer, only made the poor peasants poorer. And of the so-called 'middle peasants' (*serednyaki*), some made it into the *kulak* class, while many more were forced down into deeper penury. The biggest drawback of Stolypin's reform lay in the fact that he dealt with only half the problem. That is to say, he addressed himself solely to the restructuring of peasant agriculture and peasant land tenure. The 50 per cent of the land which remained the private property of the tiny class of noble landlords remained unaffected, and was to continue to be so until, in 1917, the peasants decided once again to take the problem into their own hands (see Chapter 12). It has often been said that what was wrong with the reforms was that they were 'too little, too late'. One might also add that they were too little and too lame.

On the eve

At the beginning of 1912, seven years after the traumatic upheavals of 1905, Russia presented a fairly stable and relatively tranquil picture to the world. Preparations were under way to celebrate the tercentenary of the Romanov dynasty. The economy was making steady progress after the earlier industrial slump which preceded the 1905 events. Stolypin's reforms were progressing, albeit slowly, despite the assassination of their architect in the Kiev opera house in 1911. (While the identity of the assassin is known – one Mordekhai Bogrov [1887–1911] – the actual motive is not, in so far as Bogrov, a Jewish former law student, was both a Socialist-Revolutionary terrorist and an agent of the *Okhrana*.) Two years previously, a group of prominent intellectuals published a remarkable anthology of essays, entitled 'Landmarks' (*Vekhi*, 1909), in which the authors, some of them ex-Marxists (including Pëtr Struve, who had drawn up the Social-Democratic Party's original programme in 1898), articulated the shock still felt in some sections of the intelligentsia at the mass fury that had been unleashed in 1905. In their writing, the 'Landmarkers' (*Vekhovtsy*), attacked the whole ethos of revolution and utilitarian morality and instead preached a message of aestheticism and quasi-mystical repentance to the Russian people. It was a sanctimonious document, smacking of religiosity and pietistic retreat from the 'accursed questions' which still faced the Russian people, and was bitterly attacked by the intelligentsia's still revolutionary wing.

But the revolutionaries themselves were at this time in a state of disarray, prone to endless factionalising and decimated by the operations of the secret police and its stool pigeons within their own camp. The Bolsheviks and Mensheviks, for instance, despite futile attempts at reconciliation, were still torn apart over a whole range of ideological and organisational issues such as whether, in the freer political climate of Duma politics, to 'liquidate' the conspiratorial underground party network, and whether the recourse to illegal, even criminal, methods to 'expropriate' party funding was a legitimate weapon in the revolutionary struggle. While the Bolsheviks continued to enjoy the benefit of huge takings from spectacular bank robberies, the seduction of rich heiresses and similar escapades, the police were having their own success in infiltrating the highest echelons of the party and picking off many of its leading members. Their most famous agent was one Roman Malinovskii (1876–1918), a close, trusted comrade of Lenin, member of the Party's Central Committee, leader of the Bolshevik faction in the Fourth Duma, and fully paid-up police informer. (His treachery was finally revealed after the Bolshevik Revolution, and he was shot on the orders of a revolutionary tribunal in 1918.) In 1912, a year packed with portents, but still outwardly calm but for one major calamity, the final split occurred between Lenin's Bolsheviks and Martov's Mensheviks at the Party's sixth conference in Prague, in which only Bolsheviks participated. From then on one may talk not of two factions of a single party, but of two separate parties. The breach was never to be mended. Also in 1912, the elections were held for the Fourth Duma, which, as indicated above, despite the presence of the far left, was of an overwhelmingly conservative complexion and, as such, cooperated meekly with the tsar's appointed government ministers, until even *its* patience began to wear thin after the outbreak of war in July/August 1914.

The 'major calamity' referred to above occurred in the far-off Lena goldfields in the depths of north-east Siberia. The conditions in which the gold miners lived and worked were notoriously harsh. Not only the rigours of the climate, but the inordinately long hours of work, atrocious accommodation, irregular pay and a draconian code of labour conduct all added to the workers' grievances, which had been simmering for several years. Just as the *Potëmkin* mutiny in 1905 had been sparked off by the rotten state of the ship's meat, so on the Lena the workers protested about the inedible condition of a ration of horsemeat which was unfit for consumption. The management's refusal to heed their complaints led to immediate strike action and the raising of the workers' demands to contain a whole raft of improvements in their working and living arrangements. The protests and strikes spread rapidly through the *taiga* from one gold-working to another, and were given a degree of cohesion and organisation by local Bolshevik activists. Eventually, the management of the parent company, Lenzoto, in cahoots with the local police and government officials, arrested a number of the strike leaders and ordered a return to work. Armed troops were also ominously deployed. Incensed by this high-handed action, a crowd of about several thousand converged on the headquarters of the Nadezhdinskii mine to hand in their individually written petitions, as requested by the management. There have been suggestions that this was a ploy on the part of the authorities to get as many people together at one time and place, in order that any military action would be more effective. As the crowd approached the settlement early in the morning of 4 April, the order was given to open fire. In the ensuing fusillade around 500 workers were killed where they stood. The response to the massacre recalled the aftermath of Bloody Sunday as a wave of sympathetic strikes and industrial unrest spread throughout Siberia and beyond. However, the remoteness of the tragedy's location meant that the repercussions were not as dramatic as the shock waves following Bloody Sunday. Hundreds of dead gold miners in remote north-east Siberia, however many and however dead, just did not evoke quite the same public reaction as the sight of countless corpses bleeding in the snow on Palace Square in front of the royal residence. And there were not many foreign journalists on the lower Lena at the time. Nevertheless, the Lena goldfields massacre did signal an upswing in labour unrest which was to rumble on throughout the country over the next two years.[16]

The revulsion from materialism and socialism experienced by the *Landmarks* writers mentioned above was illustrated by other contemporary phenomena. As well as a revival of interest in Orthodox theology, there was in many circles of high society at that time a preoccupation with spiritualism, astrology and other forms of occult transcendentalism. It was the heyday of the clairvoyant, the medium and the witch. The ready acceptance into the royal household of Rasputin – a kind of malevolent latter-day Merlin – is indicative of the weird malady which infected many areas of educated society in the aftermath of one, and on the eve of another revolution. Indeed not even the Marxists were immune from the mood of anti-materialism, and Lenin, for instance, spent a good deal of time in fighting the heresy of what he called 'god-building' (*bogostroitel'stvo*), a word he used to describe the efforts of some Marxist intellectuals, including Maksim Gorkii, to reinterpret Marxism in quasi-religious terms. Both 'god-building' and its twin heresy of 'god-seeking' (*bogoiskatel'stvo*) he witheringly dismissed as an exercise in 'ideological necrophilia'. 'Such theories,' he said, 'under the present *objective* relationship of class forces, merely adorn and sweeten the political and economic oppression of the people.'[17]

Typical, too, of the intellectual climate was the much-vaunted 'renaissance' of Russian art and letters during the reign of Nicholas II, with its preoccupation with art for art's sake, its infatuation with form, the cult of the eternal feminine and *Hagia Sophia* – 'Holy Wisdom'. In many ways Russia was at the forefront, in the avant-garde of contemporary European culture. And, indeed, there was much talent around, as testified by the names of such artistic and literary luminaries as Chekhov, Belyi, Blok, Akhmatova, Diaghilev, Chagall, Kandinskii, Stanislavskii, Stravinskii, Scriabin, Rakhmaninov *et al.*, as well as scientists like the chemist, Mendeleev, and the Nobel Prize-winning physiologist and psychologist, Pavlov. But this picture of burgeoning talent and cultural renewal is superficial and misleading. It is true that the Symbolist movement threw up one poet of major importance – Aleksandr Blok (1880–1921) – but it is interesting to note that his most outstanding work, 'The Twelve' (*Dvenadtsat'*, 1918), despite its symbolic Christian imagery, is concerned with the insistent reality of the 1917 Revolution. The so-called 'Silver Age' of Russian culture was not an era of genuine argent, but of tinsel and tawdry glitter. Except in the case of Maksim Gorkii, gone was the social commitment of Belinskii's school of 'critical realism', gone was Nekrasov's concept of the 'citizen poet'. In their place came narcissistic posturing, pretty conceits and an almost epicurean pleasure in letters as playful symbols, rather than literature as a weapon in the struggle for the common good. But of the total population of Russia, according to the 1897 census figures, only 22.3 per cent could read or write in any case. The semiotic *legerdemain* of the Symbolists was lost on the largely illiterate masses. The arcane intonations of Rozanov, the artificial constructions of Acmeism, Futurism and other self-indulgent artistic '-isms' meant little to the average, toiling peasant. Bread and land figured highly in the revolutionary slogans of 1917, *belles-lettres* did not. But the deep injustices and the contradictions of Russian society could not be wished away by squeamish intellectuals. While the poet lisped his effete and fancy verses, the groaning of the people could still be heard, and there were sufficient signs about that the superficially magnificent parade of artistic talent could camouflage only briefly the impending cataclysm. In his inaugural lecture at the University of Keele in 1969, Professor Eugene Lampert, who has already been quoted elsewhere in this book, summed up the eerie combination of cultural cleverness and political myopia present in a Russia that was already 'on the eve' of revolution as follows: 'Admiration for a marvellous window-box display is bound to be diminished … if the building incorporating it happens to be rotten to the core and/or is on fire.'[18]

War, revolution and the end of the Romanovs 1914–1917

It has been said that the Russian Revolution of 1917 was to the twentieth century what the French Revolution was to the nineteenth. It is, however, not as obvious as to how profoundly the world was changed, shaken or dominated by events in the squares of Paris in 1789 as they were by those on the streets of Petrograd in 1917.[1] Much of the international scene in terms of diplomatic, military, political, social and economic relationships throughout the entire twentieth century flowed directly or indirectly from the actions of highly politicised workers, soldiers and sailors on or around the banks of the river Neva in the space of only eight months. There was not just one, nor were there only two revolutions in Russia in that year. All over the world's largest land empire there were literally hundreds of local revolts, rebellions and mutinies which brought the 300-year-old Romanov dynasty crashing down, and later brought to power the world's first revolutionary socialist government. But, initially, both the February and the October Revolutions were an essentially metropolitan affair. The shock waves, however, with their epicentre in Petrograd, rapidly reverberated throughout the crumbling empire and eventually across the world. The post-Versailles settlement in Europe, the rise of Fascism in Italy and Nazism in Germany, the Spanish Civil War, the Second World War, the Jewish Holocaust, the Chinese Revolution, the Cold War, the Korean War, the Berlin Wall, the Cuban missile crisis, America's anti-communist incendiarism in Vietnam, all may be traced back in one way or another to the abdication of the last Romanov tsar and the later seizure of power by Lenin's Bolsheviks.

In the case of the February Revolution, however, we are faced with something of a conundrum. In 1905, the entire Russian Empire was racked with civil strife, military mutiny, peasant uprisings, national insurgencies and industrial chaos for almost 12 months. And there was also the matter of defeat in a major international war. Yet the empire – and the emperor, Nicholas the Bloody – survived. In 1917, in a period of only eight days, 23 February to 2 March, and in the space of only one city (albeit the capital), that emperor was forced to abdicate and the empire was shattered. The Romanov autocracy was dead. How did that extraordinary phenomenon come about?

War, politics and the 'Rasputin affair'

Whatever one's view of the aetiological connection between the First World War and the Revolution, it cannot be denied that the latter can be properly understood only against the background of the former. This is not the place to go into fine detail about the complex international situation which led to the outbreak of war in Europe in July/August 1914. Nor is it necessary to trace the fluctuating nature of relations between the Russian and the German Empires over the two decades or so preceding their titanic clash. Nor, again, need we go into a campaign-by-campaign account of the dreadful hostilities on Germany's eastern and Russia's western front. What particularly concerns us here is not the carnage in the mud-baths and blood-baths of eastern Europe, but the repercussions of the fighting, and both the military and political conduct of the war, on the domestic front.

Russia's defeat by Japan in 1905 had thwarted any further imperial ambitions in the Far East. Expansion in Central Asia had also gone about as far as it could go without provoking a confrontation with Britain, with which she had signed agreements in 1907 over their conflicting interests in Persia and Afghanistan. It was not surprising, therefore, that Russian statesmen and generals should have renewed their country's interest in the fraught affairs of the Balkans, particularly when that interest was enhanced by the resurgence of aggressive Panslavism in influential social and political circles in St Petersburg. Obviously not having learned the lessons of his disastrous 'short, swift war' with Japan, Nicholas may have thought that by mobilising Russian military support for Serbia, he might deflect public attention from the wave of discontent that had been flowing through the country after the Lena goldfields massacre of 1912 (see Chapter 11), and had even reached the benches of the conservative Fourth Duma. He also ignored the warnings of influential figures, including Rasputin, about the potential social chaos which would be created by war with Germany. One particularly prescient, indeed prophetic, warning over precisely that likelihood was issued by a right-wing politician and ex-Minister for Internal Affairs, Pëtr Durnovo (1845–1915). Although he did not survive to see his prognostication become reality, in February 1914 he issued a memorandum to the tsar in which his ominous and, as it turned out, accurate, prediction read in part:

> In the event of defeat, the possibility of which in a struggle with a foe like Germany cannot be overlooked, social revolution in its extreme form is *inevitable* ... [emphasis added]

> ... It will start with disasters being attributed to the government. In the legislative institutions a bitter campaign against the government will begin, which will lead to revolutionary agitation throughout the country.

> Socialist slogans will immediately ensue ... The defeated army ... will prove to be too demoralized to serve as a bulwark of law and order. The legislative institutions and the opposition intelligentsia parties ... will be powerless to stem the rising popular tide, and Russia will be flung into hopeless anarchy, the outcome of which cannot even be foreseen.[2]

Durnovo was right in almost every detail, as the following pages will demonstrate. But there are still some modern historians who believe that his prophecies were too doom-laden and Cassandra-like, that they were based on a mistaken reading of the international correlation of powers at the time, and that in any case Russia in 1914 was *not* on the brink of a revolutionary abyss which needed only a war to tip it over. Indeed, there were many signs that on all sides – political, social, economic (both industrial and agrarian) and cultural –

Russia was making steady progress towards some version of a western-style constitutional monarchy, with greater democratic freedoms based on an increasingly sound economy. There was already an elected parliament, open public debate, representative participation in legislative procedures, positive cultural and educational developments, and an industrial economy that was now less dependent on foreign investment. There was also the prospect of the creation of an independent, prosperous yeoman peasantry, once Stolypin's reforms had taken real root (see Chapter 11). Russia, in this view, was robust, rather than teetering on rebellion, and would have continued along that upward curve of development. Such arguments are, of course, specious, untenable and based upon an unsupported, counter-factual presumption about what *might* have happened, rather than what actually *did* happen – which was a revolution.

There are other historians who go beyond Durnovo's assertion that, 'In the event of defeat … social revolution in its extreme form is inevitable', and argue that all the signs were there that Russia was already set on that particular path, and that – war or no war – revolution was, if not inevitable, then extremely likely. The countless political assassinations, including the murder of the Prime Minister in 1911, the dreadful slaughter of the Siberian gold miners, the mounting tide of industrial unrest, the inadequate and incomplete nature of the agrarian settlement, the increasingly vociferous chorus of anti-government and anti-tsarist feeling in the State Duma – all of this was exacerbated by daily reports of military disaster and mayhem at the war front and bungling ineptitude in court and government circles. All these factors indicate that state and society were already lurching towards some kind of dramatic confrontation. More workers were on strike in the early months of 1914 than in 1905; there were barricades on the streets; there was a stand-off between the unpopular tsarist government and a society which from top to bottom had become increasingly aware of the shortcomings and failures of the administration. The railtrack to revolution was already laid. The war, in Trotskii's words, was the locomotive which hurtled the country into that revolution. The driver, however, in the shape of the tsar, blithely ignored the signals, which were set at red.

Two sets of circumstances which more than anything else exposed and floodlit the unpopularity and isolation of Nicholas

were, first, his decision in August 1915 to become operational commander-in-chief of the Russian armed forces at the front, and,
second, the so-called 'Rasputin affair'. Ignoring the advice of his
more perceptive ministers and members of his own entourage,
Nicholas took the fateful step to take full command in the belief that
his personal presence at army headquarters near the tiny provincial
town of Mogilёv (derived from the Russian word for a grave – *mogila*)
would literally rally the troops and fire them up with new enthusiasm
to fight, if not for their country, then for their tsar. It is difficult to
understand the utter foolishness, naivety and stubborn pigheaded-
ness of his decision, and the totally misguided and self-deluding
premises on which it was based. Nicholas had no military experience. He lacked the confidence of his general staff. And he had also
long ago forfeited his right to be looked on by his men as the 'little
father tsar' (*tsar-batyushka*). On the contrary, Nicholas the Bloody's
gory record of the Khodynka tragedy, the anti-Jewish pogroms,
Bloody Sunday, the suppression of the December uprising in
Moscow, routine knotting of the 'Stolypin necktie', the Lena goldfields massacre, and now the daily slaughter in the trenches of the
eastern front – none of this could inspire a burst of patriotic passion
in the hearts of the millions of 'peasants in uniform', many of whom
were dying with a priestly benediction, but without benefit of their
own bullets or boots.

And, of course, as commander-in-chief, he now took on not only
his duties of military leadership, but also the direct, personal responsibility for military disaster. As the war senselessly ground on under
the tsar's inept command, the increasing political disaffection of the
middle classes was famously articulated by the leader of the Kadet
Party in the Fourth Duma, Pavel Milyukov. In November 1916 he
rhetorically challenged the government's amateurish, blundering
conduct of the war in a parliamentary speech in which he finished
each paragraph with the insistent, interrogative peroration: '*Is this
stupidity or is this treason?*' The cumulative effect of his repeated
question was not lost on his listeners, and his taunting reiteration of
the word 'treason' was probably a deliberate allusion to the suspi-
cions in some quarters of a faction of allegedly pro-German
sympathisers at court and in the government – including the
Empress Alexandra (née Princess Alix of Hesse), popularly referred to
by the derogatory nickname of *nemka* – 'the German woman'.

Mention of the tsar's consort, to whom he was passionately devoted, and whom, as far as we know, he never betrayed with any extra-marital infidelities of the kind of which his libidinous forebears were so fond, brings us naturally to the subject of Grigorii Rasputin (1865[?]–1916). Such was the man's notoriety at the time, and so closely has his scandalous behaviour often been linked with the collapse of the Romanovs that it is worth dwelling briefly on the rather unsavoury nature of his influence on the course of events. He is sometimes erroneously described as the 'mad monk'. This is wrong on two counts. First, though bizarre in his behaviour, he was not mad in the clinical sense of having been medically certified as suffering from any kind of mental disability or morbid psychiatric condition. Second, he was not an ordained or inducted member of any officially recognised monastic order, nor did he possess any kind of ecclesiastical status. What he was, was a filthy, lecherous, priapic Siberian peasant; a self-appointed 'holy man' ('elder' or *starets*); a charlatan, horse-thief and drunkard who wandered on his personal pilgrim's progress from his remote hovel in Tobolsk province to be lionised in the boudoirs, bedchambers and brothels of St Petersburg. He was also attached to an extreme schismatic sect of religious perverts called the *khlysty*, who, as one of their tenets of faith, believed fervently in the doctrine of redemption through sin, especially sexual sin. The pseudo-theological logic of this is, presumably, that the more one sinned, the greater one's chances of being redeemed. Rasputin was a devout, dedicated and undeviating practitioner of what for a man of his seemingly insatiable lust was a more than convenient article of faith. Apart from their other physical indulgences, the *khlysty* also practised individual, group and self-flagellation (*khlyst* is also one of the many Russian words for 'whip').

Among his other personal accomplishments, Rasputin also had a reputation for prophesy, clairvoyance and faith-healing, the latter through the alleged power of prayer, the laying on of hands (at which he was extremely adept), hypnotism and the sheer charismatic aura of his otherwise rather repellent and malodorous presence. The excessively decadent, *début-de-siècle* atmosphere in St Petersburg when Rasputin arrived there sometime in 1905, infected as it was with various forms of occultism, sorcery, spiritualism and medical quackery, was exactly the right sort of environment in which Rasputin, holy man, healer and rake, would thrive. His reputation had preceded him, and when he was not busy debauching the willing, grateful ladies of the capital's high society, connections were established through which he was soon introduced into the royal household.

There was, of course, a special reason for this honour. The doting imperial couple had been blessed with five children, the four grand-duchesses, Olga, Tatyana, Mariya and Anastasiya, and the young tsarevich, Aleksei, heir to the Romanov Empire. The family's joy on the birth of their son in 1904 turned to grief when it was discovered that he suffered from the 'royal disease' of haemophilia, the inherited disorder of blood coagulation passed through the female line to male offspring. The condition is, naturally, extremely distressing, causing internal bleeding after minor trauma, which can pass into the joints and sometimes produce a crippling effect. The tsaritsa was a naturally highly strung, emotional and hysterical woman at the best of times, and now further inclined to spiritualism, mysticism and any other form of hocus-pocus which she believed might act as a cure or palliative for the boy's suffering. Therefore, given the combined circumstances of Aleksei's haemophilia, his mother's almost psychotic dementia and Rasputin's alleged thaumaturgical powers, it is hardly surprising that he was so readily welcomed to the Winter Palace. Ignoring other rumours of his drunken shenanigans in St Petersburg's bars and bordellos, the tsaritsa and her family were literally spellbound by Rasputin's apparent ability to staunch the bleeding, reduce the swelling and lessen the pain of the young prince. There is some medical evidence that deep hypnosis can have the effect of slowing down the body's motor system, which could induce a temporary remission of the suffering. Of the mesmeric effects of Rasputin's smouldering gaze there are also many accounts (usually those of susceptible females who had succumbed to it), but whether this is the correct psycho-physiological explanation for what occurred or not, matters not. As far as the credulous and simple-minded parents were concerned, Rasputin's 'miracle cure' – for so they regarded his ministrations – was the ultimate proof that their new-found 'friend' was truly a man of God, sent by divine guidance to heal the tsarevich, ensure the succession and save the empire for the Romanovs. The fact that he was also unquestionably a man of the people, a genuine son of the Russian soil (a good deal of which he carried beneath his fingernails), chimed in with the tsar's rather unsophisticated, quasi-Slavophil view of the special relationship between his own patriarchal role as *tsar-batyushka* and the plain folk of Russia.

But there was also another important aspect of Rasputin's shady activities which had a direct affect on the conduct of government affairs, and that was his meddling in high political appointments. Such was his hold over Nicholas and his wife through his hypnotic healing powers, that he was able on occasion to influence the tsar in his choice of government ministers. This was in return for sexual or other favours arranged for him by ambitious politicians – a crate of his favourite Madeira, say, or a fresh gypsy girl. There is almost certainly no truth in salacious innuendoes that Rasputin had sexual relations with the empress or her daughters (a subject of scurrilous popular cartoons of the time, depicting the pair of them in indecent juxtaposition) but the combination of his well-known intimacy with the royal family and his outrageous public behaviour could succeed only in bringing the court, and the government, into further disrepute. Though they were by no means all Rasputin's creatures, ministers of the crown were hired and fired in farcically rapid succession in what was described as a game of 'ministerial leapfrog'. Between 1912 and 1916, the years of the Fourth Duma, and the height of Rasputin's notoriety, Russia had four Prime Ministers, Four Procurators of the Holy Synod, four Ministers of Justice, four of Education, and no fewer than six Ministers for Internal Affairs – all of them forming, in Florinsky's felicitous phrase, 'a grotesque and sinister procession of nonentities and adventurers, pebbles – not milestones – on the road that led the monarchy to ruin'.[3]

Rasputin, neither 'mad monk' nor even a genuinely holy man, but a weird, philandering confidence trickster suffering from chronic satyriasis, was finally done to death in appropriately bizarre circumstances arranged by a member of the royal family, Prince Feliks Yusupov (1887–1967), reputedly the richest man in Russia, an Oxford graduate, a homosexual and married to the tsar's favourite niece, the beautiful Princess Irina. In December 1916, he and a handful of royalist cronies, including the ultra-right politician, Vladimir Purishkevich, exasperated by Rasputin's sexual cavorting and political meddling, inveigled him to a late-night party in the basement of the Yusupov palace, luring him with promises of wine, women and cake (though he rarely touched cake) – and an introduction to Yusupov's delectable young wife. There, according to their own account, they poisoned him with a stiff cocktail of best Madeira and potassium cyanide, then shot him three times, once in the heart region, once in the back and once in the head. Still not believing he was totally dead, the by now deranged Yusupov bludgeoned him savagely about the temples with a heavy dumbbell handle. His battered, bleeding body was then wrapped and roped in a curtain, and driven to be dumped through a hole in the ice of the frozen river Neva.[4] Other reports claim that there were no toxic substances found in his body during the autopsy, but, because of the presence of inhaled water in the lungs, gave the cause of death as 'drowning'. And there is absolutely no truth in the ridiculous story peddled on a BBC television documentary film broadcast in 2004 that the murder was masterminded and executed by an agent of the British secret service. Scarcely two months after his death, the autocracy collapsed – as Rasputin had predicted it would if he were killed. There is, of course, no causal connection between the two events. In the final analysis, the Rasputin affair was no more than a titillating side-show to the real drama now unfolding, and the scandal around his name was merely a symptom, not a cause, of the terminal malady that was dragging the discredited regime to its doom.[5]

War, politics and the approaching revolution[6]

Despite a creditable performance in some early military engagements, Russia's crushing defeat, with 300,000 casualties, at the battle of Tannenberg in August 1914 generally set the pattern for her armies' miserable fortunes for the rest of the war. Behind the lines, the repercussions of the conflict were soon felt. Economically, the effects of the war were far-reaching, though the news was not all bad for some. If war is the locomotive of revolution, it is also the gravy train for the manufacturers of armaments and other military material. Great fortunes were made out of government orders for guns, bullets, shells and uniforms. When it became clear that the fighting would not quickly be over, more and more enterprises converted to military and paramilitary production, and more and more profits were made out of the battlefront carnage. Swords were ploughed into shares.

On the other hand, of course, consumer goods production plummeted, with consequent shortages of ordinary domestic items. In an overwhelmingly rural society, even agricultural equipment was in short supply, though at the very basic level peasants left on the land got by with their traditional, locally made wooden tools. The situation was exacerbated by communication problems inside a huge country whose internal transport network was notoriously inefficient, or in many areas at certain seasons almost non-existent. (The age-old problem of *bezdorozhie* – 'roadlessness' – is dealt with in Chapter 1.) Impassable roads apart, the commandeering of engines and rolling stock to carry men and munitions to the front left little on which to ferry much needed foodstuffs from the grain-growing regions to the main centres of population. It was not the case that grain was not being grown; it was just not getting to the towns and into people's bellies. Factory workers and their families went hungry; bread queues lengthened, and the only thing that ripened on the urban landscape was discontent. In order better to coordinate efforts to meet the crisis of under-supply and over-demand, which reached a peak in 1915–16, a new non-governmental organisation was established called the War-Industries Committee. This was one of a few wartime voluntary organisations, which in this case consisted of a consortium of businessmen, arms manufacturers, Duma deputies and even workers' councils, which, despite some perverse government obstruction to their worthy efforts, to some extent offset the regime's increasingly obvious inability to cope efficiently or effectively with the economic strains and demands of total war.[7]

Financially, the country was heading for ruin. Naval blockades of the Baltic and Black Seas cut off Russia's foreign trade to north and south. Overland traffic westward through the battle zones of eastern Europe was obviously impossible. Poland and parts of Russia's western provinces were occupied by the enemy, with consequent loss not only of industrial capacity, but also of the tax-paying population. The government also shot itself in the foot, as it were, by the prohibition of alcohol sales. Excise duty on the production and selling of vodka was a lucrative source of state revenue, which now literally dried up (not that the great Russian people ceased drinking their home-distilled and often lethal liquor – *samogon*).[8] But while government income slumped, expenditure soared. The direct costs of the war rocketed from 1500 million rubles in 1914 to 14,500 million in 1916. The government's answer to the immediate financial problem was heavy foreign borrowing and the printing of millions of worthless paper rubles, which led to galloping inflation.

The mass mobilisation of 15 million conscript troops and volunteers between 1914 and 1917 also had obvious repercussions on the nation's economy. In the countryside, the redirection of so much agricultural manpower to military purposes meant that there were fewer mouths to feed in the villages. Moreover, the depletion of the male labour force did not greatly affect agricultural production, as the peasant women, children and men too old for the draft were perfectly capable of coping with the annual round of ploughing, sowing and harvesting, and consequently suffered no more than the familiar hardships of peasant existence. The army, however, the 'peasants in uniform', could not march or fight on an empty stomach. Conscription of agricultural labourers from the large private estates which produced mainly for the market resulted in reduced output at a time of increased demand. Industrial production – despite continuing demand for military equipment – also slumped as experienced craftsmen, already in short supply, were replaced by unskilled labourers, women, children and unenthusiastic prisoners-of-war.

Ever more insistently, impatiently and vociferously, the public pressed their grievances, complaining not only of military defeats at the front, but of the increasingly intolerable situation at home. Police reports on the public mood throughout 1915 and 1916 chart a strident crescendo of popular anger and frustration which threatened to break out into a frenzy of mass disturbances. One such report in October 1916 spoke in a matter-of-fact tone of 'an exceptional heightening of opposition and bitterness of temperament', of 'a situation highly favourable to any sort of revolutionary propaganda', of calls to 'first defeat the Germans here at home, and then deal with the enemy abroad', and of being 'on the eve of great events in comparison with which "1905 was but a toy"'.[9] Obviously, the short-lived emotions of national solidarity and primitive patriotism which greeted the outbreak of war had now evaporated. Large sections of the population were at the same time fed up and underfed. Industry was battered by a renewed wave of strikes, some of them, we now know, financed by German gold. Ever since the war began, the German Foreign Ministry had been authorising the channelling of thousands of marks into the coffers of Russian anti-government organisations – trade unions, left-wing parties, including the Bolsheviks, who were major beneficiaries, and the like – as part of its programme of *Revolutionierungspolitik* – that is, the policy of encouraging industrial unrest, civil disturbances, revolutionary activity and economic sabotage by financial subvention in order to undermine and disrupt the enemy's war effort from within. Rumours to this effect were rife at the time and were speculated about long after the Revolution itself, as in such works as S. P. Melgunov's *The German Golden Key to the Bolshevik Revolution,* published in Paris in 1940. Persuasive as the arguments were, solid documentary evidence was discovered only when the archives of the German Foreign Ministry in Berlin were sequestrated by allied troops at the end of the Second World War. Scholarly analysis of the records revealed beyond doubt that this was not only part of German strategy to weaken Russia and win the war, but also a useful contribution to the solvency and effectiveness of various branches of the Russian revolutionary movement.[10]

In 1915, some deputies of the centre parties in the Fourth Duma – mainly Kadets and Trudoviks – along with members of the State Council, formed themselves into the so-called 'Progressive Bloc', which called on the tsar to sack his incompetent ministers (including the 'leapfrogging' Rasputin nominees), and replace them with what they described as 'government of public confidence'. By that, they obviously meant themselves, but why the 'public' should place its 'confidence' in a bunch of wealthy, self-interested businessmen and duplicitous political careerists is a moot point, as the subsequent fate of the Provisional Government was to show in October 1917. The tsar, of course, himself had little confidence in them, and no doubt wished that the politicians would keep their mouths shut or, better still, go away. They did not, however, go away, but at the same time they were unwilling to back up their political demands with economic sanctions. Many of them, as well as sitting in the Duma, were members of the voluntary organisations (VOs), such as the War-Industries Committee and the Union of *Zemstva* and Towns (*Zemgor*), whose activities complemented, or rather compensated for, the government's own blunderings. Despite the fact that the administration more often than not hindered, rather than helped, the industrial, social and relief efforts of the VOs, their members, and those of the Progressive Bloc, were unwilling to threaten the government to withhold their services, as in many cases their own financial interests were at stake. One may charitably suppose that some feelings of crude patriotism might have had something to do with their lack of nerve, but it is not too cynical to suspect that the prospect of jeopardising their own accumulated 'fortunes of war' may also have played a part. In the final analysis, through a combination of their private interests and their pusillanimity, the Progressive Bloc succeeded only in blocking progress towards any kind of solution to the country's rapidly deteriorating social, economic, military and – ever more menacingly – political problems.

By early 1917, the volatile mixture of continued military losses and an increasingly disaffected army at all levels – troops, officers and High Command – together with mounting civilian suffering and tension on the streets of the capital, was bringing the country, seemingly inexorably, to the point of another explosion. Nicholas himself seemed blissfully unconcerned, unless it were for the measles from which his royal brood was then suffering, and about which he anxiously sought and received daily information. The embarrassing personal correspondence – all in English – between 'Nicky' and 'Sunny', from 'Hubby' to 'Wify', which passed between Mogilëv and Tsarskoe Selo in the weeks and days leading up to the greatest cataclysm in the nation's history since the Time of Troubles, reveals a ruler who seems to have been strangely detached from reality and oblivious to the storm that was about to break over the entire nation. Judging from the contents of his letters and telegrams, apart from enquiring about the family's health and addressing his wife with strings of saccharine hypocoristic apostrophes ('My Sweetest Treasure', 'My own Lovebird', 'Wify-mine', 'My own beloved Angel' and even 'My dear Mama'!), the uxorious Commander-in-Chief and Autocrat of All Russia seems to have spent most of his time at Army Headquarters dining out, playing dominoes, exercising on his trapeze (*sic* – letter of 18 November 1914), and compiling amateur meteorological bulletins. While it may be tasteless to scoff at the private endearments, it is difficult not to marvel at the tsar's sheer indifference to the critical import of what was happening all around him, both at the fighting front and, increasingly, on the streets of his capital city. To be fair, one does find the odd snippet of information about the mounting disturbances in Petrograd but, again, no real inkling of their almost apocalyptic nature. Here is what Alexandra has to say to her husband, two days into the revolution that was to cost him his crown:

> **Alix to Nikki – 25 February – Tsarskoe Selo**
> Precious, beloved Treasure,
> 8° and gently snowing – so far I sleep very well, but miss my love *more* than words can tell. The rows in town and strikes are more than provoking … It's a 'hooligan' movement, young boys and girls running about and screaming that they have no bread, only to excite – then the workmen preventing others from work – if it *were* very cold they would probably stay indoors. But this will all pass and quieten down – if the Duma would only behave itself – one does not print the worst speeches.[11]

Rowdy hooligans, screaming kids, picketing proletarians, Duma deputies behaving badly – no wonder the granddaughter of Queen Victoria was not amused. But, of course, worse was to come. Within five days of sending her message, her husband had been forced to give up his throne, finally abandoned by his General Staff while on his way back from Mogilëv to restore order. But despite the disaffection of the military, however crucial that was, it was neither the High Command, nor the Duma politicians which finally brought about the downfall of Nicholas the Bloody. It was caused by the spontaneous revolt of the politically radicalised masses, the Russian *narod*.

Insurrection and abdication

In seeking to identify the immediate *casus motus* of the February Revolution, Orlando Figes tells us: 'It all began with bread.'[12] More accurately, it was the *lack* of bread that triggered the turmoil. Disturbances in food lines of freezing, frustrated and famished shoppers in Petrograd escalated into sometimes violent protests, clashes with the police and, ultimately, military mutiny among the fretful troops garrisoned in the capital who had no desire to be sent to the front. The flashpoint came on 23 February, International Women's Day, when hundreds of female demonstrators demanding equal rights were joined on the streets by striking workers from the giant Putilov metallurgical plant. Petrograd's main thoroughfare, Nevskii prospekt, swiftly became the scene of a mêlée of strikers, protestors, policemen, students, soldiers and mounted cossaks, though as yet there was no bloodshed, and by evening relative calm had returned to the streets. Over the next three or four days, things began to turn more ugly as the detested police, under their chief, Shalfeev, came into direct, physical contact with the reassembled demonstrators. Openly revolutionary slogans were now being chanted, protesting against the monarchy and the war, red banners appeared, and what had originally started as a demand for bread and women's rights was turning into an all-out confrontation between the ever more angry people and the city authorities. Durnovo's prophecies were turning into reality. On the afternoon of Saturday the 25th, blood once more began to flow on the pavements of Petrograd. Police-chief Shalfeev, trying to whip the crowds into submission, was torn down from his horse, beaten and shot dead, and later in the day a number of people were killed by a squadron of soldiers on Nevskii prospekt. News of this only embittered the mob, but, crucially, the troops were beginning to waver. The role of the military at this point was pivotal to the outcome of the clashes. Would the peasants and workers in uniform side with their brothers and sisters on their streets, or would they obey their officers' commands to shoot the crowds into surrender? Even more crucially, would the officers even give the order to fire?

At Mogilëv, Nicholas finally set his dominoes aside and sent an instruction to Major-General Khabalov, Commander of the Petrograd Military District, to restore order by force of arms. On the following day, Sunday the 26th, that instruction was put into effect, resulting in the deaths of dozens of demonstrators in the centre of the city. The military order to fire had been given and obeyed, but civic order was not restored. The symbolism of the day – Sunday – and of the blood shed by unarmed demonstrators was not lost. But on this occasion, the wholesale slaughter of 1905's Bloody Sunday was not repeated on the same scale. The mood of the masses was more determined, more grim, and the loyalty of the soldiers less certain, less sure. Many of the junior officers were also of a different social complexion from the usual military-career class. The circumstances of all-out international war had persuaded many young men, who would otherwise not have contemplated joining the colours, to enlist in the defence of their country. But on donning their uniforms, these educated young Russians had not abandoned their progressive, vaguely democratic or more radical social aspirations or moral principles. The 'peasants in uniform' were now commanded by 'intellectuals in uniform', and in both cases their sympathy now lay overwhelmingly, not with the tsar, but with the people. It was the spontaneous mutiny of soldiers in the barracks of the Volynskii regiment, some of whom had been involved in the shooting that afternoon, that finally swung the day in favour of the revolution. They were soon joined in their rebellion by their comrades and junior officers from nearby regiments, and by the evening of 27 February it would be safe to say that almost the entire Petrograd garrison was now in a state of open and declared mutiny. Russian workers, Russian women and Russian warriors were now united in solidarity and in open defiance of the tsar and the entire political establishment. The tsar, however, still technically reigned, even if he no longer had the willpower to rule. But that was soon to change.

Alerted to the severity of the crisis by General Khabalov, the tsar set off from headquarters to return to Petrograd, maybe to try to exert his waning authority and restore some kind of order, or maybe merely to rejoin his wife and family, whom he had left after a brief conjugal visit only five days before. At all events, the royal train was diverted from its route by rebellious railway workers and forced to a standstill in a siding of the railway station at Pskov, an ancient provincial town about 200 miles south of the capital. Meanwhile, in revolutionary Petrograd, members of the self-appointed Provisional Committee of the Duma (which the tsar had prorogued on the 26th), after considerable heart searching, hand wringing and head scratching, had finally reached the bold decision to ask for the tsar's abdication. The word 'bold' is used here with deliberate irony, for it was the cowardly attitude of the Duma politicians over the previous two years or so that had made them hesitate to press their case for a 'government of public confidence' more purposefully. Now that the revolution had in effect already taken place – not in the halls of Prince Grigorii Potëmkin's Tauride Palace, where the Committee sat, but in the streets and squares outside – they felt that, rather than simply deposing Nicholas, seizing power and declaring themselves the new revolutionary government, they were at least in a strong enough position to go through the legal niceties of a formal abdication process. It was this kind of pussy-footing procrastination and preoccupation with proper procedure that was to be the hallmark of the Provisional Governments when they eventually came into being – and was, of course, one of the reasons for their ultimate undoing.

While the Provisional Committee members were dithering in the right wing of the Tauride over what to do about the tsar, other significant developments were taking place in, appropriately, the left wing. When the Revolution broke out on 23 February, most, if not all, of the leaders of the main revolutionary parties – Bolsheviks, Mensheviks and SRs – were not there to witness or take part in it. They were either abroad, in exile or in prison. Nevertheless, in the afternoon of the 27th, jubilantly expectant crowds of the capital's soldiers and citizens thronged to the Tauride Palace looking for some kind of guidance from the socialist leaders. They were eventually met with an announcement of the formation of a body calling itself the Provisional Executive Committee of the Soviet of Workers' Deputies, and a proclamation was distributed inviting all factories, enterprises, soldiers' and sailors' units to elect representatives to the first meeting of the Soviet itself, scheduled for later that evening. It will be remembered that in October 1905, the St Petersburg Soviet had been set up as a kind of makeshift workers' parliament during the 'Days of Freedom' (see Chapter 11). On this precedent, the socialist intellectuals who were to become the Executive Committee of the new Petrograd Soviet of Workers' and Soldiers' Deputies became, in effect the 'cabinet' of the resurrected popular assembly. There was not a single genuine 'worker' among them. However, there were genuine workers and soldiers aplenty (far more, in fact, of the latter than the former) to pack the first full, chaotic gathering of the new revolutionary body on the last day of February.

The fact that the mutinying soldiers of the Petrograd garrison had played such a decisive role in the Revolution, and that so many of their delegates now assembled as Soviet deputies, gave some urgency to the question of where their loyalties now lay, and whose orders they should now obey. There were still sufficient senior officers out there who might have been prepared to take punitive action against their defecting troops in what was still a very confused, volatile and violent situation, should they return to their barracks as the Military Commission of the Duma Committee had decreed. In the event, and in the agenda-less pandemonium of the Soviet's first shambolic meeting, it took its first decision and issued its famous, hastily drafted first decree, known simply as 'Order No. 1'. When its contents were read out, the Order was noisily passed by popular acclaim. The document was to have tremendous ramifications for the whole course of the continuing drama yet to be played out between February and October. What it amounted to was a democratic charter of soldiers' rights. Its full provisions were as follows.

(1) The formation of elected soldiers' committees in all units.

(2) Units not having elected a deputy to the Soviet to do so immediately.

(3) In political activities, all troop units to be subordinate to the Soviet.

(4) Orders of the Military Commission of the Duma to be obeyed only if they are in conformity with the orders of the Soviet.

(5) All arms to be placed at the disposal of the company committees, and not to be issued to officers.

(6) When off duty, all soldiers to enjoy the same rights as all citizens. Standing to attention and saluting when off duty to be abolished.

(7) Use of honorific titles for officers to be abolished and replaced by 'Mr General', Mr Colonel, etc.

Officers prohibited from addressing soldiers by the familiar *ty* ['thou', second person singular pronoun, used to address children, pets and serfs – *author*]. The Order to be read out to all units.[13]

In effect, Order No. 1 placed the entire army under the political control, if not the operational command, of the Petrograd Soviet. The consequences were to be profound.

With the almost simultaneous formation of the Provisional Committee of the Duma – in effect the pupa of the first Provisional Government – and of the Soviet of Workers' and Soldiers' Deputies, the first steps had been taken towards the development of what came to be called 'dual power' (*dvoevlastie*). The term was coined to describe the uneasy working relationship between the Provisional Governments which, nominally at any rate, exercised political power in Russia between the February and October Revolutions, and the Executive Committee of the Petrograd Soviet, which held *de facto* power by virtue of the popular backing and allegiance of the majority of the capital's citizens and soldiers. As will be seen, at that point the leaders of the Soviet did not wish to assume governmental power themselves, preferring to maintain a kind of 'watchdog' role over the actions of the Provisional Government.

While all this was going on, however, Nicholas was still stuck in his railway siding at Pskov, nominally still Tsar and Autocrat of All Russia. On the morning of 2 March, a two-man delegation from the Duma Committee, consisting of the right-wing deputy, Vasilii Shulgin (1878–1976), and the leader of the Octobrist Party, Aleksandr Guchkov (1862–1936), set off for Pskov, armed with a mandate to persuade the tsar to abdicate in favour of his son, the tsarevich Aleksei, with Nicholas's younger brother, Grand-Duke Mikhail (1878–1918), as regent. However, the final signal to Nicholas to throw in the royal towel came, not from the Duma delegates, but from General Alekseev, Chief of the General Staff and acting Commander-in-Chief. The latter, having been assured by Duma President, Mikhail Rodzyanko (1859–1924), that a new government would consist of responsible Duma politicians, and *not* the leaders of the Soviet, gave what amounted to more or less an ultimatum to the tsar that he should do the decent thing and resign both his military command and his imperial office. At that stage, Nicholas had no realistic choice in the matter, and was almost certainly resigned to the inevitable in any case. In fact, the prospect of shedding the burdens of office, even if they *were* granted to him by God, was probably a great relief. The Almighty, as far as we know, was not consulted. Those who were consulted, however, were the other officers of the General Staff, who were instructed by Alekseev to cable their own opinions to Pskov immediately. The responses were unanimous. After reading them, at around three o'clock in the afternoon of Thursday 2 March, Nicholas announced his decision to abdicate in favour of his son, Aleksei, and retired to his cabin. This he did with apparent equanimity, but, after consulting with the family physician for a prognosis relating to Aleksei's future health, Nicholas changed his mind, and altered his abdication pronouncement, passing the crown to his younger brother, Grand-Duke Mikhail, who was also not consulted.

The wording of the abdication announcement, composed by Nicholas himself, makes it absolutely clear that the only motive behind his decision was his concern that the war might be better fought to a victorious conclusion. His only passing reference to the 'internal disturbances' was to the effect that they might have 'a calamitous effect on the future conduct of the persistent war'. He then went on to explain that he was passing the crown to 'Our Brother', because he did not wish to be parted from 'Our beloved Son'. Having justified his decision, Nicholas then had the effrontery to continue:

> We enjoin Our Brother to conduct the affairs of the state in complete and inviolable union with the representatives of the people in the legislative bodies on the principles to be established by them, and to take an inviolable oath to this effect.[14]

If only Nicholas had been sensible enough to do just that at any point during the preceding decade, instead of sticking stubbornly to the mediaeval concept of divine right, brushing aside his best advisers and ignoring the voice of the people, then it is just conceivable that things might have turned out differently. For the state that the country was in, for the millions of deaths at the front, for the total breakdown of society, for his own complete isolation, Nicholas had no one to blame but himself. Appropriately, or despairingly, he ended his proclamation with the words, 'God help Russia.'

Having thus relinquished the throne of the world's largest land empire, Citizen Romanov went for a stroll, returned to his carriage, took afternoon tea and smoked a cigarette. When Guchkov and Shulgin arrived in Pskov late in the evening, both their presence and their message from the Provisional Committee of the Duma were superfluous to needs. The deed had already been done; though with the difference that the new tsar-designate was not Aleksei, but Mikhail. Some historians have over-pedantically argued that in passing the poisoned imperial chalice to his brother, Nicholas was performing an illegal act, in so far as the law on the royal succession, promulgated by the Emperor Paul in 1797, quite clearly specified the order of succession through the male line of the house of Romanov.

Had Nicholas been without a male heir, then the mantle would have fallen automatically on Mikhail. However, Nicholas *did* have a legitimate heir, and therefore Nicholas's nomination of Mikhail was constitutionally invalid. The argument is, of course, fatuous. The logic of it is that Paul's law was *also* invalid, in that it overturned the succession law of Peter the Great, which, it will be remembered, allowed each monarch to designate his own successor and caused much dynastic confusion in the mid-eighteenth century (see Chapters 4 and 5). But the principal flaw in the argument is that it overlooks the fact that the Fundamental Laws of the Russian Empire invested supreme power in the sovereign autocrat to do just whatever he liked. That, as has been said elsewhere in this book, is in the very nature of autocratic rule. If the Emperor Caligula wished to make his horse a senator, what was there to stop the Emperor Nicholas making his brother tsar? But in the final analysis, all these constitutional arguments fail to recognise that in a revolutionary situation, by definition, the established laws, values and procedures of the state no longer operate. There are no 'rules of engagement' in a revolution.

Ultimately, of course, none of this mattered, as Mikhail refused to accept the throne in any case. After listening to both republican and monarchist arguments put to him by members of the newly formed Provisional Government, Mikhail, not the brightest of intellects – in fact, if anything, even dimmer than his elder brother – at least had the literary skills necessary to read the writing on the wall that the dynasty was finally doomed. Fearing for his own personal safety, should he accept, he graciously, and prudently, declined his brother's generous offer. In 1613, after two decades of bloody national turmoil, Mikhail Fëdorovich Romanov had been selected by a popular assembly to inaugurate a new reigning dynasty. On 3 March 1917, after three years' war and eight days' popular unrest, Mikhail Aleksandrovich Romanov ended it.

Interpretations

Such earth-shaking events as the destruction of the 300-year-old royal house of Romanov, the collapse of the world's biggest empire in the throes of the hitherto most bloody war in history, and the demonstration of the devastating power of the popular forces which brought that Revolution about, have naturally been the subject of many differing interpretations. As mentioned above, there are arguments and counter-arguments about the cruciality of the Great War in relation to the Revolution, some saying that if there had been no war, there would have been no revolution, others that a revolution was on the cards in any case, and the war simply accelerated its onset. Many of the major actors in the drama of 1917, those who were eventually to end up on the losing side in the Bolshevik Revolution of October, spent the rest of their lives in foreign emigration, mulling over their defeat and writing their memoirs. People such as Milyukov, Kerenskii, Purishkevich, Rodzyanko, Sukhanov and other superannuated has-beens obviously had their own axes to grind, and saw the Revolution through the distorting prism of their own personal experiences.[15] Many of their accounts are understandably self-seeking, self-justifying and self-exculpatory to a degree which automatically debars them from any claim to impartiality or objectivity, and must therefore be treated with a good deal of circumspection.

In the Soviet Union, from the late 1920s to the 1980s, the historiography of both the February and October Revolutions was totally dominated by a strictly Marxist-Leninist (that is to say, Stalinist) methodology, according to which they were seen as the inevitable climax of a process of historical development governed by scientific laws, inexorable economic forces and the dynamics of class struggle. In this dogmatic view, even the February Revolution, which most non-Soviet historians agree was distinguished by its spontaneous, elemental, leaderless, unplanned nature – a genuine plebeian revolt of the masses against a corrupt and tyrannical regime that was morally and politically bankrupt – was attributed to the avant-garde role of the Bolshevik Party under the wise leadership of Vladimir Ilyich Lenin. In his peerless *History of the Russian Revolution*, even Trotskii, no friend of the Stalinist school, and not even a Bolshevik at the time of the February Revolution, later wrote: 'To the question, Who led the February revolution? we can then answer definitely enough: Conscious and tempered workers led for the most part by the party of Lenin.'[16]

While Trotskii typically overstates his case somewhat, there is in fact less of a contradiction than meets the eye between what he contemptuously dismisses as 'the mystic doctrine of spontaneousness'[17] and his own view of the leading role of politically conscious workers in the February days. Note that he does not say that it was the *Bolsheviks* who actually 'led' the Revolution, in the sense of organising, marshalling and marching at the head of the columns of militant factory workers, in the same way that Bolshevik commissars were to command squadrons of Red Guards during the October Revolution. What he does suggest is that the undoubted militancy of the Petrograd workers and the highly political nature of their demands, as well as the rapidity and enthusiasm of their self-mobilisation, were in no small measure due to the relentless nature of the unremitting campaign of agitation and propaganda which Bolshevik activists had been maintaining at shop-floor level ever since 1905. It was noted in the previous chapter how Lenin opposed the so-called 'liquidators' within the Social-Democratic movement in their wish to eliminate the underground party network and cease from seditious activities. His persistence, and that of the grass-roots activists, in not doing so was rewarded, paradoxically, by the spontaneous, ideologically fired-up manner in which the workers came out onto the streets in that last week of February.

That is not to say that the workers' revolution of February 1917 was an orderly, disciplined affair. On the one hand there were the peaceful marches and the calls for the overthrow of the tsar, an end to the war, more bread, the waving of the red flag, the singing of the 'Marseillaise', the toppling of royal statues and other effigies of Romanov rule. On the other, there were widespread looting and pillage, gratuitous vandalism, drunkenness, purposeless violence, rioting and 'revenge' killings – in fact an orgy of urban anarchy in which the 'class struggle' could be tragically reduced to the unprovoked murder of innocent bystanders for failing to sport a red rosette or for wearing the polished shoes and the pince-nez of the hated 'bourgeoisie'. In fact, what the Marxists called the 'bourgeois-democratic revolution', at times had all the appearance, atmosphere and accoutrements of a rampaging mob of ignorant, drunken pugilists looking for a fight. But then, revolutions are rarely gentlemanly affairs.

Some commentators, intellectually unable to come to terms with the idea that oppressive governments are on occasion overthrown by the spontaneous action of the masses, have questioned whether a revolution in the proper sense of the term actually did occur in February 1917 at all! This line of thinking is most controversially articulated by George Katkov, who pooh-poohs the assumption of 'spontaneity' as the explanation for the strength and scope of the February demonstrations in Petrograd as 'wholly gratuitous'.[18] This is uncharacteristically reminiscent of Trotskii's similar dismissal just quoted, but Katkov seeks his explanation not among the 'conscious and tempered workers' of Marxist-Leninist myth. According to Katkov, the abdication of Nicholas Romanov, whom he regards as a rather saintly, ill-served figure, was precipitated by a conspiracy orchestrated by a 'freemasonry' of self-seeking businessmen and treacherous liberal politicians, and by the German Foreign Office and military High Command, which together financially underwrote the subversion of Russia's war effort as part of their dastardly *Revolutionierungspolitik*.[19] However, Russian masons and German marks are not sufficient grounds for denying that the accumulated activities of striking workers, mutinous soldiers, revolutionary activists, anti-government politicians – all leading to the abdication of the tsar, the arrest of his Council of Ministers and the total collapse of all the institutions of tsarist authority – do not add up in common-sense terms to a 'revolution'. If, according to Katkov, theories of the spontaneity of the revolution must be dismissed as 'wholly gratuitous', then so must the evidence for his own counter-theories be equally firmly rejected as wholly exiguous.

Since Katkov's book was published in 1967, a whole school of western historians, less beholden to the old 'émigré-liberal' camp, but equally rejecting the institutionalised falsehoods and ideological gobbledegook of official Soviet writing, has produced an impressive amount of scholarship in which the Russian Revolutions have been investigated, using a combination of traditional historiography, economic analysis, sociological inquiry and the methodology of political science. What has emerged has been a refreshingly dispassionate and disinterested view – based on meticulous research – of the Revolutions 'from below', which demonstrates the full social complexity, the fluctuating rhythm, and the regional variety of the cataclysm which overtook the Romanov Empire in February 1917 and beyond.[20] In post-Soviet Russia, too, the old ideological shackles have been cast off, and the unlocking of the archives has opened up exciting new prospects for the study of the Revolution and its antecedents. However, in the rush to set the historical record straight after decades of Communist Party control and censorship, there is often an unseemly tendency to resurrect fallen idols of the old regime, to rehabilitate dishonoured figures of the past, and to wallow in a misplaced nostalgia for the symbols and totems of the historically bankrupt imperial social and political order. In place of the monolithism of Marxist-Leninism, there is now a multiplicity of mixed-quality interpretations which may still sometimes lead to the baby of truth being thrown out with the historical bathwater. Changing the metaphor, the eminent Russian historian, V. P. Buldakov, has recently written of fresh interpretations of the Revolution: 'The writing of history, long accustomed to the role of handmaiden of the state, now appears as a prostitute walking the streets of political pluralism.'[21]

The reigning Romanov dynasty was now at an end, though its *disjecta membra* and its assorted scions are still scattered around the world. What, though, of the empire over which it ruled? And what of the regime which replaced it?

Red epilogue

The story of how Russia acquired its enormous empire, spreading its tentacles from the Baltic seaboard to the Bering Strait, and from Archangelsk to Azerbaidzhan, gathering under Moscow's and St Petersburg's domination a polyglot host of nations and non-Russian peoples, has been told in the previous chapters. Having become master of these vast territories and their populations, the rulers then had the task of administering, governing and also exploiting them to the advantage of the metropolitan power. In the process – and this is one that is common to the history of all empires – the imperial authorities incurred the resentment, the dissatisfaction, the rancour and ultimately the hatred of the colonised peoples. Over the centuries, such anger and resentment expressed itself in various manifestations of anti-Russian opposition and in repeated calls for a greater or lesser degree of autonomy or outright independence from the centre. This yearning for national independence is simply a part of the universal longing for individual, personal freedom writ large. But unfortunately, while the colonial powers will defend their own liberties and independence to the last, they do not always – until compelled to do so – extend the same opportunity to those nations they have colonised or those peoples they have enslaved. It is, however, the fate of all empires to decline and fall, and this was no less true of the Romanov Empire than it was of the Roman, the Mongol, the Ottoman or the British. The hubris of centralised power is always followed inexorably by the nemesis of internal decay, dismemberment and dispersal. The process of dispersal, of the eventual winning of independence by an empire's once constituent parts, may or may not be conducted in an orderly, relatively civilised fashion, as yesterday's nationalist terrorists become tomorrow's heads of state, but it is always preceded by a long process of nationalist uprisings, protests, confrontations and anti-colonial wars.

Following the abdication of Nicholas II and the renunciation of the throne by Grand Duke Mikhail in March 1917, it was inevitable that all the administrative apparatus of the old regime would collapse in chaotic disarray. The authority of the bureaucracy, the police, the provincial governors, the colonial satraps and their staffs, and the local councils vanished as the insurgent people set up their own committees, their own elected leaders, their regional assemblies and their soviets. Even the army, which disintegrated rapidly after the passing of the Petrograd Soviet's Order No. 1, was, though technically under the control of the Soviet, becoming more like a conglomeration of semi-independent, demobilised or deserting desperadoes, without control, without leadership and now fully armed, not just with weapons, but with their civic freedoms guaranteed.

In the case of the non-Russian peoples, the opportunity for gaining or regaining their independence was eagerly seized, with no proper centralised authority to snatch it back. The writ of the Provisional Governments which nominally ruled Russia after the February Revolution did not run much further than the two capitals and the central European provinces, and even here, the machinery of coercion and control was broken, and there was little that the sorry remnants of the old authorities could do to bring the myriad individual parts of the country to order. In Russian terminology, *samoderzhavie* (autocracy) had given way to *samoupravlenie* (self-government), though *samoupravlenie* itself often gave way to *samovolie*, which means something like self-will, licence or even anarchical conduct. This meant, of course, that the bandwagon of national independence in the non-Russian borderlands was on the roll. But the whole complex, explosive, exciting and often savage process whereby independence was fought over, won, lost, regained – sometimes temporarily, sometimes permanently, sometimes never – among the many nations, peoples, ethnic groups and territorial units in the vast melting pot of the old empire is much too involved, much too labyrinthine to enter into at this point. The story of the break-up of the Russian Empire during the Civil War between 1918 and 1921, and its eventual reconstitution as the Communist-dominated Union of Soviet Socialist Republics in 1922 – a new 'Red Empire', also doomed to disintegration – must wait for another volume.[22]

As far as the central government of the country is concerned, the picture that emerged was one of continuing political uncertainty, ideological rivalry, ineffectual administration, split loyalties, confusion, unresolved class struggle and an even greater social polarisation in what Lenin described in April 1917 as 'the freest of all the belligerent countries in the world'.[23] It goes without saying that, in view of later world history, the most significant trend to develop throughout the spring, summer and early autumn was the steady growth in the popular support and influence on the course of events of Lenin's Bolshevik Party. When he returned to Petrograd from his Swiss exile on 3 April, political power was in effect split, or shared, between the first Provisional Government and the Petrograd Soviet of Worker's and Soldiers' Deputies in the arrangement known as 'dual power'. As the year ran on, it became increasingly obvious that the first, second and third Provisional Governments, like that of Nicholas II before them, were becoming more and more detached from the will of the still rebellious people. Although they passed a whole tranche of progressive legislation granting civil, political, religious and cultural freedoms, individual and collective amnesties and human rights, on the two key issues of Russia's continuing participation in the First World War, and of the redistribution of private land among the peasantry, the Provisional Governments, which represented the economic interests of big business and the landowning classes, remained fatally indecisive.

The mood of the masses was resolutely opposed to Russia's remaining in the war, as the Provisional Government had promised the allies it would. And the peasants, ever more insistent in their demands, and in any case taking the law into their own hands in a campaign of land seizures, occupations and sequestration of the nobles' estates, were once more on the rampage, and, as indicated earlier, there was precious little that what remained of the local authorities could do about it. The peasants now *were* the local authorities. The workers' and peasants' priorities were unambiguously displayed on their crimson banners and in their ubiquitous slogan of 'Bread! Peace! Land!' Another popular slogan, coined by Lenin – 'All Power to the Soviets!' – was both a clear indication of the people's impatience with the havering and hesitation of the Provisional Government, and a call for the scrapping of so-called 'dual power' (which in effect meant no power at all), the abolition of the 'bourgeois' Provisional Government and the transfer of all political power to the representative body of the revolutionary people, the Soviets. The leaders of the Petrograd Soviet, however, seemed reluctant to accept power, even when it was almost thrust upon them by a population that was becoming more pressing, more radical, more militant than even the leadership of the extremist Bolsheviks. Even Lenin, following massive demonstrations in early July, appealed to the angry crowds to go home as he judged the time to be inappropriate to seize power.

However, by early October, after the failure of what appears to have been an attempt at a right-wing military *Putsch* led by the army's Commander-in-Chief, General Kornilov (1870–1918), and after the Bolsheviks had gained a sizeable majority on both the Petrograd and the Moscow Soviets, Lenin persuaded his Party's Central Committee to vote in favour of an immediate armed seizure of power organised by the newly established Military-Revolutionary Committee of the Petrograd Soviet. The Prime Minister of the last Provisional Government, Aleksandr Kerenskii, seemed – no, *was* – powerless to prevent preparations for the coup, which were no secret once the decision was made. Working-class militancy, rural revolt, military meltdown, rocketing inflation and unrest in the borderlands all swelled the tide of revolution that was swirling around Kerenskii's boots. Reluctance to settle the land problem, procrastination over holding elections to a Constituent Assembly, and, above all, continuation of the war, clearly demonstrated the legalistically minded and increasingly arrogant Prime Minister's failure to respond effectively to the revolutionary mood of the masses. Only the Bolsheviks promised immediate 'Bread, Peace and Land'. Only the Bolsheviks could deliver 'All Power to the Soviets'.

The almost bloodless coup took place on the night of 25/26 October as detachments of Red Guards (workers' units armed by the Bolsheviks), having earlier secured the nerve centres of the city – the stations, bridges, post and telegraph offices, banks – invaded the Winter Palace and arrested the members of the last Provisional Government. They were rounded up and marched across the bridge over the Neva and incarcerated in the dungeons of the SS Peter and Paul fortress, in which so many of the Romanovs' enemies had been locked before. Kerenskii was not among them, having made good his escape in a car placed at his disposal by an official of the United States Embassy. At a meeting on the same night of the second All-Russian Congress of Soviets, power was declared to have been taken, and the world's first revolutionary socialist government was established – the Soviet of People's Commissars, with Lenin as its chairman. In the space of only eight months, the once-mighty Russian Empire had been transformed from an absolute autocracy into a revolutionary republic headed by a government of Marxists dedicated to the establishment of international socialism.

The Romanov Empire was dead, but so also were now the hopes, nurtured by some, for the establishment of a western-style constitutional democracy in Russia. Perhaps such hopes were always in vain in a country which never had any traditions of free speech, independent institutions or a civil society, and where an alternating pattern of government oppression and popular revolution was in the natural order of things. At any rate, for a quarter of the twentieth century, under the monstrous tyranny of Iosif Stalin, the long-suffering, stoical, but astonishingly resilient Russian people were to undergo another period of torment and excruciating national agony far worse than that experienced under any of the rulers of the Romanov Empire. That is not to exculpate those rulers from the burden of suffering which they inflicted on their people during the acquisition and administration of their vast domains. A psychopathic serial killer who murders 20 victims is no less a psychopathic serial killer than one who murders 200. It is only a matter of degree.

Postscript

After the abdication of the last Russian Emperor on 2 March 1917, Citizen Nicholas Aleksandrovich Romanov and his family were placed under house arrest in their summer palace at Tsarskoe Selo. Following the October Revolution, the Bolshevik government transferred them to the town of Tobolsk in west Siberia, close to the home village of their murdered mentor, Rasputin. After the outbreak of the Civil War in early 1918, in order to prevent the ex-tsar acting as an involuntary rallying figure for counter-revolutionary 'White' forces, they were moved again, this time to Yekaterinburg in the Urals, and lodged in the commandeered house of a merchant named Nikolai Ipatev. At 2 am on 17 July the family were woken from their sleep and ordered down to the cellar, where they were shot by their guards. Recent evidence seems to confirm information already committed by Trotskii to his personal diary that the execution order came ultimately from Lenin, the man whose elder brother, Aleksandr Ulyanov, had been hanged by Nicholas's father. The bodies were disfigured with acid to prevent recognition, and buried in makeshift graves.

Their remains were discovered in the 1990s and subjected to DNA testing which proved the identity of the exhumed bones beyond scientific doubt. They were later re-interred in a special side-chapel in the SS Peter and Paul Cathedral in the re-named St Petersburg. Attending the funeral was the then Russian President, Boris Yeltsin, the same man who years before, as Communist Party boss of Sverdlovsk (the old Yekaterinburg) had ordered the demolition of the still-standing Ipatev house.

In the year 2000, Nicholas Romanov was officially canonised by the Russian Orthodox Church as Nicholas the Passion Sufferer (*strastoterpets*), also known as Nicholas the Martyr (*muchenik*). But the obsequious obsequies which marked the internment of his and his family's relics can never disguise the fact that in life he was known by his own suffering subjects as Nicholas the Bloody – a fitting, sanguinary sobriquet for the last ruler of the bloodstained Romanov Empire.

At the time of writing, the chemically preserved corpse of Vladimir Lenin still lies on public display in its mausoleum on Moscow's Red Square. So far, press reports and public speculation that President Vladimir Putin intends to put out the mummified manikin for burial elsewhere remain unsubstantiated.[24]

Notes

Chapter 1

1   S. M. Solovëv, *Istoriya Rossii s drevneishikh vremen*, 15 vols (Moscow, 1960), vol. 1, pp. 60–90; V. O. Klyuchevskii, *Kurs russkoi istorii*, 5 vols (Moscow, 1937), vol. 1, pp. 35–65.

2   R. A. French, 'Russians and the Forest', in James H. Bater and R. A. French (eds), *Studies in Russian Historical Geography* (London and New York, 1983), vol. 1, pp. 23–43.

3   Raymond H. Fisher (ed.), *The Voyage of Semen Dezhnev in 1648* (London, 1981).

4   Glynn Barratt, *Russia and the South Pacific, 1696–1840*, vol. 1, *The Russians and Australia* (Vancouver, 1988); vol. 2, *Southern and Eastern Polynesia* (Vancouver, 1988).

5   See Roger Bartlett (ed.), *Land Commune and Peasant Community in Russia: Communal Forms in Imperial and Early Soviet Russia* (London, 1990), *passim*.

6   Michael T. Florinsky, *Russia: A History and an Interpretation*, 2 vols (New York, 1967), vol. 2, p. 1224.

7   Richard Pipes, *Russia under the Old Regime* (London, 1979), pp. 191–220.

8   Alan Wood, *The Origins of the Russian Revolution, 1861–1917*, 3rd edn (London, 2003), p. 7.

9   Klyuchevskii, op. cit., vol. 1, pp. 20, 21.

10 Figures from G. V. Glinka (ed.), *Aziatskaya Rossiya*, 2 vols (St Petersburg, 1914), vol. 1, pp. 64–92.

11 For a fuller discussion, see Geoffrey Hosking, *Russia: Empire and People, 1552–1917* (London, 1997), pp. xix–xxviii.

Chapter 2

1   A. D. Stokes, 'Kievan Russia', in Robert Auty and Dimitri Obolensky (eds), *An Introduction to Russian History* (Cambridge, 1976), p. 51.

2   Samuel H. Cross (ed.), *The Russian Primary Chronicle: Laurentian Text* (Cambridge, MA., 1930), pp. 144–5.

3   ibid., pp. 180–1. Russian text in N. K. Gudzii (ed.), *Khrestomatiya po drevnei russkoi literature* (Moscow, 1962), p. 18. The chronicler calculates that Vladimir kept '300 concubines in Vyshgorod, 300 in Belgorod and 200 in Berestovo', ibid.

4   *Slovo <<O zakone i blagodati>>*, in Gudzii, op. cit., pp. 30–32.

5   Michael T. Florinsky, *Russia: A History and an Interpretation*, 2 vols (New York, 1967), vol. 1, p. 31.

6   *Povest' o razorenii Batyem Ryazani v 1237*, in Gudzii, op. cit., pp. 146–54.

7   'Tatar' is a generic name for various Turkic-speaking peoples of the Mongol Empire established in northern China by Chenghiz Khan in the early thirteenth century. Most of the troops employed by Chenghiz Khan (himself a Mongol) were Tatar. Although the two terms, Mongol and Tatar, are technically distinct, they are often used interchangeably in Russian historiography, and will be so deployed in this book. The Russian spelling 'Tatar' is preferred to the English 'Tartar'.

8   *Povest' o bitve na reke Kalke*, in Gudzii, op. cit., p. 145. NB: The mediaeval Russian chronicles date the years from the Old Testament myth of the creation of the world. According to this mixture of biblical, early Christian and mediaeval calendric calculation, the year 6731 figures out at AD 1223.

9   John Fennell, *The Crisis of Medieval Russia, 1200–1304* (London, 1983), p. 121.

10 Russian text in Gudzii, op. cit., pp. 171–8.

11 I. Ya. Foinitskii, *Uchenie o nakazanii v svyazi s tyur'movedeniem* (St Petersburg, 1889), p. 158.

12 For a full discussion, see Gustave Alef, 'The Adoption of the Muscovite Two-headed Eagle: A Discordant View', *Speculum*, 41 (1966), pp. 1–21.

13 Apollinaris (d. AD 390): a controversial theologian whose teaching on the non-human nature of the mind of Christ was condemned by several Church councils, but later evolved into

Monophytism, which even denied the human nature of Christ's body. The 'ecumenical' Council of Florence in 1439 agreed the unification of the eastern and western churches under papal leadership, settled some old doctrinal disputes, but allowed the continuing use of separate liturgies. However, when news of this reached Moscow, it was received with horror. Metropolitan Isodore, who had led the Russian delegation to Florence, was stripped of office and imprisoned in the Kremlin. Any idea of a rapprochement with Rome has remained anathema to the Russian Church throughout its history.

[14] See the chapter on the origins and implications of the doctrine in I. Yu. Budovnits, *Russkaya publitsistika XVI veka* (Moscow and Leningrad, 1947), pp. 167–87, quotation p. 172.

[15] The Juadaisers were a small sect, originating in Novgorod in the late 1470s, which denied the divinity of Christ, rejected the Trinity, espoused a kind of iconoclasm, and were critical of monasticism and the Orthodox hierarchy. Although they were viciously persecuted by the official church authorities, Ivan himself took a fairly lenient attitude towards them, as did Nil Sorskii and his followers, the latter because they believed it was the work of God, not man, to condemn heretics; the former because of the Judaisers' criticism of monastic property owner-ship.

[16] Florinsky, op. cit., vol. 2, p. 208.

[17] The prime example is a series of angry, ferocious philippics directed at his erstwhile loyal lieutenant, Prince Andrei Kurbskii, who in 1564 defected to Lithuania, with which Ivan was then at war. Despite the fact that the letters' authenticity has been recently impugned, the famous 'Ivan–Kurbskii correspondence' remains one of the outstanding pieces of mediaeval Russian lit-erature; not that there is much competition. See J. L. I. Fennell (ed.) with translation, *The Correspondence between Prince A. M. Kurbsky and Tsar Ivan IV of Russia, 1564–1579* (Cambridge, 1963).

[18] W. F. Ryan, 'Introduction' to D. E. Kozhanchikov (ed.), *Stoglav* (St Petersburg, 1863, reprinted Letchworth, 1971), p. 2.

[19] R. G. Skrynnikov, 'Podgotovka i nachalo sibirskoi ekspeditsii Yermaka', *Voprosy istorii* 8 (1979), pp. 44–56; *idem, Sibirskaya ekspeditsiya Yermaka* (Novosibirsk, 1982).

[20]   V. F. Rzhiga, *I. S. Peresvetov, publitsist XVI v.* (Moscow, 1908); A. A. Zimin, *Sochineniya I. Peresvetova* (Moscow, 1956); see also Budovnits, op. cit., pp. 208–18.

[21]   *Skazanie o Magmete Saltane*, Russian text in Gudzii, op. cit., pp. 261–8; quotation, p. 263.

[22]   Budovnits, op. cit., p. 218.

[23]   The ghoulish-minded may find the lurid details in S. Gorskii, *Zheny Ioanna Groznago* (Moscow[?], 1912), pp. 4–5. Briefly stated, Viskovatyi was hanged by his feet, his head lowered into a cauldron of boiling water, his ears and nose sliced off, his arms severed from his body and his inversely suspended, mutilated living torso finally hacked in half from crotch to cranium. In her recent excellent biography of Ivan, Isabel de Madariaga describes the excrutiating process of Viskovatyi's execution slightly differently, though the details are equally horrific: I. de Madariaga, *Ivan the Terrible* (New Haven and London, 2005), p. 258.

[24]   Maureen Perrie, *The Cult of Ivan the Terrible in Stalin's Russia* (Basingstoke, 2001), p. 5.

[25]   ibid., *passim.*

[26]   M. M. Gerasimov, 'Vozvrashchennye iz proshlogo', *Nauka i zhizn'* 6 (1964), pp. 46–7.

Chapter 3

[1]   Giles Fletcher, 'Of the Russe Commonwealth', in Lloyd E. Berry and Robert O. Crummey (eds), *Rude and Barbarous Kingdom: Russia in the Accounts of Sixteenth-century English Voyagers* (Madison, Milwaukee and London, 1968), p. 140.

[2]   Chester S. L. Dunning, *Russia's First Civil War: The Time of Troubles and the Founding of the Romanov Dynasty* (Pennsylvania, 2001).

[3]   A curious footnote to this episode is that the town bell of Uglich was publicly flogged, had its 'ears' cut off and was also deported to Siberia as punishment for sounding the tocsin which summoned the townsfolk to avenge Dmitrii's death. It remained in the kremlin in Tobolsk in western Siberia until 'repatriated' to its native Uglich in 1892. See S. V. Maximov, *Sibir' i katorga* (St Petersburg, 1900), p. 369.

[4]   Dunning, op. cit. p. 60.

5   V. I. Koretskii, *Formirovanie krepostnogo prava i pervaya krest'yanskaya voina v Rossii* (Moscow, 1975), pp. 127, 131–2.

6   See Maureen Perrie, *Pretenders and Popular Monarchism in Early Modern Russia: The False Tsars of the Time of Troubles* (Cambridge, 1995).

7   Michael T. Florinsky, *Russia: A History and an Interpretation*, 2 vols (New York, 1967), vol. 1, p. 232.

8   V. O. Klyuchevskii, *Kurs russkoi istorii*, 5 vols (Moscow, 1937), vol. 3, p. 141.

9   Florinsky, op. cit., vol. 1, p. 249.

10 The phrase is borrowed from W. Bruce Lincoln, *Conquest of a Continent; Siberia and the Russians* (London, 1994).

11 R. H. Fisher, *The Russian Fur Trade, 1550–1700* (University of California, 1943), p. 29.

12 David Collins, 'Russia's Conquest of Siberia; Evolving Russian and Soviet Interpretations', *European Studies Review*, 12 (1) (1982), pp. 17–43; N. I. Nikitin, 'Voennosluzhilie lyudi i osvoenie Sibiri v XVII veke', *Istoriya SSSR*, 2 (1980), pp. 161–73.

13 N. V. Ustyugov, 'Osnovnye cherty russkoi kolonizatsii Yuzhnoi Zauralya v XVIII v.', in *Voprosy Istorii Sibiri i Dal'nego Vostoka* (Novosibirsk, 1961), pp. 67–8.

14 For a more detailed discussion, see the present author's 'From Conquest to Revolution: The Historical Dimension', in Alan Wood (ed.), *Siberia: Problems and Prospects for Regional Development* (London, 1987), pp. 36–47.

15 For a rich collection of primary sources documenting this process, see Basil Dmytryshyn, E. A. P. Crownhart-Vaughan and Thomas Vaughan (eds and translators), *Russia's Conquest of Siberia: A Documentary Record*, vol. 1, *1558–1700* (Portland, Oregon, 1985). On the historiographical debate, see Collins, op. cit.

16 There are, for instance, only six short references to the Old Believers in Richard Pipes' *Russia Under the Old Regime* (London, 1974). Geoffrey Hosking is rather more generous, and more perceptive, in his *Russia: People and Empire, 1552–1917* (London, 1997), esp. pp. 64–74. Paul Dukes makes some interesting comparisons between Russia's mid-seventeenth-century religious crisis and those in western Europe at the same time: see his *The Making of Russian Absolutism, 1613–1801*, 2nd edn (London and New York, 1990), pp. 58–62.

[17] E. Lampert, *Studies in Rebellion* (London, 1957), p. 12.

[18] For the full text, see A. N. Robinson, *Zhizneopisaniya Avvakuma i Epifaniya: issledovaniya i teksty* (Moscow, 1963). There is no adequate English translation, but see Jane Harrison and Hope Mirrlees (eds and translators), *Life of Archpriest Avvakum by Himself* (London, 1924). A discussion of Avvakum's historical significance and literary achievement is to be found in Alan Wood, 'Archpriest Avvakum and the Russian Church Schism', *Exeter Tapes*, R790, 1979; see also *idem*, 'Avvakum's Siberian Exile', in Alan Wood (ed.), *The Development of Siberia: People and Resources* (London, 1989), pp. 11–34. The fullest and most erudite account of Avvakum's role in the great Schism remains Pierre Pascal, *Avvakum et le débuts du raskol. La crise religieuse au XVIIe siècle en Russie* (Paris, 1938).

[19] Pascal, op. cit., p. 545.

Chapter 4

[1] Paul Dukes, *A History of Russia: c.882–1996*, 3rd edn (Basingstoke, 1998), p. 85.

[2] Easily the best analysis of Sofiya's regency is Lindsey Hughes, *Sophia, Regent of Russia, 1657–1704* (New Haven, 1990). NB: the dates in the title refer to Sofiya's life, not the period of her regency.

[3] Lindsey Hughes, *Russia in the Age of Peter the Great* (New Haven and London, 1998), pp. 8–20.

[4] V. O. Klyuchevskii, *Kurs russkoi istorii*, 5 vols (Moscow, 1937), vol. 4, p. 21.

[5] William Bray (ed.), *The Diary of John Evelyn*, 2 vols (London, 1966), vol. 2, p. 351.

[6] Hughes, op. cit. (1998), p. 241.

[7] Johann Georg Korb, *Diary of an Austrian Secretary of Legation at the Court of Czar Peter the Great* (London, 1863), abridged excerpts in B. Dmytryshyn (ed.), *Imperial Russia: A Source Book, 1700–1917* (New York and London, 1967), pp. 1–13.

[8] Hughes, op. cit. (1998), p. 63.

[9] Korb, quoted in Klyuchevskii, op. cit., vol. 4, p. 67.

[10] ibid., p. 69.

[11] *Polnoe sobranie zakonov rossiiskoi imperii* (*PSZRI*), vol. 4, no. 2321.

[12] Fik's distinguished bureaucratic career came to an end in 1730. He was accused of plotting against the accession of the Empress Anna Ivanovna and exiled to Siberia where he spent 11 years. See F. G. Safronov, 'Ssylka v Vostochnuyu Sibir' v pervoi polovine XVIII v.', in L. M. Goryushkin *et al.* (eds), *Ssylka i katorga v Sibiri (XVIII-nachalo XX v.)* (Novosibirsk, 1975), pp. 26–32; also Alan Wood, 'Siberian Exile in the Eighteenth Century', *Siberica*, 1 (1) (1990), pp. 38–63.

[13] A 'soul' (*dusha*) was the standard unit of calculation in the taking of the census in Russia, rather than a body or a head (poll) count. Though it had no religious significance, the impious notion of taxing the sacred essence of a person's 'soul' was regarded by the devout Russian peasantry as adding religious insult to fiscal injury. Figures calculated by Paul Milyukov, cited in Michael T. Florinsky, *Russia: A History and an Interpretation*, 2 vols (New York, 1967), vol. 1, p. 364.

[14] Florinsky, op. cit., vol. 1, p. 413.

[15] Hughes, op. cit. (1998), p. 307.

[16] Aleksandr Pushkin, *Mednyi vsadnik*, in *idem, Sochineniya v trëkh tomakh*, vol. 2 (Moscow, 1955), pp. 251–2. Translation mine. The poem was personally censored by Tsar Nicholas I, and published in full only in 1837, after the author's death. For an English prose translation of the full text, see John Fennell (ed. and translator), *Pushkin. Selected Verse* (Harmondsworth, 1964), pp. 233–55.

Chapter 5

[1] The phrase is used in a recorded discussion between Isabel de Madariaga and Lucien Lewitter on 'Peter, Catherine and the Russian State', *Audio Learning Tapes* (Sussex University, no date).

[2] For details of Menshikov's exile in Siberia, where he died in 1729, see N. A. Minenko, *Uzniki Berëzovskogo ostroga*, in L. M. Goryushkin (ed.), *Ssylka i katorga v Sibiri (XVIII–nachalo XX v.)* (Novosibirsk, 1975), pp. 59–62. The famous painting by the Russian artist, V. I. Surikov, 'Menshikov in Berëzov' (1883) hangs in the Tretyakov Gallery in Moscow.

[3] An account of the circumstances surrounding Anna's accession is to be found in Christof von Manstein, *Memoirs of Russia:*

Historical, Political, Military, 1727–44 (London, 1770), pp. 25–36.

4 Minenko, op. cit., pp. 68–9; Alan Wood, 'Siberia in the Eighteenth Century', *Siberica*, 1 (1), p. 49; S. V. Maximov, *Sibir' i katorga*, 3rd edn (St Petersburg, 1900), p. 383.

5 The circumstances of Elizabeth's coup are described in Manstein, op. cit., pp. 264–326.

6 Quoted in A. D. Kolesnikov, 'Ssylka i zaselenie Sibiri', in Goryushkin, op. cit., p. 42.

7 Michael T. Florinsky, *Russia: A History and an Interpretation*, 2 vols (New York, 1967), vol. 1, p. 480.

8 D. S. Mirsky, *A History of Russian Literature* (London, 1949, reprinted 1964), p. 41.

9 J. L. Black, 'J.-G. Gmelin and G.-F. Müller in Siberia, 1733–43', in Alan Wood and R. A. French (eds), *The Development of Siberia: People and Resources* (Basingstoke, 1989), pp. 38–9.

10 There is a large literature on the life and work of Gerhard Müller in Russian, German and English. For an entertaining account of Müller's and Gmelin's experience and personal relations in Siberia, see Black, op. cit., pp. 35–49; also J. L. Black and D. K. Buse, *G.-F. Müller in Siberia, 1733–1743* (Fairbanks, 1989). Müller's monumental history of Siberia has recently been edited and reprinted in three volumes by the Russian Academy of Sciences' Institute of Ethnology and Anthropology as, G. F. Miller, *Istoriya Sibiri*, 3 vols (Moscow, 1999, 2000, 2001).

11 J. L. Black, 'Rediscovering Siberia in the Eighteenth Century: G. F. Müller and the *Monthly Compositions, 1755–1764*', *Siberica*, 1 (2) (Winter 1990–91), pp. 112–26.

12 See Carol S. Leonard, *Reform and Regicide: the Reign of Peter III of Russia* (Bloomington and Indianapolis, 1993), *passim*.

Chapter 6

1 V. O. Klyuchevskii, *Kurs russkoi istorii*, 5 vols (Moscow, 1937), vol. 5, p. 54.

2 Translated extracts from the *Nakaz* are contained in Basil Dmytryshyn (ed.), *Imperial Russia: A Source Book* (New York and London, 1967), pp. 67–94. See also Paul Dukes, *Catherine the Great and the Russian Nobility* (Cambridge, 1967).

3 Dmytryshyn, op. cit., pp. 67–94.

4   '*Parturiunt montes, nascetur ridiculus mus*', Horace, *Ars poetica*, 139.

5   Klyuchevskii, op. cit., vol. 5, pp. 81–2.

6   Translated excerpts from the archive materials, illustrating the opinions of nobles from central and northern Russia and Ukraine, a discussion of serfdom, the views of merchants and townsmen, and instructions given to representatives of the state peasants can be found in George Vernadsky (ed.), *A Source Book for Russian History from Early Times to 1917*, 3 vols (New Haven and London, 1972), vol. 2, pp. 431–41.

7   Klyuchevskii, op. cit., vol. 5, p. 83.

8   Quoted in David Warnes, *Chronicle of the Russian Tsars* (London, 1999), p. 134.

9   In Russian historical terminology, the Russian suffix '-*shchina*' is often attached to the name of an individual who has lent his name to a particularly notorious, often violent, passage of events in Russian history: e.g. the *Nikolaevshchina* (the reign of Tsar Nicholas I, see Chapter 8) and the *Yezhovshchina* (named after N. I. Yezhov, head of Joseph Stalin's political police, the NKVD, during the 'Great Terror' of the 1930s).

10   On early pretenders, see Maureen Perrie, *Pretenders and Popular Monarchism in Early Modern Russia: The False Tsars of the Time of Troubles* (Cambridge, 1995).

11   The English-language literature on the *Pugachëvshchina* is quite extensive, though a complete history of the rebellion still awaits its chronicler. Among the most useful secondary sources are: John T. Alexander, *Autocratic Politics in a National Crisis: The Imperial Russian Government and Pugachev's Revolt, 1773–1775* (Bloomington, Indiana, and London, 1969); *idem., Catherine the Great: Life and Legend* (New York and Oxford, 1989), pp. 162–83; Isabel de Madariaga, *Russia in the Age of Catherine the Great* (London, 1981), pp. 239–55; Paul Avrich, *Russian Rebels, 1600–1800* (New York, 1972), pp. 180–273; Philip Longworth, *The Cossacks* (London, 1969), pp. 187–224. Russian archival sources are reviewed in R. V. Ovchinnikov, *Krest'yanskaya voina v Rossii v 1773–1775 godakh: Vosstanie Pugacheva* (Leningrad, 1966). Russia's greatest poet, Aleksandr Pushkin, wrote an incomplete history of the Pugachëv rebellion, *Istoriya Pugachevskogo bunta*, 2 vols (St Petersburg, 1834), but is better remembered for his

fictional story based on factual events in the insurgent areas, 'The Captain's Daughter' (*Kapitanskaya dochka*, 1836), English translation in Alexander Pushkin, *The Queen of Spades and Other Stories*, translated by Rosemary Edmonds (London, 1962), pp. 187–317.

12 Russian proverb, 'Out of mud you can make a prince' (*iz gryazi – da v knyazi*). The remark was attributed to Timofei Myasnikov, one of Pugachëv's entourage, quoted in Avrich, op. cit., p. 192. Original text in N. F. Dubrovin, *Pugachev i ego soobshchniki*, 3 vols (St Petersburg, 1884), vol. 1, pp. 218–21.

13 Isabel de Madariaga, 'Catherine II and the Serfs: A Reconsideration of Some Problems', *Slavonic and East European Review*, LII, no. 126 (1974), pp. 34–62.

14 Quoted in Avrich, op. cit., p. 245.

15 For Eric Hobsbawm's discussion of 'social banditry', see his *Bandits* (Harmondsworth, 1971), pp. 1–29 and *passim*.

16 The 'Rules Relating to Measures for the Preservation of National Order and Public Tranquillity' promulgated by Tsar Alexander III in August 1881, following the assassination of his father by Populist terrorists (see Chapters 9 and 10), and the 'Prevention of Terrorism' Act forced through the British Houses of Parliament in 2005, both severely restricting citizens' civil rights, liberties and access to due judicial procedure, are cases in point.

17 Letter to Melchior Grimm, cited in John T. Alexander, *Catherine the Great* (Oxford, 1989), p. 185.

18 D. S. Mirsky, *A History of Russian Literature* (London, 1964), p. 154.

19 Klyuchevskii, op. cit., vol. 5, p. 96.

20 For a translation of the full text of the Charter, see Paul Dukes, *Russia under Catherine the Great: Volume One: Selected Documents on Government and Society* (Newtonville, MA, 1978), pp. 162ff.

21 V. I. Semevskii, *Krest'yane v tsarstvovanii Yekateriny II* (St Petersburg, 1901), quoted in Michael T. Florinsky, *Russia: A History and an Interpretation*, 2 vols (New York, 1967), vol. 1, pp. 575–6.

22 See, for instance, Alexander Polovtsoff, *The Favourites of Catherine the Great* (London, 1940), and Bernard Gip, *The Passions and Lechery of Catherine the Great* (London, 1971), the latter luridly illustrated with photographs of Catherine's 'porno-

graphic furniture'. More scholarly analyses are to be found in de Madariaga, op. cit. (1981), pp. 343–57, and Alexander, op. cit. (1989), pp. 201–26.

23 For further entertaining detail, see Alexander, op. cit. (1989), pp. 337–9.

24 Alexander, de Madariaga and Dukes all seem to concur on this. For the most recent, lengthy, and somewhat inflated encomium of Potëmkin, see Simon Sebag Montefiore, *Prince of Princes: The Life of Potemkin* (London, 2000).

25 Alexander, op. cit. (1989), p. 226.

26 For a detailed analysis of foreign settlement in the late eighteenth century, see R. P. Bartlett, *Human Capital: The Settlement of Foreigners in Russia, 1762–1804* (Cambridge, 1979).

27 Montefiore, op. cit., p. 383.

28 A useful biography is David Marshall Lang, *The First Russian Radical: Alexander Radishchev, 1749–1802* (London, 1959).

29 A. N. Radishchev, *Puteshestvie iz Peterburga v Moskvu* (Moscow/Leningrad, 1964), pp. 185–6.

30 Klyuchevskii, op. cit., vol. 5, pp. 210–12.

Chapter 7

1 Michael T. Florinsky, *Russia: A History and an Interpretation*, 2 vols (New York, 1967), vol. I, p. 623.

2 S. B. Okun', *Istoriya SSSR (Lektsii). Chast' I. Konets XVIII-nachalo XIX veka* (Leningrad, 1974), p. 132.

3 Far the best monograph on Speranskii's life and work remains Marc Raeff, *Michael Speransky, Statesman of Imperial Russia, 1772–1839* (The Hague, 1957). See also his *Siberia and the Reforms of 1822* (Seattle, 1956).

4 *M. M. Speranskii: proekty i zapiski* (Moscow, 1961), pp. 43–4.

5 Quoted in Florinsky, op. cit., vol. 2, p. 675, footnote.

6 R. E. Pipes, 'The Russian Military Colonies', *Journal of Modern History*, 22 (3) (1950), pp. 205–19.

7 Alexander's unofficial beatification is echoed in the resemblance of his features with those of the angel which surmounts the huge Alexander Column in St Petersburg's Palace Square. The monolithic 704-ton column, marking the victory over Napoleon, was suggested by the architect Montferrand, erected in 1832, completed and unveiled in 1834.

8 On Pushkin's bizarre life and character, see T. J. Binyon, *Pushkin: A Biography* (London, 2002).

9 Anatole G. Mazour, *The First Russian Revolution, 1825: The Decembrist Movement* (Stanford, 1961).

10 *Bol'shoi entsiklopedicheskii slovar'* (Moscow, 1994), p. 1256.

11 Quoted in Mazour, op. cit., p. 84.

12 ibid., p. 94.

13 Edited extracts from the texts of Muravëv's constitutional project and Pestel's *Russkaya Pravda,* with useful commentary, are to be found in Marc Raeff, *The Decembrist Movement* (Englewood Cliffs, N.J., 1966), pp. 100–56.

14 Janet M. Hartley, *Alexander I* (London, 1994), p. 202.

15 A. S. Mel'nikova *et al., Konstantinovskii rubl': Novye materialy i issledovaniya* (Moscow, 1991).

Chapter 8

1 English translation, A. E. Presniakov, *Emperor Nicholas I of Russia: The Apogee of Autocracy, 1825–1855* (Gulf Breeze, 1974).

2 *Ssylka v Sibir': Ocherk eya istorii i sovremennago polozheniya* (St Petersburg, 1900), *Prilozheniya,* p. 1. Figures include accompanying family dependents.

3 Nicholas V. Riasanovsky, *Nicholas I and Official Nationality in Russia, 1825–1855* (Berkeley, 1959).

4 Richard Pipes, *Russia under the Old Regime* (Harmondsworth, 1977, reprinted 1978), p. 313.

5 ibid., p. 293.

6 The term 'remarkable decade' is taken from the title of an essay, *Zamechatel'noe desyatiletie,* by P. V. Annenkov, translated by I. R. Titunik (ed. A. P. Mendel) as *The Extraordinary Decade: Literary Memoirs* (Ann Arbor, 1968).

7 Parts of this section are borrowed from the present author's article, 'The Resurgent Russian Intelligentsia', in Bikhu Parekh (ed.), *Dissent and Disorder: Essays in Social Theory* (Toronto, 1971), pp. 81–95, esp. pp. 81–3.

8 Martin Malia, *Alexander Herzen and the Birth of Russian Socialism* (New York, 1965), p. 43.

9 P. Ya. Chaadaev, 'Letters on the Philosophy of History', in Marc Raeff (ed.), *Russian Intellectual History: An Anthology* (New York, 1966), pp. 160–73.

[10] ibid., p. 165.

[11] Chaadaev's *Apology …* is discussed in Andrzej Walicki, *The Slavophile Controversy: History of a Conservative Utopia in Nineteenth-Century Russian Thought* (Oxford, 1975), pp. 105–9.

[12] The *filioque* (Latin, 'and the Son') controversy surrounds the question of whether, in Christian dogma, the Holy Spirit proceeds from the Father *and the Son*. To non-Christians, the point is bafflingly arcane, but it continues to constitute one of the major doctrinal differences between the western and eastern branches of the Church.

[13] Walicki, op. cit., p. 220.

[14] K. S. Aksakov, 'On the Internal State of Russia', in Raeff, op. cit., p. 231.

[15] ibid., pp. 234–9.

[16] For a stimulating comparative analysis of all three, see E. Lampert, *Studies in Rebellion* (London, 1957).

[17] Lampert, op. cit., p. 110.

[18] ibid., p. 41.

[19] Quoted in ibid., p. 82.

[20] The Schlüsselburg fortress was one of the tsarist regime's most dreaded penal institutions. Located 40 miles east of St Petersburg on the edge of Lake Ladoga, it was the place of incarceration, and occasionally execution, of some of Russia's most famous revolutionaries.

[21] V. G. Belinskii, 'Letter to N. V. Gogol', in Raeff, op. cit., pp. 254–6.

[22] Lampert, op. cit., pp. 224–5.

[23] On 'The Birth of Russian Socialism', see Malia, op. cit. *passim*, and Franco Venturi, *Roots of Revolution* (London, 1960), pp. 1–35.

[24] For a recent English translation of his semi-fictional *Zapiski iz mertvogo doma*, see F. Dostoevskii, *The House of the Dead*, trans. by David McDuff (Harmondsworth, 1985).

[25] Michael T. Florinsky, *Russia: A History and an Interpretation*, 2 vols (New York, 1967), vol. 2, p. 850. Marx's *Manifesto* was first published as *Manifest der Kommunistischen Partei* (London, 1848), translated into English in 1888 with a new preface by Engels: K. Marx and F. Engels, *Manifesto of the Communist Party* (reprinted Moscow, 1965).

[26] Presniakov, quoted in S. B. Okun', *Ocherki istorii SSSR: vtoraya chetvert' XIX veka* (Leningrad, 1957), p. 298.

[27] A. V. Nikitenko, *Zapiski i dnevnik* (St Petersburg, 1904), vol. I, p. 553.

Chapter 9

1 See Eric Hobsbawm, *The Age of Capital, 1848–1875* (London, 1962), pp. 1–3 and *passim*. On 'Bourgeois and Proletarians', see Chapter I of K. Marx and F. Engels, *The Manifesto of the Communist Party* (reprinted Moscow, 1965), pp. 39–59.

2 'Rech' Aleksandra II predvoditelyam Moskovskogo dvoryanstva', in S. S. Dmitriev (ed.), *Khrestomatiya po istorii SSSR*, vol. II (Moscow, 1948), p. 11.

3 N. A. Dobrolyubov, 'What is Oblomovshchina?', in *idem, Selected Philosophical Works* (Moscow, 1956), pp. 174–217; quotation, p. 205.

4 Alfred J. Rieber, 'The Politics of Emancipation', in *idem* (ed.), *The Politics of Autocracy: Letters of Alexander II to Prince A. I. Bariatinskii, 1857–1864* (Paris and The Hague, 1966), pp. 15–58.

5 A. K. Dzhigelegov *et al.* (eds) *Velikaya reforma: Russkoe obshchestvo i krest'yanskii vopros v proshlom i nastoyashchem* (Moscow, 1911), vol. 1, p. 258.

6 'Vcherashnii den', chasu v shestom,/ Zashel ya na Sennuyu;/Tam bili zhenshchinu knutom,/Krest'yanku moloduyu ...*, in N. A. Nekrasov, *Stikhotvoreniya* (Moscow, 1965), p. 30.

7 Richard Pipes, *Russia under the Old Regime* (Harmondsworth, 1987), p. 152.

8 'Polozhenie 19 fevralya 1861 g. o krest'yanakh, vyshedshikh iz krepostnoi zavisimosti', in Dmitriev, op. cit., pp. 46–53; translated excerpts in George Vernadsky (ed.), *A Source Book for Russian History from Early Times to 1917*, 3 vols (New Haven and London, 1972), vol. 3, pp. 600–2; the full text of the 'Manifesto' is contained in Basil Dmytryshyn (ed.), *Imperial Russia: A Source Book, 1700–1917* (New York, 1957), pp. 221–5.

9 Original text in Dmitriev, op. cit., p. 46.

10 From an unpublished report in the archives of the Third Section, quoted in E. Lampert, *Sons against Fathers: Studies in Russian Radicalism and Revolution* (Oxford, 1965), p. 32.

11 V. Dal', *Tolkovyi slovar' zhivago russkago yazyka* (St Petersburg and Moscow, 1881), vol. II, pp. 330–1.

12 Alan Wood, 'The Use and Abuse of Administrative Exile to Siberia', *Irish Slavonic Studies*, 6 (1985), pp. 48–56; *idem*, 'Administrative Exile and the Criminals' Commune in Siberia', in Roger Bartlett (ed.), *Land Commune and Peasant Community in*

Russia: Communal Forms in Imperial and Early Soviet Society (Basingstoke, 1990), pp. 395–414.

[13] Russian peasant mores in general are nicely summarised in Orlando Figes, *A People's Tragedy: The Russian Revolution, 1891–1917* (London, 1996), pp. 84–102.

[14] See Daniel Field, *Rebels in the Name of the Tsar* (Boston and London, 1989), pp. 31–111.

[15] W. Bruce Lincoln, *The Great Reforms: Autocracy, Bureaucracy and the Politics of Change in Imperial Russia* (Dekalb, IL, 1990).

[16] The most scholarly account of Russian Populism remains Franco Venturi's *Il Populismo Russo* (Italy, 1952), translated as *Roots of Revolution*, introduced by Isaiah Berlin (London, 1960). It is difficult to envisage how this classic study could be improved on in any significant way.

[17] *Revolyutsionnaya situatsiya v Rossii v 1859–1861 gg.*, 7 vols (Moscow, 1960–78).

[18] N. P. Ogarëv, N. N. Obruchev *et al.*, 'Chto nuzhno narodu?', *Kolokol*, 1 July 1861, p. 102; reproduced in A. V. Zapadov (ed.), *Khrestomatiya po istorii russkoi zhurnalistiki XIX veka* (Moscow, 1965), pp. 232–9.

[19] Text in Dmitriev, op. cit., pp. 96–9.

[20] Venturi, op. cit., p. 129.

[21] Lampert, op. cit., p. 95.

[22] Quoted in Venturi, op. cit., pp. 139–40.

[23] ibid., p. 159.

[24] During the ritual of 'civil execution' (*grazhdanskaya kazn'*), the condemned person is chained to a post on a public scaffold where his sentence is read out to him. He is then made to kneel, bare-headed, stripped of his citizen's rights, a sword broken over his head, and taken back in a tumbrel to the fortress to begin his sentence of imprisonment or exile. For a full description of Chernyshevskii's humiliating treatment, see M. N. Gernet, *Istoriya tsarskoi tyur'my*, 5 vols (Moscow, 1961), vol. 2, pp. 285–9.

[25] Michael Prawdin, *The Unmentionable Nechaev* (London, 1961).

[26] N. Flerovskii, *Polozhenie rabochego klassa v Rossii* (St Petersburg, 1869).

[27] Daniel Field, 'Peasants and Propagandists in the Russian Movement to the People of 1874', *Journal of Modern History*, 59 (1987), pp. 415–38.

28 John J. Stephan, *Sakhalin: A History* (Oxford, 1971), pp. 65–82.

29 James R. Gibson, 'Tsarist Russia in Colonial America', in Alan Wood (ed.), *The History of Siberia: From Russian Conquest to Revolution* (London and New York, 1991), p. 112.

Chapter 10

1 Richard Pipes, *Russia under the Old Regime* (Harmondsworth, 1987), p. 303.

2 Konstantin P. Pobedonostsev, *Reflections of a Russian Statesman* (University of Michigan, 1965), p. 49.

3 K. Marx, 'Preface to the Russian Edition, 1882' of the *Manifesto of the Communist Party* (reprinted Moscow, 1965), p. 11.

4 Translated excerpts from the Statute of 14 August are to be found in George Kennan, *Siberia and The Exile System*, 2 vols (New York, 1981), vol. 2, pp. 507–9.

5 ibid., pp. 29–59.

6 On Siberian exile in general, see Alan Wood, 'Crime and Punishment in the House of the Dead', in Olga Crisp and Linda Edmondson (eds), *Civil Rights in Imperial Russia* (Oxford, 1989), pp. 215–33.

7 Quoted by Hans Rogger, *Russia in the Age of Modernisation and Revolution, 1881–1917* (London, 1983), p. 11.

8 A. E. Lutskii, *Istoriya SSSR, 1861–1917* (Moscow, 1956), pp. 127–8.

9 ibid., p. 123.

10 Full text in S. S. Dmitriev, *Khrestomatiya po istorii SSSR, tom III, 1857–1894* (Moscow, 1948), pp. 432–3.

11 Police Department figures, with further statistical information, reproduced in ibid., pp. 402–8.

12 Hugh Seton-Watson, *The Russian Empire, 1801–1917* (Oxford, 1967), p. 466.

13 Source: P. A. Khromov, *Ekonomicheskoe razvitie Rossii v XIX–XX vekakh* (Moscow, 1950), pp. 453–4.

14 Source: ibid., p. 462.

15 For a scholarly, entertaining account of the building of the 'Trans-Sib', see Steven G. Marks, *Road to Power: The Trans-Siberian Railroad and the Colonization of Asian Russia, 1850–1917* (London, 1991).

16 All statistical information from F. A. Brockhaus and I. A. Efron (eds), *Entsiklopedicheskii slovar': Rossiya* (St Petersburg, 1898), pp. 224–6.

17 This section is a revised and expanded version of part of Chapter 4 of the present author's *The Origins of the Russian Revolution, 1861–1917*, 3rd edn (London, 2003), pp. 27–31.

18 Marx, op. cit., p. 12.

19 Lutskii, op. cit., p. 140.

20 The translation '*Workers* Party', rather than '*Labour* Party' (Russian – *rabochaya partiya*), is preferred here to emphasise the Marxist distinction between industrial 'workers' and 'peasants'.

21 V. I. Lenin, *What is to be Done?* (1902), Penguin Classics edition, introduced by Robert Service (Harmondsworth, 1988), p. 107.

22 ibid., p. 118.

Chapter 11

1 Martin McCauley (ed.), *From Octobrists to Bolsheviks: Imperial Russia 1905–1917* (London, 1984), pp. 46–7.

2 On the security police, see D. C. B. Lieven, 'The Security Police, Civil Rights and the Fate of the Russian Empire, 1855–1917', in Olga Crisp and Linda Edmondson (eds), *Civil Rights in Imperial Russia* (Oxford, 1989), pp. 235–62, and A. T. Vassilyev, *The Ochrana* (London, 1930). See also B. Nikolajewsky, *Aseff the Spy: Russian Terrorist and Police Stool* (New York, 1934), and especially Anna Geifman, *Entangled in Terror: The Azef Affair and the Russian Revolution* (Wilmington, 2000).

3 See Dimitry Pospielovsky, *Russian Police Trade Unionism* (London, 1971).

4 Walter Sablinsky, *The Road to Bloody Sunday* (Princeton, 1976), pp. 247–8.

5 ibid., pp. 264–8. A final figure of 1000 casualties, maximum, seems the safest estimate.

6 ibid., p. 271.

7 Michael T. Florinsky, *Russia: A History and Interpretation*, 2 vols (New York, 1967), vol. 2, p. 1275.

8 For a rather confusing account of the confusion, see Richard Hough, *The Fleet that had to Die* (London, 1958, reprinted 1975), pp. 32–49.

9   John Bushnell, *Mutiny amid Repression: Russian Soldiers and the Revolution of 1905–1906* (Bloomington, 1985).

10 Abbreviated excerpts from the Fundamental Laws are contained in Basil Dmytryshyn (ed.), *Imperial Russia: A Source Book, 1700–1917* (New York, 1967), pp. 317–24.

11 The precise psephological statistics vary according to source, though the differences are minuscule. Figures given here are from E. Oberländer, 'The Role of the Political Parties', in George Katkov *et al.* (eds), *Russia Enters the Twentieth Century* (London, 1971).

12 *Shorter Oxford English Dictionary.*

13 E. A. Lutskii, *Istoriya SSSR, 1861–1917* (Moscow, 1956), p. 265.

14 See Donald W. Treadgold, *The Great Siberian Migration* (Princeton, 1957).

15 L. M. Goryushkin, 'Migration, Settlement and the Rural Economy of Siberia, 1861–1914', in Alan Wood (ed.), *The History of Siberia: From Russian Conquest to Revolution* (London and New York, 1991), pp. 140–57.

16 Unfortunately, M. Melancon, *The Lena Goldfields Massacre and the Crisis of the Late Tsarist State* (Texas, 2006), was not available to me at the time of writing.

17 Quoted by B. R. Bociurkiw, 'Lenin and Religion', in Leonard Schapiro and Peter Reddaway (eds), *Lenin: the Man, the Theorist, the Leader* (London, 1967), pp. 121–3.

18 E. Lampert, *Decadents, Liberals, Revolutionaries: Russia 1900–1918* (Keele, 1969), p. 18.

Chapter 12

1   The capital of the Russian Empire since 1712, St Petersburg was renamed as Petrograd shortly after the outbreak of the war with Germany in 1914. St Petersburg (*Sankt Peterburg*) was thought to be too Germanic-sounding in a time of war with that country. The city was re-renamed as Leningrad in 1924, and reverted to St Petersburg in 1991.

2   Edited text in Thomas Riha (ed.), *Readings in Russian Civilization*, 2 vols (Chicago, 1964), vol. 1, pp. 457–70.

3   Michael T. Florinsky, *Russia: A History and an Interpretation*, 2 vols (New York, 1967), vol. 2, p. 1365.

4   The accounts of Purishkevich and Yusupov are reproduced in
     Andrei Maylunas and Sergei Mironenko, *A Lifelong Passion.
     Nicholas and Alexandra: Their Own Story* (London, 1966), pp.
     494–504.
5   There is a large literature on Rasputin, much of it of doubtful
     value, but see Harold Shukman, *Rasputin* (Stroud, 1997); René
     Füllöp-Miller, *Rasputin, The Holy Devil* (New York, 1928); A. de
     Jonge, *The Life and Times of Grigorii Rasputin* (London, 1982).
     Despite its title, Edvard Radzinsky's melodramatic *Rasputin: The
     Last Word* (London, 2000) is unconvincing in its theatrical
     attempts to reconstruct Rasputin's last moments, based on spec-
     ulation rather than scholarship.
6   This section draws on Chapter 5 of the present author's *The
     Origins of the Russian Revolution, 1861–1917*, 3rd edn (London,
     2003), pp. 39–49.
7   See Lewis H. Siegelbaum, *The Politics of Industrial Mobilization
     in Russia, 1914–1917: A Study of the War-Industries Committees*
     (London and Basingstoke, 1983).
8   For a thoroughly researched and entertaining investigation into
     the relationship between vodka, government and people in
     Russia, see Stephen White, *Russian goes Dry: Alcohol, State and
     Society* (Cambridge, 1996).
9   Police report on social conditions in October 1916, published in
     Krasnyi Arkhiv, 17 (1926), pp. 6–7.
10   Z. A. B. Zeman (ed.), *Germany and the Revolution in Russia,
     1915–1918. Documents from the Archives of the German Foreign
     Ministry* (London, 1958). The whole question of *Revolutionier-
     ungspolitik* is discussed in George Katkov, *Russia, 1917: The
     February Revolution* (London, 1969), pp. 108–73. For a fascinat-
     ing account of the activities of one of the chief go-betweens
     operating clandestinely between the German authorities and
     the Russian revolutionaries, see Z. A. B. Zeman and W. B.
     Scharlau, *Merchant of Revolution: The Life of Alexander Israel
     Helphand (Parvus), 1867–1924* (Oxford, 1965).
11   Maulunas and Mironenko, op. cit., pp. 538–9.
12   Orlando Figes, *A People's Tragedy: The Russian Revolution,
     1891–1917* (London, 1996), p. 307.
13   Order No. 1 was published in the news bulletin of the Petrograd
     Soviet, *Izvestiya*, on 2 March 1917.

14 Full text in George Vernadsky (ed.), *A Source Book for Russian History from Early Times to 1917*, 3 vols (New Haven and London, 1972), vol. 3, p. 883.

15 See, e.g., P. N. Milyukov, *Political Memoirs, 1905–1917* (Ann Arbor, 1967); Alexander Kerensky, *The Kerensky Memoirs: Russia and History's Turning Point* (London, 1966); V. M. Purishkevich, *Dnevnik* (Moscow, 1990); M. V. Rodzianko, *The Reign of Rasputin: An Empire's Collapse* (London, 1927); N. N. Sukhanov, *The Russian Revolution: Eyewitness Account*, 2 vols (London, 1955).

16 Leon Trotsky, *History of the Russian Revolution*, 3 vols (London, 1967), vol. 1, p. 154.

17 ibid., p. 152.

18 Katkov, op. cit., p. 551.

19 ibid., *passim*.

20 Marc Ferro, *The Russian Revolution of February 1917* (Englewood Cliffs, NJ, 1972); *idem, October 1917: A Social History of the Russian Revolution* (London and Boston, 1980); D. Koenker, *Moscow Workers and the 1917 Revolution* (Princeton, 1981); S. A. Smith, *Red Petrograd: Revolution in the Factories, 1917–1918* (Cambridge, 1983); Allan K. Wildman, *The End of the Russian Imperial Army: The Old Army and the Soldiers' Revolt, March–April 1917* (Princeton, 1980), and *The End of the Russian Imperial Army: The Road to Soviet Power and Peace* (Princeton, 1987).

21 V. P. Buldakov, 'The October Revolution: Seventy-five Years On', *European History Quarterly*, 22 (4) (1992), p. 499.

22 Arthur E. Adams, *Bolsheviks in the Ukraine: The Second Campaign, 1918–1919* (New Haven, 1963); Firuz Kazemzadeh, *The Struggle for Transcaucasia, 1917–1921* (New York, 1951); Alexander Garlan Park, *Bolshevism in Turkestan, 1917–1927* (New York, 1957); Richard Pipes, *The Formation of the Soviet Union: Communism and Nationalism, 1917–1923* (Cambridge, MA., 1964); Jonathan D. Smele, *Civil War in Siberia: The Anti-Bolshevik Government of Admiral Kolchak 1918–1920* (Cambridge, 1996); N. G. O. Pereira, *White Siberia: The Politics of Civil War* (Montreal and London, 1996); John J. Stephan, *The Russian Far East: A History* (Stanford, 1994), pp. 99–155. See also the useful articles on 'Nationality and Regional Questions' by R. G. Suny, O. Arens and A. Ezergailis, M. B. Olcott, A. Wood and

M. von Hagen, in Edward Acton *et al.* (eds), *Critical Companion to the Russian Revolution, 1914–1921* (London, Sydney and Auckland, 1997), pp. 659–740.

23 V. I. Lenin, '*Aprel'skie tezisy*', first published in the Bolshevik newspaper, *Pravda,* 7 April 1917, reprinted in English by Progress Publishers as Lenin, *The April Theses*, 3rd edn (Moscow, 1970).

24 In February 2001 the St Petersburg weekly, *Sankt-Peterburg Zhizn'*, carried a report based on sources allegedly from within Putin's *apparat* that the president had taken the 'firm' and 'principled' decision to remove Lenin's body in 2002 from its mausoleum for burial in the Ulyanov family plot in the Volkovskoe cemetery. The relocation has not yet occurred.

Select bibliography

Most of both the English- and Russian-language sources consulted during the writing of this book are fully cited in the notes to the individual chapters. What follows is a highly selective list of works in English only, which provide further reading and study aids to amplify the contents of the present volume. Items are arranged in both thematic and chronological order. Many of the works listed contain their own extensive bibliographies, to which further reference may be made for more intensive, in-depth reading, including articles in scholarly journals, details of which are not given here.

Bibliographies

Clendenning, P. H., and Bartlett, R., *Eighteenth Century Russia: A Select Bibliography of Works Published since 1955* (Newtonville, MA, 1981).

Crowther, Peter, A., *A Bibliography of Works in English on Early Russian History to 1800* (Oxford, 1969).

Egan, D. R. and Egan, M. A., *Russian Autocrats from Ivan the Great to the Fall of the Romanov Dynasty: An Annotated Bibliography of English Language Sources to 1985* (Metuchen, NJ, and London, 1987).

Frame, Murray, *The Russian Revolution, 1905–1921: A Bibliographic Guide to Works in English* (London, 1995).

Horak, Stephen M., *Russia, the USSR and Eastern Europe: A Bibliographic Guide to English Language Publications, 1964–1974* (Littleton, 1978), *1975–1980* (Littleton, 1982), *1981–1955* (Littleton, 1987).

Horecky, Paul L., *Russia and the Soviet Union: A Bibliographical Guide to Western-language Publications* (Chicago and London, 1965).

Pearson, Raymond, *Russia and Eastern Europe, 1789–1985: A Bibliographical Guide* (Manchester, 1989).

Shapiro, David, *A Select Bibliography of Works in English on Russian History, 1801–1917* (Oxford, 1962).

Reference

Acton, Edward *et al.* (eds), *Critical Companion to the Russian Revolution, 1914–1921* (London, Sydney and Auckland, 1997).

Auty, Robert and Obolensky, Dimitri (eds), *An Introduction to Russian History* (Cambridge, 1976).

Brown, Archie *et al.* (eds), *The Cambridge Encyclopedia of Russia and the Former Soviet Union*, 2nd edn (Cambridge, 1982).

Channon, John, *The Penguin Historical Atlas of Russia* (Harmondsworth, 1995).

Gilbert, Martin, *The Routledge Atlas of Russian History*, 4th edn (London, 2006).

Longley, David, *The Longman Companion to Imperial Russia, 1689–1917* (London, 2000).

Paxton, John, *Imperial Russia: A Reference Handbook* (Basingstoke, 2001).

Pushkarev, Sergei G., *Dictionary of Russian Historical Terms from the Eleventh Century to 1917* (New Haven, 1970).

Raymond, Boris and Duffy, Paul, *Historical Dictionary of Russia* (Lanham, 1998).

Shukman, Harold (ed.), *The Blackwell Encyclopedia of the Russian Revolution* (Oxford, 1988).

Warnes, David, *Chronicle of the Russian Tsars: The Reign-by-reign Record of the Rulers of Imperial Russia* (London, 1999).

Documents and source materials

Dmytryshyn, Basil (ed.), *Imperial Russia: A Source Book, 1700–1917* 2nd edn (Hinsdale, IL, 1974).

Golder, Frank (ed.), *Documents on Russian History, 1914–1917* (Gloucester, MA, 1964).

Kowalski, Ronald (ed.), *The Russian Revolution, 1917–1921* (London and New York, 1997).

McCauley, Martin (ed.), *The Russian Revolution and the Soviet State, 1917–1921: Documents* (London, 1980).

McCauley, Martin (ed.), *Octobrists to Bolsheviks: Imperial Russia, 1905–1917* (London, 1984).

McCauley, Martin and Waldron, Peter (eds), *The Emergence of the Modern Russian State, 1855–81* (London, 1988).

Raeff, Marc (ed.), *Russian Intelletual History: An Anthology* (New York, 1966).

Riha, Thomas (ed.), *Readings in Russian Civilization,* 3 vols in 1 (Chicago and London, 1964).

Vernadsky, George *et al.* (eds), *A Source Book for Russian History from Early Times to 1917*, 3 vols (New Haven, 1972).

General histories

Acton, Edward, *Russia* (London and New York, 1986).

Bartlett, Roger, *A History of Russia* (Basingstoke, 2005).

Cracraft, James (ed.), *Major Problems in the History of Imperial Russia* (Lexington, MA, 1994).

Dukes, Paul, *A History of Russia, c.882–1996*, 3rd edn (Basingstoke, 1998).

Figes, Orlando, *Natasha's Dance: A Cultural History of Russia* (Harmondsworth, 2002).

Florinsky, Michael T., *Russia: A History and an Interpretation*, 2 vols (New York, 1967).

Hosking, Geoffrey, *Russia: People and Empire, 1552–1917* (London, 1997).

Hosking, Geoffrey, *Russia and the Russians* (Harmondsworth, 2001).

Hosking, Geoffrey and Service, Robert (eds), *Reinterpreting Russia* (London, 1999).

Klyuchevsky, Vasili O., *A History of Russia*, 5 vols (New York, 1960).

Mavor, James, *An Economic History of Russia*, 2 vols (New York, 1965).

Pipes, Richard, *Russia under the Old Regime* (London, 1974).

Pokrovsky, Mikhail, *A History of Russia from the Earliest Times to the Rise of Capitalism* (London, 1931).

Seton-Watson, Hugh, *The Russian Empire, 1801–1917* (Oxford, 1967).

Vernadsky, George, *A History of Russia* 5th edn (New Haven, reprint 1968).

Biographies and prosopographies

1. Individual rulers

Ivan III

Fennell, John L. I., *Ivan the Great of Moscow* (London, 1961).
Grey, Ian, *Ivan III and the Unification of Russia* (Harmondsworth, 1973).

Ivan IV

Bobrick, Benson, *Ivan the Terrible* (Edinburgh, 1990).
de Madariaga, Isabel, *Ivan the Terrible* (New Haven, 2006).

Boris Godunov

Grey, Ian, *Boris Godunov: The Tragic Tsar* (London, 1973).

The False Dmitrii

Barbour, Philip L., *Dimitry, Called The Pretender: Tsar and Great Prince of All Russia, 1605–1606* (London, 1967).

Mikhail

Bain, R. Nisbet, *The First Romanovs, 1613–1725* (New York, 1967).

Aleksei

Bain, op. cit.
Longworth, Philip, *Alexis: Tsar of All the Russias* (London, 1984).

Sofiya

Hughes, Lindsey, *Sophia: Regent of Russia, 1657–1704* (New Haven, 1990).

Peter I

Bushkovitch, Paul, *Peter the Great: The Struggle for Power, 1671–1725* (Cambridge, 2001).

Hughes, Lindsey, *Russia in the Age of Peter the Great* (New Haven and London, 1998).

Hughes, Lindsey, *Peter the Great: A Biography* (New Haven and London, 2002)

Klyuchevsky, Vasili, *Peter the Great*, trans. by Liliana Archibald (London, 1958).

Swift, John, *Peter the Great* (London, 2000).

Catherine I, Anna, Elizabeth and Peter III

Bain, R. Nisbet, *The Daughter of Peter the Great* (New York, 1970).

Leonard, Carol S., *Reform and Regicide: The Reign of Peter III of Russia* (Bloomington, 1993).

Longworth, Philip, *The Three Empresses: Catherine I, Anne and Elizabeth of Russia* (London, 1972).

Catherine II

Alexander, John T., *Catherine the Great: Life and Legend* (Oxford, 1989).

de Madariaga, Isabel, *Russia in the Age of Catherine the Great* (London, 1981).

de Madariaga, Isabel, *Catherine the Great: A Short History* (New Haven and London, 1990).

Dixon, Simon, *Catherine the Great* (Harlow and New York, 2001).

Raeff, Marc (ed.), *Catherine the Great: A Profile* (London, 1972).

Paul

Ragsdale, H. (ed.), *Paul I: A Reassessment of his Life and Reign* (Pittsburgh, 1979).

Walizsewski, Kazimierz, *Paul I of Russia, The Son of Catherine the Great* (Hamden, CT., 1969).

Alexander I

Almedingen, Edith M., *The Emperor Alexander I* (London, 1964).

Hartley, Janet M., *Alexander I* (London and New York, 1994).

McConnell, Allen, *Tsar Alexander I: Paternalistic Reformer* (Northbrook, IL, 1970).

Palmer, Alan, *Alexander I: Tsar of War and Peace* (London, 1974).

Nicholas I

Lincoln, W. Bruce, *Nicholas I: Emperor and Autocrat of All the Russias* (London, 1978).

Presniakov, Alexander E., *Emperor Nicholas I of Russia: The Apogee of Autocracy, 1825–1855* (Gulf Breeze, FL, 1974).

Riasanovsky, Nicholas, *Nicholas I and Official Nationality in Russia* (Berkeley, CA, 1959).

Alexander II

Graham, Steven, *Tsar of Freedom; The Life and Reign of Alexander II* (New Haven, 1935).

Mosse, W. E., *Alexander II and the Modernization of Russia* (London, 1992).

Pereira, N. G. O., *Tsar-Liberator: Alexander II of Russia, 1818–1881* (Newtonville, MA, 1983).

Alexander III

Zaionchkovsky, P. A., *The Russian Autocracy under Alexander III* (Gulf Breeze, FL, 1976).

Nicholas II

Carrère d'Encausse, Hélène, *Nicholas II: The Interrupted Transition* (New York and London, 2000).

Ferro, Marc, *Nicholas II: The Last of the Tsars* (Harmondsworth, 1992).

Lieven, Dominic, *Nicholas II: Emperor of All the Russias* (London, 1993).

2. Other prominent personalities (alphabetical order by author)

Abraham, R., *Alexander Kerensky: First Love of the Revolution* (London and New York, 1987).

Ascher, Abraham, *P. A. Stolypin: The Search for Stability in Late Imperial Russia* (Stanford, CA, 2001).

Avrich, Paul, *Russian Rebels, 1600–1800* (on Pugachëv, *inter al.*; New York, 1972).

Binyon, T. J., *Pushkin: A Biography* (London, 2002).

Deutscher, Isaac, *The Prophet Armed; Trotsky, 1879–1921* (New York and London, 1954).

Footman, David, *Red Prelude: A Life of A. I. Zhelyabov,* 2nd edn (London, 1968).

Fülöp-Miller, René, *Rasputin: The Holy Devil* (London, 1967).

Jenkins, Michael, *Arakcheev: Grand Vizier of the Russian Empire* (London, 1969).

Lampert, Eugene, *Studies in Rebellion* (on Belinskii, Bakunin and Herzen; London, 1957).

Lampert, Eugene, *Sons against Fathers: Studies in Russian Radicalism and Revolution* (on Chernyshevskii, Dobrolyubov and Pisarev; Oxford, 1965).

Lang, David, *The First Russian Radical: Alexander Radishchev, 1749–1802* (London, 1959).

Longworth, Philip, *The Art of Victory: The Life and Achievements of Generalissimo Suvorov, 1729–1800* (London, 1965).

Menshutkin, Boris N., *Russia's Lomonosov: Chemist, Courtier, Physicist, Poet* (Princeton, NJ, 1952).

Montefiore, Simon Sebag, *Prince of Princes: The Life of Potemkin* (London, 2000).

O'Meara, Patrick, *The Decembrist Pavel Pestel: Russia's First Republican* (Basingstoke and New York, 2003).

Radzinsky, Edvard, *Rasputin: The Last Word* (London, 2000).

Riha, Thomas, *A Russian European: Paul Miliukov in Russian Politics* (Notre Dame, IN., 1969).

Service, Robert, *Lenin: A Biography* (Basingstoke, 2000).

Shukman, Harold, *Rasputin* (Stroud, 1997).

Volkogonov, Dmitri, *Lenin: Life and Legacy* (London, 1994).

Land, peoples and imperial expansion

Armstrong, Terence, *Russian Settlement in the North* (Cambridge, 1965).

Bater, James H. and French, R. A. (eds), *Studies in Russian Historical Geography,* 2 vols (London and New York, 1983).

Doroshenko, D., *History of the Ukraine* (Edmonton, 1939).

Fisher, Raymond H., *The Russian Fur Trade, 1550–1700* (University of California, 1943).

Forsyth, James, *A History of the Peoples of Siberia: Russia's North Asian Colony, 1581–1990* (Cambridge and New York, 1992).

Gibson, James R., *Feeding the Russian Fur Trade: Provisionment of the Okhotsk Seabord and the Kamchatka Peninsula, 1639–1856* (Madison, 1969).

Gibson, James, R., *Imperial Russia in Frontier America* (New York, 1976).

Hosking, Geoffrey, *Russia and the Russians: A History* (Harmondsworth, 2001).

Hrushevsky, M., *A History of Ukraine* (Yale, 1941).

Kappeler, Andreas, *The Russian Empire: A Multiethnic History* (London and New York, 2001).

Kerner, R. J., *The Urge to the Sea: the Role of Rivers, Portages, Ostrogs, Monasteries and Furs*, 2nd edn (New York, 1971).

Lincoln, W. Bruce, *The Conquest of a Continent: Siberia and the Russians* (London, 1994).

Parker, W. H., *An Historical Geography of Russia* (London, 1968).

Suny, Ronald, *The Making of the Georgian Nation* (Bloomington, IN, 1995).

Wood, Alan (ed.), *The History of Siberia: From Russian Conquest to Revolution* (London, 1991).

Note: works suggested in the following sections, which follow the chapter order, are – apart from a few repeated titles – in addition to the individual biographies listed above.

Kievan, Mongol and Muscovite Russia

Blum, Jerome, *Lord and Peasant in Russia from the Ninth to the Nineteenth Century* (New York, 1965).

Crummey, Robert O., *The Formation of Muscovy, 1304–1613* (London and New York, 1987).

de Madariaga, Isabel, *Ivan the Terrible* (New Haven, 2005).

Dukes, Paul, *The Making of Russian Absolutism, 1613–1801*, 2nd edn (London and New York, 1990).

Dunning, Chester S. L., *Russia's First Civil War: The Time of Troubles and the Founding of the Romanov Dynasty* (Pennsylvania, 2001).

Fennell, J. L. I., *The Emergence of Moscow, 1304–1359* (London, 1968).

Fennell, John, *The Crisis of Medieval Russia, 1200–1304* (London and New York, 1983).

Grekov, B., *Kiev Rus* (Moscow, 1959).

Gudzy, N. K. *History of Early Russian Literature* (New York, 1949).

Hughes, Lindsey, *Sophia: Regent of Russia, 1657–1704* (New Haven, 1990).

Kliuchevsky, V. O., *A Course in Russian History: The Seventeenth Century* (Chicago, 1968).

Longworth, Philip, *Alexis: Tsar of All the Russias* (London, 1984).

Michels, Georg B., *At War with the Church: Religious Dissent in Seventeenth-century Russia* (Stanford, CA, 1999).

Mousnier, Roland, *Peasant Uprisings in Seventeenth-century France, Russia and China* (London, 1971).

Rybakov, B., *Early Centuries of Russian History* (Moscow, 1965).

Staden, Heinrich von, *The Land and Government of Muscovy: A Sixteenth-century Account* (Stanford, CA, 1967).

Vernadsky, George, *A History of Russia*, vol. 2, *Kievan Russia* (New Haven and London, 1948).

Vernadsky, George, *A History of Russia*, vol. 3, *The Mongols and Russia* (New Haven and London, 1953).

Vernadsky, George, *A History of Russia*, vol. 4, *Russia at the Dawn of the Modern Age* (New Haven and London, 1959).

The age of Peter the Great

Anisimov, Evgenii V., *The Reforms of Peter the Great: Progress through Coercion in Russia* (Armonk, NY, and London, 1993).

Cracraft, James, *The Church Reform of Peter the Great* (London, 1971).

Cracraft, James (ed.), *Peter the Great Transforms Russia*, 3rd edn (Lexington, MA, 1991).

Cracraft, James, *The Petrine Revolution in Russian Culture* (Cambridge, MA, 2004).

Hughes, Lindsey, *Russia in the Age of Peter the Great* (New Haven and London, 1998).

Lentin, Antony, (ed.) *Peter the Great: His Law on Imperial Succession in Russia 1722* (Oxford, 1996).

Peterson, Claes, *Peter the Great's Administrative and Judicial Reforms: Swedish Antecedents and the Process of Reception* (Stockholm, 1979).

Riasanovsky, Nicholas, *The Image of Peter the Great in Russian History and Thought* (New York, 1985).

Sumner, B. H., *Peter the Great and the Ottoman Empire* (Hamden, CT., 1965).

Sumner, B. H., *Peter the Great and the Emergence of Russia* (New York, 1976).

The period of palace revolutions

Dixon, Simon, *The Modernization of Russia, 1676–1825* (Cambridge, 1999).

Dukes, Paul, *The Making of Russian Absolutism, 1613–1801*, 2nd edn (London, 1990).

Hartley, Janet M., *A Social History of the Russian Empire, 1650–1825* (London and New York, 1999).

Raeff, Marc, *Origins of the Russian Intelligentsia: The Eighteenth-century Nobility* (New York, 1966).

Raeff, Marc, *Plans for Political Reform in Imperial Russia, 1730–1905* (Englewood Cliffs, NJ, 1966).

Shcherbatov, Mikhail M., *On the Corruption of Morals in Russia* (London, 1969).

The age of Catherine the Great

Alexander, John T., *Autocratic Politics in a National Crisis: The Imperial Russian Government and Pugachev's Revolt, 1773–1775* (Bloomington, IN, 1969).

Bartlett, Roger (ed.), *Russia in the Age of Enlightenment* (Basingstoke, 1990).

de Madariaga, Isabel, *Russia in the Age of Catherine the Great* (London, 1981).

de Madariaga, Isabel, *Politics and Culture in Eighteenth-century Russia: Collected Essays* (London and New York, 1998).

Dukes, Paul, *Catherine the Great and the Russian Nobility: A Study Based on the Legislative Commission of 1767* (London, 1967).

Dukes, Paul, (ed.) *Catherine the Great's Instruction (Nakaz) to the Legislative Commission of 1767* (Newtonville, MA, 1977).

Jones, R. E., *The Emancipation of the Russian Nobility, 1762–1785* (Princeton, 1973).

Maroger, Dominique, *Memoirs of Catherine the Great* (London, 1955).

Montefiore, Simon Sebag, *Prince of Princes: The Life of Potemkin* (London, 2000).

Radishchev, Aleksandr N. (ed. R. P. Thaler), *Journey from St Petersburg to Moscow* (Cambridge, MA, 1958).

Ransel, D. L., *The Politics of Catherinian Russia: The Panin Party* (New Haven, 1975).

Reddaway, William F., *Documents of Catherine the Great* (London, 1971).

Segel, Harold B. (ed.), *The Literature of Eighteenth-century Russia: A History and Anthology of Russian Literary Materials* (New York, 1967).

Thomson, Gladys S., *Catherine the Great and the Expansion of Russia* (Westport, CT., 1985).

Tompkins, Stuart R., *The Russian Mind from Peter the Great through the Enlightenment* (Norman, OK, 1953).

Paul, Alexander I and the Decembrists

Barratt, Glynn, *Voices in Exile: The Decembrist Memoirs* (Montreal and London, 1974).

Barratt, Glynn, *The Rebel on the Bridge: A Life of the Decembrist Baron Andrey Rozen, 1800–84* (London, 1975).

Czartoryski, Adam G., *Memoirs of Prince Adam Czartoryski and his Correspondence with Alexander I* (New York, 1971).

Eidelman, Natan, *Conspiracy against the Tsar: A Portrait of the Decembrists* (Moscow, 1985).

Grimsted, Patricia K., *The Foreign Ministers of Alexander I* (Berkeley, CA, 1969).

Jenkins, Michael, *Arakcheev: Grand Vizier of the Russian Empire* (London, 1969).

Lobanov-Rostovsky, Andrei, *Russia and Europe, 1789–1825* (New York, 1968).

Mazour, Anatole, *The First Russian Revolution, 1825: The Decembrist Movement* (Stanford, CA, 1961).

O'Meara, Patrick, *K. F. Ryleev: A Political Biography of the Decembrist Poet* (Princeton, NJ, 1984).

O'Meara, Patrick, *The Decembrist Pavel Pestel: Russia's First Republican* (Basingstoke and New York, 2003).

Palmer, Alan, *Napoleon in Russia* (London, 1967).

Raeff, Marc, *Siberia and the Reforms of 1822* (Seattle, 1956).

Raeff, Marc, *Michael Speransky: Statesman of Imperial Russia, 1772–1839* (The Hague, 1957).

Raeff, Marc (ed.), *The Decembrist Movement* (Englewood Cliffs, NJ, 1966).

Saunders, David, *Russia in the Age of Reaction and Reform, 1801–1881* (London and New York, 1992).

Tarle, Evgenii V., *Napoleon's Invasion of Russia, 1812* (London, 1942).

Thackeray, Frank W., *Antecedents of Revolution: Alexander I and the Polish Kingdom, 1815–1825* (New York, 1980).

Zamoyski, Adam, *1812: Napoleon's Fatal March on Moscow* (London, 2004).

Zetlin, Mikhail, *The Decembrists* (New York, 1958).

The reign of Nicholas I

Annenkov, Pavel V. (ed. Arthur P. Mandel), *The Extraordinary Decade: Literary Memoirs* (Ann Arbor, MI, 1968).

Binyon, T. J., *Pushkin: A Biography* (London, 2002).

Curtiss, John S., *The Russian Army under Nicholas I* (Durham, NC, 1965).

Curtiss, John S., *Russia's Crimean War* (Durham, NC, 1979).

Custine, Marquis de, *Letters from Russia* (Harmondsworth, 1991).

Goldfrank, D. M., *The Origins of the Crimean War* (London and New York, 1994).

Herzen, Alexander, *My Past and Thoughts: Memoirs* (London, 1974).

Hingley, Ronald, *Russian Writers and Society, 1825–1904* (London, 1967).

Lampert, E., *Studies in Rebellion* (London, 1957).

Malia, Martin, *Alexander Herzen and the Birth of Russian Socialism, 1812–1855* (New York, 1965).

McNally, R. T., *Chaadayev and his Friends: An Intellectual History of Peter Chaadayev and his Russian Contemporaries* (Tallahassee, FL, 1971).

Monas, Sydney, *The Third Section: Police and Society under Nicholas I* (Cambridge, MA, 1961).

Nikitenko, A., *Diary of a Russian Censor* (Amherst, MA, 1975).

Presniakov, A. E., *Emperor Nicholas I of Russia: The Apogee of Autocracy, 1825–1855* (Gulf Breeze, FL, 1974).

Riasanovsky, Nicholas, *Nicholas I and Official Nationality in Russia, 1825–1855* (Berkeley, CA, 1959).

Riasanovsky, Nicholas, *Russia and the West in the Teaching of the Slavophiles* (Gloucester, MA, 1965).

Seddon, J. H., *The Petrashevtsy: A Study of the Russian Revolutionaries of 1848* (Manchester, 1985).

Squire, Paul S., *The Third Department: The Political Police in the Russia of Nicholas I* (Cambridge, 1968).

Tolstoy, Leo N., *The Sebastopol Sketches* (Harmondsworth, 1986).

Walicki, Andrzej, *The Slavophile Controversy: History of a Conservative Utopia in Nineteenth-century Russian Thought* (Oxford, 1975).

Emancipation and reform

Adams, Arthur E. (ed.), *Imperial Russia after 1861: Peaceful Modernization or Revolution?* (Boston, MA, 1965).

Black, Cyril (ed.), *The Transformation of Russian Society: Aspects of Social Change since 1861* (Cambridge, MA, 1960).

Blum, Jerome, *Lord and Peasant in Russia from the Ninth to the Nineteenth Century* (New York, 1965).

Eklof, Ben *et al.* (eds), *Russia's Great Reforms, 1855–1881* (Bloomington, IN, 1994).

Eklof, Ben and Frank, Stephen P. (eds), *The World of the Russian Peasant: Post-emancipation Culture and Society* (Boston, MA, and London, 1990).

Emmons, Terence, *The Russian Landed Gentry and the Peasant Emancipation of 1861* (London, 1968).

Emmons, Terence, *The Emancipation of the Russian Serfs* (New York, 1970).

Emmons Terence and Vucinich, Wayne S. (eds), *The Zemstvo in Russia: An Experiment in Local Self-government* (Cambridge and New York, 1982).

Field, Daniel, *The End of Serfdom: Nobility and Serfdom in Russia, 1855–1861* (Cambridge, MA, 1976).

Lincoln, W. Bruce, *Nikolai Miliutin: An Enlightened Russian Bureaucrat* (Newtonville, MA, 1977).

Lincoln, W. Bruce, *The Great Reforms: Autocracy Bureaucracy and the Politics of Change in Imperial Russia* (Dekalb, IL, 1990).

Macey, David A. J., *Government and Peasant in Russia, 1861–1906: The Prehistory of the Stolypin Reforms* (Dekalb, IL, 1987).

Miller, Forrestt A., *Dmitrii Miliutin and the Reform Era in Russia* (Nashville, TN, 1968).

Moon, David, *The Russian Peasantry, 1600–1930: The World the Peasants Made* (London and New York, 1999).

Mosse, W. E., *Alexander II and the Modernization of Russia* (London, 1992).

Pearson, Thomas S., *Russian Officialdom in Crisis: Autocracy and Local Self-government, 1861–1900* (Cambridge and New York, 1989).

Rieber, Alfred J., *The Politics of Autocracy* (Paris, 1966).

Robinson, Geroid T., *Rural Russia under the Old Régime: A History of the Landlord–Peasant World and a Prologue to the Peasant Revolution of 1917* (New York, 1957).

Zaionchkovsky, P. A., *The Abolition of Serfdom in Russia* (Gulf Breeze, FL, 1978).

Revolutionary Populism

Acton, Edward, *Alexander Herzen and the Role of the Revolutionary Intellectual* (Cambridge, 1979).

Billington, James, *Mikhailovsky and Russian Populism* (Oxford, 1958).

Broido, Vera, *Apostles into Terrorists: Women and the Revolutionary Movement in the Reign of Alexander II* (London, 1977).

Figner, Vera, *Memoirs of a Revolutionist* (London, 1927).

Footman, David, *Red Prelude: A Life of A. I. Zhelyabov*, 2nd edn (London, 1968).

Gleason, A., *Young Russia: The Genesis of Russian Radicalism in the 1860s* (Chicago and London, 1983).

Hardy, D., *Petr Tkachev: The Critic as Jacobin* (Seattle, WA, and London, 1977).

Hardy, D., *Land and Freedom: The Origins of Russian Terrorism* (Westport, CT, 1987).

Herzen, Alexander, *From the Other Shore and The Russian People and Socialism* (Cleveland, OH, 1963).

Kropotkin, Peter, *Memoirs of a Revolutionist* (New York, 1962).

Lampert, E., *Sons against Fathers: Studies in Russian Radicalism and Revolution* (Oxford, 1965).

Lavrov, Petr L., *Historical Letters* (University of California Press, 1967).

Offord, Derek, *Nineteenth-century Russia: Opposition to Autocracy* (London, 1999).

Pomper, Philip, *Peter Lavrov and the Russian Revolutionary Movement* (Chicago, 1972).

Pomper, Philip, *Sergei Nechaev* (New Brunswick, NJ, 1979).

Pomper, Philip, *The Russian Revolutionary Intelligentsia*, 2nd edn (Wheeling, IL, 1993).

Prawdin, Michael, *The Unmentionable Nechaev* (London, 1961).

Venturi, Franco, *Roots of Revolution: A History of the Populist and Socialist Movements in Nineteenth Century Russia* (London, 1960).

Walicki, Andrzej, *The Controversy over Capitalism: Studies in the Social Philosophy of the Russian Populists* (Oxford, 1969).

Weeks, Albert L., *The First Bolshevik: A Political Biography of Peter Tkachev* (New York, 1968).

Reaction and industrialisation

Byrnes, Robert F., *Pobedonostsev: His Life and Thought* (Bloomington, IN, 1968).

Crisp, Olga, *Studies in the Russian Economy before 1914* (London, 1976).

Falkus, M. E., *The Industrialisation of Russia, 1700–1914* (London, 1972).

Gatrell, Peter, *The Tsarist Economy, 1850–1917* (London, 1986).

Gerschenkron, Alexander, *Economic Backwardness in Historical Perspective* (Cambridge, 1962).

Kennan, George, *Siberia and the Exile System*, 2 vols (New York, 1891).

Laue, Theodore von, *Sergei Witte and the Industrialization of Russia* (New York, 1963).

Lenin, V. I., *The Development of Capitalism in Russia* (Moscow, 1967).

Lyashchenko, Pëtr A., *History of the National Economy of Russia to the 1917 Revolution* (New York, 1949).

Marks, Steven G., *Road to Power: The Trans-Siberian Railroad and the Colonization of Asian Russia, 1850–1917* (London, 1991).

Offord, Derek, *The Russian Revolutionary Movement in the 1880s* (Cambridge, 1986).

Pobedonostsev, Konstantin P., *Reflections of a Russian Statesman* (Ann Arbor, MI, 1965).

Rogger, Hans, *Russia in the Age of Modernisation and Revolution, 1881–1917* (London and New York, 1983).

Walkin, Jacob, *The Rise of Democracy in Pre-Revolutionary Russia* (London, 1963).

Zaionchkovsky, P. A., *The Russian Autocracy under Alexander III* (Gulf Breeze, FL, 1976).

Russian Marxism and the Social Democratic movement

Ascher, Abraham, *Pavel Axelrod and the Development of Menshevism* (Cambridge, MA, 1972).

Baron, Samuel H., *Plekhanov: Father of Russian Marxism* (London, 1963).

Getzler, I., *Martov: A Political Biography* (Cambridge, 1992).

Haimson, Leopold, *The Russian Marxists and the Origins of Bolshevism* (Boston, MA, 1966).

Keep, John, *The Rise of Social Democracy in Russia* (Oxford, 1963).

Lane, David, *The Roots of Russian Communism: A Social and Historical Study of Russian Social Democracy, 1898–1907* (London, 1975).

Lenin, V. I. (ed. by Robert Service), *What is to be Done?* (Harmondsworth, 1988).

Mendelsohn, Ezra, *Class Struggle in the Pale: The Formative Years of the Jewish Workers' Movement in Tsarist Russia* (Cambridge, 1970).

Service, Robert, *Lenin: A Political Life*, vol. 1, *The Strengths of Contradiction* (London, 1985).

Service, Robert, *Lenin: A Political Life*, vol. 2, *Worlds in Collision* (London, 1985).

Wildman, Allan K., *The Making of a Workers' Revolution: Russian Social Democracy, 1891–1903* (Chicago, 1967).

Wolfe, Bertram D., *Three Who Made a Revolution* (Harmondsworth, 1966).

Other political movements

Avrich, Paul, *The Russian Anarchists* (Princeton, NJ, 1967).

Crisp, Olga and Edmondson, Linda (eds), *Civil Rights in Imperial Russia* (Oxford, 1989).

Fischer, George, *Russian Liberalism: From Gentry to Intelligentsia* (Cambridge, MA, 1958).

Galai, Shmuel, *The Liberation Movement in Russia, 1900–1905* (Cambridge, 1973).

Geifman, Anna, *Entangled in Terror: The Azef Affair and the Russian Revolution* (Wilmington, DE, 2000).

Pearson, Raymond, *The Russian Moderates and the Crisis of Tsarism, 1914–1917* (Basingstoke, 1977).

Perrie, Maureen, *The Agrarian Policy of the Socialist-Revolutionary Party from its Origins through the Revolution of 1905–07* (Cambridge and New York, 1976).

Pipes, Richard, *Struve: Liberal on the Left, 1870–1905* (Cambridge, MA, 1970).

Pipes, Richard, *Struve: Liberal on the Right, 1905–1944* (Cambridge, MA, 1980).

Riha, Thomas, *A Russian European: Paul Miliukov in Russian Politics* (Notre Dame, IN, 1969).

Foreign policy and the Russo-Japanese War

Blackstock, Paul (ed.), *The Russian Menace to Europe: Articles, Speeches and Letters by Karl Marx and Friedrich Engels* (London, 1953).

Connaughton, Richard, *The War of the Rising Sun and the Tumbling Bear: a Military History of the Russo–Japanese War* (London and New York, 1988).

Geyer, D., *Russian Imperialism: The Interaction of Domestic and Foreign Policy, 1860–1914* (Leamington Spa, 1987).

Jelavich, Barbara, *A Century of Russian Foreign Policy, 1814–1914* (Philadelphia, 1964).

Nish, Ian, *The Origins of the Russo-Japanese War* (London and New York, 1985).

Taylor, A. J. P., *The Struggle for Mastery in Europe, 1848–1918* (Oxford, 1954).

Warner, Denis and Warner, Peggy, *The Tide at Sunrise: A History of the Russo-Japanese War* (London, 1975).

White, John A., *The Diplomacy of the Russo-Japanese War* (Princeton, NJ, 1964).

1905 and the Duma period

Ascher, Abraham, *The Revolution of 1905,* vol. 1, *Russia in Disarray* (Stanford, CA, 1988).

Ascher, Abraham, vol. 2, *Authority Restored* (Stanford, CA, 1992).

Ascher, Abraham, *P. A. Stolypin: The Search for Stability in Late Imperial Russia* (Stanford, CA, 2001).

Badayev, Aleksei E., *The Bolsheviks in the Tsarist Duma* (London and Chicago, 1987).

Bushnell, John, *Mutiny amid Repression: Russian Soldiers in the Revolution of 1905–1906* (Bloomington, IN, 1985).

Florinsky, Michael T., *The End of the Russian Empire* (New York, 1961).

Fülöp Miller, René, *Rasputin: The Holy Devil* (London, 1967).

Harcave, Sidney, *First Blood: The Russian Revolution of 1905* (London, 1964).

Hosking, Geoffrey, *The Russian Constitutional Experiment: Government and Duma, 1907–14* (Cambridge, 1973).

Katkov, George, Oberländer, Erwin *et al.* (eds), *Russia Enters the Twentieth Century, 1894–1917* (London, 1971).

Levin, Alfred, *The Second Duma: A Study of the Social Democratic Party and The Russian Constitutional Experiment* (Hamden, CT, 1966).

Lieven, Dominic, *Russia's Rulers under the Old Regime* (New Haven and London, 1989).

Miliukov, Pavel N., *Political Memoirs, 1905–1917* (Ann Arbor, MI, 1967).

Pearson, Raymond, *The Russian Moderates and the Crisis of Tsarism, 1914–1917* (London, 1977).

Pospielovsky, Dimitry, *Russian Police Trade Unionism: Experiment or Provocation?* (London, 1971).

Read, Christopher, *Religion, Revolution and the Russian Intelligentsia, 1900–1912* (London, 1979).

Rodzianko, M. V., *The Reign of Rasputin: An Empire's Collapse. Memoirs of M. V. Rodzianko* (London, 1927).

Sablinsky, Walter, *The Road to Bloody Sunday: Father Gapon and the St Petersburg Massacre of 1905* (Princeton, NJ, 1976).

Shukman, Harold, *Rasputin* (Stroud, 1997).

Trotsky, Leon, *1905* (Harmondsworth, 1972).

War and revolution

The literature on the Russian Revolution is – as befits its universal significance – enormous, and of varied quality. What follows is a short selection of some of the more useful, mainly recent, works, with an emphasis on the 'revisionist' school of interpretation.

Acton, Edward, *Rethinking the Russian Revolution* (London, 1990).

Adams, Arthur and Suny, Ronald (eds), *The Russian Revolution: and Bolshevik Victory*, 3rd edn (Lexington, DC, 1990).

Burdzhalov, E. N., *Russia's Second Revolution: The February 1917 Uprisings in Petrograd* (Bloomington, IN, 1987).

Ferro, Marc, *The Russian Revolution of February 1917* (Englewood Cliffs, NJ, 1972).

Figes, Orlando, *A People's Tragedy: The Russian Revolution, 1891–1924* (London, 1996).

Fitzpatrick, Sheila, *The Russian Revolution, 1917–1932* (Oxford, 1982).

Frankel, Edith R. *et al.* (eds), *Revolution in Russia: Reassessments of 1917* (Cambridge, 1992).

Gatrell, Peter, *Russia's First World War: A Social and Economic History* (London, 2005).

Hasegawa, Tsuyoshi, *The February Revolution: Petrograd 1917* (Seattle, WA, 1981).

Kaiser, Daniel H. (ed.), *The Workers' Revolution in Russia, 1917: The View from Below* (Cambridge, 1987).

Katkov, George, *Russia 1917: The February Revolution* (London, 1967).

Keep, John, *The Russian Revolution: A Study in Mass Mobilisation* (London, 1976).

Koenker, Diane and Rosenberg, William G., *Strikes and Revolution in Russia, 1917* (Princeton, NJ, 1989).

Liebman, Marcel, *The Russian Revolution: Origins, Phases and Meaning of the Bolshevik Victory* (London, 1970).

Lieven, Dominic, *Russia and the Origins of the First World War* (London, 1983).

Lincoln, W. Bruce, *Passage through Armageddon: The Russians in War and Revolution, 1914–1918* (Oxford, 1994).

Melgunov, S. P., *The Bolshevik Seizure of Power* (Oxford, 1972).

Pipes, Richard, *The Russian Revolution, 1899–1919* (London, 1990).

Rabinowitch, Alexander, *The Bolsheviks Come to Power: The Revolution of 1917 in Petrograd* (Bloomington, IN, 1968).

Read, Christopher, *From Tsar to Soviets: The Russian People and their Revolution 1917–1921* (London, 1996).

Service, Robert, *The Russian Revolution, 1900–1927*, 3rd edn (London, 1999).

Siegelbaum, Lewis H., *The Politics of Industrial Mobilization in Russia, 1914–1917: A Study of the War-Industries Committees* (London, 1983).

Smith, Steve A., *Red Petrograd: Revolution in the Factories, 1917–1918* (Cambridge, 1983).

Stone, Norman, *The Eastern Front: 1914–1917* (London, 1975).

Sukhanov, N. N., *The Russian Revolution 1917: Eyewitness Account*, 2 vols (New York, 1962).

Trotsky, Leon, *History of the Russian Revolution*, 3 vols (London, 1967).

Wildman, Allan K., *The End of the Russian Imperial Army*, 2 vols (Princeton, NJ, 1980 and 1987).

Wood, Alan, *The Origins of the Russian Revolution, 1861–1917*, 3rd edn (London and New York, 2003).

Zeman, Z. A. B. (ed.), *Germany and the Revolution in Russia, 1915–1918* (London, 1958).

Index